'This excellent collection by leading South Asian and European scholars could not be more timely. Their essays, grounded in field work and with analytical finesse, make notable contributions to our understanding of the complexities and contradictions of capitalist development across India's major economic sectors today. The authors provide new insights on longstanding issues in the light of current change in India, as well as addressing new topics like India's much vaunted "knowledge economy", money laundering and capital flight.'

Henry Bernstein

'Is Indian capitalism really different? This important book addresses this question through a focus on patterns of accumulation and how they interact with other economic, social, political and cultural processes, providing fascinating insights into the singularities, diversities and complexities of capitalism – and economy and society in general – in India.'

Jayati Ghosh

'The set of papers in this volume trace the dynamics of capitalist development in India focusing on activities where the mass of the labour force is concentrated and subjected to manifold exploitation.'

K.P. Kannan

Indian Capitalism in Development

Recognising the different ways that capitalism is theorised, this book explores various aspects of contemporary capitalism in India. Using field research at a local level to engage with larger issues, it raises questions about the varieties and processes of capitalism, and about the different roles played by the state.

With its focus on India, the book demonstrates the continuing relevance of the comparative political economy of development for the analysis of contemporary capitalism. Beginning with an exploration of capitalism in agriculture and rural development, it goes on to discuss rural labour, small town entrepreneurs, and technical change and competition in rural and urban manufacturing, highlighting the relationships between agricultural and non-agricultural firms and employment. An analysis of processes of commodification and their interaction with uncommodified areas of the economy makes use of the 'knowledge economy' as a case study. Other chapters look at the political economy of energy as a driver of accumulation in contradiction with both capital and labour, and at how the political economy of policy processes regulating energy highlights the fragmentary nature of the Indian state. Finally, a chapter on the processes and agencies involved in the export of wealth argues that this plays a crucial role in concealing the exploitation of labour in India.

Bringing together scholars who have engaged with classical political economy to advance the understanding of contemporary capitalism in South Asia, and distinctive in its use of an interdisciplinary political economy approach, the book will be of interest to students and scholars of South Asian Politics, Political Economy and Development Studies.

Barbara Harriss-White was formerly Director of Oxford University's Contemporary South Asian Studies programme, and Director of the Department of International Development at Queen Elizabeth House. She is now Emeritus Professor of Development Studies and Senior Research Fellow in Area Studies, Oxford University, UK. Since 1969 she has been studying and teaching Indian political economy, focusing on rural development, informal capitalism and many aspects of deprivation.

Judith Heyer was formerly a Tutorial Fellow of Somerville College, and Lecturer in the Department of Economics, at Oxford University. She is now an Emeritus Fellow of Somerville College. She has written extensively on Kenya and India, specialising in rural development and political economy.

Routledge contemporary South Asia series

1 **Pakistan**
Social and cultural transformations in a Muslim nation
Mohammad A. Qadeer

2 **Labor, Democratization and Development in India and Pakistan**
Christopher Candland

3 **China–India Relations**
Contemporary dynamics
Amardeep Athwal

4 **Madrasas in South Asia**
Teaching terror?
Jamal Malik

5 **Labor, Globalization and the State**
Workers, women and migrants confront neoliberalism
Edited by Debdas Banerjee and Michael Goldfield

6 **Indian Literature and Popular Cinema**
Recasting classics
Edited by Heidi R.M. Pauwels

7 **Islamist Militancy in Bangladesh**
A complex web
Ali Riaz

8 **Regionalism in South Asia**
Negotiating cooperation, institutional structures
Kishore C. Dash

9 **Federalism, Nationalism and Development**
India and the Punjab economy
Pritam Singh

10 **Human Development and Social Power**
Perspectives from South Asia
Ananya Mukherjee Reed

11 **The South Asian Diaspora**
Transnational networks and changing identities
Edited by Rajesh Rai and Peter Reeves

12 **Pakistan–Japan Relations**
Continuity and change in economic relations and security interests
Ahmad Rashid Malik

13 **Himalayan Frontiers of India**
Historical, geo-political and strategic perspectives
K. Warikoo

14 **India's Open-Economy Policy**
Globalism, rivalry, continuity
Jalal Alamgir

15 **The Separatist Conflict in Sri Lanka**
Terrorism, ethnicity, political economy
Asoka Bandarage

16 **India's Energy Security**
Edited by Ligia Noronha and Anant Sudarshan

17 **Globalization and the Middle Classes in India**
The social and cultural impact of neoliberal reforms
Ruchira Ganguly-Scrase and Timothy J. Scrase

18 **Water Policy Processes in India**
Discourses of power and resistance
Vandana Asthana

19 **Minority Governments in India**
The puzzle of elusive majorities
Csaba Nikolenyi

20 **The Maoist Insurgency in Nepal**
Revolution in the twenty-first century
Edited by Mahendra Lawoti and Anup K. Pahari

21 **Global Capital and Peripheral Labour**
The history and political economy of plantation workers in India
K. Ravi Raman

22 **Maoism in India**
Reincarnation of ultra-left wing extremism in the twenty-first century
Bidyut Chakrabarty and Rajat Kujur

23 **Economic and Human Development in Contemporary India**
Cronyism and fragility
Debdas Banerjee

24 **Culture and the Environment in the Himalaya**
Arjun Guneratne

25 **The Rise of Ethnic Politics in Nepal**
Democracy in the margins
Susan I. Hangen

26 **The Multiplex in India**
A cultural economy of urban leisure
Adrian Athique and Douglas Hill

27 **Tsunami Recovery in Sri Lanka**
Ethnic and regional dimensions
Dennis B. McGilvray and Michele R. Gamburd

28 **Development, Democracy and the State**
Critiquing the Kerala model of development
K. Ravi Raman

29 **Mohajir Militancy in Pakistan**
Violence and transformation in the Karachi conflict
Nichola Khan

30 **Nationbuilding, Gender and War Crimes in South Asia**
Bina D'Costa

31 **The State in India after Liberalization**
Interdisciplinary perspectives
Edited by Akhil Gupta and K. Sivaramakrishnan

32 **National Identities in Pakistan**
The 1971 war in contemporary
Pakistani fiction
Cara Cilano

33 **Political Islam and Governance
in Bangladesh**
*Edited by Ali Riaz and
C. Christine Fair*

34 **Bengali Cinema**
'An Other Nation'
Sharmistha Gooptu

35 **NGOs in India**
The challenges of women's
empowerment and accountability
Patrick Kilby

36 **The Labour Movement in the
Global South**
Trade unions in Sri Lanka
S. Janaka Biyanwila

37 **Building Bangalore**
Architecture and urban
transformation in India's Silicon
Valley
John C. Stallmeyer

38 **Conflict and Peacebuilding in
Sri Lanka**
Caught in the peace trap?
*Edited by Jonathan Goodhand,
Jonathan Spencer and
Benedict Korf*

39 **Microcredit and Women's
Empowerment**
A case study of Bangladesh
*Amunui Faraizi, Jim McAllister
and Taskinur Rahman*

40 **South Asia in the New World
Order**
The role of regional cooperation
Shahid Javed Burki

41 **Explaining Pakistan's Foreign
Policy**
Escaping India
Aparna Pande

42 **Development-induced
Displacement, Rehabilitation
and Resettlement in India**
Current issues and challenges
*Edited by Sakarama Somayaji and
Smrithi Talwar*

43 **The Politics of Belonging in India**
Becoming Adivasi
*Edited by Daniel J. Rycroft and
Sangeeta Dasgupta*

44 **Re-Orientalism and South Asian
Identity Politics**
The oriental other within
*Edited by Lisa Lau and
Ana Cristina Mendes*

45 **Islamic Revival in Nepal**
Religion and a new nation
Megan Adamson Sijapati

46 **Education and Inequality in
India**
A classroom view
Manabi Majumdar and Jos Mooij

47 **The Culturalization of Caste in
India**
Identity and inequality in a
multicultural age
Balmurli Natrajan

48 **Corporate Social Responsibility
in India**
Bidyut Chakrabarty

49 **Pakistan's Stability Paradox**
Domestic, regional and
international dimensions
*Edited by Ashutosh Misra and
Michael E. Clarke*

50 **Transforming Urban Water Supplies in India**
The role of reform and partnerships in globalization
Govind Gopakumar

51 **South Asian Security**
Twenty-first century discourses
Sagarika Dutt and Alok Bansal

52 **Non-discrimination and Equality in India**
Contesting boundaries of social justice
Vidhu Verma

53 **Being Middle-class in India**
A way of life
Henrike Donner

54 **Kashmir's Right to Secede**
A critical examination of contemporary theories of secession
Matthew J. Webb

55 **Bollywood Travels**
Culture, diaspora and border crossings in popular Hindi cinema
Rajinder Dudrah

56 **Nation, Territory, and Globalization in Pakistan**
Traversing the margins
Chad Haines

57 **The Politics of Ethnicity in Pakistan**
The Baloch, Sindhi and Mohajir ethnic movements
Farhan Hanif Siddiqi

58 **Nationalism and Ethnic Conflict**
Identities and mobilization after 1990
Edited by Mahendra Lawoti and Susan Hangen

59 **Islam and Higher Education**
Concepts, challenges and opportunities
Marodsilton Muborakshoeva

60 **Religious Freedom in India**
Sovereignty and (anti) conversion
Goldie Osuri

61 **Everyday Ethnicity in Sri Lanka**
Up-country Tamil identity politics
Daniel Bass

62 **Ritual and Recovery in Post-Conflict Sri Lanka**
Eloquent bodies
Jane Derges

63 **Bollywood and Globalisation**
The global power of popular Hindi cinema
Edited by David J. Schaefer and Kavita Karan

64 **Regional Economic Integration in South Asia**
Trapped in conflict?
Amita Batra

65 **Architecture and Nationalism in Sri Lanka**
The trouser under the cloth
Anoma Pieris

66 **Civil Society and Democratization in India**
Institutions, ideologies and interests
Sarbeswar Sahoo

67 **Contemporary Pakistani Fiction in English**
Idea, nation, state
Cara N. Cilano

68 **Transitional Justice in South Asia**
A study of Afghanistan and Nepal
Tazreena Sajjad

69 **Displacement and Resettlement in India**
The human cost of development
Hari Mohan Mathur

70 **Water, Democracy and Neoliberalism in India**
The power to reform
Vicky Walters

71 **Capitalist Development in India's Informal Economy**
Elisabetta Basile

72 **Nation, Constitutionalism and Buddhism in Sri Lanka**
Roshan de Silva Wijeyeratne

73 **Counterinsurgency, Democracy, and the Politics of Identity in India**
From warfare to welfare?
Mona Bhan

74 **Enterprise Culture in Neoliberal India**
Studies in youth, class, work and media
Edited by Nandini Gooptu

75 **The Politics of Economic Restructuring in India**
Economic governance and state spatial rescaling
Loraine Kennedy

76 **The Other in South Asian Religion, Literature and Film**
Perspectives on otherism and otherness
Edited by Diana Dimitrova

77 **Being Bengali**
At home and in the world
Edited by Mridula Nath Chakraborty

78 **The Political Economy of Ethnic Conflict in Sri Lanka**
Nikolaos Biziouras

79 **Indian Arranged Marriages**
A social psychological perspective
Tulika Jaiswal

80 **Writing the City in British Asian Diasporas**
Edited by Seán McLoughlin, William Gould, Ananya Jahanara Kabir and Emma Tomalin

81 **Post-9/11 Espionage Fiction in the US and Pakistan**
Spies and 'terrorists'
Cara Cilano

82 **Left Radicalism in India**
Bidyut Chakrabarty

83 **"Nation-State" and Minority Rights in India**
Comparative perspectives on Muslim and Sikh identities
Tanweer Fazal

84 **Pakistan's Nuclear Policy**
A minimum credible deterrence
Zafar Khan

85 **Imagining Muslims in South Asia and the Diaspora**
Secularism, religion, representations
Claire Chambers and Caroline Herbert

86 **Indian Foreign Policy in Transition**
Relations with South Asia
Arijit Mazumdar

87 **Corporate Social Responsibility and Development in Pakistan**
Nadeem Malik

88 **Indian Capitalism in Development**
Edited by Barbara Harriss-White and Judith Heyer

89 **Bangladesh Cinema and National Identity**
In search of the modern?
Zakir Hossain Raju

Indian Capitalism in Development

Edited by Barbara Harriss-White
and Judith Heyer

LONDON AND NEW YORK

First published 2015
by Routledge
2 Park Square, Milton Park, Abingdon, Oxon OX14 4RN

and by Routledge
711 Third Avenue, New York, NY 10017

First issued in paperback 2017

Routledge is an imprint of the Taylor & Francis Group, an informa business

© 2015 selection and editorial matter, Barbara Harriss-White and Judith Heyer; individual chapters, the contributors

The right of the editors to be identified as the authors of the editorial material, and of the authors for their individual chapters, has been asserted in accordance with sections 77 and 78 of the Copyright, Designs and Patents Act 1988.

All rights reserved. No part of this book may be reprinted or reproduced or utilised in any form or by any electronic, mechanical, or other means, now known or hereafter invented, including photocopying and recording, or in any information storage or retrieval system, without permission in writing from the publishers.

Trademark notice: Product or corporate names may be trademarks or registered trademarks, and are used only for identification and explanation without intent to infringe.

British Library Cataloguing in Publication Data
A catalogue record for this book is available from the British Library

Library of Congress Cataloging in Publication Data
Harriss-White, Barbara
Indian capitalism in development/Barbara Harriss-White and Judith Heyer.
 pages cm. – (Routledge contemporary South Asia series; 88)
 Includes bibliographical references and index.
 1. Capitalism–India–21st century. 2. India–Economic policy–21st century. 3. Rural development–India–21st century. 4. Economic development–India–21st century. I. Heyer, Judith. II. Title.
 HC435.3.H373 2015
 330.954–dc23   2014016156

ISBN 13: 978-1-138-49151-9 (pbk)
ISBN 13: 978-1-138-77994-5 (hbk)

Typeset in Times New Roman
by Wearset Ltd, Boldon, Tyne and Wear

To the next generation of scholars who we hope will take forward some of the ideas in this book.

Contents

List of illustrations	xvii
Notes on contributors	xviii
Preface	xxii
Acknowledgements	xxiv
List of abbreviations	xxv

1 Introduction   1
BARBARA HARRISS-WHITE AND JUDITH HEYER

2 Primitive accumulation and the 'transition to capitalism' in neoliberal India: mechanisms, resistance, and the persistence of self-employed labour   23
SHAPAN ADNAN

3 Regional patterns of agrarian accumulation in India   46
JENS LERCHE

4 Agrarian relations and institutional diversity in Arunachal Pradesh   66
DEEPAK K. MISHRA

5 First transaction, multiple dimensions: the changing terms of commodity exchange in a regulated agricultural market in Madhya Pradesh   84
MEKHALA KRISHNAMURTHY

6 The political economy of microfinance and marginalised groups: implications of alternative institutional strategies   102
D. NARASIMHA REDDY

xvi *Contents*

7 **Labour in contemporary south India** 118
ISABELLE GUÉRIN, G. VENKATASUBRAMANIAN AND
SÉBASTIEN MICHIELS

8 **Emerging spatio-technical regimes of accumulation in the globalising south and implications for labour** 136
M. VIJAYABASKAR

9 **Commodification, capitalism and crisis** 153
UMAR SALAM

10 **A heterodox analysis of capitalism: insights from a market town in South India after the Green Revolution** 170
ELISABETTA BASILE

11 **Money laundering and capital flight** 190
KANNAN SRINIVASAN

12 **Power-hungry: the state and the troubled transition in Indian electricity** 208
ELIZABETH CHATTERJEE

13 **Technology and materiality: South Asia in the twenty-first century** 226
SANJEEV GHOTGE

Glossary 244
Index 246

Illustrations

Figure

3.1 Landholdings – major size groups, 2005/2006   52

Tables

3.1	Employment by sector as percentage of total employment in India	47
3.2	Employment in agriculture and manufacturing in major Indian states, 2009/2010	48
3.3	Agricultural productivity indicators (Rs.1000)	49
3.4	Trend growth rates in GDP, percentage per year, 1975/1976 to 2010/2011	50
3.5	Average monthly per capita expenditure for the top decile of the rural population in 2009/2010	51
3.6	Irrigation and tractor intensity in Indian states	53
4.1	Size-class distribution of operational holdings (Arunachal Pradesh): 1970/1971 to 2010/2011	68
4.2	Share of ST operated holdings in Arunachal Pradesh: 1980/1981 to 2010/2011	69
4.3	Land relations in the study villages	73
4.4	Labour relations in the study villages	74
6.1	Growth of active borrowers in India's top 11 MFIs, 2005 to 2009	107
6.2	Growth of active borrowers in top four MFIs of AP origin, 2002 to 2009	108
10.1	Private firms in Arni	177
10.2	Gross output in the Arni samples	178
12.1	Status of reform across Indian states	218

Contributors

Shapan Adnan has worked extensively on agrarian relations, and more recently on primitive accumulation in rural areas in Bangladesh. His publications include 'Classical and contemporary approaches to agrarian capitalism', *Economic and Political Weekly* (1985) 20(30); 'Agrarian structure and agricultural growth trends in Bangladesh: the political economy of technological change and policy interventions', in B. Rogaly, B. Harriss-White and S. Bose (eds), *Sonar Bangla?: Agricultural Growth and Agrarian Change in West Bengal and Bangladesh* (1999); 'Departures from everyday resistance and flexible strategies of domination: the making and unmaking of a poor peasant mobilization in Bangladesh', *Journal of Agrarian Change* (2007) 7(2); 'Land grabs and primitive accumulation in deltaic Bangladesh: interactions between neoliberal globalization, state interventions, power relations and peasant resistance', *Journal of Peasant Studies* (2013) 40(1).

Elisabetta Basile, Professor of Development Economics at the University of Rome 'La Sapienza', completed an Oxford D.Phil. thesis on the evolution of capitalism in the town of Arni and its region. She has written on rural development in Italy, the institutional embeddedness of Indian capitalism, capital labour transformations in the Indian informal economy, and the methodology of neoclassical economics. Her recent publications include (edited with I. Mukhopadhyay) *The Changing Identity of Rural India* (2009); *Capitalist Development in India's Informal Economy* (2013); and (edited with G. Lunghini and F. Volpi) *Pensare il capitalismo. Nuove prospettive per l'economia politica* (2013).

Elizabeth Chatterjee is a Fellow of All Souls College, and a D.Phil. candidate at the Oxford Department of International Development. Her research examines the persistent failures of electricity policy and the changing Indian state in the era of liberalization. She published 'Dissipated energy: Indian electric power and the politics of blame', *Contemporary South Asia* (2012) 20(1). A travel book based on her fieldwork experiences, *Delhi: Mostly Harmless*, was published by Random House India in December 2013.

Sanjeev Ghotge is Research Director at the World Institute of Sustainable Energy in Pune. He has written on the environmental impacts of agriculture, large dams, conventional energy and mining, especially on poorer communities. He has worked on renewable energy and climate change. His publications include 'A political manifesto for the greening of India', *Capitalism, Nature, Socialism* (2004) 15(4); 'Agriculture: its relation to ecology and society', *Financing Agriculture* (2004) 35(3); and (with others) *Power Drain: Hidden Subsidies to Conventional Power in India* (2008).

Isabelle Guérin is currently Senior Research Fellow at the Institute of Research Development at CESSMA (Centre d'Etudes en Sciences Sociales sur les Mondes Africains, Américains et Asiatiques), Paris. She has done fieldwork on bonded labour in brick kilns and rice mills in Tamil Nadu, and has also written on the political economy of microfinance and debt relations. Her academic interests span from the political and moral economy of money, debt and labour, to social economy, NGO interventions, empowerment programmes and linkages with public policies. She has jointly edited a number of books and special issues of journals recently (with Jan Breman and Aseem Prakash) *India's Unfree Workforce, Old and New Practices of Labour Bondage* (2009); (with Jens Lerche and Ravi Srivastava) *Labour Standards in India, Global Labour Journal Special Issue* (2012); (with Solene Morvant-Roux and Magdalena Villareal) *Microfinance, Debt and Over-Indebtedness: Juggling With Money* (2013).

Barbara Harriss-White was formerly Director of Oxford University's Contemporary South Asian Studies programme, and Director of the Department of International Development at Queen Elizabeth House. She is now Emeritus Professor of Development Studies and Senior Research Fellow in Area Studies, Oxford University. Committed to a political economy practised through field research, she has published widely. Recent books include *India Working* (2003); (with S. Janakarajan and others) *Rural India Facing the 21st Century* (2004); (edited with A.Sinha) *Trade Liberalisation and India's Informal Economy* (2007); (edited with F. Stewart and R. Saith) *Defining Poverty in Developing Countries* (2007); *Rural Commercial Capital and the Left Front* (2008), winner of the 2009 Edgar Graham Prize for original scholarship in development; (edited with Elisabetta Basile) *India's Informal Capitalism and Its Regulation, Special Issue of International Review of Sociology* (2010); (with others) *Dalits and Adivasis in India's Business Economy* (2014); and (edited with Delia Davin) *China-India Pathways of Economic and Social Development* (2014).

Judith Heyer was for three decades until 2005 Lecturer in Economics, Oxford University, before which she held posts in Nairobi University's Institute for Development Studies and Economics Department. She is now an Emeritus Fellow of Somerville College, Oxford. A specialist in rural development, much of her earlier work focused on Kenya. Her more recent writing has drawn on fieldwork in western Tamil Nadu over more than three decades, and focused on the oppression of Dalits in the agrarian economy, the exclusion of Dalits in the process of industrialisation, the role of social policy in the rise in

xx *Contributors*

material standards of living of Dalits, and the withdrawal of Dalit women from wage labour. She has written and/or edited a number of books, including (edited with Barbara Harriss-White) *The Comparative Political Economy of Development: Africa and South Asia* (2010).

Mekhala Krishnamurthy is an Associate Professor in the Department of Sociology at Shiv Nadar University, India. She has worked on women's courts and dispute resolution, community health workers and public health systems, agricultural commodity markets and regulation, and rural development, livelihoods and land acquisition. Her publications include (with P.S. Vijay Shankar) the 'Introduction' to a Special Issue on Agricultural Commodity Markets, *Economic and Political Weekly* (Review of Rural Affairs, 2012); 'States of wheat: the changing dynamics of public procurement in Madhya Pradesh' in the same issue; 'Margins and mindsets: enterprise, opportunity and exclusion in a market town in Madhya Pradesh' in Nandini Gooptu (ed.) *Enterprise Culture in Neoliberal India: Studies in Youth, Class, Work and Media* (2013); and 'Agricultural commodity markets: regional variations' in the *India Rural Development Report 2014* (forthcoming).

Jens Lerche is currently a Reader in the Department of Development Studies at the School of Oriental and African Studies (SOAS), University of London, and has been editor of the *Journal of Agrarian Change* since 2008. His work focuses on agrarian questions and rural labour in India, and on Dalits. His publications include 'Transnational advocacy networks and affirmative action for Dalits in India', *Development and Change* (2008) 39(2); 'Labour regulations and labour standards in India: decent work?', *Global Labour Journal* (2012) 3(1); and 'The agrarian question in neoliberal India: agrarian transition bypassed?', *Journal of Agrarian Change* (2003) 13(3). His books include (edited with K. Kapadia and T.J. Byres) *Rural Labour in Contemporary India* (1999) and (edited with R. Jeffery and C. Jeffrey) *Development Failure and Identity Politics in Uttar Pradesh* (2014).

Sébastien Michiels is currently a Ph.D. student in development economics at Bordeaux IV University (GREThA), and affiliated to the French Institute of Pondicherry. His thesis deals with contemporary forms of migration in rural south India.

Deepak K. Mishra is currently an Associate Professor in Economics, Centre for the Study of Regional Development, School of Social Sciences, Jawaharlal Nehru University, New Delhi. He has worked as a field economist in both Odisha and Arunachal Pradesh, published on the development of both states and is currently working on rural transformations in Odisha. His publications include (with B. Harriss-White and V. Upadhyay) (2009) 'Institutional diversity and capitalist transition: the political economy of agrarian change in Arunachal Pradesh, India', *Journal of Agrarian Change* (2009) 9(4) and (with A. Sarma and V. Upadhyay) *The Unfolding Crisis in Assam's Tea Plantations: Employment and Occupational Mobility* (2012).

Contributors xxi

D. Narasimha Reddy was formerly at the University of Hyderabad where he was until recently the holder of the Sankaran Chair. He is currently ICSSR National Fellow, Council for Social Development, Hyderabad, and Visiting Professor at the Institute of Human Development in Delhi. He has had a long involvement in the study of the rural economy of Andhra Pradesh, as well as being involved in apex discussions and debates on India as a whole. His publications include *Towards Understanding WTO Doha Development Round* (2005); *Labour Regulation, Industrial Growth and Employment: A Study of Recent Trends in Andhra Pradesh* (2008); (edited with Srijit Mishra) *Agrarian Crisis in India* (2009); and 'Agrarian crisis and challenges in reviving Small Farmer economy' in the *India Social Development Report 2010* (2011).

Umar Salam is currently a D.Phil. student at Oxford University working under the supervision of Barbara Harriss-White on the commodification of the knowledge economy in India and Pakistan.

Kannan Srinivasan has been a journalist since 1980. His most recent publication is 'A subaltern fascism?' in Jairus Banaji (ed.) *Fascism: Essays on Europe and India* (2013).

G. Venkatasubramanian is a researcher at the Department of Social Sciences at the French Institute of Pondicherry, India. He has been working on socio-geographical questions for the past 15 years. His areas of interests include migration, labour standards, livelihood and rural–urban linkages. At present he is associated with two international research programmes dealing with debt bondage and rural–urban linkages.

M. Vijayabaskar is currently a Research Fellow at the Madras Institute of Development Studies in Chennai. His Ph.D. was on the knitwear industry in Tiruppur. He has since worked on the IT sector in Bangalore, SEZs in Tamil Nadu, and with production in other centres and sectors in Tamil Nadu. His publications include 'Labour under flexible accumulation: the case of the Tiruppur knitwear cluster' in K. Das (ed.) *Industrial Clusters: Cases and Perspectives* (2005); 'Global crises, welfare provision and coping strategies of labour in Tiruppur', *Economic and Political Weekly, Review of Labour* (2011) 46(22); 'The institutional milieu of skill formation: a comparative study of two textile regions' in M. Ohara, M. Vijayabaskar and Hong Lin (eds) *Industrial Dynamics in China and India: Firms, Clusters, and Different Growth Paths* (2011); and 'The politics of silence' in Rob Jenkins, Loraine Kennedy and Partha Mukhopadhyay (eds) *Power, Policy and Protest: The Politics of India's Special Economic Zones* (2014).

Preface

This book is the result of a conference held in Oxford to celebrate Barbara Harriss-White's formal retirement after 42 years of research and teaching on development in India, a quarter century of which was in Oxford. At the heart of the meeting was a score of committed field researchers, many eminent in their fields, all engaged with, critiquing or developing aspects of her work, who came together from around the world – from India, Bangladesh, Pakistan, Australia, the USA, France, Italy, the Netherlands and the UK – to pool their expertise on the political economy of Indian capitalism.

The timing is significant: Barbara Harriss-White and the generation of scholars to which she belongs are passing the baton to a new generation of researchers, above all in South Asia, when the key question of the moment was what liberalisation was really going to mean for India. In this context two of Barbara's distinctive preoccupations – the role of the socially regulated informal economy, accounting for 90 per cent of all jobs and 60 per cent of India's GDP, and the implications of liberalised capitalist growth for the future of the ecosphere – are rising inexorably up the policy agenda.

What gives Indian capitalism its social and political character? How is capital acquired and labour freed for productive deployment? Why are India's accumulation pathways so diverse? Why does petty production expand through multiplication and not concentration of capital? Why do diverse technologies, oppressive forms of labour and forms of organisation of firms and their families co-exist persistently? Why does the state regulate the economy through social institutions rather than its own laws? Why does it allow such significant capital flight? What puts the brakes on commodification? How is Indian capital destroying resource 'sinks' and 'taps'? These are some of the major questions that are at stake – and at issue in this book – with implications for livelihoods, food security, caste and gender relations, class formation, corruption, and the rule of law.

Answers to these questions can be attempted at many different levels. Among policy-makers the most common answers are based on large-scale statistics framed by highly abstract economic models drawn from marginalist economic theory. The distinctive contribution of the work carried out by Barbara Harriss-White and her colleagues, students and former students is to look for empirical evidence through the optic of heuristic theories of an appropriate scale. Their

Preface xxiii

commitment is to link theory to closely observed empirical reality, not to big numbers whose basis in social and economic reality is all too often tenuous. Our view is that large-scale theory and macro-level policy is only as useful as the quality of the theory that has framed the collection of the data relied on to support them, and of the work that went into gathering those data; and therefore that the prime duty of scholars is to do the hard and sometimes disillusioning work needed to generate trustworthy data against which higher level theory may be tested, and higher level policies evaluated.

The chapters in the book all exemplify this theme and this commitment. Whether in the vivid account of the north Indian market studied by Mekhala Krishnamurthy, the complex play of state power in the energy/power sector revealed by Liz Chatterjee, the complicity of London and New York in India's money laundering sleuthed by Kannan Srinivasan, the dramatic evolution of microfinance for the poor as big business exposed by D.N. Reddy, the subject is really the same throughout: the fast-moving spread of capitalist production relations, the commodification of land, all forms of labour, exchange and all products, the tightening links between local and national and international markets, the reworking of pre-capitalist social relations in new market-based structures, and the ubiquitous spread of relations of unequal power, incomes and life chances that accompany these transitions and ongoing transformations. These terms too are abstractions. What the chapters in this book do is to both theorise them and put flesh on them in a way that scrupulous field research makes possible. In the process they call into question many prevalent development myths, and many problematic dimensions of conventional policy wisdom.

With its companion volume, *The Comparative Political Economy of Development*, also published by Routledge – in 2010 in celebration of the work in Africa and India of Judith Heyer upon her formal retirement from Oxford – this book not only sums up an era of work and thought on India, but takes forward the analysis of global capitalism as it engulfs one of the world's largest, richest, most diverse and challenging regional arenas in a way that we hope concerned scholars and policy makers will value.

Judith Heyer and Barbara Harriss-White

Acknowledgements

We wish particularly to thank conference participants and their home institutions for help with travel costs. We are grateful to Wolfson College, Oxford, All Souls College, Oxford, and Oxford University's Department of Anthropology, as well as the Conference Fund of Oxford Development Studies, the School of Interdisciplinary Area Studies' Contemporary South Asian Studies Programme and the Support Fund of the Department of International Development, Oxford University, for resources making it possible to host such a successful conference overall as well as making it possible to bring people from India to participate in the conference. We are grateful to Tanya Vale for taking responsibility for the organisation of the conference far beyond the call of duty, and to Indrajit Roy for help at the time of the conference itself. We are also grateful to Dorothea Schaefter and others at Routledge for their interest and support.

Abbreviations

ABD	Accumulation by Dispossession
AICC	All India Congress Committee
AP	Andhra Pradesh
APDRP	Accelerated Power Development and Reforms Programme
APERP	Andhra Pradesh Economic Restructuring Project
APMC	Agricultural Produce Marketing Committee
APP	Association of Power Producers
APST	Arunachal Pradesh Scheduled Tribe
BCCI	Bank of Credit and Commerce International
BJP	Bharatiya Janata Party
BKS	Bharatiya Kisan Sangh
BSES	Bombay Suburban Electric Supply Ltd
BUPN	*Bhumi Uchchhed Pratirodh Committee*
CAG	Comptroller and Auditor General of India
CGAP	Consultative Group to Assist the Poorest
CIF	Community Investment Fund
CMSA	Community Managed Sustainable Agriculture
CMT	Cutting, Machining and Trimming
CPI (M)	Communist Party of India (Marxist)
CPI-ML	Communist Party of India Marxist-Leninist
DIPP	Department of Industrial Policy and Promotion
FDI	Foreign Direct Investment
FEMA	Foreign Exchange Management Amendment
GAIL	Gas Authority of India Ltd
GBC	Global Business Company
GCA	Gross Cropped Area
GHG	Greenhouse Gas
GR	Green Revolution
GSDP	Gross State Domestic Product
HYV	High Yielding Variety
IAS	Indian Administrative Service
IBC	International Business Corporation
ICT	Information and Communications Technology

xxvi *Abbreviations*

IEA	International Energy Agency
IPO	Initial Public Offering
IPP	Independent Power Producer
IPPAI	Independent Power Producers Association of India
IPPC	Integrated Pollution Prevention and Control
JLG	Joint Liability Group
KCC	Kisan Credit Card
KP	Kisan Panchayat
LIC	Life Insurance Corporation
MACS	Mutually Aided Cooperative Societies
MBC	Most Backward Class, member of Most Backward Class
MBT	Mutual Benefit Trust
MD	Managing Director
MFA	Multi-Fibre Agreement
MFI	Micro Finance Institution
MLA	Member of the Legislative Assembly
MNC	Midnight Notes Collective
MOU	Memorandum of Understanding
MS	Mandal Samakhya
MSP	Minimum Support Price
MWC	Mahindra World City
NABARD	National Bank for Agriculture and Rural Development
NALSAR	National Academy of Legal Studies and Research
NAPM	National Alliance of People's Movements
NBFC	Non-Bank Financial Company
NEFA	North-East Frontier Agency
NHPC	National Hydroelectric Power Corporation
NREGA, MGNREGA	Mahatma Gandhi National Rural Employment Guarantee Act
NSAS	National Social Assistance Scheme
NSS, NSSO	National Sample Survey, National Sample Survey Organisation
NTPC	National Thermal Power Corporation
ONGC	Oil and Natural Gas Corporation Ltd
PCP	Petty Commodity Production
PESA	Panchayats (Extension to the Scheduled Areas)
PLR	Priority Sector Lending Rate
PMK	Paattali Makkal Katchi
PN	Participatory Note
POSCO	Indian subsidiary of Korean conglomerate
PPSS	*POSCO Pratirodh Sangram Samiti*
PV	Photo-voltaic
RBI	Reserve Bank of India
RE	Renewable Energy
SAARC	South Asia Association for Regional Cooperation
SAPAP	South Asia Poverty Alleviation Programme

SC	Scheduled Caste, member of a Scheduled Caste
SEB	State Electricity Board
SEBI	Securities and Exchange Board of India
SERP	Society for the Elimination of Rural Poverty
SEZ	Special Economic Zone
SHG	Self Help Group
SHG-BL	Self Help Group Bank Lending
SIDBI	Small Industries Development Bank of India
SKS	Swayam Krushi Sangham
SML	SHARE Microfinance Ltd
SOE	State Owned Enterprise
SOMO-ICN	Stichting Onderzoek Multinationale Ondernemingen – India Committee of the Netherlands
SSIF	Spandana Spoorthy Innovative Financials
ST	Scheduled Tribe, member of a Scheduled Tribe
TCPA	Tonnes Carbon Per Annum
TUF	Technology Upgradation Fund
VO	Village Organisation
ZS	Zilla Samakhya

1 Introduction

Barbara Harriss-White and Judith Heyer

This book is the work of a group of political economists committed to using first-hand research as a basis for analysing the development of capitalism in India and for engaging with theoretical ideas about it. Capitalism bestrides the contemporary world like a colossus and is so naturalised in thought that alternatives are hard to imagine. Yet the word 'capitalism' is airbrushed from the index of most general texts in economics and is synonymous with 'irrelevant' Marxist approaches to development. The writers of this book however, whether they are institutionalists, Weberians or historical materialists, find it impossible to understand the dynamics of development in India without defining it as capitalist, and without, for the most part, engaging critically with Marx's *Capital*.

The ways in which capitalism is theorised have ramifications both for our understanding and for interventions in its dynamics. Theories guide the analytical moves between general logic and historically specific circumstances (Banaji 2010). In arguing that a plurality of theoretical approaches is needed,[1] Tony Lawson, the feminist institutional economist and philosopher, provides justification for the pluralism of this book (Lawson 2003).

An understanding of the development of capitalism in the contemporary world requires knowledge of what is happening on the ground. The continual transformation of forces and relations of production, the exploitation of natural resources and of labour, relations with the state and with powerful social collectives that together provide a structure of accumulation are all uneven in their combinations and balances, their trajectories and effects. The fine detail of lived experience mediated by first-hand research, in the factory and field, on farms, in villages, in marketplaces, in offices and in the archives, makes possible an engagement with theory, both deductively, in testing hypotheses on the ground, and inductively, in fieldwork that allows for surprises and challenges preconceptions.

Barbara Harriss-White's fieldwork over four decades in rural and small town Tamil Nadu, West Bengal and Arunachal Pradesh has emphasised the diversity of capitalist trajectories, the social heterogeneity of the capitalist class, the significance of relations of distribution for those of production, the roles of commodity markets in efficiency, exploitation and resource extraction; the ways in which structures of social authority are deployed in processes

2   B. Harriss-White and J. Heyer

of class formation and accumulation and the nexus of interest between local capital and the state which generates both informal economic activity and a parallel or shadow state. The contributors to this book were invited to use their own theoretical perspectives on capitalism to interrogate Indian ground realities. They responded in different ways. Some chapters are more theoretical, using empirical material to illustrate their arguments; others are more empirical, informed by theory.

The book's contributors raise questions about the varieties, institutions and dynamics of contemporary capitalism in India and about the regulative roles of the state. The opening chapter assesses Marx's concept of primitive accumulation and uses it to look at the diverse ways in which primitive accumulation is occurring in India today. This is followed by chapters tracking the constituent processes of capitalism in sectors involving the mass of the labour force: chapters on accumulation in agriculture, and on institutional diversity in agriculture; on agricultural markets; and on credit and finance. Together, they explore the range of capitalist trajectories in agricultural and rural development, the particular institutions of capitalism which make it distinctively 'Indian', and the role of the Indian state. The following chapters examine the persistent vulnerability of labour, both agricultural and non-agricultural; the way in which technical change affects the quality as well as the quantity of employment, the role of commodification in the development of capitalism which is proceeding with little resistance in India as everywhere else, and the institutional framework within which small-town capitalists try to stabilise the cycles of profit and investment. A chapter on the processes and agencies involved in the export of Indian wealth argues that this plays crucial roles not only in clandestine accumulation but also in concealing the exploitation of labour. This is followed by a chapter on the political economy of policy processes which examines the fragmented institutions of India's regulative state. The final chapter foregrounds energy as the material dynamo of accumulation, exploring what may be the most serious challenge capitalism has faced to date, since non-renewable raw materials are being used up without precedent, and energy is being dissipated as heat-retaining gases in the atmosphere.

There are distinct limits to the scope of this project. It does not cover India's corporate sector.[2] We have not looked at corporate and state banking and finance.[3] We do not explicitly examine the political changes in the state ('liberalisation') which incentivise foreign direct investment and the role being played by FDI.[4]

What follows in this introduction is a brief review of some of the many debates surrounding issues taken up in individual chapters of the book.

1 Primitive accumulation/accumulation by dispossession

The scramble for raw materials, and their subsequent development based on labour, coal and other fossil fuels are some of the most well-remarked aspects of India's twenty-first-century capitalism. This is a form of what Marx called

Introduction 3

primitive accumulation (PA) (Marx 1976: 500–502).[5] He made clear that PA was a dual process. The first part of the dual process is the point of departure for productive capitalist investment, re-configuring nature as private property. The second part is the freeing of labour to work for wages. In *Capital* this is a process lasting for centuries before the era of manufacturing capitalism.

Adnan, in Chapter 2, interrogates Marx's theory of PA, evaluating its relevance to capitalist development. He maintains that PA is necessary for twenty-first-century capitalist development because the latter relies on expansion of the forces of production while the former facilitates and renews it (Adnan 2013). As Adnan shows here, the process is both contested on the ground and debated in theory. Harvey's concept of accumulation by dispossession, developed to describe something similar, neglects both the formation of the labour force and the productive purpose of the seizure of resources: the need for non-capitalist processes to precede capitalism. Adnan critiques both purpose and intentionality, arguing that PA is necessarily prior to the productive development of the resources seized. He questions the use of force: deliberate acts of violent seizure are one end of a continuum of social processes, the other end of which is 'voluntary' relinquishment of control over resources through market exchange. Marx himself listed speculation, restricted practices and price manipulation as components of the process in Britain. Further, Adnan argues that the *simultaneous* role of primitive accumulation in freeing labour to work for wages may actually be a special case of the general process of transforming property relations so that capital must hire labour in order that commodities be produced. Where a landless workforce predates land seizures, the second part of the dual process of PA ensures the continuing supply of labour that can be exploited rather than its creation for the first time. Resistance to the process may take open and hidden forms, and be violent or non-violent. The state itself may further these processes and/or yield to, or buy off, resistance.

The new era of acquisition of land in forest areas by global and Indian capital for mining and mineral exploitation is PA *par excellence* (see Rajshekhar's meticulous work in India's *Economic Times Bureau* (Raja and Rajshekhar 2012) on the politics of coal blocks, and Rajshekhar (2013) on the politics of hydel). Much of the acquisition of land and eviction of labour for Special Economic Zones (SEZs), for infrastructure such as motorways, and for urban development and property speculation, is a form of PA too (Karnad 2008) depriving people of assets, transferring control and undermining livelihoods.

The economic consequences of loss of land and other land-based assets include not only a swollen casual labour force but also a proliferation of tiny firms unable to accumulate in the informal, unregistered, non-farm economy, written into the labour laws as labour not as capital combined with labour (Sankaran 2008) and theorised as the formal (rather than real) subsumption of labour to capital (Banaji 1977). The political consequences of a lack of elementary compensation and rehabilitation to displaced people are visible as never before and include the turn to non-parliamentary, revolutionary politics (Dhagamwar *et al.* 2003; Shah 2010; Kunnath 2011).

2 The agrarian question

While, with very few exceptions, India's transition to capitalism is well and truly over, debates in India still rage over whether agriculture is indeed capitalist (and undergoing constant transformation under capitalism) or 'semi-feudal',[6] the latter buttressed by the persistence in some regions and the re-emergence in others of debt bondage, landlordism, share tenancy and servile relations to landowners (Rao 2012).

The agrarian question is concerned with the political conditions for agriculture to make the transition to capitalism while performing some vital economic roles for the non-agricultural economy as it does this (Lerche *et al.* 2013). Agriculture must be squeezed to provide raw materials (e.g. cotton), labour, finance and food. In turn the income of the agrarian population must grow to support a home market for the products of industry. Henry Bernstein (2006) has argued that since finance capital for industrialisation can bypass both national frontiers and domestic agriculture, all that is left of the agrarian question for the twenty-first century is the politics of classes of labour. Tom Brass has counter-argued (2007) that lumping all forms of work together as labour is just as politically and analytically flawed as is the neoliberal economic approach in which labour is a market.

This debate is important because India's widespread agrarian poverty is far from being a starting point for development. It is the outcome of decades of development of a type of capitalism that creates pauperised petty production and prevents accumulation from it both in and outside agriculture (Harriss-White 2012b). Yet it cannot be doubted that differentiation and the accumulation of surplus are also proceeding apace (Lerche, Chapter 3, this volume). While these contradictory processes often occur in the same place at the same time, there are also important regional differences in the balance of forces and pathways.[7]

Lerche addresses these issues in Chapter 3, looking at patterns of surplus accumulation in agriculture, and the sectors to which the surplus is directed, and finding great diversity in both. He finds that surplus is by no means always directed into manufacturing, as is assumed in much of the literature on the 'agrarian question'. Lerche uses state-level data on land productivity and the distribution of landholdings as indicators of the regional diversity of surplus accumulation in agriculture. He notes that agrarian accumulation also takes place outside agriculture. His discussion of the relationship between surplus accumulation in agriculture and accumulation in manufacturing and non-agricultural activities draws on case study material from Punjab and Tamil Nadu as well as state-level statistics. It is not possible to go very far on the basis of state-level statistics here. Lerche stresses at many points in his chapter the fact that his analysis is tentative, raising questions that need to be investigated at more disaggregated levels. Mishra (Chapter 4) focuses on Arunachal Pradesh which is outside the core of states that are usually at the heart of debates about agrarian change in India. He uses field evidence to examine the diversity of institutions in Arunachal Pradesh where the state has been and continues to be heavily implicated in the perpetuation of

Introduction 5

non-capitalist institutional forms. He shows that while the transition to capitalism is well established in Arunachal Pradesh, capitalist and non-capitalist institutions, market and non-market institutions, continue to coexist with capitalist agriculture. He also makes the more general point that capital can enter through the state administration and the development of infrastructure as much as anything else – as has been the case in Arunachal Pradesh.

The identification, analysis of dynamics and explanation of regions of capital are needed if only to interrogate the argument that liberalisation put the Indian economy on a regional convergence path (refuted both by Bandyopadhyay (2012), and by Lerche here). The results of such interrogation have serious implications both for planning and equity.

A set of forces argued both to encourage and prevent differentiation and accumulation is relations of exchange. While debt is well established as a powerful differentiating force (Guérin *et al.* 2013b), critics have queried whether interlocked contracts block India's agrarian transition, preserving it in stagnant 'semi-feudal' thraldom, or instead are being constantly reworked to sustain capitalist accumulation (Janakarajan 1986). The vast mass of Indian farmers in the twenty-first century consists of part-time producers working micro-holdings. In 2011, the average holding size was 1.2 ha. Productive activity is suffused by both old terms of exchange such as interlocked contracts and new ones such as those of microfinance (Reddy, Chapter 6, this volume; Augsburg and Fouillet 2010). The bulking of consignments of marketed surplus is also now starting to take place through new contracts (forward contracts tightly specified for quality and timing) for a new scale of agribusiness and big retail (Reardon and Minton 2011; Vijay-shankar and Krishnamurthy 2012). While agriculture is leaking labour as never before, the balance between labour-displacing and livelihood-creating effects of the new exchange relations and distribution chains has not yet been established and is politically controversial.

3 Agricultural and food markets

Food distribution has always been a poor relation of food production. Despite India's PDS (Public Distribution System) receiving the largest subsidy in Asia, food is still distributed overwhelmingly by means of market exchange. Capitalist food markets perform a triple role (Jan and Harriss-White 2012). First, via prices and costs, markets shape the distribution of returns to production and signal incentives for future production decisions. The efficiency with which they do this has been the dominant concern in research on agricultural markets which has shown that Indian agricultural markets persist in being far from allocatively efficient (Palaskas and Harriss-White 1993; Chand 2012). The common occurrence of large numbers of more or less licensed firms, which one is tempted at one's peril to interpret as evidence for competition and thus efficiency, masks the equally common coexistence of local oligopolies with petty trade, the latter often dependent on the former. Second, agricultural commodity markets are also arenas of exploitation, a fact ignored by those who airbrush out post-harvest activities that are productive as well as necessary and are carried out by mercantile firms (Harriss-White 1996a). Not confined to buying and selling, their 'impure' commercial capital is an active element in rural and urban class formation. The third role of food markets is extractive. Financial resources leave agriculture invisibly through the terms of trade and visibly through the profits and investments of farmers and traders controlling rural surpluses. The institutional character of food markets is explained as much by the balance between their three roles as by the physical characteristics of each commodity.

Food markets are complex systems in which physical stages and firms are far from congruent, and horizontal and vertical conditions for transactions are meshed. Order is established by state regulations which in India contrive both to replace market exchange with state trading where markets are inefficient or consumption is inadequate, and to regulate markets when conditions permit (Harriss-White 1996b; Krishnamurthy, Chapter 5, this volume). Wherever the state cannot or will not regulate, or has been bought off, customary rules replace the state in the informal economy (Harriss-White 2003). Business associations play important roles here. Many rules and norms are also grounded in social institutions of caste, ethnicity, religion, locality and gender that are reworked to become economic regulators through which capitalism is structured and accumulation stabilised.

Krishnamurthy shows how agricultural markets in Harda, Madhya Pradesh (MP) have changed as new production regimes have been established, state policy has changed and MNCs have become involved. Her chapter starts with a discussion of the abolition of commission agents in Harda's regulated market yard showing that both the politics of the early 1980s in MP and the increasing prosperity of agriculturalists were crucial to the success with which this change was implemented. Increasingly prosperous agriculturalists were able to survive detachment from commission agent credit as they had benefited from the spread of irrigation following the opening of a major new canal. The other major change discussed by Krishnamurthy is the introduction of weighbridges at the end of the 1990s which signalled the increased power of farmers who spearheaded this change.

4 Microfinance

Money, the essential lubricant of production, distribution and consumption, is both a stock and a flow: the 'ectoplasm' of global capital. In fact money is far from being seamless (Gregory 1997; Hart 2000). It is construed, and, as Reddy shows here, commodified, through socially engineered organisations ranging from banks to pawnbrokers, in processes shaped through social institutions such as caste and gender. Weak and vulnerable groups have long been snared in credit and debt (Fouillet *et al.* 2013), and the new wave of microfinance has been promoted as an answer to such exploitative relationships.

Yet much recent research on microfinance has been gendered, showing how the formal institutions of microfinance have had ambivalent effects on women,

Introduction 7

capable at one and the same time of being emancipating and disempowering (Guérin *et al.* 2013a; Johnson 2005; Garikipati 2012). Simultaneous ambivalence is not theorised well in social science. Reddy, in Chapter 6, describes the contradictory effects of the spread of new waves of microfinance among the hitherto financially excluded in Andhra Pradesh (AP), starting with the development of state supported micro-credit institutions in the 1990s. He shows that the AP state, which went much further than any other state with the development of micro-credit institutions in the 1990s and early 2000s, was remarkably successful in coupling micro-credit with supporting services for rural low-income households. Reddy then describes how unregulated private finance capital emerged in the 2000s engaging in a range of malpractices while piggy-backing on the 1990s developments. The fact that the growth of the private microfinance institutions was strongly backed by the 'international community' was important here. Reddy ends with an account of the AP state government's attempts to regulate private microfinance institutions, and the ways in which the Government of India thwarted them. AP passed its own Bill in 2010. The Government of India passed a much weaker Bill in 2012. As of 2014, both remained on the statute books.

New forms of financial control are set to incorporate the majority of the Indian workforce, consisting of hitherto financially excluded and vulnerable labour, through unique identity numbers, mobile banking correspondents, and the routing of social benefits through cash transfers. Hailed in terms of liberation, progress and empowerment, just as the extension of private microfinance institutions were, this is a development calling for critical scrutiny given what happened in the case of microfinance in AP.[8]

5 Labour

Marx, distinguishing labour power from labour itself, cautioned against seeing labour as a commodity under capitalism (Marx 1844/1959: ch. 4). Yet, apart from the family, there is still no consensus over the key institutional preconditions for the production of labour under capitalism. Wolf (2007) has suggested education, courts and health care, while others suggest gender, caste, ethnicity and religion (Harriss-White 2003; Heyer 2010, 2012, 2014). In India these institutions constitute a structure of discrimination as well as of reproduction essential to accumulation (Prakash and Harriss-White 2010).

Labour is increasingly mobile and its migration has contradictory motives and effects. While distress in the sending site, or the search for liberation from social and economic fetters there, and/or consumer aspirations may propel migration, higher wages at the destination may lure them (Guérin *et al.*, Chapter 7, this volume). The new and totalising regimes of (capitalist) migrant labour control and neo-bondage are exacerbated by migrants being displaced from sites of enforcement of their rights to minimum wages and social benefits and effectively disenfranchised in their destination sites (Breman 2007; Picherit 2012).

8 B. Harriss-White and J. Heyer

There is no sign of the equalisation of the wage in capitalist labour markets (Heyer 2014; Srinivasan forthcoming). Within a given occupational sector returns to rural labour are highly differentiated, by caste, gender and region (Heyer 2014; Guérin *et al.*, Chapter 7, this volume). Dalits and adivasis have least upward mobility in India's labour markets (Kumar *et al.* 2002; Heyer 2010, 2012).

The unresolved questions about labour have a bearing on the capacity of labour to act politically in its own interests amid the daily grind of work, to resist new regimes of control and to struggle for social security rights outside work (Vijayabaskar 2011; Heyer 2012).

Guérin *et al.*, in their chapter, focus on rural labour which is engaged in non-agricultural as much as in agricultural work. Drawing on fieldwork in north-eastern Tamil Nadu, they show that much rural labour is forced to be 'dynamic': switching occupations, migrating off and on, and commuting varying distances. Yet the work that is found through such initiative remains both precarious in its terms and conditions, and vulnerable to contingencies.

Guérin *et al.* also argue that as commodification intensifies its grip, aspirations based on a culturally defined standard of private consumption become generalised. Wages and returns to own-account enterprise are the compulsory precondition of these naturalised but ever growing levels of consumption. An inability to achieve the required consumption level means relative poverty. As absolute levels of material deprivation have declined, rising consumer aspirations, for example, for private education and health care, are fuelling rising reservation wages. The new compulsions of consumption continue to lead rural labourers into exploitative conditions of employment (Guérin *et al.*, Chapter 7, this volume; Cavalcante forthcoming). Credit linked to labour arrangements plays a coercive role.

6 Technical change

Technology both shapes development and is in turn shaped by markets, state policies, and the choices that capitalists make to lower costs and raise the productivity of labour. Competition is crucial to the progress of capitalism and technical change is one of the dynamos of competition. Competition is generally and formally carried out through pressures to adopt new cost-cutting techniques and pressures to accumulate in order to invest in them. However, as Lenin observed,[9] much competition is to avoid competing, so practices such as the ensuring of loyalty through branding and/or through debt, the mobilisation of social institutions to bar entry and carve out and protect market shares, together with attempts to endow each supplying firm with unique attributes, may be seen as technologies of competition too (Harriss-White 1996b, 2008). India's capitalism has many features which defy the principle of competition. Technical change does not necessarily displace the costliest factor. In agro-processing, wave after wave of technical change has displaced the least costly element: casual, low caste female labour, across the board. Instead of the most efficient technology (which includes the technologies of organisation of firms) prevailing over less efficient ones, a plurality of technologies co-exist in a stable fashion (Harriss-White 2005). In Chapter 8, Vijayabaskar explores the way in which new technologies have been introduced into different segments of the textile industry in the Coimbatore/Tiruppur region, enabling new forms of exploitation of labour. Here, a plurality of new technologies has enabled firms to employ increasingly less labour on ever more adverse terms. Space, in the form of changes in location and configurations specific to location, plays an important role. The new technologies he discusses are all the outcomes of the reaction of capital not only to changes in markets but also to changes in state policies.

These features of technical change and competition are important because new techniques adapted for India's socially segmented capitalism are unrevolutionary when they do not cut costs of production and when they displace least-cost elements. As well as being capital-biased they are often formally and informally subsidised by the state.

7 Commodification

While industrial, commercial and financial capital centralises and concentrates itself through the exploitation of innovative technical change, scale economies, and the displacement of labour (often through primitive means involving coercion), another process distinctive of capitalism is at work. This is the process of commodification (Salam, Chapter 9, this volume). Left to its own devices, capital invades subsistence production (J. Harriss 1981; Thorner 1982) and productive and reproductive domestic work carried on outside the money economy (Huws 2003; Harriss-White 2005); it turns the physical and emotional needs of the body (whether labouring or not) into commodities (R. Sunder Rajan 1999/2000; K. Sunder Rajan 2006); it invades the non-market activity of the public sphere, including health, education and knowledge (Leys 2001, 2007; see also Salam, Chapter 9, this volume); it creates markets in the political sphere (McDonald 2010); it invades the non-market disposal of waste (Gill 2009; Hodges 2013, forthcoming). It does the same to common property and common pool resources (Jodha 1990), including now the very air that we breathe (Lohmann 2006).

Development is increasingly defined in terms of the acquisition, spread, control and application of knowledge, with the 'knowledge society' as its ultimate goal. The concept of 'knowledge economy' refers to an economy in which knowledge is no longer confined in institutions protecting its social privileges, but instead is made 'freely' available, but for a price, through markets. In this economy, knowledge becomes a vast collection of commodities along with increasing numbers of institutions (e.g. private universities, think-tanks) and practices (e.g. intellectual property rights and patents, research funding, curricula, consultancies, careers) previously organised according to non-market principles.

Salam, in Chapter 9, discusses (1) how commodification takes place and in whose interests; (2) what is altered by commodification and what effects this has

10   *B. Harriss-White and J. Heyer*

on those involved; and (3) the complex relationships between what is commodified and what is uncommodified. He shows that India's rapidly growing commodified knowledge economy and its aspirations for a knowledge society require an uncommodified knowledge commons, resting in what he calls a 'unity of opposites' rather than a contradiction. It follows that commodification cannot expand without de-commodification, which is just as essential to the wider health and reproduction of society as a whole as it is to the knowledge sector undergoing privatisation.

8 The multiple structures of capital

While the weakness of labour as a political force raises questions about its complicity in capital's hegemony, the question whether it is corporate capital or provincial family business or even a regime of local intermediate classes (operating mostly out of the ambit of state regulation in the informal economy) that exercise hegemony over the Indian economy and polity is still the object of contemporary debate (McCartney and Harriss-White 1999). 'Multiple structures' (the term is owed to Soviet scholarly attempts to make sense of India's capitalism) allude to the heterogeneity of India's capitalist class, fractured as it is, like labour, but perhaps counter-intuitively by region, ethnicity, religion and caste, sector, scale and the form of ownership. Given sharp differences in ownership, governance and economic interests, between finance and industrial capital in the corporate sector (Banaji and Mody 2001), the further question of whether fractions of the capitalist class can themselves exist in contradiction, as necessary but opposed interests driving development, has also been posed. P.S. Jha (1981), for instance, has argued that intermediate capitalists have a direct interest in scarcity while corporate capital does not, that intermediate capital hegemonises its (family) labour forces into complicity while corporate capital opposes labour in open contradiction.

There is a further debate between the social structure of accumulation school which argues that a matrix of institutions forms to stabilise accumulation while also co-evolving over time, ultimately contributing to crises of accumulation (McDonough 2007), and the Marxist institutionalists who see class struggle as the prime mover of the economy while recognising the interaction of class dynamics with political and economic agency expressed through a range of social manifestations of status and authority (Basile, Chapter 10, this volume).

There are also persistent differences of opinion over whether the social institutions through which most applied economists see the economy as being regulated are pre-capitalist residuals, or outliers (Hodgson 2001), or institutions of a non-capitalist economy (Sanyal 2007), or better conceived as culture, or even 'history', or 'impurities' (Hodgson 2001) in an otherwise pure 'canonical' capitalism. Against these debates is ranged an interpretation of capital as reworking the institutions that can serve the process of accumulation and jettisoning those that act as obstacles.

Institutional change then involves the destruction, creation, reworking and persistence of institutions. Even apparent institutional persistence cannot be assumed to reflect stasis but involves conflicts of agency when forces encouraging institutional change are well matched by those opposing it.

Basile, in Chapter 10, develops a Marxist institutionalist framework in which class struggle is the prime mover and class relations are intertwined with local structures deeply rooted in culture and history. She applies her framework to the analysis of the evolution of small-scale capitalism and caste over several decades in a rural market town in Tamil Nadu that has been studied extensively by Harriss-White and her students and colleagues (Harriss-White forthcoming). Basile's analysis is enriched by the fact that it is not reduced to an account of the evolution of capitalism in which social structures passively reflect the development of class forces, nor does it see changing social structures as operating independently of class forces. Thus caste acts as a mediator limiting capital/labour and capital/capital conflicts, while these conflicts themselves remain the basic drivers of capitalist development.

9 International finance

Our book explores capital – understanding it to be a relation of exploitation between owners of private property and a labour force that is less well endowed with, or devoid of, private property. Capital is also commonly understood as financial assets and flows. International finance now dominates the political scene as never before, exerting far more influence over policy than manufacturing capital (Patnaik 2009). It plays ambivalent roles. While in the race for high interest rates it facilitates international technological transfers, by doing so it both increases national debt and tends to destabilise it. It may flow counter-intuitively from jurisdictions in which capital–labour endowments are low to those in which they are high. Even before the financial crisis, and more so afterwards, countries with less dependence on international finance were associated with higher rates of growth (Mohanty 2012). One of its most insidious features is its requirement for material growth to generate returns exceeding the interest on loans, fuelling the pressures on resources that this implies. Its influence on policy is far-reaching. Reddy's examination of the case of microfinance is but one example of this.

Srinivasan in Chapter 11 examines a different aspect of international finance that is very difficult to research: the use of international financial channels and institutions to hide the surpluses of Indian capital. He focuses on the processes and agencies involved in both the devious but legal and the outright illegal hiding of wealth and its flight overseas that play a crucial role in concealing the exploitation of labour in India. The complicity of Western nations, finance centres and institutions makes this all appear above board. India's capitalist economy is not simply informalised; a sizeable part is criminalised. Liberalisation has eased the process of accumulation offshore. It is estimated that 'the total value of illicit assets held abroad represents about 72 per cent of the size of India's underground economy which has been estimated at 50 per cent of India's GDP' (Kar 2010: vii). Capital flight may leach as much as 16 per cent of GDP,

12 *B. Harriss-White and J. Heyer*

some of which returns through Mauritius as FDI which is eligible for tax breaks. While commentators on capital flight deplore its negative effects on the tax base, the public sector and domestic productive investment (Kar 2010), Srinivasan emphasises its effects on the workforce as well.

10 The state and policy

Marxists have generally viewed policy as an epiphenomenon and the state as the executive arm of the bourgeoisie (Marx and Engels 1848/1998). This is inadequate for the complexity of the political requirements of the Indian capitalist class, for the deep structures of informal practices embedded in the state, and for the state's changing – more or less autonomous – developmental role (Evans 1995). Scholars interrogating the 'actually existing' Indian state and its policy activity, as Chatterjee does in Chapter 12, find that it is a complex congeries of ideas and practices. Over the decades, attempts have been made to systematise them (see e.g. Corbridge *et al.* 2012; Fernandez 2012; Gupta 2012; Harriss 1984; Jenkins 2000; Kohli 1987; Schaffer 1984; Sud 2012; Trubek and Galanter 1974). In the churning relations of bureaucratic politics a mass of political strategies and tactics, deployed throughout the bureaucracy, contrive frequently to turn formally intended beneficiaries into victims, and to regulate the economy in the interests of its elites. While few systematically probe the non-monolithic nature of the Indian state, its autonomy in directing development has been questioned (Evans 1995; Chatterjee, Chapter 12, this volume), and the extent to which it has been captured (Mitra's dual and unequal alliance; Chatterjee, this volume), or expresses a coalition of interests (Bardhan's tripartite coalition), or represents a political settlement that has been forged between interests in the triad of investment, compensation and rent exactions are issues that are still unresolved (see Khan and Jomo 2001; McCartney 2010).

What we know about the Indian state in action is derived from knowledge gathered through direct experience in the field, and this is limited. Existing research reveals the extent to which there are informal models of control, informal practices of protection, taxation, regulation and distribution, a 'parallel' or 'shadow' or 'private interest' or 'private status' state coexisting in uneasy relations with the visible, formal one. There is less consensus, even among field economists and political scientists, over whether social norms (and the effects inside the state of institutions of religion, ethnicity, caste, gender and the informal politics of parties) bring a *different* order to the regulation of capitalism from that designed through due process by formal institutions of government. Alternatively, formal but unenforced law may exert indirect effects on informal agents, firms and workers, who operate 'as if' formal law were implemented when it isn't (Olsen and Morgan 2010). Be that as it may, the extent to which informal practices pervade India's formal state (Fernandez 2010) is such as to question the formal–informal duality.

The Indian state is fragmented, as is patently obvious, for example, when states pursue very different policies the one from the other. Jos Mooij's outstanding early

Introduction 13

research on the politics of food distribution showed that state borders could mark radically different approaches to the food economy (Mooij 1999). John Harriss (2001) revealed the degree of state-level discontinuity in the combination of local party politics and non-party expressions of class politics in addressing poverty. Chatterjee (Chapter 12, this volume) also finds radically different approaches to the reform of the electricity sector across states.

Chatterjee asks why the actually existing state has failed to pursue pro-business policies with respect to the electricity sector, a sector which is crucial to business success. Using both Marxist and Weberian theory, she starts by tracking attempts to 'depoliticise' electricity policy, i.e. to reduce the influence of agrarian and consumer interests, particularly at the state level. This resulted in a repoliticisation of the bureaucracy at higher levels, strengthening the influence of business interests. Chatterjee stresses the porosity, fragmentation and organisational complexity of the state, arguing that this makes it difficult for business interests to capture it. She concludes that far from directly serving the interests of capital, 'India's contemporary "capitalist state" remains simultaneously more ambivalent, more indispensable, and more chaotic than much theory might suggest'.

11 Nature

At the start of *Capital* Marx wrote, 'labour is not the only source of material wealth ... labour is its father and the earth its mother'. Until recently however, the mother has been taken for granted and forgotten.[10] For capital, mother nature is a 'tap' supplying material resources. The body's 'internal organs' interact with 'external organs' (tools and raw materials) to create useful products in a process increasingly mediated by markets. However, under capitalism, physical resources are not restituted to nature. Contradictions, necessary oppositions, underlie the dynamism of capital, not only between capital and labour but between capital and the resources it transforms (the Club of Rome's much criticised insight (Meadows *et al.* 1972)). The 'metabolic rift' (Marx 1981: 949) identifies commodity production and distribution as being in contradiction with the Earth's finite capacities to provide raw materials and to de- and re-compose waste into commodifiable raw materials.[11] As in the chemical cycles in European industrial agriculture and in the solid and liquid waste that streamed visibly from nineteenth-century cities such as London, so now in India, land fertility is sustained by non-renewable chemical fertiliser imported from ever greater distances, and small-town India is stifling in its own non-biodegradable waste, excrement and fumes. The material and energy exchanges between nature and society are exhausting nature as a 'sink' as well as as a 'tap'. Planetary sinks are on track to set catastrophic limits to the entire system of global capital. With nature stylised as consisting of sectors with 'safe spaces' for exploitation, the process of capitalist development has already reached and exceeded three of the nine 'planetary boundaries' which support it (Rockstrom *et al.* 2009). Currently there is no answer from history anywhere to the political question of how to stop

14   *B. Harriss-White and J. Heyer*

or reverse the processes described above before they threaten the biosphere upon which all life depends. India has contributed only 2.5 per cent to cumulative atmospheric stocks of CO_2 and currently emits only 6 per cent of the annual gaseous pollution – one-twentieth per caput of that of the USA in both cases – but is considered highly vulnerable to the effects of global warming, with limited room for manoeuvre in relation to these planetary processes.[12]

Ghotge, in the final chapter in this book, draws attention to the differing epistemologies of matter in social science and science which has led to a belated integration of the latter into the former. He then shows how late it was before energy was admitted by economists as a third means or factor of production responsible for growth. The geopolitics of fossil fuel in particular has shaped the military industrial complexes of the world as well as the strong political resistance to renewable energy. India is no exception. Ghotge shows how the refusal to act with reason on evidence, and the refusal to acknowledge the speed and the strength of the underlying bio-geo-chemical processes, is contributing to the development of increasingly serious problems in the longer term. He argues however that there remain ways in which India can still contribute to what is known as 'mitigation', and he suggests priorities. In agriculture: solar-pumped irrigation water; in industry and services: renewable energy and mass transport based on it, materials efficiency and the reuse of waste. He concludes that already existing technologies that are small in scale, flexible, and modular in production might be wrenched from (state) corporate capital to bring about not simply a less devouring footprint on nature but also major changes in the global class configurations in which those of India are situated.

Conclusion

In its engagement with a wide range of theoretical debates using the insights of ground-level research, our book starts to show how the transitions to, and current transformations of, capitalism give it a character and create a particular model of development that are both distinctively Indian. Its key elements are its poorly educated and poorly skilled, casualised, rightless and badly paid, caste- and gender-stratified labour force; the persistence and ubiquity of petty production/self-employment which expands by multiplication not accumulation; small family businesses which are hemmed in by vernacular language frontiers; new state-level capital aspiring to national markets, and state and national capital exporting and importing its surpluses internationally, much in the informal and underground economies. These elements are enduringly reinforced by a powerful state-owned sub-economy that has embraced liberalisation yet resisted privatisation, and by state-backed power over the acquisition of land-based resources with scant regard for the compensation of victims. India's 'model' features a mass of regulative law that is observed in the breach and an economy that is – deliberately – socially regulated. India's rights-based redistributive project aimed at improving the conditions under which labour is

Introduction 15

produced and reproduced, is heavily fought for by elements of civil society and the Indian academy but makes slow progress. Half of India's women are illiterate, and dalits, adivasis and Muslims are disfavoured. While this book examines the model, more research is needed to flesh out the interconnections of its elements.

As Ghotge explains in Chapter 13, now that capitalism has outstripped the planet's capacity to accommodate it in the atmosphere, the lithosphere, the hydrosphere and the biosphere, what can be done? This is not a melodramatic question but a practical one. It is being answered in very specific ways. The future is being foreseen and planned through a new generation of global models based on heroic assumptions, including those about the responsive capacities of individual nations and states (Nelson *et al.* 2010; Stern 2013). The grip of foresight science on society, policy, management and the public expresses an approach to the expert public communication of science which rejects social science and deploys carefully depoliticised language. This is evident in consensual scientific 'assessments'[13] and engineering scenarios which ignore people as stakeholders, workers, consumers and voters (EPSRC 2012).

To enrich the understanding of India's development and to provide a solid base from which to determine what might be done in future, the time is overripe for a renaissance of political economy, based on knowledge of ground realities and crafted at the scales through which the theories and ideas about Indian's capitalism in development have been addressed in this book.

Notes

1 First, because there is no theory of everything in social science; second, because progress requires opening theory up to collective 'democratic' scrutiny.
2 For critical political economy analyses, see Mukherjee-Reed (2003) on corporate capital, Banaji and Mody (2001) on corporate governance, Upadhya (2009) on the new wave of capital, D'Costa (2005) for the auto industry, and Saraswati (2012) for India's IT. For capital in India's energy infrastructure, see Chatterjee and Ghotge (Chapters 12 and 13, respectively this volume).
3 See Bhattacharya *et al.* (2009) on banking. For microfinance and money laundering see Reddy and Srinivasan (Chapters 6 and 11, respectively, this volume).
4 See Dasgupta (2008 and n.d.) for a Marxian analysis of liberalisation.
5 The word 'primitive' is also translated as 'previous', 'prior', 'original' and 'primary'.
6 For example, Brass (2007). The contributors to our book show how while caste and gender distort labour markets in a manner akin to the effects of debt bondage, they are not the less capitalist labour markets for this.
7 There are outliers in which agrarian relations are dominated by landlordism and debt bondage (Rao 2012). There are others in which agrarian capitalism has hardly begun penetrating (Shah 2013).
8 See e.g. Rajshekhar (http://economictimes.indiatimes.com/news/news-by-industry/banking/finance/banking/psu-banks-express-reservation-against-usage-of-aadhaar-number-for-cash-transfers/articleshow/19551284.cms http://economictimes.indiatimes.com/news/economy/policy/governments-move-to-shelve-aadhaar-based-direct-benefit-transfer-blow-for-uidai/articleshow/29622644.cms).
9 The labour force was to resist competition by sabotaging it (www.marxists.org/archive/lenin/works/1917/dec/25.htm).

16   B. Harriss-White and J. Heyer

10 This insight is attributed to Frederick Soddy by Martinez Alier and Schlupmann (1987: 131).

11 Whether the metabolic rift is a consequence of capitalist development or is instead constitutive of it is debated by Jason Moore (2011).

12 United Nations Statistics Division (2010). Carbon dioxide emissions (CO_2), calculated from human-produced, direct emissions of carbon dioxide only. Excludes other greenhouse gases; land-use, land-use-change and forestry (LULUCF); and natural background flows of CO_2.

13 For example, for population and consumption (Sulston *et al.* 2012), biodiversity loss (Cardinale *et al.* 2012) and nuclear fission (Wood *et al.* 2012).

References

Adnan, S. (2013) 'Land grabs and primitive accumulation in deltaic Bangladesh: interactions between neoliberal globalization, state interventions, power relations and peasant resistance', *Journal of Peasant Studies*, 40(1): 87–128.

Agnihotri, S. (2000) *Sex Ratio Patterns in the Indian Population*, New Delhi: Sage Publications.

Augsburg, B. and Fouillet, C. (2010) 'Profit empowerment: the microfinance institution's mission drift', *Perspectives on Global Development and Technology*, 9(3–4): 323–351.

Banaji, J. (1977) 'Capitalist domination and the small peasantry: Deccan districts in the late nineteenth century', *Economic and Political Weekly*, 12: 33–34.

—— (2010) *Theory as History*, Leiden, and Boston, MA: Brill.

Banaji, J. and Mody, G. (2001) Corporate governance and the Indian private sector', *QEH Working Paper Number 73* (http://eprints.soas.ac.uk/10919/1/qehwps73.pdf).

Bandyopadhyay, S. (2012) 'Convergence club empirics: evidence from Indian states', *Research in Economic Inequality*, 20: 175–203.

Barua, K. (2010) 'Variation in wage earnings among agricultural labourers', *Indian Journal of Labour Economics*, 53(4): 677–686.

Basile, E., Lutringer, C. and Harriss-White, B. (eds) (forthcoming) *Mapping India's Capitalism: Old and New Regions*, Basingstoke: Palgrave Macmillan.

Bernstein, H. (2006) 'Is there an agrarian question in the 21st century?', *Canadian Journal of Development Studies*, 27(4): 449–460.

Bhaduri, A. (1983) *The Economic Structure of Backward Agriculture*, London: Academic Press.

Bhattacharya, S. and Chakrabarti, D. (2013) 'Financial liberalisation, financing constraint and India's manufacturing sector', *Economic and Political Weekly*, 48(6): 61–67.

Brass, T. (2002) 'Rural labour in agrarian transitions: the semi-feudal thesis revisited', *Journal of Contemporary Asia*, 32(4): 256–273.

—— (2007) 'Weapons of the weak and weakness of the weapons', *Journal of Peasant Studies*, 34(1): 111–153.

Breman, J. (2007) *The Jan Breman Omnibus: Comprising Of Peasants, Migrants and Paupers; Wage Hunters and Gatherers; The Labouring Poor in India*, New Delhi: Oxford University Press.

Breman, J., Guérin, I. and Prakash, A. (eds) (2009) *India's Unfree Workforce: Of Bondage Old and New*, New Delhi: Oxford University Press.

Cardinale, B.J., Emmett Duffy, J., Gonzalez, A., Hooper, D.U., Perrings, C., Venail, P., Narwani, A., Mace, G.M., Tilman, D., Wardle, D.A., Kinzig Gretchen, A.P., Daily, C., Loreau, M., Grace, J.B., Larigauderie, A., Srivastava, D.S. and Naeem, S. (2012)

Introduction 17

'Biodiversity loss and its impact on humanity', *Nature*, 486(7401) (www.nature.com/nature/journal/v486/n7401/full/nature11148.html).

Cavalcante, M. (forthcoming) 'Feeling rich with empty stomachs: agrarian crisis and rural consumption choices', in B. Harriss-White (ed.) *Middle India and Urban-Rural Development: Four decades of Change in Tamil Nadu*, New Delhi: Springer.

Chand, R. (2012) 'Development policies and agricultural markets', *Economic and Political Weekly*, 47(52): 53–56.

Corbridge, S., Harriss, J. and Jeffrey, C. (2012) *India Today: Economy, Politics & Society*, Cambridge: Polity Press.

Dasgupta, C. (2008) *State and Capital in Independent India: From Dirigisme to Neoliberalism*, Ph.D. thesis, School of Oriental and African Studies, University of London.

—— (n.d.) *Globalisation, Corporate Legal Liability and Big Business Houses in India* (www.cisd.soas.ac.uk/Editor/assets/chirashreedasgupta_final.pdf).

D'Costa, A. (2005) *The Long March to Capitalism: Embourgeoisement, Internationalisation and Industrial Transformation in India*, Basingstoke: Palgrave Macmillan.

Dhagamwar, V., De, S. and Verma, N. (2003) *Industrial Development and Displacement*, New Delhi: Sage.

EPSRC (Engineering and Physical Sciences Research Council) (2012) Low Carbon Pathways consortium of E-on; government; and nine universities, 18 April, London (www.lowcarbonpathways.org.uk/).

Evans, P. (1995) *Embedded Autonomy; States and Industrial Transformation*, Princeton, NJ: Princeton University Press.

Fernandez, B. (2012) *Transformative Policy for Poor Women: A New Feminist Framework.* Burlington, VT, and Surrey, UK: Ashgate.

Financial Times (2010) 'The age of "indovation" dawns', 15 June.

Foster, J.B. (2002) 'Marx's ecology in historical perspective', *International Socialism*, 96 (http://pubs.socialistreviewindex.org.uk/isj96/foster.htm).

Fouillet, C., Hudon, M. and Harriss-White, B. (2013) 'Microfinance and Development Studies', Special Issue, *Oxford Development Studies*.

Garikapati, S. (2013) 'Microcredit and women's empowerment: have we been looking at the wrong indicators?', Special Issue, *Oxford Development Studies*.

Gill, K. (2009) *Of Poverty and Plastic*, New Delhi: Oxford University Press.

Gregory, C. (1997) *Savage Money: The Anthropology of Commodity Exchange*, Amsterdam: Harwood Academic Publishers.

Guérin, I. (forthcoming) 'Bonded labour and the agrarian question in Tamil Nadu', *Journal of Agrarian Change.*

Guérin, I., Kumar, S. and Agier, I. (2013a) 'Women's empowerment: power to act or power over other women? Lessons from Indian microfinance', *Special Issue, Oxford Development Studies.*

Guérin, I., Morvant-Roux, S. and Villareal, M. (2013b) *Microfinance, Debt and Over-Indebtedness, Juggling with Money*, London: Routledge.

Gupta, A. (2012) *Red Tape: Bureaucracy, Structural Violence, and Poverty in India*, Durham, NC: Duke University Press.

Harriss, B. (1984) *State and Market*, New Delhi: Concept Publication Company.

Harriss, J. (1981) *Capitalism and Peasant Farming*, Bombay, Calcutta, New Delhi, Madras: Oxford University Press.

—— (1999) 'Comparing political regimes across Indian states, Part One', *Economic and Political Weekly*, 34(48): 3367–3377.

Harriss-White, B. (1996a) *A Political Economy of Agricultural Markets in South India*, New Delhi: Sage.

—— (1996b) 'Order ... Order ... Agrocommercial microstructures and the state – the experience of regulation', in S. Subrahmanyam and B. Stein (eds) *Institutions and Economic Change in South Asia: Historical and Contemporary Perspectives*, New Delhi: Oxford University Press.

—— (2003) *India Working*, Cambridge: Cambridge University Press.

—— (2005) 'Commercialisation, commodification and gender relations in post harvest systems for rice in South Asia', *Economic and Political Weekly*, 40(25): 2530–2542.

—— (2008) *Rural Commercial Capital: Agricultural Markets in West Bengal*, New Delhi: Oxford University Press.

—— (2012a) '"Ecological economics" – in and after Marx', in B. Fine and A. Saad Filho (eds) *An Encyclopaedia of Marxist Economics*, Cheltenham: Edward Elgar.

—— (2012b) 'Capitalism and the common man', *Agrarian South: Journal of Political Economy*, 1(2): 109–160.

—— (ed.) (forthcoming) *Middle India and Urban-Rural Development: Four Decades of Change in Tamil Nadu*, New Delhi, Springer.

Harrisss-White, B. and Heyer, J. (eds) (2010) *The Comparative Political Economy of Development: Africa and South Asia*, London and New York: Routledge.

Harriss-White, B. and Vidyarthee, K. (2010) 'Stigma and regions of accumulation: dalits and adivasis in India's business economy in the 1990s', in B. Harriss-White and J. Heyer (eds) *The Comparative Political Economy of Development: Africa and South Asia*, London and New York: Routledge.

—— (2014) 'Regions of dalit and adivasi discrimination in India's business economy', in *Dalits and Adivasis in India's Business Economy – Three Essays and an Atlas*, New Delhi: Three Essays Press.

Hart, K. (2000) *Money in an Unequal World: The Memory Bank*, London: Profile Books.

Heyer, J. (2010) 'The marginalisation of dalits in a modernising economy', in B. Harriss-White and J. Heyer (eds) *The Comparative Political Economy of Development*, London and New York: Routledge.

—— (2012) 'Labour standards and social policy: a South Indian case study', *Global Labour Journal*, 3(1): 91–117.

—— (2013) 'Integration into a global production network: impacts of labour in Tiruppur's rural hinterlands', *Oxford Development Studies*, 41(3): 307–321.

—— (2014) 'Dalit women becoming "housewives": lessons from the Tiruppur region 1981/2–2008/9', in C. Still (ed.) *Mobility of Marginalisation: Dalits in Neo-Liberal India*, New Delhi: Routledge.

Hill, P. (1986) *Development Economics on Trial: The Anthropological Case for a Prosecution*, Cambridge: Cambridge University Press.

Hodges, S. (2013) 'Medical garbage and the making of neoliberalism in India', *Economic and Political Weekly*, 48(48): 112–119.

—— (forthcoming) *Biotrash: Money, Medicine and Garbage in India*.

Huws, U. (2003) *The Making of the Cybertariat*, London: Merlin.

Jan, M.A. and Harriss-White, B. (2012) 'The three roles of agricultural markets', *Economic and Political Weekly*, 47(52): 39–52.

Janakarajan, S. (1986) *Aspects of Market Interrelationships in a Changing Agrarian Economy*, Ph.D. thesis, University of Madras.

Jenkins, R. (2000) *Democratic Politics and Economic Reform in India*, Cambridge: Cambridge University Press.

Introduction 19

Jha, P.S. (1981) *The Political Economy of Stagnation*, New Delhi: Oxford University Press.

Jodha, N.S. (1990) 'Depletion of common property resources in India: micro-level evidence', in G. McNicoll and M. Cain (eds) *Rural Development and Population: Institutions and Policy*, New York: Oxford University Press.

Johnson, S. (2005) 'Gender relations, empowerment and microcredit: moving on from a lost decade', *European Journal of Development Research*, 17(2): 224–248.

Kar, D. (2010) 'The drivers and dynamics of illicit financial flows from India: 1948–2008', *Global Financial Integrity* (www.gfintegrity.org/).

Karnad, R. (2008) 'The hunting party returns', *Tehelka Magazine*, 5(20), 24 May.

Khan, M. and Jomo, K.S. (2001) *Rents, Rent Seeking and Economic Development in Asia*, Cambridge: Cambridge University Press.

Kohli, A. (1987) *The State and Poverty in India: The Politics of Reform*, Cambridge: Cambridge University Press.

Kumar, S., Heath, A. and Heath, O. (2002) 'Changing patterns of social mobility: some trends over time', *Economic and Political Weekly*, 37(40): 4091–4096.

Kunnath, G. (2011) *Rebels from the Mud Houses: Dalits and the Making of the Maoist Revolution in Bihar*, New Delhi: Social Science Press.

Lawson, T. (2003) *Reorienting Economics*, London and New York: Routledge.

Lerche, J., Shah, A. and Harriss-White, B. (2013) 'Agrarian questions and Left politics in India', *Journal of Agrarian Change*, 13(3): 337–350.

Lefebvre, H. (1991) *The Production of Space*, Oxford: Blackwell.

—— (2009) *State, Space, World: Selected Essays*, Minneapolis: University of Minnesota Press.

Lenin, V.I. (1917/1997) *How to Organise Competition?* (www.marxists.org/archive/lenin/works/1917/dec/25.htm).

Leys, C. (2001) *Market Driven Politics*, London: Verso.

—— (2007) *Total Capitalism*, London: Merlin.

Lohmann, L. (2006) *Carbon Trading: A Critical Conversation of Climate Change, Privatisation and Power*, Stockholm: Stockholm Institute/Dag Hammarskjold Foundation.

McCartney, M. (2010) *Political Economy, Growth and Liberalisation in India, 1991–2008*, London: Routledge.

McCartney, M. and Harriss-White, B. (1999) 'The 'intermediate regime' and 'intermediate classes' revisited: a critical political economy of Indian economic development from 1980 to Hindutva', *Queen Elizabeth House Working Paper, no. 34*.

McDonald, H. (2010) *Ambani and Sons*, New Delhi: Roli.

McDonough, T. (2007) 'Social structures of accumulation theory: the state of the art', *Review of Radical Political Economics*, 40(2): 153–173.

Martinez Alier, J. and Schlupmann, K. (1987) *Ecological Economics: Energy, Environment and Society*, Oxford: Blackwell.

Marx, K. (1976) *Capital Vol. I*, London: Lawrence and Wishart.

—— (1981) *Capital Vol. III*, New York: Vintage.

—— (1844/1959) *Economic and Philosophical Manuscripts: Theories of Surplus-Value*, Moscow: Progress Publishers.

Marx, K. and Engels, F. (1848/1998) *The Communist Manifesto, Introduction*, by Martin Malia, New York: Penguin Group.

Meadows, D.L., Randers, J. and Behrens, W.W. III (1972) *Limits to Growth*, New York: New American Library for the Club of Rome.

20 B. Harriss-White and J. Heyer

Mishra, D.K. (forthcoming) 'Why map India's capitalism? An introduction', in E. Basile *et al.* (eds) *Mapping India's Capitalism: Old and New Regions*, Basingstoke: Palgrave Macmillan.

Mohanty D (2012) 'Global capital flows and the Indian economy – opportunities and challenges', Kanpur: IIT/Basel: Bank for International Settlements (www.bis.org/review/r120201a.pdf).

Mooij, J. (1999) *Food Policy and Politics*, New Delhi: Oxford University Press.

Moore, J.W. (2011) 'Transcending the metabolic rift: towards a theory of crises in the capitalist world-ecology', *Journal of Peasant Studies*, 38(1): 1–46.

Mukherjee-Reed, A. (ed.) (2003) *Corporate Capitalism in Contemporary Asia*, Basingstoke: Palgrave Macmillan.

Nelson, G. *et al.* (2010) *Food Security, Farming, and Climate Change to 2050*, IFPRI, Washington, DC (www.ifpri.org/publication/food-security-farming-and-climate-change-2050).

Olsen, W.K. (1996) *Rural Indian Social Relations*, New Delhi: Oxford University Press.

Olsen, W.K. and Morgan, D. (2010) 'Institutional change from within the informal sector in Indian rural labour relations', *International Review of Sociology*, 20(3): 535–555.

Palaskas T.B. and Harriss-White, B. (1993) 'Testing marketing integration: new approaches with case material from the West Bengal food economy', *Journal of Development Studies*, 30(1): 1–57.

Palmer-Jones, R.W. and Sen, K.K. (2003) 'What has luck got to do with it? A regional analysis of poverty and agricultural growth in rural India', *Journal of Development Studies*, 40(1): 1–31.

Patnaik, P (2009), *The Value of Money*, New York and Chichester: Columbia University Press.

Picherit, D. (2012) 'Migrant labourers' struggles between village and urban migration sites: labour standards, rural development and politics in South India', *Global Labour Journal*, 3(1): 143–162.

Polanyi, K. (1947) *The Great Transformation*, London: Doubleday.

Prakash, A. and Harriss-White, B. (2010) 'Social discrimination and economic citizenship', *Working Paper 8, Oxfam-India*, New Delhi (www.oxfamindia.org/sites/default/files/VIII.%20Social%20Discrimination%20in%20India-%20A%20Case%20for%20Economic%20Citizenship.pdf).

Radjou, N., Prabhu, J. and Ahuja, S. (2012) *Jugaad Innovation*, New Delhi: Random House India.

Raja, J.S. and Rajshekhar, M. (2012) 'Coal block allocations: private profiteering from a public asset', *Economic Times*, 2 August (http://articles.economictimes.indiatimes.com/2012-08-02/news/33001108_1_coal-block-allocations-power-plant-wardha-power).

Rajshekhar, M. (2013) 'Contours of a hydelpower frenzy', Fractured Earth: Reflections on a Planet that lacks both Equitable and Sustainable Development (http://mrajshekhar.wordpress.com/2013/05/06/the-hydelpower-scam/).

Raju, S. (forthcoming) 'Mapping the world of women's work in India', in E. Basile *et al.* (eds) *Mapping India's Capitalism, Old and New Regions*, Basingstoke: Palgrave Macmillan.

Rao, N.V. (2012) *Understanding Maoists: Notes of a Participant Observer from Andhra Pradesh*, Kolkata: Archana Das & Subrata Das.

Reardon, T. and Minten, B. (2011) 'The quiet revolution in India's food supply chains', *IFPRI Discussion Papers 1115*, Washington, DC: International Food Policy Research Institute (IFPRI).

Rockstrom *et al.* (2009) 'A safe operating space for humanity', *Nature*, 461: 472–475.

Rogaly, B. (1997) 'Embedded markets: hired labour arrangements in West Bengal agriculture', *Oxford Agrarian Studies*, 25(2): 209–223.

Samuel, J., Raja, D. and Rajshekhar, M. (2012) 'Coal block allocations: private profiteering from a public asset', *Economic Times Bureau, New Delhi*, 2 August.

Sankaran, K. (2008) 'Informal economy, own account workers and the law: an overview', *WIEGO Law Pilot Project on the Informal Economy*, retrieved from http://wiego.org/sites/wiego.org/files/resources/files/fow_background_note.pdf (29 accessed May 2012).

Saraswati, J. (2012) *Dot.compradors: Power and Policy in the Development of the Indian Software Industry*, London: Pluto Press.

Schaffer, B. (1984) 'Toward responsibility', in B. Schaffer and E. Clay (eds) *Room for Manoeuvre*, London: Heinemann.

Schumpeter, J.A. (1942/1994) *Capitalism, Socialism and Democracy*, London: Routledge.

Shah, A. (2010) *In the Shadows of the State: Indigenous Politics, Environmentalism and Insurgency in Jharkhand, India*, Durham, NC: Duke University Press.

—— (2013) 'The agrarian question in a Maoist guerrilla zone: Land, labour and capital in the forests and hills of Jharkhand, India', *Journal of Agrarian Change*, 13(3): 424–450.

Sinha, A. (2005) *The Regional Roots of Development Politics in India*, Bloomington: Indiana University Press.

Srinivasan, M.V. (forthcoming) 'Segmentation processes and labour market mobility of self-employed workers in Arni', in B. Harriss-White (ed.) *Middle India and Urban-Rural Development: Four decades of Change in Tamil Nadu*, New Delhi: Springer.

Stern, N. (2013) www.guardian.co.uk/environment/2013/jan/27/nicholas-stern-climate-change-davos.

Sud, N. (2012) *Liberalization, Hindu Nationalism and the State*, New Delhi: Oxford University Press.

Sulston, Sir John, and a multidisciplinary team (2012) *People and the Planet*, London: Royal Society.

Sunder Rajan, K. (2006) *Biocapital: The Constitution of Postgenomic Life*, Durham, NC: Duke University Press.

Sunder Rajan, R. (ed.) (1999/2000) *Signposts: Gender Issues in Post-Independence India*, New Delhi: Kali for Women; reprinted by Rutgers University Press, New Brunswick, NJ.

Thorner, A. (1982) 'Semi-feudalism or capitalism – contemporary debate on classes and modes of production in India', *Economic and Political Weekly*, 17(50 and 51): 1908–1961 and 1993–1999.

Trubek, D.M. and Galanter, M. (1974) 'Scholars in self estrangement', *Wisconsin Law Review*, pp. 1062–1103.

United Nations Statistics Division (2010) *Millennium Development Goals Indicators: Carbon Dioxide Emissions (CO₂), Thousand Tonnes of CO₂*, New York: United Nations.

Upadhya, C. (2009) 'Emergence of new business classes', *Economic and Political Weekly*, 44(18): 21–24.

Vijayshankar, P.S. and Krishmamurthy, M. (2012) 'Understanding agricultural commodity markets', *Economic and Political Weekly*, 47(52): 34–37.

Wolf, F.O. (2007) 'Reproduction, accumulation and the division of labour: what Capital II is really about', *Historical Materialism Conference Paper*, SOAS, London.

Wood, J. *et al.* (2012) *Benefits and Limitations of Nuclear Fission for a Low Carbon Economy*, Brussels: European Union (ec.europa.eu/research/energy/.../study2012_synthesis_report.pdf).

2 Primitive accumulation and the 'transition to capitalism' in neoliberal India

Mechanisms, resistance, and the persistence of self-employed labour[1]

Shapan Adnan

1 Introduction

Marx's conceptualization of 'so-called primitive accumulation' drew upon available historical accounts of his time, particularly the enclosure of private and common lands of tenant farmers and attached labourers by landlords and capitalist farmers in Britain. The formation of a class of wage workers by the dispossessed groups was presented as the obverse of the concentration of land by the expropriating classes. The *simultaneity* of these 'two transformations' was integral to Marx's (1976: 874) construct of primitive accumulation. The unique set of *convergences* in this stylized historical account, combining the acts of expropriation and the creation of propertyless workers mediated by extraeconomic coercion and legal enactments, made it something of a special case.

However, Marx also conceived of primitive accumulation as an ongoing process, which adopted different forms and modalities in specific socialhistorical contexts (Marx 1976: 876; Perelman 1984: 8–12). Subsequent changes in the features of evolving capitalism and the means used to procure its inputs have led to a reformulations of the concept. Particularly influential among these has been the notion of 'accumulation by dispossession' (ABD) advanced by Harvey (2005) in the context of neoliberal globalization.

In this chapter, I have made a preliminary attempt to assess the features and outcomes of primitive accumulation in India in the context of neoliberal globalization. India has already experienced a considerable degree of capitalist development and possesses a well-developed ('mature') capitalist sector operating in relation to coexistent non-capitalist sectors. This raises a number of critical questions about the role and relevance of ongoing primitive accumulation in the contemporary Indian economy, as follows:

1   What are the distinctive mechanisms of primitive accumulation operating in neoliberal India, as well as their driving factors and limiting constraints?
2   To what extent has primitive accumulation been followed by the formation of wage labour and the 'transition to capitalism', as posited in Marx's schema?

24   *S. Adnan*

3   Does the experience of neoliberal India indicate the need to reformulate the concept of primitive accumulation and its causal interlinkages with capitalist production?

4   Should primitive accumulation be considered as a part of 'movements within mature capitalism' or an analytically distinct process?

Given constraints of time and space, it has not been feasible to provide a comprehensive theoretical review of the concepts of primitive accumulation and ABD. Nor has it been possible to cover all the empirical evidence on primitive accumulation in neoliberal India. Instead, I have analysed selected case studies from different states of India as relevant to the arguments put forward. The empirical evidence used is taken from secondary sources, including published materials and online websites on land grabs and related aspects of primitive accumulation in India.

Section 2 provides a brief review of theoretical concepts and key issues pertaining to primitive accumulation and ABD in the context of capitalist development. Section 3 outlines the salient features of neoliberal policy shifts in India. Distinct mechanisms of land grabs in neoliberal India, as well as resistance to them, are analysed in Section 4. The impacts of neoliberal policies, including income deflation, are outlined in Section 5. Section 6 critically reviews major explanations of the persistence and preponderance of self-employed labour, drawing out the implications for the 'transition to capitalism'. Section 7 integrates the key conclusions on the mechanisms and determinants of primitive accumulation and puts forward theoretical reflections emerging from the analysis of neoliberal India.

2   Theoretical aspects of primitive accumulation: issues and problems

2.1   Characteristics of primitive accumulation

The *separation* of direct producers from their means of production and subsistence lies at the core of Marx's (1976: 874–876) notion of primitive accumulation. Such *mechanisms* of primitive accumulation need to be analytically distinguished from those mediating capitalist accumulation, namely (i) expanded reproduction, and (ii) centralization of capital.

Primitive accumulation requires that distinct social classes come to control these separated resources (*qua* capital and labour). It is also necessary that such resources are transformed into *compatible forms of property* that can be potentially deployed in capitalist production (i.e. transactable commodities). Such changes in 'social–property relations' and the class structure are integral to the concept of primitive accumulation (Dobb 1963: 185–186; Wood 2002: 31–37; 2006: 19–20; Brenner 2006: 97–98). It follows that no amount of quantitative resource transfer, by itself, corresponds to primitive accumulation unless there is concomitant *transformation* of the *class structure and property rights*.

Primitive accumulation in neo-liberal India 25

However, there is no teleological presupposition that primitive accumulation will be necessarily followed by the deployment of the separated resources into capitalist production. In particular, the labour of the dispossessed producers may not always be incorporated into capitalist wage employment.[2]

2.2 Accumulation by dispossession

Harvey's (2005) conceptualization of 'accumulation by dispossession' (ABD) broadens and updates Marx's construct of primitive accumulation by incorporating new mechanisms emerging in the context of globalized capitalism (MNC 2001: 4) and 'neoliberal imperialism' (Brenner 2006: 102; Ashman and Callinicos 2006: 115–117; Fine 2006: 143). It highlights manipulation of the international financial system to orchestrate crisis and impose devaluation on vulnerable states, particularly through structural adjustment programmes administered by the IMF and World Bank. Such processes can result in drastic reductions in the prices of their assets and labour, which can then be 'profitably recycled back into the circulation of capital' (Harvey 2005: 150–156).

Neoliberal globalization also puts private corporations under intense competitive pressure, impelling them to grab resources at very low – even zero – costs wherever possible (Harvey 2005: 149). If necessary, those holding such resources may be dispossessed by undermining their protective social and legal institutions (Luxemburg 2003: 348–351; Brenner 2006: 99; De Angelis 2004: 73–76). Large-scale loss of assets can be caused through speculation and manipulation orchestrated by major institutions of finance capital, constituting 'the cutting edge of accumulation by dispossession' (Harvey 2005: 142–147; 2006: 142; cf. Moyo *et al.* 2012: 193).

Harvey's formulation of ABD has been the object of a number of theoretical critiques. First, as pointed out by Brenner (2006: 99) and Wood (2006: 19–23), ABD is largely defined in terms of the (quantitative) transfer of resources without reference to the necessary changes in 'social-property relations' that are 'constitutive of capitalist production'. Second, some aspects of Harvey's formulation of ABD are indistinguishable from processes of asset transfer and redistribution that take place routinely in the normal workings of the capitalist economy (Ashman and Callinicos 2006: 119–120; Fine 2006: 143–146). This can lead to the conflation of primitive and capitalist accumulation, which 'blurs the conceptualization [of ABD] and blunts the basic thrust of his argument' (Brenner 2006: 98–102). Third, such instances also raise the issue of *causal sequence and directionality*, since the *preconditions* of capitalist production appear to have been conflated with its *consequences*. These theoretical problems pertaining to ABD are also encountered in the experience of neoliberal India and are discussed further in the concluding section (7).

2.3 Mechanisms of primitive accumulation

Although primitive accumulation is widely thought to involve only the use of extra-economic coercion, a close reading of Marx's text, as well as the empirical

26   *S. Adnan*

evidence, provides a far more nuanced view of the wide range of possible ways it can work. In particular, mechanisms of dispossession, such as financial speculation, manipulation of market prices, taxation, credit, debt and fraud, do not necessarily entail the use of force and violence (Marx 1976: 919–922; De Angelis 2004; Harvey 2005: 145; 2006: 166; Adnan 2013: 92–93).

Even though such alternative mechanisms of primitive accumulation are very different from deliberate and forcible enclosure, they lead to comparable outcomes: the dispossession of producers and the concentration of their erstwhile resources among the expropriating classes (Perelman 1984; De Angelis 2001: 11; 2004: 78–79). For instance, the reproduction of self-provisioning households and communities can be undermined if their avenues of survival are closed down by market and state interventions (e.g. unfavourable changes in relative prices and taxation) (Perelman 1984: 46–58; Burawoy 1985: 217–219; De Angelis 2004: 77–78). Such a mechanism of primitive accumulation is *indirect*, because dispossession is a 'by-product' of processes primarily geared to other objectives and hence constitutes an *unintended consequence* (De Angelis 2004: 77–79).

2.4 Factors driving and limiting primitive accumulation

The reproduction and expansion of capitalist production propels ongoing primitive accumulation by generating recurrent demand for land, labour and other inputs (Marx 1976: 912). Consequently, the very functioning of capitalism drives a continuing process of '*ex novo* separation' of such resources from those owning or controlling them in coexisting non-capitalist sectors (De Angelis 2001: 9; 2004: 77). Ongoing primitive accumulation can also involve encroachment into altogether 'new commons' or untapped resource frontiers (Perelman 1984: 16–17; De Angelis 2004: 75–77; Harvey 2005: 147–148). Viewed in this perspective, primitive accumulation is necessary not just at the *origin* of capitalism but also during the continuing reproduction and expansion of capitalist production (Perelman 1984: 10–11; MNC 2001: 1). The processes of primitive and capitalist accumulation are thus functionally interlinked and interact reiteratively over historical time (Adnan 1984: 28, fn. 28; Harriss-White 2006: 1241–1246; 2012: 129).

Nonetheless, the causal interlinkages between these two accumulative processes need further clarification. On the one hand, it is evident that once capitalist production has begun it becomes a critical driver of primitive accumulation in subsequent phases (Perelman 1984; MNC 2001: 1–2). On the other hand, this does not explain why and how (other) processes of primitive accumulation take place that are not driven by capitalism, but nonetheless make available resources such as land and labour that can be potentially deployed in capitalist production. Explication of this aspect of the complex causal interlinkages between primitive accumulation and capitalist production is taken up in the conclusion (Section 7).

Moreover, primitive accumulation also entails transformation of social–property and class relations, which cannot be explained 'simply in terms of the needs of capital accumulation'. These involve critical socioeconomic and political trans-

Primitive accumulation in neo-liberal India 27

formations which need to be explained in their own terms (e.g. through analysis of structural changes in the economy and political conflicts in local and global arenas) (Brenner 2006: 100). Given these considerations, the factors constraining primitive accumulation and the resultant contestations assume significance.

Critical limits to primitive accumulation are posed by the resistance of groups and communities that are actually dispossessed or threatened by dispossession (De Angelis 2001: 12–18; 2004: 72–74). Correlatively, the classes and agencies gaining from primitive accumulation attempt to undermine such resistance through forcible repression or co-option of dispossessed groups, giving rise to social and political conflicts (De Angelis 2001: 12–18; 2004: 68–69; Brenner 2006: 99).

In this context, the role of the state is critical and can cut both ways, as evidenced in earlier historical instances (e.g. the enclosures in Britain) (Moore 1966: 13–24). The state can either play a protective role by supporting non-capitalist producers against encroachment of their resources, or its administration and security forces can facilitate mechanisms of primitive accumulation and the repression of resistance in the interest of capital.

2.5 Constraints to the growth of wage labour and persistence of the self-employed

In the Marxian schema of capitalist development, the social groups dispossessed by primitive accumulation are envisaged to become employed as wage workers with the growth of capitalist production (Perelman 2001: 7–9). However, such groups are not necessarily transformed immediately, because the capitalist sector may not be able to generate sufficient wage employment. Furthermore, even after having been employed, wage workers may be made redundant by industrial restructuring and labour-displacing technological innovation, pushing them into the 'industrial reserve army' (Marx 1976: 781–787). Comparable lack of wage employment faced by dispossessed or retrenched groups has been noted in the contemporary world economy, including neoliberal India, as taken up below (Harvey 2005: 161; Moyo *et al.* 2012: 187).

3 Policy changes in India under neoliberal globalization

The Indian economy has been critically restructured by 'the rise to hegemony of a new kind of international finance capital based on a process of globalisation of finance' (P. Patnaik 2008: 109). From the beginning of the 1990s, the Indian government adopted 'massive programmes of privatisation and structural adjustment' (U. Patnaik 2012: 234; Walker 2008: 559). Its post-Independence regulatory framework – dubbed the 'license-permit raj' – was replaced by a neoliberal policy package, including deregulation, trade liberalization, financial sector reforms and devaluation (Bhaduri 2008; Sanyal 2007: 242–245; Shah 2008: 80). The priority given to attracting foreign investment and preventing capital flight led the Indian government to adopt policies that opened up the

28   *S. Adnan*

domestic economy. These also served to retain the 'confidence of the investors' as well as multilateral financial institutions regulating global capital flows, particularly the World Bank and IMF (P. Patnaik 2008: 109).

The lifting of restrictions on private corporate investment by the Indian central government also triggered an unprecedented 'race to the bottom' among the regional state (*rajya*) governments, which vied with each other to offer concessionary terms to corporate capital (Bhaduri 2008; P. Patnaik 2011: 3; Levien 2012: 944–946). This reflected a 'virtual consensus among all major political parties about the priorities of rapid economic growth led by private investment' (Chatterjee 2008a: 57). Even traditionally left-wing state governments led by the CPI (M) in West Bengal and Kerala joined the competition.

These drastic policy shifts opened up new arenas of primitive accumulation in neoliberal India, operating in direct and indirect ways. I take up three critical aspects of these processes for further analysis, as follows:

1   Mechanisms of grabbing land and natural resources by the state and private corporations, as well as forms of resistance arising in response.
2   Impacts of the neoliberal policy regime, focusing upon income deflation and the undermining of peasant production.
3   'Dispossession without proletarianization': limits to the growth of wage labour and the persistence of the self-employed, as well as the implications for the postulated 'transition to capitalism'.

4   Land grabs and resistance

The neoliberal era has been marked by massive expropriation of land and natural resources by foreign and domestic corporations for deployment in agricultural and industrial production in India and abroad (P. Patnaik 2011; 2012: 31–32; U. Patnaik 2012: 240–241; Sebastian 2012: 21–27; Walker 2008: 589). Primitive accumulation has encroached into 'new commons' or untapped resource frontiers, including forests, minerals, fisheries, groundwater and surface water bodies (Basu 2007: 1284; Walker 2008: 580–581; Vasudevan 2008: 42). The term 'land grab' is used henceforth as shorthand for the expropriation of this wide variety of natural resources, characterized by diverse forms of property rights ranging from de jure ownership to de facto possession (Bhaduri 2008: 13).

4.1   Special Economic Zones

The pre-eminent institution used to attract investment and provide a *systematic* framework for land grabs began to be put together with the adoption of the Special Economic Zone Policy by the central Indian government in 2000.[3] This process was institutionalized by the promulgation of the Special Economic Zone (SEZ) Act of 2005, which led to such zones being approved and established all over India with astonishing speed.[4] The SEZs constituted 'hyperliberalized economic enclaves – with minimal taxes, tariffs and regulations', aimed at

Primitive accumulation in neo-liberal India   29

'promoting exports, attracting FDI, developing infrastructure, and generating employment' (Levien 2012: 934–935; Walker 2008: 587–588).

Financial investments in the SEZs were made by Western transnationals as well as 'Indian multinationals', including 'large diversified corporate houses' and real estate developers. The state governments made contracts with these private corporations, transferring large tracts of land and mineral rights to them on highly concessionary terms (Bharadwaj 2009). Such contracts typically required the developers to allocate half, or even less, of the SEZ area for industrial purposes. This allowed the remaining area to be allotted to profitable commercial facilities catering to upper- and middle-class 'lifestyles', such as residential complexes, shopping malls, hotels and golf-courses (Walker 2008: 588–589; Levien 2012: 934). Such patterns of land use frequently resulted in financial speculation in real estate, particularly in sites close to major urban centres (cf. Harvey 2005: 158).

4.2 State acquisition and compensation practices

While the SEZs and other development projects provided land to corporate investors, they did so by dispossessing the people who lived in these areas. This was typically done through compulsory state acquisition of their private and customary lands by invoking the archaic Land Acquisition Act of 1894 (Walker 2008: 589). Its draconian provisions made use of the legal principle of *eminent domain*, which empowered the state to acquire *private* land for *public* purposes, overriding objections by those dispossessed in the process (Vasudevan 2008: 41). Such coercive power of the state was exercised to acquire large blocks of *contiguous lands* for transfer to private corporations (Levien 2012: 944–946). In effect, state authorities manipulated the rhetoric of *public* purpose to acquire lands for allocation to the corporate sector for *private* profit-making, serving as 'land brokers' *par excellence* (Bhaduri 2008; Walker 2008: 580; Levien 2012: 941–945; cf. Adnan 2013: 117).

Furthermore, the Indian central and state governments promulgated laws and policies that facilitated corporate interests in getting hold of land and natural resources (e.g. the National Mining Policy) (Sebastian 2012: 10; Bharadwaj 2009).[5] The rights and entitlements of vulnerable groups were denied by undermining protective legal-institutional rules and procedures, also constituting instances of primitive accumulation. For instance, constitutional provisions and laws protecting adivasi rights were dismantled or ignored by the state in order to enable private corporations to gain access to forests, minerals and other resources. Restrictions on the acquisition of tribal lands without the consent of the concerned communities, stipulated in the PESA (1996) Act, were often circumvented by illegal means.[6] The West Bengal state government was prepared to flout its own land-use policy by transferring agricultural lands to an Indian multinational for constructing a car factory in the Singur SEZ (Basu 2007: 1283). Correspondingly, the Hyderabad Urban Development Authority violated the Urban Land Ceiling Act in order to give retroactive legal sanction to illegal encroachments by powerful groups (Whitehead 2012: 32).

30 S. Adnan

Moreover, the law recognized only those with formal rights or titles as eligible for payment of compensation for acquired lands. Excluded were all those whose livelihoods depended upon common or customary 'rights of use' on open access lands and water bodies (Walker 2008: 582–590). Even when compensation was paid, the acquired lands were valued well below open market prices. Paying low rates of compensation enabled the state to make windfall gains, since it 'literally stole the land and then made large profits' through higher rates charged to private developers (Levien 2012: 947–948; Walker 2008: 582). Such practices are characteristic of ABD (Harvey 2005: 149–150).

4.3 Land grabs, resistance and repression

Certain types of resource grabs have been based on sheer market power or technological superiority, indicative of direct primitive accumulation *without the use of force and violence*. For instance, municipal authorities in Bangalore acquired areas in IT corridors through 'e-titling and GIS planning' in ways that simply 'erased' from the city's land records the erstwhile customary rights of local landholders (Whitehead 2012: 32). Private corporations producing soft drinks extracted 'pure groundwater as a free raw material' from great depths using expensive capital-intensive technology that could not be matched by local peasant producers (Bhaduri 2008: 13; cf. Walker 2008: 564–565).

However, much more typical of land grabs in neoliberal India has been the use of legal or illegal force, inclusive of explicit violence wherever necessary. Urban land grabs have been based on discriminatory use of state power to divide the affected population and pre-empt the possibility of collective resistance. For instance, while the law was enforced to demolish and acquire the settlements of working class squatters in Delhi, it was amended to 'regularize' the illegal constructions and violation of zoning codes by well-to-do traders and homeowners (Baviskar and Sundar 2008: 88–89). A comparable process was observed in Hyderabad, where the Urban Development Authority acquired the lands occupied by slum-dwellers, while illegal encroachments made by powerful groups were regularized (Whitehead 2012: 32).

Explicit use of violence has characterized land grabs for SEZs as well as repression of the resulting resistance. In Odisha, local inhabitants agitating against the lack of adequate compensation and rehabilitation following state acquisition of their lands for the Kalinganagar SEZ were violently repressed by the police (Walker 2008: 583–584). The police forcibly evicted villagers protesting against 'enclosure' of their lands for an automobile factory in Singur SEZ of West Bengal (Walker 2008: 591).

Typically, people resisting forcible land grabs by the state and corporate interests formed organizations to mobilize supporters for collective action (Tilly 1978: 78), as evidenced in the responses to state acquisition of lands for SEZs in Odisha, West Bengal and Chhattisgarh.[7] Furthermore, overarching associations such as the National Alliance of People's Movements (NAPM) have been formed to coordinate the various local-level protests against land grabs as well as oppose legislation facilitating such acts (Walker 2008: 590).

Primitive accumulation in neo-liberal India 31

Resistance to land grabs by dispossessed groups has usually involved *socially accepted* forms of protest in India, such as handing over petitions and memoranda, street demonstrations and blockades of concerned offices (*gherao*). However, such non-violent protests have often proved futile against the forces imposing dispossession. Consequently, some affected groups have had little option but to take up more violent means (Harriss-White 2012: 142–143).[8] In particular, Maoist movements have been the foremost among those opposing 'displacement and dispossession from land-based livelihoods' in India through armed struggle (Walker 2008: 582–583; Kunnath 2012: 104–107; Sebastian 2012: 19–20).

The forest-clad and mineral-rich state of Chhattisgarh provides an extreme case of state repression of armed resistance against land grabs by local adivasi (tribal) inhabitants allied to the Communist Party of India (Maoist). The state authorities have signed dozens of MOUs with foreign and domestic corporations and issued them with prospecting and mining licences, enabling the latter to acquire minerals and forest resources at very low costs (Walker 2008: 593–595; Bharadwaj 2009). Local adivasis suffering from such land grabs and forced displacement by the state and corporate forces have been impelled to take up armed resistance in collaboration with the Maoists (Jha 2013).

In response, the central Indian and Chhattisgarh state governments have embarked upon counter-insurgency operations to crush the Maoist-adivasi movement, leading to 'Operation Green Hunt' involving 70,000 paramilitary forces (Sebastian 2012; Jha 2013). In addition to the Central Reserve Police Force, this operation has been actively joined by the *Salwa Judum*, a private vigilante force, partly recruited and financed by corporate interests (Mohanty 2006: 3167; Walker 2008: 593–595).The combined strength of the state and private corporations has been used to forcibly relocate the Chhattisgarh adivasis from their villages to 'strategic hamlets', subjecting them to systematic violence, intimidation and extra-judicial killings. The mineral-rich lands around the deserted adivasi settlements have been taken over to set up SEZs for extraction of resources by private corporations.

Many such struggles against dispossession across the country have given rise to 'land wars' constituting 'the single most contentious issue' in neoliberal India (Walker 2008: 590). The political fallout from violent repression of protesters in the Nandigram SEZ of West Bengal in March 2007 'led to a cancellation of the project, a temporary moratorium on SEZs and a reduction in their maximum allowed size' (Levien 2012: 933). Other instances of resistance have led to cancellation, postponement or downsizing of projects, including 'two massive SEZs … in Mumbai and Gurgaon, the South Korean POSCO steel SEZ in [Odisha] … and all the SEZs approved in the state of Goa' (Levien 2012: 934). In some cases, as in Chhattisgarh, the dispossessed groups have been able to recapture some of the expropriated lands, or capture new areas from the state, constituting 'counter-enclosures' and 'new commons' (De Angelis 2004: 73–76; Walker 2008: 597–598; Borras and Franco 2010). Insofar as these struggles have succeeded in reducing the pace and volume of land grabs, such acts of social and

32   S. Adnan

political resistance have also imposed *limits* upon the inroads of primitive accumulation in neoliberal India.

5 Impacts of neoliberal policy regimes

Since 1991, the neoliberal policies implemented by successive Indian governments have activated a number of other causal mechanisms mediating primitive accumulation. Among these were fiscal contraction and other severely income-deflating policies, as well as measures reducing the entitlements of the poor (U. Patnaik 2012: 249).

First, neoliberal policies promoted the substitution of 'a whole range of "upmarket" tertiary sector capitalist enterprises, such as shopping malls, for the old, self-employed petty providers of services' (P. Patnaik 2012: 35–37). These resulted in contemporary forms of 'deindustrialization', redefined broadly to include the 'displacement of petty producers from all sorts of activities and not from industry alone' (P. Patnaik 2008: 109).

Second, neoliberal policies enabled transnational corporations and Indian big business to gain increased control over the marketing of products of peasants and other petty producers. Trade liberalization opened up the Indian market to foreign competition by removing restrictions on entry, and adherence to WTO 'compulsions' resulted in the withdrawal of tariffs and subsidies that had formerly provided protection to the domestic economy, particularly the agricultural sector (Shah 2008: 80). Marketing and distribution were increasingly taken over from numerous small intermediaries by transnational corporations and Indian big business, resulting in 'a redistribution of income from the producers to these giant intermediaries' (P. Patnaik 2008: 109; 2012: 36–37).

Third, a sharp decline in state expenditure benefiting the poor resulted from several neoliberal policy shifts involving reduction in welfare payments, public investment, rural development and employment-generation programmes (P. Patnaik 2008: 109; 2012: 35–37; Shah 2008: 80). These cuts in public expenditure reduced the entitlements of peasants and artisans, constituting primitive accumulation in an *anticipatory* sense as compared to actual dispossession.

Furthermore, these neoliberal policies resulted in a 'pronounced worsening of income distribution' across the whole economy, inclusive of the capitalist sector 'where the share of profits in value added [rose] dramatically at the expense of wages'.[9] Such reduction in the purchasing power of wage workers in the capitalist sector constituted part of the 'normal' process of *capitalist* accumulation (P. Patnaik 2012: 37). Overall, the complex impacts of neoliberal policies in India resulted in several distinct strands of primitive accumulation operating in parallel with capitalist accumulation.[10]

In addition to impoverishing small producers and wage workers in the *short term*, the cumulative impacts of neoliberal policy regimes served to undermine the viability of peasant production in the *longer term* (P. Patnaik 2008: 113). Poor peasants faced collapse when they could no longer afford to purchase production inputs with their own resources. Those undertaking production by borrowing from moneylenders were often constrained to settle cumulative debts through 'distress sale' of mortgaged lands or assets (Walker 2008: 573–579). The lands and resources of such ruined peasants became available for investment in capitalist production.

Unlike land grabs, implementation of these neoliberal policies did not involve explicit violence, even though they clearly entailed the use of force, in the sense of being backed by Indian state power. Since the proximate objectives of these policies were quite different from the deliberate capture of land and other resources, such outcomes constituted *unintended* consequences, corresponding to *indirect* forms of primitive accumulation.

6 'Dispossession without proletarianization'

In order to assess the outcomes of primitive accumulation in neoliberal India, it is necessary to ascertain what has happened to the peasants and petty commodity producers dispossessed by the mechanisms noted above. Deprived of their means of production, this segment of the labour force has been faced with the need to find alternative avenues of survival. Have its members been steadily transformed into wage workers, as postulated in the Marxian schema of capitalist development? Or, have they ended up in forms of self-employment? In either case, what are the implications for the postulated 'transition to capitalism'?

6.1 Jobless growth and the persistence of self-employed labour

A striking feature of the Indian economy under liberalization has been 'jobless growth' (Sanyal 2007: 245–247; Bhaduri 2008: 11; Sanyal and Bhattacharyya 2009: 36–37). This has been attributed in part to the increased pressure of international competition on the Indian economy due to neoliberal globalization. Private corporations have been compelled to invest in capital-intensive machinery to raise labour productivity, leading to downsizing of their workforce and growth of the 'industrial reserve army' (Bhaduri 2008).

As distinct from wage workers retrenched by the dynamics of capitalism, Sanyal (2007: 53–58) has pointed to the generation of a continuous stream of dispossessed producers by ongoing primitive accumulation who are 'excluded' from the circuit of capital.[11] Despite the analytical differences between them, both groups have found very few opportunities for wage employment owing to jobless growth in the formal sector, while also being deprived of redistributive welfare benefits and social services due to neoliberal cuts in public expenditure (Bhaduri 2008: 12–13; Walker 2008: 562). Thus, the combined effects of capitalist and primitive accumulation have resulted in a significant segment of the Indian labour force lacking access to wage employment that has been constrained to survive through various forms of petty self-employment in the informal sector (cf. Amin 2003; Moyo *et al.* 2012).[12] In the Indian context, this phenomenon has been termed 'dispossession without proletarianization'.[13]

34 *S. Adnan*

Comparing data on the composition of the Indian labour force between 1999/2000 and 2004/2005, Sanyal and Bhattacharyya conclude that there is 'a clear trend towards self-employment as the main source of livelihood for the informal labour force'.[14] The persistence and preponderance of the self-employed in the contemporary Indian labour force assumes significance because it suggests that *primitive accumulation has not been followed by substantive transformation of the dispossessed into wage workers*. Nor does the prospect appear to be likely in the near future, given the very low rates of employment generation in the capitalist sector (Sanyal 2007: 248). Sanyal invokes this scenario to question the very possibility of transition to capitalism in India despite ongoing primitive accumulation, as well as the theoretical relevance of the Marxian schema of capitalist development (2007: 39–40, 62).

Harriss-White (2012: 117–118) has also pointed to the veritable 'explosion of self-employment' in neoliberal India, noting that petty commodity production (PCP) 'is numerically the commonest form of production and contributes roughly as much to GDP as the corporate sector' (109). PCP is 'more common than wage work', accounting for '53 per cent of total "livelihoods" including those in agriculture' (117). Reflecting on the prospects of this category of self-employed producers, she observes: '[PCP] is not transitional. If it is but a stage in the differentiation of individual capitals, it is constantly being replenished and reproduced.... Its existence does not imply a teleology of development' (117–118).

This view is suggestive of a dynamic balance between two opposed processes through which PCP units are being simultaneously undermined and regenerated. To illustrate, even though primitive accumulation through land grabs and income deflation is resulting in the continuing disintegration of peasant and artisanal production units, the producers so dispossessed are actively reconstituting themselves into other kinds of PCP that operate at a lower level of income and security, given their lack of substantive means of production.

The prospects of 'the transition to capitalism' in India thus appear to hinge critically upon the factors determining the preponderance and stability of PCP among the labour force. The issues involved are explored further by critically reviewing two major arguments advanced to explain the persistence of self-employed labour in neoliberal India.

6.2 Linkages of PCP with markets and circuits of capital

Leaving aside retrenched and currently employed wage workers, Sanyal and Bhattacharyya (2009: 36–40) divide the rest of the Indian labour force into two subcategories. The first consists of 'non-capitalist producers tied to capital via subcontracting or outsourcing and from whom capital extracts their surplus'. In contrast, the second is defined by its 'exclusion' from the capitalist sector of the economy owing to its lack of linkages with the 'circuit of capital'.

Crucial to this formulation is the innovative argument by Sanyal that the 'excluded' component of the labour force is *not* a 'precapitalist residue', but rather a constantly replenished by-product of ongoing primitive accumulation

Primitive accumulation in neo-liberal India 35

(Sanyal 2007: 39; Sanyal and Bhattacharyya 2009: 37–38).[15] Consequently, this continuously regenerated segment of the labour force will continue to persist, implying that capitalist development may not necessarily lead to the disappearance of self-employed producers in India.

However, the proposition that there are self-employed units in the contemporary Indian economy that are entirely 'excluded' from the circuit of capital is extremely difficult to substantiate. Sanyal and Bhattacharyya (2009: 38–41) themselves note that the survival of such producers is significantly mediated by the market.[16] To the extent that self-employed producers participate in non-labour input and product markets that are also used for transactions by capitalist producers and merchant-moneylenders, they cannot avoid interacting with the circuits of *productive* and *unproductive* capital respectively (Marx 1981: 728–745, 915–938; Adnan 1985).[17] Thus, rather than presupposing the total 'exclusion' of a category of self-employed producers from the circuit of capital, it is analytically more promising to explore the *differential implications* of their interactions with the circuits of productive and unproductive capital.

Relevant evidence is provided by Levien's (2012) ethnographic study of the Mahindra World City (MWC) SEZ in rural Rajasthan. In contrast to the postulated delinking (exclusion) from the circuit of capital, households whose lands were acquired display systematic *increase in market participation*, since they now have to buy the goods that could have been produced earlier from their own lands (and attendant livestock). More generally, the local economy displayed increasing degrees of commoditization following land acquisition, resulting from significant changes in the relations of production and the growth of finance capital through speculation in real estate, differentially affecting various castes and classes (Levien 2012: 949–965).

Typically, the better-off households with more compensation money invested in unproductive rather than productive 'circuits of capital', extracting surplus by deploying usurious and merchants' capital, while also buying land to collect pre-capitalist ground rent and 'eat' commission as land brokers (Levien 2012: 956–963). Correlatively, poorer households were transformed from one kind of PCP (land-holding peasants) to other kinds of self-employed operators selling a variety of products and services (also PCP), while being subject to forms of market-based exploitation through circuits of unproductive capital and rent extraction. Significantly, very few of the dispossessed population gained stable wage employment in the high-tech capitalist enterprises established in the SEZ. Such uneven outcomes of land grabs for the MWC SEZ corresponded to a somewhat modified form of *dispossession without proletarianization*, displaying variations in the degree of '*relative proletarianization*' among different classes (Levien 2012: 954).

It is somewhat paradoxical that land grabs propelled by finance capital, aimed at establishing advanced capitalism in a high-tech SEZ, resulted in the renewed operation of traditional mechanisms of 'precapitalist' exploitation among the dispossessed rural households (Levien 2012: 962–963). Indeed, the evidence from the MWC SEZ suggests that the actual consequences of primitive accumulation through land grabs may not have corresponded to either the Marxian

36 *S. Adnan*

schema of 'transition to capitalism' or the Sanyal-Bhattacharyya hypothesis of the persistence of self-employed producers *excluded* from the circuit of capital. Following Burawoy (1996; 2001), Levien (2012: 960–965) regards these outcomes as embodying a kind of 'involutionary process of economic change', indicative of 'a peculiar form of agrarian transformation' that does *not* appear to be heading towards sustained growth of productive capital among the peasant classes dispossessed by the SEZ.

Reflecting on the direction of causation at work, Levien observes:

> Harvey's concept of ABD marks a definitive break with primitive accumulation traditionally conceived by … freeing it for application to a panoply of contemporary forms of dispossession of private and social wealth … that *emanate from, rather than create the pre-conditions for*, advanced capitalism.
>
> (Levien 2012: 938 [emphasis added])

This view, which appears to be theoretically anomalous insofar as it inverts the position of primitive accumulation (ABD) to being the *consequence* of capitalism rather than its *precondition*, is taken up for further discussion in the conclusion (Section 7).

6.3 The 'reversal' of primitive accumulation or its effects

Sanyal (2007: 36–37 and 59–61) argues that the influence of formal democracy and human rights in contemporary India has made it politically unacceptable to dispossess social groups through primitive accumulation without providing them with alternative means of survival. The very political and ideological conditions of legitimation and reproduction of the capitalist 'accumulation economy' require transfer of a part of its profits to 'the victims of primitive accumulation'. Accordingly, dispossessed social groups in India have been made the targets of 'welfarist governmentality', enabling them to survive as self-employed producers. Sanyal (2007: 59–61, 218–221) terms such flow of development resources as the 'reversal of primitive accumulation', which ensures the continued reproduction of the dispossessed as an *aggregate* category. This is put forward as an explanation of the persistence of self-employed producers following primitive accumulation.

Chatterjee (2008a: 55–56; 2008b: 91) endorses Sanyal's view that the imperatives of political legitimation require redistribution of a share of the profits of the capitalist sector to the dispossessed through transfer of development resources. However, he modifies Sanyal's argument to note that it is *not the process* of primitive accumulation as such, but rather its *effects*, which are *reversed*.

However, the theoretical basis and empirical validity of these views are open to serious question. Sanyal's (2007: 59–61) notion of the 'reversal' of primitive accumulation is theoretically problematic because it is conceived of simply as a *quantitative* flow of resources in the opposite direction, *without* any reference to

Primitive accumulation in neo-liberal India 37

the concomitant 'reversal' of social-institutional and class *relations* (as specified in Section 2).[18] Chatterjee (2008a: 55–56), too, does not point out this theoretical difficulty, while his reformulation of the argument in terms of the reversal of the 'effects' of primitive accumulation does not explain why state-mediated redistribution is primarily motivated by this consideration rather than by others.[19]

Moreover, the empirical evidence clearly indicates that the Indian state has withdrawn from welfare and supportive facilities benefiting the poor, in accordance with neoliberal imperatives (Basu and Das 2009: 159; Baviskar and Sundar 2008: 87–89). Virtually all policies that had been aimed at providing support to the poor during the period preceding the 1990s have been dismantled, far exceeding the 'ameliorative interventions of the state'. Shah (2008: 80) notes that such 'withdrawal from its earlier welfare and developmental role' by the Indian state is precisely 'the opposite of what Chatterjee suggests'. 'In short, any evidence of the State taking steps to make primitive accumulation bearable, to *reverse its effects* by providing alternative means of livelihood to the dispossessed population, seems to be totally missing' (Basu and Das 2009: 159).

Ironically, the formal existence of parliamentary democracy and humanitarian norms in neoliberal India has not actually prevented violent mechanisms of primitive accumulation from being used to grab land and natural resources required by capitalist accumulation. As noted above, land acquisition for SEZs has involved the use of violence by the state, inclusive of brutal counter-insurgency operations, as well as 'officially condoned criminal violence' by private armies. Such violent roles of the state in enforcing dispossession and repressing resistance contrast sharply with the enlightened vision of welfarist governmentality and redistributive 'development' projected by Sanyal (2007) and Chatterjee (2008a: 55).

7 Overview of primitive accumulation

In this section I have integrated the major conclusions of the preceding analysis regarding the mechanisms, driving forces and limiting factors of primitive accumulation in contemporary India. Theoretical reflections on primitive accumulation, as well as its causal roles and linkages with capitalist production, are also put forward.

7.1 Mechanisms and determinants of primitive accumulation in neoliberal India

Particular mechanisms of primitive accumulation have played significant roles in neoliberal India, ranging from SEZs mediating land grabs, to income deflation induced by neoliberal policies. These direct and indirect mechanisms have made available land, labour and other resources that could be potentially deployed in capitalist production. Taken together, they constitute a *diverse repertoire* from which *alternative mechanisms and strategies* of primitive accumulation have been flexibly chosen to suit particular circumstances (cf. Burawoy 1985: 214–219; Harvey 2006: 159; Tilly 1978: 151–158).

38   *S. Adnan*

Factors driving primitive accumulation

Interactions among the factors driving and limiting primitive accumulation have shaped the dynamics of the process in neoliberal India. The state has played crucial roles in facilitating direct and indirect mechanisms of primitive accumulation. It has reassured foreign and domestic corporations that the resources required for their expansion would remain available *despite possible resistance*. The might of the Indian state has been used to crush opposition put up by dispossessed peasants, adivasis and other adversely affected groups. Such roles have served to keep India attractive for FDI by maintaining the confidence of finance capital as well as regulatory institutions such as the IMF and the World Bank. Taken together, these *national and international* institutions, coordinated by the imperatives of neoliberal globalization, have served as key drivers of ongoing primitive accumulation.

In parallel, domestic and transnational corporations have been acquiring new territories and types of resources, pushing the resource frontiers of India. In certain instances, these corporations have hired private militias to crush the resistance of dispossessed groups, making use of illegal violence, sometimes in collusion with the state (Walker 2008; Sebastian 2012: 13–16). Private corporate interests have also sought state support for undermining the pre-existing social institutions and legal provisions that had protected the resource rights of dispossessed groups (cf. Luxemburg 2003: 348–351; De Angelis 2004: 75).

Limits to primitive accumulation: resistance and repression

The adverse impacts of ongoing primitive accumulation in neoliberal India have triggered a politics of resistance that is qualitatively different from classic working-class struggles against capitalism (cf. Harvey 2005: 162–169; Sanyal and Bhattacharyya 2009: 41–43; Borras and Franco 2010). Protests against the grabbing of lands, forests and mineral resources, as well as social movements against large-scale displacements caused by construction of 'special economic zones, expressways and other infrastructure projects ... have become the key markers' of the resistance against primitive accumulation (Das 2012: 33–35). These also include struggles by slum-dwellers against eviction for 'urban development', as well as the opposition of petty retailers to displacement by 'department stores and shopping malls' (Sanyal and Bhattacharyya 2009: 40–43; Walker 2008).

This kind of resistance has typically involved the *multi-class* mobilization of entire communities, including not only peasants and adivasis holding land, but also occupational groups without such rights whose livelihoods depend upon open-access land and water resources (Sanyal and Bhattacharyya 2009: 42–43). The growing coalescence and coordination of localized resistance through overarching associations has imposed significant limits upon primitive accumulation in neoliberal India (Vasudevan 2008: 43; Nilsen 2010: 201, cited by Das 2012: 35–37; Levien 2012: 933–934; cf. De Angelis 2001: 3).[20]

Primitive accumulation in neo-liberal India   39

Correlatively, attempts to counter such resistance by dividing and repressing the concerned groups have also been in evidence. These include the deployment of security forces and private armies, leading to counter-insurgency operations in extreme cases (Sebastian 2012: 13–16). In some instances, such conflicts have led to intensified backlash against the resisting groups, resulting in further seizure of their lands and resources (Walker 2008: 595–599).

Viewed as a whole, capitalist production has been a key driver of primitive accumulation, while resistance by dispossessed groups has attempted to impose social and political limits upon it (P. Patnaik 2012: 38; De Angelis 2004). The resultant outcomes have cut both ways (cf. Adnan 2013: 119). In certain instances, successful resistance has been able to slow down and reduce the inroads of primitive accumulation. In others, repression and co-option have served to undermine or divide such resistance, thereby accentuating the pace and extent of primitive accumulation. Such dynamics of interaction between expropriation and resistance have shaped the *trajectory and contested limits* of primitive accumulation in neoliberal India.

7.2 *Reflections on the concept and role of primitive accumulation*

Primitive accumulation as a generic concept

The state and corporate interests in contemporary India have undertaken primitive accumulation by making use of mechanisms and institutions that were particularly suited to the prevailing circumstances. For instance, the institution of the SEZ was 'invented'[21] and replicated due to its suitability in the context of neoliberal globalization. Obviously, not all such mechanisms of dispossession were in operation at the time when Marx conceived of primitive accumulation. While some of them can be subsumed under Harvey's notion of ABD, this may not be applicable to others, such as income deflation. The particular mechanisms of dispossession that gained prominence in the social-historical circumstances of neoliberal India need to be incorporated into a reformulated construct of primitive accumulation.

Viewed in a longer term perspective, the mechanisms and mediating institutions of primitive accumulation in India may be regarded as having shifted with changing historical circumstances.[22] By the same token, new modalities of primitive accumulation may be expected to emerge in the future, as the social organization of production itself undergoes change.

These considerations suggest that primitive accumulation needs to be reformulated as a *generic* concept that can accommodate variations in the mechanisms and mediating institutions supplying inputs to evolving capitalist production under changing historical circumstances (Adnan 2012; 2013: 123). Viewed in this perspective, Marx's nineteenth-century construct of primitive accumulation has been 'updated' by Harvey as ABD in the context of neoliberal globalization at the end of the twentieth century (Brenner 2006: 102). Further reformulation of this generic concept may be expected as its modalities continue to change with the evolving production systems of the future.

40   *S. Adnan*

Recursive relationship between primitive accumulation and capitalist production

The experience of neoliberal India also sheds light on the complex causal inter-linkages between primitive and capitalist accumulation. As noted above, capital-ist production itself has been a force driving land grabs through the *deliberate* dispossession of peasants and indigenous peoples. Actually existing capitalism has therefore been directly involved in expropriating resources *via primitive accumulation*, over and above the appropriation of surplus value from wage labour through the labour market. In these varied instances, the direction of cau-sation is *from capitalist production to primitive accumulation* (Marx 1976: 912).

However, not all mechanisms resulting in primitive accumulation are deliber-ately or necessarily aimed at procuring inputs for capitalist production. This con-sideration applies pre-eminently to indirect mechanisms, such as neoliberal policies which had very different primary objectives but nonetheless led to the dispossession of peasants and artisanal producers. To the extent that the land, labour and commodities released by such processes were subsequently deployed in capitalist production, these constituted *unintended consequences* of such indi-rect mechanisms. In these instances, the direction of causation is *from primitive accumulation to capitalist production.*

Further insights may be derived by synthesizing these two causal relation-ships with opposed directionality and drawing out the logical implications. I hypothesize that they constitute obverse facets of an *integrated and recursive causal relationship* between primitive accumulation and capitalist production (Adnan 2012; 2013: 123–124). A corollary of this hypothesis is that primitive accumulation can constitute either the *precondition* or the *consequence* of cap-italist production, depending upon the particular phase of their interactive dynamics.

Such a reconceptualization of the causal interrelationship between capitalist production and primitive accumulation as two-way and recursive also *provides theoretical space* for the resolution of the apparent paradoxes noted above. Thus, the critique that certain aspects of ABD correspond to *consequences* rather than *preconditions* of capitalist production may no longer pose such a theoretical anomaly, given a *recursive* view of the causal relationship between the two pro-cesses.[23] Correspondingly, it is possible to reconcile within this framework of recursive causation Levien's (2012: 938–939) view that ABD is the *con-sequence, rather than the precondition*, of advanced capitalism.[24]

Primitive accumulation and actually existing capitalism

The preceding analysis of neoliberal India also helps to clarify whether primitive accumulation is a part of 'movements within mature capitalism' or an analytically distinct process. Clearly, it is necessary to distinguish between primitive and cap-italist accumulation, in the first place, to be able to decompose the complex con-sequences of neoliberal policy interventions into the parallel operations of these

Primitive accumulation in neo-liberal India   41

two types of accumulative processes (P. Patnaik 2012: 35–37). The distinction is also essential for specifying the two-way and recursive causal relationship between primitive accumulation and capitalist production. Moreover, it helps to resolve the apparent theoretical anomalies in the directionality of the causal interlinkages between them. All of these considerations indicate that primitive accumulation constitutes an analytically distinct process that coexists and interacts with the capitalist sector of the Indian economy without being subsumed by it.

These issues and considerations are not simply a matter of defining and categorizing primitive accumulation. Rather, analytical clarity about primitive accumulation and its complex causal interlinkages with capitalist production and accumulation is essential for understanding the features of actually existing capitalism in neoliberal India (Adnan 2012; 2013: 124).

Notes

1 I am particularly indebted to Judith Heyer for critical comments as well as her patience and insistence in getting me to revise this chapter. I thank Schams A. Ahad, Amiya K. Bagchi, Pranab K. Basu, Dwaipayan Bhattacharya, Sudipta Bhattacharyya, Nandini Gooptu, Barbara Harriss-White, Jens Lerche, David Ludden, J. Mohan Rao and Alpa Shah for comments and discussions on the issues covered.
2 Comments from J. Mohan Rao helped to clarify this point.
3 However, many of the Indian state governments had also set up their own specialized agencies earlier for attracting foreign and domestic investment (Walker 2008: 581).
4 As of June 2012, there were about 143 SEZs in operation throughout India and an additional 634 SEZs had been formally/principally approved by the Government of India. Source: Wikipedia http://en.wikipedia.org/wiki/Special_economic_zone#India (accessed 28 March 2014).
5 Such laws included the Special Economic Zone (SEZ) Act, 2005 and the Unlawful Activities (Prevention) Act, 2008. The Chhattisgarh Public Security Act of 2005 was used to evict tribal groups in order to take over their mineral-rich lands for subsequent reallocation to private corporations (Walker 2008: 558).
6 For instance, community (*gram sabha*) consent to the acquisition of land is reported to have been 'manufactured at gun point by the law and order machinery of the state' (Bhaduri 2008: 13).
7 Such organizations include the *POSCO Pratirodh Sangram Samiti (PPSS)* in Odisha, the *Bhumi Uchchhed Pratirodh Committee (BUPN)* in Nandigram, and the *Raigarh Bachao Shangarsh Samiti* in Chhattisgarh (Walker 2008: 585–591).
8 Such instances highlight the conditions under which non-violent and covert modes of resistance may be transformed into violent and overt ones (cf. Adnan 2007: 214–215; 2013: 118–119).
9 The share of wages in the organized manufacturing sector of India declined steadily to less than 15 per cent of value-added during the neoliberal period (P. Patnaik 2012: 37).
10 This innovative analysis of the differential impacts of neoliberal policies, distinguishing between forms of actual and *anticipatory* primitive accumulation as well as 'normal' capitalist accumulation, is largely attributable to the work of Prabhat Patnaik (2008; 2012).
11 The notion of 'exclusion' is somewhat problematic in this context, given that the units dispossessed by ongoing primitive accumulation were not necessarily 'included' within circuits of capital in the first place. A more accurate description would be that they are *not linked* to circuits of capital.

42 *S. Adnan*

12 This does not imply any normative judgement in terms of 'glorification or celebration' of the self-employed or petty commodity producers as being preferable to wage workers – or vice versa.

13 For instance, Sanyal and Bhattacharyya (2009: 35) and Basu and Das (2009: 158).

14 Sanyal and Bhattacharyya (2009: 39–40), citing data from the National Commission for Enterprises in the Unorganized Sector.

15 Sanyal (2007: 53–58) explicitly distinguishes this category from Marx's industrial reserve army by stressing its *continuous generation by ongoing primitive accumulation.*

16 Sanyal and Bhattacharyya (2009: 41) observe that such 'informal home-based' producers are involved in the considerable industrial production in the Dharavi slum of Mumbai.

17 Usurious and merchants' capital correspond to unproductive capital and are involved in non-capitalist or 'precapitalist' forms of exploitation. They are analytically distinct from productive capital which appropriates surplus value through production based on wage labour, leading to capitalist accumulation (Adnan 1984; 1985).

18 Sanyal (2007: 59) defines 'reverse primitive accumulation' in two ways: (1) redistribution of the pre-existing stock of the 'means of labour'; and (2) 'a part of the surplus product in the capitalist sector [that] is not transformed into new capital but transferred to the surplus population to constitute the conditions of existence of non-capitalist production'.

19 In the general case, redistributive programmes by the state can be aimed at compensating for relative deprivation or inequality caused by a whole multitude of factors that may not necessarily have anything to do with either primitive accumulation or the 'reversal' of its effects. However, this argument is not concerned with questioning the role and relevance of *governmentality* in the *political management* of inequality and exploitation.

20 While in the first instance such resistance is directed against primitive accumulation, it also amounts to *resistance against capitalism* insofar as it constrains the supply of resources needed for the reproduction and expansion of capitalist production.

21 The Indian SEZs were influenced by the model of 'economic development zones' in contemporary China (Walker 2008: 587).

22 However, the historical analysis of mechanisms of primitive accumulation in India lies outside the scope of this chapter.

23 As pointed out by Brenner (2006: 98–102), Ashman and Callinicos (2006: 119–120) and Fine (2006: 143–146) with reference to Harvey's (2005) formulation of ABD.

24 Nonetheless, as noted above, ABD (*qua* primitive accumulation) can also be the precondition of capitalist production, depending upon the specific phase of their interaction in a dynamic context.

References

Adnan, Shapan (1984) *Peasant production and capitalist development: A model with reference to Bangladesh*, PhD Thesis, University of Cambridge.

—— (1985) 'Classical and contemporary approaches to agrarian capitalism', *Economic and Political Weekly*, 20(30): PE-53–64.

—— (2007) 'Departures from everyday resistance and flexible strategies of domination: the making and unmaking of a poor peasant mobilization in Bangladesh', *Journal of Agrarian Change*, 7(2): 183–224.

—— (2012) 'Primitive accumulation to accumulation by dispossession: understanding capitalist development in South Asia', paper presented at a conference in honour of Barbara Harriss-White, held at University of Oxford, 4–5 July (mimeo).

Primitive accumulation in neo-liberal India 43

—— (2013) 'Land grabs and primitive accumulation in deltaic Bangladesh: interactions between neoliberal globalization, state interventions, power relations and peasant resistance', *Journal of Peasant Studies*, 40(1): 87–128.

Amin, Samir (2003) 'World poverty, pauperization & capital accumulation', *Monthly Review*, website: monthlyreview.org/.

Ashman, Sam and Callinicos, Alex (2006) 'Capital accumulation and the state system: assessing David Harvey's *The New Imperialism*', *Historical Materialism*, 14(4):107–131.

Basu, Pranab Kanti (2007) 'Political economy of land grab', *Economic and Political Weekly*, 42(14): 1281–1287.

Basu, Deepankar and Das, Debarshi (2009) 'Political economy of contemporary India: some comments', *Economic and Political Weekly*, 44(22): 157–159.

Baviskar, Amita and Sundar, Nandini (2008) 'Democracy versus economic transformation?', *Economic and Political Weekly*, 43(46): 87–89.

Bhaduri, Amit (2008) 'Predatory growth', *Economic and Political Weekly*, 43(16): 10–14 (19 April).

Bharadwaj, Sudha (2009) 'Gravest displacement, bravest resistance: the struggle of adivasis of Bastar, Chhattisgarh against imperialist corporate landgrab', *Sanhati*, 1 June, pp. 1–39. http://sanhati.com/excerpted/1545/. Downloaded 19 February 2013.

Borras, S.M. Jr. and Franco, J. (2010) *Towards a Broader View of the Politics of Global Land Grab: Rethinking Land Issues: Reframing Resistance*, Initiatives in Critical Agrarian Studies (ICAS), Land Deal Politics Initiative (LDPI) and Transnational Institute (TNI): ICAS Working Paper Series No. 001.

Brenner, Robert (2006) 'What is, and what is not, imperialism?', *Historical Materialism*, 14(4): 79–105.

Burawoy, Michael (1985) *The Politics of Production: Factory Regimes under Capitalism and Socialism*, London: Verso, New Left Books.

—— (1996) 'The state and economic involution: Russia through a China lens', *World Development*, 24(6): 1105–1117.

—— (2001) 'Transition without transformation: Russia's involutionary road to capitalism', *East European Politics and Societies*, 15(2): 269–290.

Chatterjee, Partha (2008a) 'Democracy and economic transformation in India', *Economic and Political Weekly*, 43(16): 53–62.

—— (2008b) 'Classes, capital and Indian democracy', *Economic and Political Weekly*, 43(46): 89–93.

Das, Budhaditya (2012) 'Resisting development, theorizing resistance', *Economic and Political Weekly*, 47(33): 33–37. (Review of Alf Gunvald Nilsen (2010) *Dispossession and Resistance in India: The River and the Rage*, London and New York: Routledge).

De Angelis, Massimo (2001) 'Marx and primitive accumulation: the continuous character of capital's "enclosures"', *The Commoner*, No. 2, September. www.commoner.org.uk/01deangelis.pdf (accessed 16 June 2012).

—— (2004) 'Separating the doing and the deed: capital and the continuous character of enclosures', *Historical Materialism*, 12(2): 57–87.

Dobb, Maurice (1963) *Studies in the Development of Capitalism*, London: Routledge & Kegan Paul.

Fine, Ben (2006) 'Debating the "new" imperialism', *Historical Materialism*, 14(4): 133–156.

Harriss-White, Barbara (2006) 'Poverty and capitalism', *Economic and Political Weekly*, 41(13): 1241–1246 (1 April).

44 S. Adnan

Harriss-White, Barbara (2012) 'Capitalism and the common man: peasants and petty production in Africa and South Asia', *Agrarian South: Journal of Political Economy*, 1(2): 109–160.

Harvey, David (2005) *The New Imperialism*, Oxford: Oxford University Press.

—— (2006) 'Comment on commentaries', *Historical Materialism*, 14(4): 157–166.

Jha, Prem Shankar (2013) 'Mr PM think twice before jumping the gun', *Tehelka*, 24(10), 15 June. http://tehelka.com/mr-pm-think-twice-before-jumping-the-gun/.

Kunnath, George (2012) *Rebels from the Mud Houses: Dalits and the Making of the Maoist Revolution in Bihar*, New Delhi: Social Science Press.

Levien, Michael (2012) 'The land question: special economic zones and the political economy of dispossession in India', *Journal of Peasant Studies*, 39(3–4): 933–969.

Luxemburg, R. (2003) *The Accumulation of Capital*, London and New York: Routledge.

Marx, Karl (1976) *Capital: A Critique of Political Economy, Volume 1*, London: Penguin.

Marx, Karl (1981) *Capital: A Critique of Political Economy, Volume 3*. London: Penguin.

MNC (Midnight Notes Collective) (2001) (1990) 'The new enclosures', *The Commoner*, September. (Reprinted from *Midnight Notes*, #10, 1990.)

Mohanty, Monoranjan (2006) 'Challenges of revolutionary violence: the Naxalite movement in perspective', *Economic and Political Weekly*, 41(29): 3163–3168 (22 July).

Moore, Barrington Jr. (1966) *Social Origins of Dictatorship and Democracy: Lord and Peasant in the Making of the Modern World*, Boston, MA: Beacon Press.

Moyo, Sam, Yeros, Paris and Jha, Praveen (2012) 'Imperialism and primitive accumulation: notes on the new scramble for Africa', *Agrarian South: Journal of Political Economy*, 1(2): 181–203.

Nilsen, Alf Gunvald (2010) *Dispossession and Resistance in India: The River and the Rage*, London and New York: Routledge.

Patnaik, Prabhat (2008) 'The accumulation process in the period of globalisation', *Economic and Political Weekly*, 43(26–27): 108–113 (28 June).

—— (2011) 'Things, not people', *Frontline*, 28: 21. www.frontline.in/navigation/?type=static&page=archive. Downloaded 9 February 2013.

—— (2012) 'The peasant question and contemporary capitalism: some reflections with reference to India', *Agrarian South: Journal of Political Economy*, 1(1): 27–42.

Patnaik, Utsa (2012) 'Some aspects of the contemporary agrarian question', *Agrarian South: Journal of Political Economy*, 1(3): 233–254.

Perelman, Michael (1984) *Classical Political Economy: Primitive Accumulation and the Social Division of Labour*, Totowa, NJ: Rowman & Allanheld.

—— (2001) 'The secret history of primitive accumulation and classical political economy', *The Commoner*, No. 2, September.

Sanyal, Kalyan (2007) *Rethinking Capitalist Development: Primitive Accumulation, Governmentality and Post-colonial Capitalism*, London, New York and New Delhi: Routledge.

Sanyal, K. and Bhattacharyya, R. (2009) 'Beyond the factory: globalisation, informalisation of production and the new locations of labour', *Economic and Political Weekly*, 44(22): 35–44.

Sebastian, Gilbert (2012) 'The big U-turn: new forms of primitive accumulation and the shift in patriotic sensibilities in India', paper presented at an all-India seminar on 'Parliamentary Democracy and Neoliberalism in India', 18–19 October, organized by the Institute of Parliamentary Affairs, Government of Kerala, in association with the Department of Economics, University College, Thiruvananthapuram (mimeo).

Shah, Mihir (2008) 'Structures of power in Indian society: a response', *Economic and Political Weekly*, 43(46): 78–83 (15 November).

Tilly, Charles (1978) *From Mobilization to Revolution*, Reading, MA: Addison-Wesley.

Vasudevan, Ramaa (2008) 'Accumulation by dispossession in India', *Economic and Political Weekly*, 43(11): 41–43 (15 March). (Review of The Perspectives Team (2007) *Abandoned: Development and Displacement*, New Delhi: Perspectives.)

Walker, Kathy Le Mons (2008) 'Neoliberalism on the ground in rural India: predatory growth, agrarian crisis, internal colonization, and the intensification of class struggle', *Journal of Peasant Studies*, 35(4): 557–620.

Whitehead, Judith (2012) 'The neo-liberal city: a critical geography', *Economic and Political Weekly*, 47(13): 31–33. (Review of Banerjee-Guha, Swapna (ed.) (2010) *Accumulation by Dispossession: Transformative Cities in the New Global Order*, New Delhi: Sage.)

Wikipedia (2014) Main article: *List of Special Economic Zones in India*. http://en.wikipedia.org/wiki/Special_economic_zone#India (accessed 28 March 2014).

Wood, Ellen Meiksins (2002) *The Origins of Capitalism: A Longer View*, London and New York: Verso.

—— (2006) 'Logics of power: a conversation with David Harvey', *Historical Materialism*, 14(4): 9–34.

3 Regional patterns of agrarian accumulation in India[1]

Jens Lerche

1 Introduction

The objective of this chapter is to increase our understanding of regional patterns of agrarian capital accumulation in India. 'Regional aspects of agrarian development in India' is an oft-studied theme, but not with a focus on accumulation. By 'agrarian capital accumulation' we understand the process of expansion of value through surplus value production within agriculture and its appropriation. This is at the core of capitalist agriculture. Who accumulates, through which processes and how much? And what happens to the accumulated capital? An investigation of these issues will also throw light on the wider social and economic relations of which they are part.

Recent studies dealing with aspects of this issue at an all-India level include Amit Basole and Deepankar Basu (2011), Hans Binswanger-Mkhize (2013), V.K. Ramachandran (2011) and Lerche (2011; 2013). None of these studies has investigated regional trajectories, however.

The focus here is on those classes who accumulate capital through farming activities in India's regions. The study is informed by an overall understanding of the character of agrarian transition(s) in India today, and focuses on regional patterns and developments in relation to this. It is also concerned with other social groups who, together with agrarian capitalists, make up the regional agrarian, small-town and rural-dominant classes. These wider relations are dealt with in less depth, not least due to the inconsistent and thin literature on such issues.

In this chapter the topic is investigated empirically, from an agrarian vantage point, drawing on existing state-level statistical survey data as well as on existing case studies. Given the paucity of the data and studies relevant to this topic, the investigation will necessarily be preliminary. State-level data do show regional differences. However, they also cover up differences within states. Economic activities may well straddle state boundaries, increasingly so today, as agribusiness, traders and moneylenders, and rural labourers as well as farmers do not necessarily confine their concerns to their 'local' area. Moreover, government statistical data are limited by the categories used and can only serve as proxy indicators for class relations and capital accumulation.

Regional patterns of agrarian accumulation 47

2 Agricultural accumulation and economic development in other sectors

The role of the agricultural sector in India is changing. In the early 1980s more than two-thirds of the country's working population were employed in agriculture. In 2009 to 2010 this had fallen to close to the 50 per cent mark (see Table 3.1). The move away from agriculture is part of the pattern that is expected to occur in an agrarian transition (see e.g. Byres 1996). Labour and small farmers are squeezed out of an increasingly class-differentiated and capital-intensive agrarian sector, and left to find employment in the growing non-agricultural sectors, especially manufacturing. However, in India, as in many other developing countries, the move out of agriculture is not primarily to manufacturing but to the service sector and to construction (see Table 3.1). GDP-wise it is also not manufacturing that has taken over from agriculture as the leading contributor to the economy.[2]

This general picture hides important regional differences. Table 3.2 lists employment in agriculture and manufacturing in 2009/2010 in all Indian states with more than 20 million inhabitants. There are significant differences between states. In Kerala the proportion of the workforce working in agriculture has fallen to 28 per cent, and West Bengal, Tamil Nadu, Punjab, Haryana and Jharkhand also have fewer than half of their workforces in agriculture. On the other hand, a number of states in central, eastern and northeastern India have more than 60 per cent of their workforces in agriculture. In Chhattisgarh the percentage is above 70 per cent.

Table 3.2 also shows that lower levels of employment in agriculture tend to coincide with higher levels of employment in manufacturing. There has been a stronger shift (more precisely, a less weak shift) from agricultural to manufacturing employment in Kerala and West Bengal, followed by Tamil Nadu, Haryana and Punjab. In the overwhelmingly agricultural states of Bihar, Assam, Madhya Pradesh and Chhattisgarh agricultural employment is more than ten times as important numerically as manufacturing employment.[3] Thus, state-level developments are more diverse than the picture painted by the all-India figures.

In the classic agrarian transitions, the surplus generated by the newly highly productive capitalist agriculture kick-started growth in other sectors, while the

Table 3.1 Employment by sector as percentage of total employment in India

	1983	1993–1994	1999–2000	2004–2005	2009–2010
Agriculture	68.5	64.0	56.5	56.5	53.2
Industry	11.5	11.7	11.8	13.0	11.9
Construction	2.2	3.2	4.4	5.7	9.6
Services	17.6	21.1	23.5	24.8	25.3
Total	99.8	100.0	100.0	100.0	100.0

Source: Ramaswami (2007: 48); Mehrotra *et al.* (2012: 63, 67), based on NSS data.

48   J. Lerche

Table 3.2 Employment in agriculture and manufacturing in major Indian states, 2009/2010

	Agriculture	*Manufacturing*
Kerala	27.8	13.0
W Bengal	42.8	19.0
Tamil Nadu	44.0	17.1
Punjab	44.2	12.8
Haryana	44.3	15.4
Jharkhand	45.8	7.7
Rajasthan	52.8	6.3
Maharashtra	52.2	11.1
Gujarat	53.1	13.9
Andhra Pradesh	54.1	11.7
Karnataka	55.2	10.4
Uttar Pradesh	56.1	10.7
Odisha	60.6	8.9
Bihar	61.9	5.8
Assam	63.6	4.0
Madhya Pradesh	68.7	6.1
Chhattisgarh	74.1	5.9
All India	52.9	11.0

Source: Government of India (2011a, table S36).

Note
Minor differences between Tables 3.1 and 3.2 are due to a narrower definition of agriculture and manufacturing in Table 3.2. Agriculture: agriculture, hunting and forestry but not fishing. Manufacturing: does not include: mining and quarrying; electricity, gas and water supply; construction.

emerging agrarian capitalists formed a new and growing market for non-agricultural produce (Byres 1996). Whether the overall inter-sectoral economy in India is organised in such a way that value is transferred from agriculture to industry or vice versa is virtually impossible to establish. Instead, the focus here will be on the more basic issue: what are the levels and patterns of agrarian capital accumulation and who appropriates it? Without sizeable capital accumulation based on farming it is unlikely that this sector can play the role of a powerhouse in capitalist development. This will be followed by a case-based analysis of the extent to which, and how, capital accumulated in agriculture is invested in other sectors.

An indicator of the production of surplus value in agriculture is the Gross Domestic State Product (GDSP) from agriculture. Here I have calculated GDSP from agriculture per acre of land and per person working in agriculture. Top scores on both indicators are likely to reflect high levels of capital accumulation through capital-intensive agrarian production and high labour productivity.

The calculations may be found in Table 3.3. Linking this to the previous discussion, the top-ranking states measured in GDSP per person, and per acre, are among the five states achieving the lowest levels of employment in agriculture, and thus, seemingly having experienced most of an agrarian transition. Kerala

Regional patterns of agrarian accumulation 49

and Punjab lead the group, followed by Haryana. West Bengal – which is the state with the highest proportion of its working population in manufacturing – has very high levels of value addition per acre but this is based on lower GDSP/person (i.e. less high productivity per person), and thus, potentially, lower income and/or lower levels of accumulation per person. For most of the very low-scoring states the immediate explanation of this is low levels of irrigation (see below), which in turn is often associated with overall low levels of agrarian capitalist development.

There is clearly not a straightforward relationship between agrarian surplus and industrialisation. Only in Kerala and Punjab does the agricultural sector appear to produce a significant surplus. At the same time, Kerala and Punjab are only just above the national average regarding manufacturing employment. The runners-up, Haryana and West Bengal, are some distance behind these two states but have higher levels of industrialisation. In Haryana's case, the industrialisation level is likely to reflect primarily the expansion of industrial estates into its territory from neighbouring Delhi. Tamil Nadu, on the other hand, is one of the two states which are most industrialised but its level of agrarian surplus is little more than average. Perhaps agriculture does not, after all, play a crucial role in the creation of capital for industrialisation in India. Another possibility is that it does do so, but that these figures cannot capture this, either because capital is invested in industrial development but outside the 'home' state, or owing to

Table 3.3 Agricultural productivity indicators (Rs.1000)

	GDSP per arable acre	*GDSP per cultivators and agricultural labourers*
Kerala	65.1	64.0
West Bengal	71.6	31.3
Tamil Nadu	29.3	17.4
Punjab	60.7	71.9
Haryana	44.4	38.5
Jharkhand	12.7	8.1
Rajasthan	7.7	12.6
Maharashtra	17.6	16.5
Gujarat	12.6	14.3
Andhra Pradesh	26.4	19.4
Karnataka	22.6	22.3
Uttar Pradesh	31.7	17.1
Orissa	17.1	13.2
Bihar	34.0	10.5
Assam	37.7	24.2
Madhya Pradesh	10.1	9.5
Chhattisgarh	9.8	7.4
India	23.5	18.3

Source: Ministry of Agriculture (2007); Indiastat (n.d.a).

Note
GSDP: gross state domestic product.

50 *J. Lerche*

major regional differences within agriculture in the home state. It may be concluded that the relationship between levels of capital accumulation in agriculture and industrial development varies across states and that, in order to understand this interrelationship, one must undertake a concrete and specific analysis as opposed to attempting to simply 'read off' the relationship from high-level agrarian transition theory.

3 Indian agriculture – accumulation and crisis for whom?

Who accumulates within agriculture?

The next step is to investigate the accumulation processes *within* agriculture, including who accumulates and how, and how this relates to (1) accumulation outside of agriculture by farmers, and (2) accumulation by capital engaged in agribusiness and thus extracting agricultural surplus as well.

Here we first focus on accumulation within agriculture. Some argue that, overall, very little accumulation takes place in agriculture (Patnaik 2006). This view is based, in part, on the common argument that Indian agriculture is in crisis. However, agriculture as a *productive* sector has not been in crisis since 2003/2004 (see Table 3.4). Growth rates have more or less recovered, agricultural investments have reached new record highs and terms of trade are more positive for agriculture then they were even in the late 1980s (Chand and Parappurathu 2012; Lerche 2011; 2013; Ramachandran 2011).

Even if agriculture as a productive sector is not in crisis, there has indeed been real hardship for many farmers, as evidenced by, for example, the 2007 Government of India report on agricultural indebtedness (GoI 2007). This however relates to class-specific regional trajectories that cannot be captured even by state-level average growth figures. The question this raises is: who accumulates, when there is hardship for some rural groups?

Based on the Ministry of Agriculture 'cost of cultivation of principal crops for India' annual surveys (Ministry of Agriculture n.d.) Emumalai Kannan (2014) has calculated the average net income (gross income minus all expenditures) per acre in Punjab, West Bengal, Karnataka and Maharashtra. He shows that the variation in average regional income per acre is quite extreme, the

Table 3.4 Trend growth rates in GDP, percentage per year, 1975/1976 to 2010/2011

	1975/1976– 1988/1989	*1988/1989– 1995/1996*	*1997/1998– 2002/2003*	*2004/2005– 2010/2011*
GDP agriculture at factor cost (%)	2.4	3.2	0.5	3.3

Source: Chand and Parappurathu (2012) (based on National Accounts Statistics), except 1997/1998–2002/2003: Government of India (2012).

Note
Agriculture: 'Agriculture and allied' sector; 2004/2005 prices.

income per acre during the period 2001/2002 to 2007/2008 in Punjab being 6.0 to 7.0 times as high as in Maharashtra, 3.6 times as high as in Karnataka and 3.0 times as high as in West Bengal. The straightforward conclusion is that agrarian accumulation is much more substantial in the old Green Revolution areas of the northeast of India (Punjab, but probably also Haryana and the westernmost parts of Uttar Pradesh which are normally seen as not lagging far behind Punjab) than it is in most other parts of India.

The consumer expenditure levels of the rural populations of India point to a roughly similar regional picture (see Table 3.5).[4] It is the agriculturally highly productive states that have the highest average levels of consumer expenditure. Expenditure data for the top 10 per cent of households are also listed in the table. Inequality, judged by expenditure, is much more pronounced in the states with the highest levels of consumer expenditure. The implication is that regional rural inequalities in levels of accumulation combine with social class inequalities so that the accumulation is disproportionately concentrated in the hands of the best-off groups in the best-off states.

The high degree of inequality within the very productive states of Punjab and Haryana may also be inferred from land size distribution figures. The official figures show a major variation in land sizes from state to state (see Figure 3.1). It

Table 3.5 Average monthly capita expenditure for top decile of the rural population in 2009/2010

	Average expenditure for top decile		Average expenditure for all deciles	
	Rs.	State ranking	Rs.	State ranking
Kerala	5001	1	1835	1
Punjab	4128	2	1649	2
Haryana	3527	3	1510	3
Andhra Pradesh	2895	4	1234	4
Rajasthan	2789	5	1179	5
Tamil Nadu	2625	6	1160	6
Maharashtra	2438	7	1153	7
Gujarat	2362	8	1110	9
Karnataka	2190	9	1020	8
Madhya Pradesh	2162	10	903	12
Assam	1949	11	1003	10
West Bengal	1931	12	952	11
Uttar Pradesh	1911	13	899	13
Odisha	1754	14	818	15
Jharkhand	1705	15	825	14
Chhattisgarh	1642	16	784	16
Bihar	1504	17	780	7
All India	2517		1054	

Source: Government of India (2011b).

Note
Based on average MPCE-MMRP (Modified Mixed Reference Period MPCE).

is not known how much underreporting of, for example, village-level ex-landlord holdings (which in some cases may run into 100+ hectares) skew the picture. Combining the data with what is generally known about land sizes in India, it stands to reason that larger holdings are significantly more common in Punjab and Haryana than elsewhere in the country: at the core of the Green Revolution in Punjab and Haryana are the large farmers (i.e. farmers owning more than ten hectares) who have had access to sufficient capital to invest in modern technology. Taking irrigation and number of tractors per acre as simple indicators of agrarian investment, Punjab and Haryana are in a league of their own, with practically all farmland irrigated and very high levels of mechanisation (see Table 3.6). There may well be pockets in other states that display similar levels of investment but such pockets are lost in the overall picture from the concerned states. The state with least irrigation is Jharkhand (2.4 per cent irrigation), which is also at the bottom end with regard to labour productivity per hectare and household expenditure levels.

The preponderance of marginal (<1 hectare) farmers in states such as Tamil Nadu, West Bengal and Kerala makes for a very different agriculture to that of Punjab and Haryana. It is difficult to accumulate from such small holdings. However, even in these states there are landowners who accumulate. In Kerala this is done through growing high-value tropical cash crops such as ginger, vanilla, cashew and medicinal plants, and a move into higher value vegetable and other cash crops requiring a great deal of investment – a trend which is also discernible in other states where oilseed, cotton, fruit and vegetable production is gaining ground (Birthal *et al.* 2007; International Cotton Advisory Committee 2009).

The major capitalist farmers from the agriculturally most developed states are, however, in a league of their own. In the past decade they have shown their

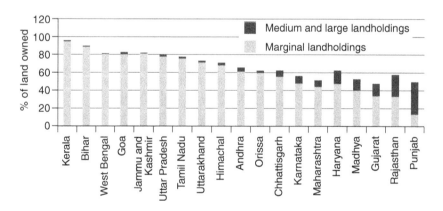

Figure 3.1 Landholdings – major size groups, 2005/2006 (source: Government of India (2008)).

Notes
Marginal: less than 1 hectare of land.
Medium and large: more than 4 hectares of land.

Table 3.6 Irrigation and tractor intensity in Indian states

State-wise percentage of net irrigated area over area of agricultural land 2009/2010			Tractor intensity per 1000 ha	
State	Percentage	Rank	Intensity	Rank
Punjab	96.8	1	71.4	1
Haryana	82.3	2	61.0	2
Uttar Pradesh	70.3	3	31.1	3
Gujarat	34.2	8	18.5	4
Tamil Nadu	35.2	7	18.5	5
Bihar	51.7	5	16.2	6
Madhya Pradesh	39.8	6	14.9	7
Rajasthan	22.9	13	12.7	8
Andhra Pradesh	26.5	10	12.6	9
Karnataka	26.3	11	9.5	10
Maharashtra	15.4	15	7.9	11
West Bengal	54.7	4	4.6	12
Odisha	30.6	9	4.5	13
Kerala	16.8	14	3.1	14
Assam	6.1 (07–08)	16	1.9	15
Chhattisgarh	23.8	12	–	–
Jharkhand	2.4	17	–	–
India	34.7		17.0	

Sources: Irrigation: Indiastat (n.d.b); tractor intensity: Singh (2006).

economic strength by seeking out cheaper additional lands for their ventures outside the 'hothouses' of their home states where land is expensive and land ceilings are sometimes too vigorously implemented for their taste. For example, farmers from Punjab, Haryana and western UP have been buying up land in the state of Chhattisgarh (Anonymous 2009; Jha 2009) and abroad (e.g. in Georgia and Ethiopia) (Anonymous n.d.; Burke 2013; Dogra 2013) while Kerala farmers have been leasing land in neighbouring Karnataka, especially for growing vanilla (Rajesh 2013; Sathish 2011).

The least investigated aspect of accumulation in the countryside is that of non-agrarian accumulation. The general picture seems to one of major capitalist farmers increasingly accumulating from non-agricultural sources as well, but the extent of this is not clear. There appear to be several types of non-agricultural accumulation: (1) government office-related accumulation; (2) trading, agro-processing and moneylending; (3) land sale for industrial/urban usage, and (4) overseas migration.

Regarding government office-related accumulation, Pattenden (2011) has shown that in a village in Karnataka around half the income of the group of mainly major capitalist farmers came from misuse of government funds and undue access to government contracts. Others have also pointed to the political office-related accumulation of this group (see e.g. Ramachandran *et al.* (2010) in

54   *J. Lerche*

Andhra Pradesh, and Jeffrey (2003) in Uttar Pradesh). In addition, large capitalist farmers tend to invest in urban-based education for their offspring, especially their sons, so that they will be able to access government jobs, or perhaps take up a professional job in the USA, Canada or Europe (Jamikow *et al.* 2013; Jeffery *et al.* 2008; Ramachandran *et al.* 2010).

Local trading, agroprocessing and moneylending are often interlinked. Today, these types of accumulation often relate to the up- and downstream integration of farming into the wider agro-industrial complex.[5] The relatively few recent case studies of this indicate that it is common for farmers to be tied to traders and agro-commercial capital via pre-harvest moneylending, enabling traders to pay less for their produce. Large capitalist farmers often double up as traders, etc. and so themselves command a better price for their produce, as documented by case studies from Andhra Pradesh (Ramachandran *et al.* 2010), Orissa (Mishra 2008) and, to a lesser extent, Punjab (Gill 2004). Harriss-White shows that, by 2010, the tie-in with traders and agro-commercial capital in a region studied by her in Tamil Nadu had loosened somewhat (Harriss-White 2010). In West Bengal another study indicates that this may have been replaced by buyers linked to large-scale, often multinational companies who offer lower prices to all (Rakshit 2011). Harriss-White's West Bengal study (2008) also states that this is a possibility. Not much is known about how recent changes in government regulation of agricultural produce markets have impacted on this (Vijayshankar and Krishnamurthy 2012). An increase in contract farming has also been noted, mainly in relation to non-traditional crops, and cotton, with a variety of tie-ins and market relations involved. As elsewhere, such relations tend to exclude smaller farmers, and/or involve new middlemen (Frontline 2013: 30, 14; Narayan 2012; S. Singh 2002; 2005).

Harriss-White's detailed study of West Bengal shows that whereas the lower echelons of the trading chain would often reinvest their profits in agriculture, higher up the chain, especially among the owners of large-scale mills who accumulated most of the agrarian surplus, investments would also go into transport, wholesale commerce, finance and urban property (Harriss-White 2008).

Finally, accumulation also takes place through the sale of land for industrial and other urban purposes. Most cases reported show that non-farming groups benefit from these transactions (Sud (2009) for Gujarat; newspaper and magazine articles, e.g. zeenews.com (2012) for Rajasthan; Shalini Singh (2012; 2013) for Haryana; Anonymous (2011) for Punjab). However, powerful major landowners may also benefit from land sale and land speculation, as shown by Levien (2011) in Rajasthan. Mario Rutten (1995) also reports that capitalist farmers in villages in Gujarat speculated in land, and Heyer (forthcoming) shows that even smaller landowners benefited from land sale in Tamil Nadu villages. The general conclusion may well be that the landed groups who are *most likely* to be able to gain from land expropriation are major capitalist farmers with strong political connections.

4 Agrarian surplus in the wider economy

It is now time to return to the extent to which accumulated agrarian surpluses penetrate the wider non-agrarian economy and contribute to industrial development. Harish Damodaran, among others (e.g. Raman Mahadevan 2011), has studied the historical role played by different castes and communities in Indian industrialisation, with a focus on the history of major Indian industrial groups but also with an eye to smaller capitalists and wider networks of capital. Damodaran identifies three 'general trajectories of industrial transition of communities': (1) the *bazaar-to-factory* route, dominant in north and central India; (2) *office-to-factory*, with Bengal as the paradigmatic case, and (3) *field-to-factory*, common in the south and the west (Damodaran 2008: 315).

The bazaar-to-factory route was dominated by the classical trading communities belonging mainly to the north Indian trading castes of Bania and Vaishya origin such as the Marwaris, especially from Rajasthan and Gujarat. Their trading and moneylending networks came to dominate huge swathes of north, east and central India from the nineteenth century onward, working with colonial businessmen and financing the growth of cash crops, including, for example, opium for the world market. They moved into industrial production from the latter half of the nineteenth century onward, while maintaining a grip on agricultural produce trading as well (Damodaran 2008: 8–47; Mahadevan 2011). For example, in West Bengal and Chhattisgarh, Marwaris and other Bania groups are still prevalent among the large agroprocessing operators (Harriss-White 2008; Das Gupta forthcoming). However, it should be added that the classic trade-based industrial groups have lost out in the past decades. Newspaper articles claim, for example, that while in 1990 the Marwaris controlled 24 per cent of business in India, by 2000 this had fallen to 2 per cent (Niyogi 2002), attributing this to the close-knit family and community economic relationships which used to be their strength but which are now proving to be less effective than modern capitalist ways of organising finance and production (Anonymous 2012).

The field-to-factory route emerged in South India which in the nineteenth century was outside the realm of the north Indian trading castes. Here various farming groups succeeded in accumulating through high-value cash crop production and modernised agricultural production methods. From the early twentieth century onward these groups, as well as local landlords, first engaged in agricultural produce trading and then in agroprocessing (e.g. the setting up of rice mills, cotton ginning factories, and spinning and weaving mills). Examples include the Kamma, Reddy and Raja farming castes in Andhra Pradesh and the Naidus in Tamil Nadu (Damodaran 2008: 92–152; Mahadevan 2011; Upadhya 1988). In western India, where the trading castes were present, Damodaran argues that it was only possible for local dominant farming castes to gain a foothold in agro-commercial activities through pooling their resources in cooperatives with strong support from the local dominant political force and governments which they dominated. The sugar cane cooperatives in Maharashtra and Gujarat are a case

56 *J. Lerche*

in point (Damodaran 2008: 216–258). However, Rutten shows that the presence of the trading castes did not stop all capitalist farmers moving from agricultural to industrial accumulation in this part of India. Whereas farmers in a tobacco-growing village studied by him were unable to gain a foothold in the trading of tobacco leaves due to the dominance of a small number of merchants in this sector, potato-producing farmers in a nearly village were able to become agricultural traders themselves, and from there to grow into rural industrialists, not the least due to the more open potato market, with many buyers (Rutten 1995: 237–239).

5 Two case studies: Punjab and Tamil Nadu

A focus on specific states will provide a more detailed understanding of the accumulation of agrarian surplus and its impact on the wider economy. In the following we will outline aspects of the developments in Punjab and Tamil Nadu. These are states where agrarian accumulation clearly takes place, but, equally clearly, this accumulation follows somewhat different trajectories.

Punjab is the classic Green Revolution state, and its agriculture still outperforms that of all other states in India. To summarise the characteristics outlined above: Punjab has the highest value of output per acre of all states. Measured as GSDP per arable acre, it is ranked third among the states while income per acre is significantly ahead of other states, judging from the four-states comparison undertaken by Kannan (2014). Its agriculture is the most mechanised in India.

In addition to Punjab having the highest agrarian income of all the Indian states, the rural economy in Punjab is also one of the most unequal in the country. Landownership is *the* most unequal in the country and land concentrations have been increasing from the 1970s onward (Government of Punjab 2004).[6] Per-capita expenditure in the rural sector is the second most unequal in the country. During the agricultural crisis years at the turn of the twenty-first century small and marginal farmers did suffer and farmer suicides increased, but accumulation among the top echelons of farmers seems not to have suffered (Jodhka 2006; K. Singh 2009). Reverse tenancy, whereby small and marginal farmers rent out their land to major capitalist farmers, is common and increasing (Dutta 2012). The Punjab government appears to support large farmers over smaller ones, not only through its public procurement system but also in its subsidy policy. For example, it provides subsidies for transplantation machines used by major capitalist farmers. Corporate farming and contract farming are growing phenomena in the state as well (S. Singh 2012).

Over the past decade, growth within Punjab's own agricultural sector has levelled off, and accumulating Punjabi farmers have sought out new investment avenues. One is the purchasing or leasing of land both in other states and internationally where land prices are lower than in Punjab (see above). Another is to move out of agriculture. Large farmers own town houses and have their children educated in urban schools (Jodhka 2006). A recent survey of 40 villages in Punjab showed that relatively few large farmers had left active farming (5 per

Regional patterns of agrarian accumulation   57

cent of large farmers against 11 per cent of all farmers) since the early 1990s. Large farmers who did so would tend to lease out their land while also engaging in non-farm activities. The most common moves among large farmers were from active farming, to living off renting out their land and trading in agricultural produce (Singh *et al.* 2009). According to a case study covering locations in two districts in Punjab, traders are also the main providers of informal credit to farmers who are tied into harvest sales to them. True to form, small farmers are charged higher interest rates than large farmers (Gill 2004). Moreover, it has been argued that the lowest-level traders, the commission agents (*arhatiyas*), have strengthened their position (Dutta 2012; S. Singh 2012).

The indications are clear: large capitalist farmers dominate accumulation within agriculture in Punjab. The state procurement system in the state means that compared to other states, a smaller proportion of the agricultural surplus ends up in the hands of traders and agro-commercial capital. Traders and agro-commercial capital are, nevertheless, important.

It is noticeable that the economic strength of the large capitalist farmers who by all accounts have succeeded in amassing a sizeable agrarian surplus has not led to the industrial development of the state. In fact, P. Singh (2008) argues that most of the industrial development in Punjab has been spearheaded by migrants from Pakistan after Partition and is in no way related to Punjab's agrarian surplus. Explanations abound, including that, given the profitability of capitalist agriculture in Punjab until recently, there has been little reason for large farmers to invest outside agriculture.[7] However, Damodaran's focus on the role of the trading communities seems more plausible. He argues that the Banias, Marwaris, etc. are so dominant in commodity and money markets in this part of India that it has been difficult for capitalist farmers to branch out; successful farmers-turned-industrialist cases in Punjab are extremely rare. Even engaging in agro-processing has proved difficult. The state has not been willing to provide the support necessary to go down the cooperative route taken in Gujarat and Maharashtra. However, a case study of the grain market in Khanna in Punjab reveals that since the beginning of the twenty-first century a significant number of farmers have succeeded in becoming 'commission agents', the lowest level of grain trader. By 2006, 76 per cent of these agents were also local farmers, compared to only a handful in the 1980s (Damodaran 2008: 259–296). This tallies with the case studies referred to above (Singh *et al.* 2009) and it is of course possible that this in the longer run would lead to the emergence of agrarian-based industrial development in Punjab, similar to Rutten's Gujarat case. The reason for this first foothold outside agriculture is less clear. It is also unclear why the north Indian trading groups, in spite of their earlier successes in venturing into industrial production, have not done so in Punjab.

Tamil Nadu is chosen as the second example, due to its levels of industrialisation. It is the second most industrialised of the major states in India, both in terms of employment and in terms of contribution of manufacturing to the National State Domestic Product (Vijayabaskar 2010). At the same time, the proportion of working population in agriculture is similar to that of Punjab, i.e.

58   *J. Lerche*

well below the national average. This indicates that the Tamil Nadu economy has not only been moving away from agriculture but also towards manufacturing as opposed towards the service sector. However, it should also be noted that recently manufacturing employment in Tamil Nadu has decreased.[8]

The agricultural sector in Tamil Nadu is a great deal less productive than that of Punjab. Irrigation and productivity indicators are only average and while its paddy-based Green Revolution was reasonably successful the growth generated from this has plateaued (Harriss-White 2010). Small and marginal landowners dominate, according to official statistics as well as to case studies from various parts of the state (Bouton 1985; Chari 2004). Other village case studies point to rural social inequality, as do the expenditure tables above, and the existence of larger 'elite' or 'landlord' holdings as well (Colatei and Harriss-White 2004; Djurfeldt *et al.* 2008; Harriss *et al.* 2010). These social groups also dominate non-agricultural incomes. Agrarian accumulation in many parts of the state is also being curtailed by an extreme groundwater shortage, which implies the high cost of providing deep tubewell water (Janakarajan 2004; Heyer 2012; Harriss-White 2010).

At the same time, high growth rates have been achieved in new high-value commodities such as gherkins and marigold, and cotton, often linked to agribusiness processing units and contract farming (Narayan 2012). Moreover, Harriss-White argues that in her case study area, accumulation for the top end of agricultural producers has improved as new government regulation of the trading in agricultural produce, and the availability of bank loans, have enabled more farmers to escape interlinked credit and produce markets (Harriss-White 2010). Judging by the 2002/2003 income figures, non-agricultural income formed a significantly higher proportion of the overall income of the large farmers in Tamil Nadu than in any other state but one (42 per cent in Tamil Nadu).[9] The move towards non-agricultural sources of accumulation among the accumulating rural classes seems to have gone further than elsewhere, with the possible exception of Kerala (see above).

It is in its industrial development that Tamil Nadu stands out. Its (by Indian standards) high levels of employment in manufacturing may in part be related to large-scale formal sector firms located in the state, including those related to international investments. It was one of the first states to set up Special Economic Zones (SEZs) to attract private investments and by 2010 it had nearly 50 notified SEZs (Vijayabaskar 2010). However, this was predicated on earlier waves of industrialisation in which agrarian surplus played a pivotal role.

The Coimbatore region played an important role. Based on the introduction of new 'Cambodia' cotton seeds in 1904 to 1905, the local petty landlord elite from the Kammevar (or Kamma) Naidu[10] community began investing in cotton ginning and, later, also in spinning and weaving in Coimbatore. This grew into a major textile and engineering industry hub, and by the 1930s Coimbatore had become a diversified industrial town, with Naidus as well as others the major investors. Gounders became the drivers of the neighbouring, extremely fast-growing garment town of Tiruppur, starting in the 1950s but taking off properly in the 1980s. However, their widely celebrated story was *not* primarily one of agrarian surplus invested in industry. The Tiruppur garment hub proliferated in its early years through the gradual transformation of Gounder garment workers from the countryside into garment producers. This could be called a 'Workers-to-Capital' trajectory, something which was not unheard of in the early days of the garment industry when entry barriers with regard to capital investment were low. A similar trajectory appears to have unfolded in Ludhiana (Mezzadri 2009). Gounders were aided by investments or loans from their agrarian caste and kin but this was far from always the case. By the early 1980s the Gounders had become dominant among the Tiruppur garment industrialists (Chari 2004: 205–228; Damodaran 2008: 138–174).

In a more recent development, Harriss-White has shown that capitalist farmers have succeeded in gaining a foothold in agro-industry-related accumulation, especially rice trading, in North Arcot district of Tamil Nadu (Harriss-White 1996). Since then, in the past decade, 'rural agro-capital' (i.e. 'the village machine-lords, water-lords and landlords') have also been able to rent in mills from existing larger producers (Harriss-White 2010: 67). However, in her studies of the market town Arni she concluded that agrarian accumulation only played a minor role in urban investments outside the agro-commercial area (Harriss-White 2010).

Nevertheless, compared to Punjab, in Tamil Nadu there is a history of agrarian surplus finding its way into trading, agro-processing and some wider industrial activities. This has partly been through the activities of major capitalist farmers but also through investments of other types of 'rural agro-capital' in industry.

6 Conclusion

The overall role of the agricultural sector in India is changing, but regionally at very different speeds. With agricultural sector employment ranging between 74 and 28 per cent (Chhattisgarh and Kerala) this is evident. However, it is not only the speed but also underlying trajectories of agrarian capital accumulation that differ.

This is not a well-studied area and to deal with it through state-level statistics and local case studies, as has been attempted here, is bound to lead to a partial picture. Perhaps that is why, at this point in time, there are several elements in the picture and they do not fit neatly together. *Within agriculture*, the original Green Revolution state of Punjab stands out. This is where agriculture appears to be most profitable and most unequal, spearheaded by an elite of major capitalist farmers running highly profitable capital-intensive farming businesses. Only Kerala, with its quite different specific reasons (including availability of capital from overseas migration, plantation crop history and high wages in agriculture, relative to other states), appears to be able to scale similar heights of profitable capital-intensive agriculture. The overwhelmingly agriculturally dominated states such as Chhattisgarh are at the other extreme.

60   *J. Lerche*

There is no evidence that the profitability of agriculture is falling for all agricultural classes across India, nor that this has called a halt to the rise in capitalist farming, as argued by some. Capitalist farming is alive and kicking, as is agrarian accumulation for significant groups of capitalist farmers. There is no sign that all farmers suffer under the yoke of global agribusiness; on the contrary, rural class differences, reinforced by regional differences, are creating an even wider gap between major capitalist farmers and the poor farmers and labourers.

Less is known about accumulation by agricultural capitalists outside agriculture but it stands to reason that the avenues open to dominant capitalist farmers coalesce around state-related accumulation, education and urban/overseas jobs; trading, agri-processing and moneylending; as well as possible land sale. In some states, especially but not only in the south, agricultural capitalists have also moved into industrial production.

The question of *investment of agrarian surplus in the wider economy* is a different angle on accumulation outside of agriculture, related to the classic formulation of the agrarian question, i.e. the transformation from an agricultural to an industrial society. The evidence from Indian states is that there is no neat fit between agricultural development and industrial investments. The experience of Punjab outlined here fits well with a classic class-based left-wing analysis of industrial development, casting the moneylenders-cum-traders as the villains who in many parts of India have monopolised the higher echelons of agribusiness as well as the entry-level territory of industrial production.

The Tamil Nadu sketch, as well as evidence from other states, show that there are cases where agricultural capitalists have succeeded in moving into agribusiness and onward to industrial accumulation. The common factor here seems to be the absence of class- and caste-based blockages in the agribusiness sector. The more general studies of caste, business and industry in India's regions lend credence to this interpretation, especially its historical perspective. However, it also leaves much unexplained regarding present-day developments, including in Punjab where it may be that the boundaries of the control of the trading communities are being pushed back.

If there is an overall conclusion to be drawn from this chapter, it may be that there is no a priori relationship between agrarian accumulation and industrialisation; and there is no a priori relationship between neoliberalism and the ability to accumulate within agriculture. There is a need to empirically ground theories regarding the agrarian question today, and while much work on this needs to be done in India, this is, hopefully, one step along that path.

Notes

1 I am grateful to Judith Heyer for her insightful comments. The usual disclaimers apply.
2 In 2012, the contribution of the service sector to GDP was 56.4 per cent while manufacturing and mining only contributed 26.4 per cent. Agriculture's share was 17.2 per cent (Index Mundi n.d.).

Regional patterns of agrarian accumulation 61

3 The very low levels of non-agrarian employment in the labour outmigration states of east and central India raise the question of whether seasonal migrant workers have been properly counted by the NSS.
4 The NSSO consumer expenditure figures only measure how much a household spends on consumer-related expenditure: they do not measure overall income levels and do not include investment-related expenditure.
5 The classic Indian debate on interlocking, development of capitalism in agriculture, and the role herein of landlords and traders involved scholars such as Amit Bhaduri, Krishna Bharajwaj, Pranab Bardhan and Ashok Rudra. It has been summarised and developed further by Ravi Srivastava (1989).
6 Land concentration measures such as concentration of 'operational holdings' increased from 1970/1971 to 2000/2001. In the period 1980/1981 to 1990/1991 land concentration decreased but this had been more than overturned already by 1995/1996 (Government of Punjab 2004).
7 If this were the case, the same argument should apply to other successful farming groups in India who, however, did go on to invest outside agriculture.
8 In the period 2004 to 2010, sector-wise employment growth in Tamil Nadu was: agriculture −4.6%; manufacturing −2.4%; non-manufacturing +7.0% and services −0.2%. Non-manufacturing consists of the subsectors gas, electricity, mining and construction (Government of India 2011c: 129).
9 No other state had more than 28 per cent of its income from non-agricultural sources, with the exception of Rajasthan, which, at that time, was in its fifth consecutive drought year, leading to near-zero income from agriculture.
10 Kamma Naidu according to Chari (2004); Kammevar Naidu according to Damodaran. The Kammevar Naidu community were 'originally migrants affiliated to the Kammas of Andhra Pradesh' (Damodaran 2008: 142).

References

Anonymous (2009) 'Buying farm land in Chhattisgarh to be tougher', *Indian Express*, 19 February, www.indianexpress.com/news/buying-farm-land-in-chhattisgarh-to-be-tougher/425271 (accessed 22 February 2013).

—— (2011) 'After Haryana, Punjab faces farmers' anger on land acquisition'. *Economic Times*, 30 July, http://articles.economictimes.indiatimes.com/2011–07–30/news/29833230_1_forcible-land-land-acquisition-acquisition-process (accessed 22 February 2013).

—— (2012) 'Marwari businesses at crossroads', *Times of India*, 14 November, http://timesofindia.indiatimes.com/business/india-business/Marwari-businesses-at-crossroads/articleshow/17211830.cms (accessed 22 February 2013).

—— (n.d.) 'Punjab farmers make successful beginning in Ethiopia', *Punjab Newsline*, www.punjabnewsline.com/content/punjab-farmers-make-successful-beginning-ethiopia/28064 (accessed 16 March 2013).

Basole, Amit and Basu, Deepankar (2011) 'Relations of production and modes of surplus extraction in India: Part I – agriculture', *Economic and Political Weekly*, 46(14): 41–58.

Binswanger-Mkhize, Hans (2013) 'The stunted structural transformation of the Indian economy', *Economic and Political Weekly*, 48(26–27): 5–13.

Bouton, Marshall (1985) *Agrarian Radicalism in South India*, Princeton, NJ: Princeton University Press.

Birthal, P.S., Joshi, P.K., Roy, Devesh and Thorat, Amit (2007) 'Diversification in Indian agriculture towards high-value crops: the role of smallholders', *IFPRI Discussion Paper* 00727, www.ifpri.org/sites/default/files/publications/ifpridp00727.pdf (accessed 22 February 2013).

62   J. Lerche

Blaut, J.M. (1994) 'Robert Brenner in the tunnel of time', *Antipode*, 26 (4): 351–376.

Burke, Jason (2013) 'Punjabi farmers find pastures new (and cheap) in Georgia', *Guardian*, 7 January, www.guardian.co.uk/world/2013/jan/07/georgia-punjab-migrants-farming (accessed 22 February 2013).

Byres, Terence J. (1996) *Capitalism from Above and Capitalism from Below, An Essay in Comparative Political Economy*, Basingstoke: Macmillan.

Chand, Ramesh and Parappurathu, Shinoj (2012) 'Temporal and spatial variations in agricultural growth and its determinants', *Economic and Political Weekly*, 47(26–27): 55–64.

Chari, Sharad (2004) *Fraternal Capital: Peasant-Workers, Self-made Men, and Globalization in Provincial India*, Stanford, CA: Stanford University Press; and Delhi: Permanent Black.

Colatei, Diego and Harriss-White, Barbara (2004) 'Social stratification and rural households', in Barbara Harris-White and S. Janakarajan (eds) *Rural India Facing the 21st Century, Essays on Long Term Village Change and Recent Development Policy*, London: Anthem Press: 115–158.

Damodaran, Harish (2008) *India's New Capitalists: Caste, Business, and Industry in a Modern Nation*, Basingstoke: Palgrave Macmillan.

Das Gupta, Sejuti (forthcoming) *Class Interest and Political Decisions: Agricultural Policies in Three Indian States, Chhattisgarh, Gujarat and Karnataka*, University of London, School of Oriental and African Studies, Ph.D. thesis.

Djurfeldt, Göran, Athreya, Venkatesh, Jayakumar, N., Lindberg, Staffan, Rajagopal, A. and Vidyasagar, R. (2008) 'Agrarian change and social mobility in Tamil Nadu', *Economic and Political Weekly*, 43(45): 50–61.

Dogra, Chander Suta (2013) 'From Taran Taran to Tbilisi, in search of a farming paradise', *The Hindu*, 6 January, www.thehindu.com/news/national/from-taran-taran-to-tbilisi-in-search-of-a-farming-paradise/article4280302.ece (accessed 15 March 2013).

Dutta, Swarup (2012) 'Green revolution revisited: the contemporary agrarian situation in Punjab, India', *Social Change*, 42(2): 229–247.

Gill, Anita (2004) 'Interlinked agrarian credit markets: case study of Punjab', *Economic and Political Weekly*, 39(33): 3741–3751.

Government of India (various years) *Agricultural Statistics at a Glance*, New Delhi: Ministry of Agriculture, Department of Agriculture and Cooperation, http://agricoop.nic.in/Agristatistics.htm (accessed 22 February 2013).

—— (2005) *Income, Expenditure and Productive Assets of Farmer Households, 2003, NSS 59th Round*, New Delhi: Ministry of Statistics and Programme Implementation, NSS Report No. 497.

—— (2007) *Report of the Expert Group on Agricultural Indebtedness*, New Delhi: Ministry of Finance, Department of Economic Affairs, July, www.igidr.ac.in/pdf/publication/PP-059.pdf (accessed 22 February 2013).

—— (2008) *A Special Programme for Marginal and Small Farmers*, New Delhi: National Commission for Enterprises in the Unorganised Sector (NCEUS).

—— (2011a) *Key Indicators of Employment and Unemployment in India 2009–2010, NSS 66th Round (NSS/KI 66/1.0)*, New Delhi: Ministry of Statistics and Programme Implementation.

—— (2011b) *Level and Pattern of Consumer Expenditure 2009–10, NSS 66th Round (66/1.0/1)*, Ministry of Statistics and Programme Implementation, NSS Report 538.

—— (2011c) *Report of the Working Group on Employment, Planning & Policy for the Twelfth Five Year Plan (2012–2017)*, New Delhi: Planning Commission, http://planningcommission.nic.in/aboutus/committee/wrkgrp12/wg_emp_planing.pdf (accessed 15 March 2013).

Regional patterns of agrarian accumulation 63

—— (2012) *State-wise Growth Rate (Annual Average in %) of Agriculture Sector in India: 1996–97 to 2008–09*, Planning Commission, http://planningcommission.nic.in/data/datatable/0904/tab_39.pdf (accessed 22 February 2013).

Government of Punjab (2004) *Human Development Report 2004 Punjab*, http://pbplanning.gov.in/HDR/merged_hdr.pdf (accessed 2 February.2013).

Harriss, J., Jeyaranjan, J. and Nagaraj, K. (2010) 'Land, labour and caste politics in rural Tamil Nadu in the 20th century: Iruvelpattu (1916–2008)', *Economic and Political Weekly*, 45(31): 47–61.

Harriss-White, Barbara (1996) *A Political Economy of Agricultural Markets in South India: Masters of the Countryside*, New Delhi: Sage.

—— (2008) *Rural Commercial Capital. Agricultural Markets in West Bengal*, New Delhi: Oxford University Press.

—— (2010) *Local Capitalism and the Foodgrains Economy of Northern Tamil Nadu, 1973–2010*, New Delhi: Three Essays Press, http://wiego.org/sites/wiego.org/files/publications/files/Harriss-White_Capitalism.Foodgrains.TamilNadu.pdf (accessed 22 February 2013).

Heyer, Judith (2012) 'Labour standards and social policy: a South Indian case study', *Global Labour Journal*, 3(1): 91–117.

—— (forthcoming) 'Rural Gounders on the move in western Tamil Nadu: 1981/2 to 2008/9', in Praveen Jha, Himanshu and Gerry Rodgers (eds) *Longitudinal Research in Village India: Methods and Findings*, New Delhi: Oxford University Press.

Index Mundi (n.d.) *India GDP – Composition by Sector*, www.indexmundi.com/india/gdp_composition_by_sector.html (accessed 22 February 2013).

Indiaagronet (n.d.) *Ceiling Limits on Land Holdings*, www.indiaagronet.com/indiaagronet/AGRI_LAW/CONTENTS/Ceiling.htm (accessed 22 February 2013).

Indiastat (n.d. a) *Agricultural Area Landuse*, www.indiastat.com/table/agriculture/2/agriculturalarealanduse/152/549424/data.aspx (accessed 22 February 2013).

—— (n.d. b) *Selected State/Source-wise Gross Irrigated Area in India (1997/1998 to 2009/2010)*, Indiastat.com (accessed 22 February 2013).

International Cotton Advisory Committee (2009) *Cotton Fact Sheet India*, www.icac.org/econ_stats/country_facts/e_india.pdf (accessed 22 February 2013).

Jamikow, Tanya, Williams, Liana and Tallapragada, Chiranjeevi (2013) 'A future orientation to agrarian livelihoods', *Economic and Political Weekly*, 48(26–27): 129–138.

Jan, Muhammad Ali and Harriss-White, Barbara (2012) 'The three roles of agricultural markets: a review of ideas about agricultural commodity markets in India', *Economic and Political Weekly*, 47(52): 39–52.

Janakarajan, S. (2004) 'Irrigation: the development of an agro-ecological crisis', in Barbara Harris-White and S. Janakarajan (eds) *Rural India Facing the 21st Century, Essays on Long Term Village Change and Recent Development Policy*, London: Anthem Press: 59–77.

Jeffrey, Craig (2003) 'Soft states, hard bargains: rich farmers, class reproduction and the local state in rural north India', in J. Lerche and R. Jeffery (eds) *Social and Political Change in Uttar Pradesh: European Perspectives*, New Delhi: Manohar: 225–246.

Jeffrey, Craig, Jeffery, Patricia and Jeffery, Roger (2008) *Degrees Without Freedom? Education, Masculinities, and Unemployment in North India*, Stanford, CA: Stanford University Press.

Jha, Dhirendra K. (2009) 'Jatland in Chhattisgarh', *Open > features*, 26 September, www.openthemagazine.com/article/nation/jatland-in-chhattisgarh (accessed 22 February 2013).

64   *J. Lerche*

Jodhka, Surinder (2006) 'Beyond "crises": rethinking contemporary Punjab agriculture', *Economic and Political Weekly*, 41(16): 1530–1537.

Kannan, Emumalai (2014) 'Trends in agricultural incomes: an analysis at select crops and states level in India', *Journal of Agrarian Change*, early view.

Lerche, Jens (2011) 'Agrarian crisis and agrarian questions in India', *Journal of Agrarian Change*, 11(1): 104–118.

—— (2013) 'The agrarian question in neoliberal India: agrarian transition bypassed?', *Journal of Agrarian Change*, 13(3): 382–404.

Levien, Michael (2011) 'Special Economic Zones and accumulation by dispossession in India', *Journal of Agrarian Change*, 11(4): 454–483.

Mahadevan, Raman (2011) 'Revisiting Indian capitalists in colonial India: some critical reflections', in D. Narayana and R. Mahadevan (eds) *Shaping India: Economic Change in Historical Perspective*, New Delhi: Routledge: 129–148.

Mehrotra, Santosh, Gandhi, Ankita, Sahoo, Bimal Kishore and Saha, Partha (2012) 'Creating employment in the twelfth Five-Year Plan', *Economic and Political Weekly*, 47(19): 63–73.

Mezzadri, Alessandra (2009) *The Architecture of Production and Labour Control in the Indian Garment Industry: Informalisation and Upgrading in the Global Economy*, University of London, School of Oriental and African Studies, unpublished Ph.D. thesis, http://ethos.bl.uk/SearchResults.do;jsessionid=35D3EF9D202C99801340CD82D26A D95A (accessed 22 February 2013).

Ministry of Agriculture, Government of India (2007) *Agricultural Statistics at a Glance 2007*, Directorate of Economics and Statistics, http://eands.dacnet.nic.in/At_A_Glance-2007/Indicator.htm (accessed 22 February 2013).

—— (n.d.) *Cost of Cultivation*, Directorate of Economics and Statistics, http://eands.dacnet.nic.in/Cost_of_Cultivation.htm (accessed 22 February 2013).

Mishra, D.K. (2008) 'Structural inequalities and interlinked transactions in agrarian markets: results of a field survey', in S.K. Bhaumik (ed.) *Reforming Indian Agriculture, Towards Employment Generation and Poverty Reduction*, New Delhi: Sage: 231–268.

Narayan, Sudha (2012) 'Inflections in agricultural evolution: contemporary commodity complexes and transactional forms in interior Tamil Nadu', *Economic and Political Weekly*, 47(52): 84–94.

Niyogi, Subhro (2002) 'Marwaris losing business acumen', *Times of India*, 6 May, http://articles.timesofindia.indiatimes.com/2002–05–06/kolkata/27120926_1_marwaris-founding-family-cent-family-owned-businesses (accessed 22 February 2013).

Patnaik, Utsa (2006) 'The agrarian crisis and importance of peasant resistance', *People's Democracy*, 30(5), http://pd.cpim.org/2006/0129/01292006_utsa.htm (accessed 22 February 2013).

Pattenden, Jonathan (2011) 'Gatekeeping as accumulation and domination: decentralisation and class relations in rural South India', *Journal of Agrarian Change*, 11(2): 164–194.

Rajesh, Ravi (2010) 'Kerala farmers lease land in K'taka for ginger production', *The Financial Express*, 21 October, www.financialexpress.com/news/kerala-farmers-lease-land-in-k-taka-for-ginger-production/700242 (accessed 22 February 2013).

Rakshit, Santanu (2011) 'Capital intensification, productivity and exchange – a class based analysis of agriculture in West Bengal in the current millennium', *Journal of Agrarian Change*, 11(4): 505–535.

Ramachandran, V.K. (2011) 'The state of agrarian relations in India today', *The Marxist*, 27(1–2): 51–89, www.cpim.org/marxist/201101-agrarian-relations-vkr.pdf (accessed 22 February 2013).

Regional patterns of agrarian accumulation 65

Ramachandran, V.K., Rawal, Vikas and Swaminathan, Madhura (eds) (2010) *Socio-economic Surveys of Three Villages in Andhra Prades, A Study of Agrarian Relations*, New Delhi: Tulika Books.

Ramaswamy, K.V. (2007) 'Regional dimensions of growth and employment', *Economic & Political Weekly*, 42(47): 47–56.

Reddy, D. Narasimha and Mishra, Srijit (2009) 'Agriculture in the reforms regime', in D. Narasimha Reddy and S. Mishra (eds) *Agrarian Crisis in India*, New Delhi: Oxford University Press: 3–43.

Rutten, Mario (1995) *Farms and Factories: Social Profile of Large Farmers and Rural Industrialists in West India*, New Delhi: Oxford University Press.

Sathish, G.T. (2011) 'Farmers find leasing out land to ginger growers profitable', *The Hindu*, 1 April, www.hindu.com/2011/04/01/stories/2011040164511100.htm (accessed 22 February 2013).

Singh, Gyanendra (2006) 'Estimation of a mechanisation index and its impact on production and economic factors – a case study in India', *Biosystems Engineering*, 93(1): 99–106.

Singh, Karam (2009) 'Agrarian crisis in Punjab: high indebtedness, low returns, and farmers' suicides', in D. Narasimha Reddy and Srijit Mishra (eds) *Agrarian Crisis in India*, New Delhi: Oxford University Press.

Singh, Pritam (2008) *Federalism, Nationalism and Development: India and the Punjab Economy*, London: Routledge.

Singh, Shalini (2012) 'Behind Haryana land boom, the Midas touch of Hooda', *The Hindu*, 30 October, www.thehindu.com/news/national/behind-haryana-land-boom-the-midas-touch-of-hooda/article4048394.ece (accessed 22 February 2013).

—— (2013) 'Behind realty rush in Haryana, a gilt-edged licence raj', *The Hindu*, 4 February, www.thehindu.com/news/national/behind-realty-rush-in-haryana-a-giltedged-licence-raj/article4375630.ece (accessed 22 February 2013).

Singh, Sukhpal (2002) 'Contracting out solutions: political economy of contract farming in the Indian Punjab', *World Development*, 30(9): 1621–1638.

—— (2005) *The Political Economy of Contract Farming*, New Delhi: Allied Publishers.

—— (2012) 'Institutional and policy aspects of Punjab agriculture: a smallholder perspective', *Economic and Political Weekly*, 47(4): 51–57.

Srivastava, Ravi (1989) 'Interlinked modes of exploitation in Indian agriculture during transition: a case study', *Journal of Peasant Studies*, 16(4): 493–522.

Sud, Nikita (2009). 'The Indian state in a liberalizing landscape', *Development and Change*, 40(4): 645–665.

Upadhya, Carol Boyak (1988) 'The farmer-capitalists of coastal Andhra Pradesh', *Economic and Political Weekly*, 23(27): 1376–1382; and 23(28): 1433–1442.

Vijaybaskar, M. (2010) 'Saving agricultural labour from agriculture: SEZs and politics of silence in Tamil Nadu', *Economic and Political Weekly*, 45(6): 36–43.

Vijayshankar, P.S. and Krishnamurthy, Mekhala (2012) 'Understanding agricultural commodity markets', *Economic and Political Weekly*, 47(52): 34–37.

zeenews.com (2012) 'Farmers agitate against land acquisition in Rajasthan', 27 October, http://zeenews.india.com/news/rajasthan/farmers-agitate-against-land-acquisition-in-rajasthan_807931.html (accessed 22 February 2013).

4 Agrarian relations and institutional diversity in Arunachal Pradesh

Deepak K. Mishra

While it has long been recognised that in a large economy like India regional diversity and unevenness in the process of capitalist transition are important in understanding the development of capitalism, the precise role of 'regional variations' in creating different trajectories of regional capitalist development is a question that remains under-investigated, and nowhere more so than in relation to the uniquely diverse northeastern region of India. Arunachal Pradesh, one of the states, has many distinct features that have shaped its recent economic and social transformation. Arunachal is a mountainous border state located in the extreme northeast corner of India, marked by an extraordinary degree of ecological and socio-cultural diversity (Misra 1979; Das 1995). Home to more than 100 tribes and sub-tribes, this thinly populated state remained largely un-administered during colonial rule. Among the specificities of the state that have shaped its economic transformation are: the postcolonial state as the prime mover of modernisation; the military and security agencies as key contributors in building roads and other infrastructure; the low land–man ratio of this mountainous region; ethnic community rights over land and forests; and restrictions on the movement of labour into the state (Mishra 2013).

By examining the complex interactions between non-capitalist and capitalist modes of production, exchange and accumulation within and outside agriculture, we will see that institutional diversity and identity remain key transformative dimensions of the Arunachal economy.[1] The specific ecological and institutional features of the region shape its transformation (and are simultaneously transformed by it), resulting not only in socio-ecological diversity but also in distinct patterns of economic interaction among state, market and community institutions. This chapter seeks to unpack these multi-level interactions in an attempt to understand aspects of the economic trajectory of Arunachal and the degree to which its specificities have facilitated or constrained accumulation pathways. Linking these specificities to the fundamental transformative processes of capitalist accumulation, the chapter seeks to examine the ways in which capitalist and non-capitalist institutions continue to interact and transform the local economy.

The changing agrarian structure

In Arunachal, landownership has for long been community-based, with institutional mechanisms like village councils to manage collective property rights over land and forest[2] (Misra 1979; Das 1995; Roy Burman 2002; Dutta 2003). The shifting cultivation system, *jhum*, the main system of cultivation in the past, is being gradually replaced by settled cultivation on the slopes and valleys. Although officially community institutions continue to control land,[3] under the mutually reinforcing interventions of state and market forces, private property rights have emerged in many parts of the state (Mishra 2001; Roy and Kuri 2001: 53–59; Harriss-White *et al.* 2009). Moreover, collective rights have diverse and context-specific operational meanings[4] (Bordoloi 1998). With gradual changes in the economy, actually existing communal property rights are being transformed in complex ways.

Of the total geographical area of Arunachal Pradesh only around 5 per cent is available for cultivation. The scope for further expansion of land under cultivation is not yet exhausted, but its cost limits this process. As per the Agricultural Census of 2010/2011, around 20 per cent of operational holdings were marginal, operating on less than 3 per cent of the total operated area, and around 38 per cent were small or marginal. On the other hand, the 6 per cent of large holdings covered nearly 25 per cent of the operated area. Between 1970/1971 and 2010/2011 there was a significant increase of the share of marginal, small and semi-medium holdings, while that of the medium- and large-size classes declined (Table 4.1). The prominent feature of the agrarian structure as captured through the distribution of operational holdings is the increase in the share of smaller holdings. The average size of holding declined from 6.19 ha in 1970/1971 to 3.51 ha in 2010/2011, partly showing increasing population pressure on agricultural land.[5]

It is important to note that semi-medium and medium-size holdings together accounted for 57 per cent of holdings and 65 per cent of area. This is due to the relatively large holdings in *jhum* cultivation. The area under *jhum* cultivation is on the decline and when farmers switch over to wet rice cultivation in the valleys and plains the size of operational holdings generally declines (Mishra 2006).

Within the different size classes, the decline has, however, not been uniform. Several factors other than the abandonment of large *jhum* plots for smaller permanent holdings are at work. These include the shift of manpower from rural/agricultural occupations to urban/non-agricultural occupations; increasing population pressure on fertile plains land which is scantily available; and the influx of migrant labourers as tenants (Mishra 2006). However, given the increasing popularity of horticulture and the drive for land occupation among the neo-rich, the possibility of underreporting of areas under the large-size category cannot be overlooked.[6] Another distinctive feature of the agrarian structure is the relative share of holdings operated by Arunachal's Scheduled Tribes (STs). The data from the Agricultural Census suggest that agriculture in the state is pursued largely through self-cultivation and that to date land leasing has a marginal

68   *D.K. Mishra*

Table 4.1 Size-class distribution of operational holdings (Arunachal Pradesh): 1970/1971 to 2010/2011

Year		Size-class of holdings (share in %)				
		Marginal	Small	Semi-medium	Medium	Large
1970/1971	No.	7.7	12.0	25.9	36.4	18.1
	Area	0.7	2.8	11.6	35.0	49.9
1976/1977	No.	9.7	18.3	27.4	27.3	17.3
	Area	1.0	4.4	12.8	28.3	53.6
1980/1981	No.	16.5	20.8	28.1	28.1	6.5
	Area	2.3	6.9	17.8	38.9	34.2
1985/1986	No.	17.2	18.9	31.2	27.0	5.8
	Area	2.7	7.0	21.8	40.2	28.3
1990/1991	No.	17.4	18.4	32.0	27.2	5.0
	Area	2.9	7.5	24.0	42.1	23.5
1995/1996	No.	19.3	19.4	29.0	26.7	5.8
	Area	3.0	7.6	22.4	43.3	23.7
2000/2001	No.	14.0	18.8	34.1	27.8	5.3
	Area	1.9	6.7	24.6	43.5	23.3
2005/2006	No.	20.3	23.1	28.1	24.6	3.9
	Area	3.1	9.1	23.6	46.7	17.5
2010/2011	No.	19.6	17.7	31.8	25.6	6.0
	Area	3.1	6.8	24.5	40.3	25.3

Source: Government of Arunachal Pradesh, Agricultural Census, various years.

presence. From 1980/1981 to 1995/1996, there was a marginal decline in the share of STs, both with respect to number of holdings and with respect to area operated, but thereafter the share of ST-operated holdings increased (Table 4.2). As the operational holdings belonging to STs account for around 98 per cent of the holdings in the state, the size class distribution of ST-operated holdings, by and large, follows the same pattern as that of total holdings. This in itself is significant, particularly with reference to the experience in central and eastern Indian states (such as Odisha, Andhra Pradesh, Jharkhand and Chhattisgarh), where large-scale land alienation from tribal communities has been reported (Ambagudia 2010). The fact that legal restrictions on the transfer of land controlled by tribal populations to non-tribal people have been effective in restricting land alienation in Arunachal Pradesh has influenced the agrarian transition. But the recent increase in the area under ST-operated holdings, particularly in the relatively larger size classes of holdings, needs further investigation. It may result from the increasing drive towards land capture by tribal elites or it may be the result of deliberate underreporting of the area and holdings.

Insights from field survey

There is a huge gap between the characteristics of the agrarian structure of Arunachal Pradesh that may be derived from the successive rounds of Agricultural

Agrarian relations and diversity in Arunachal 69

Table 4.2 Share of ST operated holdings in Arunachal Pradesh: 1980/1981 to 2010/2011

Year		Marginal	Small	Semi-medium	Medium	Large	All
1980/1981	No	96.4	93.9	92.6	98.9	99.6	95.7
	Area	96.8	95.1	93.9	99.1	96.9	97.1
1985/1986	No	87.9	92.9	93.2	98.4	99.6	94.0
	Area	94.4	93.7	94.8	98.7	99.5	97.6
1990//1991	No	93.8	93.8	97.4	99.0	99.9	96.7
	Area	93.1	94.6	97.8	99.1	99.5	98.4
1995/1996	No	88.4	88.8	93.3	98.3	99.4	93.1
	Area	87.7	88.7	93.9	98.5	99.5	96.6
2005/2006	No	94.3	94.6	95.8	99.4	99.6	96.3
	Area	94.2	93.7	96.0	99.4	100.0	98.2
2010/2011	No	90.5	100.0	100.0	100.0	85.7	98.2
	Area	91.7	100.0	100.0	99.4	99.0	99.0

Source: Government of Arunachal Pradesh, Agricultural Census, various years.

Census data and the insights from field research. Here we use the findings of three different rounds of field surveys in rural Arunachal Pradesh. The first round of research was conducted in 1999, when household-level primary data were collected from 111 households in four villages of West Kameng district, selected on the basis of levels of infrastructure, distance from urban areas and farming systems.[7] The focus of this study was to explore production relations in agriculture. The second round of field surveys was undertaken in 2003/2004, and its focus was on determinants of participation in the rural non-farm economy. In this survey, six villages from two districts with relatively high shares of workers in the non-farm sector were selected on the basis of distance from the urban centres, so as to represent the different types of growth of the rural non-farm sector. After the selection of the study villages, households were selected randomly from among the households residing in the villages. In total, 288 households were covered. The third round of surveys, undertaken in 2007 in collaboration with Barbara Harriss-White and Vandana Upadhyay, focused on village-level institutions. Eleven villages in five districts were covered in that round.

Access to land

Our field surveys, particularly the first round in West Kameng district, revealed structures and changes in agrarian relations: the predominance of smallholders; inequality in the distribution of landownership (the top 15 per cent control around 40 per cent of the land, while the bottom 74 per cent control only 43.5 per cent of the land and the Gini coefficient of land distribution is high (0.416)); relatively low but increasing landlessness with causes ranging from customary inheritance laws, indebtedness, rural-to-rural migration and migration from other states and adjacent countries so that the landless population had a varied ethnic composition. The privatisation of land rights was a gendered process – in none

70 D.K. Mishra

of the households were women found to be owners of land, although they were found to be de facto managers of farm operations. Land sale markets were gradually emerging, with a few instances of transfer of land through mortgage, sale and informal contracts in all of the sample villages (Mishra 2002).

Land leasing was not captured in the official data. Agricultural Census data suggest that the agrarian structure in the state continues to be dominated by owner-cultivators. Our own surveys and other micro-studies from different parts of the state have reported that a land-lease market has already developed in parts of the state, with labourers from neighbouring states and countries migrating to the rural areas as tenants (Roy and Kuri 2001; Mishra 2002; Harriss-White *et al.* 2009). The Agricultural Censuses however do not report an upward trend in tenancy. Our field surveys found that in 2000/2001, sharecropping accounted for the largest proportion of leased-in area, followed by 'other terms', while fixed money accounted for around 13 per cent of the area leased in. From 1995/1996 to 2000/2001, there was a remarkable rise in the share of area under sharecropping. It is quite likely then that the extent of leasing in is being underreported in Agricultural Census data. As per NSS 59th round data in 2002/2003, 9.8 per cent of households in rural Arunachal Pradesh leased in land. Of the total area owned, the leased-in area accounted for 12.35 per cent (NSSO 2003: 28). While sharecropping accounted for around 15 per cent of the area leased out, nearly 85 per cent of the area was recorded under 'other terms' (NSSO 2003: 30). Our field survey in West Kameng district suggested that of the total households surveyed 69 per cent were owner cultivators, 22 per cent were part-owner and part-tenant, 7 per cent were pure tenants and only 2 per cent were landless labourers. The second survey in six relatively well-connected villages in Papum Pare and West Kameng districts revealed that among all the sample households, 34 per cent were landless, 42 per cent were marginal landowners and only 5 per cent owned more than 10 acres of land, but more importantly, landlessness varied from a low of 2.6 per cent in one of the villages to as high as 48 per cent in another of the villages (Mishra 2007). Thus there is significant variation in tenancy and landlessness. Both aspects of the agrarian structure are also ethnicised. Most of the tenants belong to migrant, non-ST communities. Similarly, most among the landless are migrants, as people not belonging to the Arunachal Pradesh Scheduled Tribe (APST) do not have rights over land. The ethnic dimension has significant implications for the ways in which land and labour markets operate in the state, since 'outsiders' are more likely to be treated much more oppressively than 'insiders'. The sharp ethnic division between the tenants and landlords and the employers and agricultural labourers has meant weaker bargaining power of the 'outside' labour force and their dependence on their employers/landlords for personal security. These factors in turn affect the wage rates, rents and general working conditions of the migrant workers.

In the third survey, it was observed that in some parts of the state, such as East Siang district where the availability of flatter land suitable for wet rice cultivation has made agrarian accumulation possible, a new large landowner class has emerged. Some of these landowners have used surpluses from non-agricultural sources (such as businesses and services) to purchase fertile

Agrarian relations and diversity in Arunachal 71

farmland. These landowners have leased out their land to tenants from Assam and elsewhere. They have managed to extract exorbitant rents through a variety of means. These large landowners have benefited from government subsidies to agriculture and have responded to opportunities provided by markets within and outside the state, but a range of coercive and exploitative practices marks their relationship with tenants.[8] Another crucial aspect of the emergence of this neo-landlord class is their appropriation of community resources through the active mobilisation and capture of state institutions. From elsewhere in Arunachal, we have evidence of politicians establishing tea and horticultural gardens on land effectively recognised as their private property, which has been created by clearing collectively owned pastures or forests.

Labour use and livelihood diversification

In the past, agricultural production was interwoven with community institutions and labour was mobilised collectively as a shared resource. Even now, production relations are dominated by exchange and family labour. A wage labour market has emerged unevenly – more in areas under wet rice cultivation than in other areas. Exchange labour has increasingly taken the form of wage labour with wage payments in kind and reciprocity is atrophying. The field survey of agricultural labour-use patterns in West Kameng district showed that: (1) households depend on a number of different sources of livelihood, but the pattern of livelihood diversification is gendered: while men spend nearly 68 per cent of their working days in agriculture, women spend 83 per cent of their working days in agriculture; (2) while men have diversified into non-farm and non-rural occupations, the burden of maintaining social obligations and reciprocity has fallen on women. Exchange labour, mostly done by women, was found to be higher in the relatively well-connected village near an urban area (Mishra 2002).

The non-farm labour survey revealed the spatial concentration of non-farm activities in certain villages (e.g. villages near urban, administrative centres; roadside villages; villages near labour camps; settlements near army cantonments), and its significantly low presence in interior villages. The spatial concentration of non-farm activities partly reflects the ecological constraints in a mountain economy, but it also shows the fragmented and locale-specific nature of economic diversification, which itself has resulted in part from the nature of government intervention (Mishra 2007). Public administration, construction and petty trading emerge as main occupations in the non-farm economy. There appear to be very weak links between agricultural productivity and the growth of the rural non-farm economy.

Cropping pattern and input use

Arunachal's agriculture uses low levels of inputs and has low productivity. Of the gross cropped area (GCA) only 15 per cent is irrigated and only 25 per cent is under HYV seeds, and in 1999/2000 the consumption of chemical fertiliser

72   D.K. Mishra

was as low as 2.9 kg/ha of GCA. The patterns of input use and types of owner-ship of productive farm assets clearly indicate that agrarian relations in Aru-nachal Pradesh, though changing very fast, remain less commercialised than elsewhere in India.[9] Apart from the gradual shift to permanent cultivation, two other aspects of land use need noting. *First*, the cropping pattern in the state has undergone significant changes. The percentage of area under food grains has declined, particularly since 1980. Out of nine major crops produced, the share of food grains came down from nearly 87 per cent in the early 1980s to nearly 77 per cent from 2000 to 2003. *Second*, in recent years, horticulture and spice cultivation have expanded.[10] Our field surveys and secondary data reveal the highly region- and crop-specific nature of the process of commercialisation. While basic food crops are almost entirely for self-consumption, vegetables, fruits and spices are cultivated almost entirely on a commercial basis. However, we found very little evidence of the classic linkages between farm and non-farm sectors. The growth of the non-farm sector was the result of the expansion of public administration and infrastructure development initiated by the state, and was not driven by investment of surplus from agriculture.[11]

Institutional diversity and capitalist transformation in agriculture

The last round of field investigations in 11 villages in five districts of Arunachal Pradesh documents institutional diversity in almost every aspect of the agrarian economy (Harriss-White *et al.* 2009). The simultaneous existence of market and non-market institutions within a given village or territory is an important aspect of the transition to capitalism in Arunachal Pradesh.

From the village-level survey we see that while 'informal' private property rights over agricultural land have appeared in most villages, land market trans-actions are few and are often subject to community control. Although the existence of wage labour is reported from all but one of the villages, family and exchange labour continues to play a significant role. Land leasing is widespread, but has a greater significance in the fertile littorals of East Siang district, where tribal land-owners have imposed highly exploitative contracts on tenants from outside the state. Credit markets remain fragmented and of limited economic significance, but land alienation through debt bondage within the tribal community was noted in a few villages. There appears to be hardly any correlation between physical remote-ness and the lack of emergence of private property, or between physical accessibil-ity and the weakening of non-market institutional arrangements.

Thus, the privatisation of landownership rights does not necessarily mean the existence or emergence of a land market.[12] Individual or private rights over land are necessary but not sufficient conditions for the transfer of ownership: the consent of the village community is also necessary (Table 4.3). The moral and political authority of the village does not simply wither away as a result of the emergence of individual rights over agricultural land. Although the land-lease market was reported to be operating in as many as eight of the 11 study villages, two kinds of land leasing need to be distinguished. The first has emerged within

Table 4.3 Land relations in the study villages

Sl no.	Features	Alternatives and no. of villages (of the total 11 villages)
1	Type of cultivation	Only settled cultivation – 9 Both settled and jhum (shifting cultivation) – 2
2	Major crops grown	Rice – 9; Maize – 5; Millet – 5; Wheat – 2; Horticulture (fruits) – 4; Vegetables – 11
3	Landownership	Privately owned (informally) – but restrictions imposed by village institutions on land sales to outsiders – 9 Privately owned (informally) – but considered to be the property of Gompa (Buddhist monastery) – 2
4	Land revenue payment to non-state authorities	Paid to the village council – 2 Paid to Gompa (as rent) – 2 No land revenue paid, but payments to the village fund reported – 7
5	Land sales (agricultural land)	Frequent – 4 Few – 3 None – 4
6	Land leasing	Frequent – 5 Few – 3 None – 3
7	Landlessness	Very high (>20%) – 0 Low – 8 None – 3
8	Availability of irrigation	For most of agricultural land – 6 Available, but for a few – 1 Not available – 4
9	Irrigation provision and management	By state government departments – 4 Provided by the state and managed by the village council – 1 Provided and managed by the village council – 2 Entirely private – 4
10	Ownership of grazing land	Entirely private – 4 Entirely collective – 2 Partly private and partly collective – 5

Source: Adapted from Harriss-White *et al.* (2009); Field Survey (2007).

74 D.K. Mishra

the clan/village community in response to outmigration to urban or non-agricultural jobs. Here the primary objective is often, but not always, to retain inheritance rights. Thus the terms of lease are unspecified and ambiguous. The other kind of land leasing is to migrant tenants from outside the state (mainly from Assam) or outside the country (Nepalese migrants in Western Arunachal Pradesh and Bangladeshi migrants in East Siang and other districts). The incidence and frequency of such land leasing depends on factors such as the availability and accessibility of land for labour-intensive wet rice cultivation and not on the degree of commercialisation of agriculture. The commercialisation of agriculture and production for the market does not necessarily involve dependence on wage labour (Table 4.4). The overwhelming importance of family labour was confirmed in all the study villages, irrespective of the type of cultivation (*jhum* or wet rice cultivation), the crops produced, the property rights over land or the size and reliability of the marketed surplus.[13] Commercialisation and market participation have even created conditions for forms of bondage and labour un-freedom hitherto unknown in the tribal context.[14] While wage labour was reported in the majority of villages, the incidence of landlessness among the tribal population itself was typically low. Most of the landless are migrants from other states and countries, who, in any case, do not have the right to own land in Arunachal Pradesh. Thus a significant commercialisation of the output market may be found in the absence of well-known processes of de-peasantisation and local differentiation.[15]

It is the non-agricultural surplus that has been the moving force behind agrarian transition in the 2007 survey villages (Harriss-White *et al.* 2009). Except in a few plains areas where wet rice cultivation is being pursued (mostly by migrant tenants), the surplus is low and cannot form a base for agrarian accumulation. Investment in agriculture has mostly come from non-agricultural sources. Access to political power and to the material resources of the state have been key factors in the creation and circulation of the social surplus. Until 1993 another source of non-agrarian surplus for local elites was the timber trade.

Table 4.4 Labour relations in the study villages

Sl no.	Features	Alternatives and no. of villages (of the total 11 villages)
1	Casual wage labour in agriculture/ forest	Exists – 11 Does not exist – 0
2	Family labour exchange labour	Exists – 11 Does not exist – 0
3	Exchange labour	Exists and significant – 7 Exists but declining – 2 Does not exist any longer – 2
4	Non-farm casual labour	Exists – 10 Does not exist – 1

Source: Adapted from Harriss-White *et al.* (2009); Field Survey (2007).

Agrarian relations and diversity in Arunachal 75

Although timber was controlled by large-scale capital from outside the state, the local business class managed to corner a substantial share as junior partners and facilitators. The processes through which commonly owned forests were plundered by traders in active collaboration with local elites and the local bureaucracy provides a useful example of three-way interactions among state, market and community institutions.

Since labour was the most valuable input in the traditional economy of the tribes, the regulation and socialisation of labour power was a key activity of their community institutions. Most agricultural and forest-related activities were collectively organised, acting as an in-built check on inter-household inequality. There was no explicit 'quota' rule specifying the range and quantities of forest products that individuals and households could collect from the commonly owned forests. Low population density, norms for subsistence consumption and the social regulation of labour combined to prevent threats to natural resources in forests. But the mobilisation of migrant labour by state agencies, including the Army and the Border Roads Organisation, and their quartering in interior villages, gradually led to the emergence of a migrant labour market.

The timber trade, dominated by traders from outside the state, intensified the inmigration of outside labour for felling and transporting timber. Local elites alone could obtain permits to cut down trees, and the elite capture of the state machinery ensured that by law permission was granted exclusively to them. Permits were then sold to outsider traders and contractors who organised massive plunder of the forest wealth of Arunachal, until the practice was stopped by an order of the Supreme Court of India in 1993. In this process, local institutional mechanisms lost much of their credibility and were often out-manoeuvred by neo-rich beneficiaries from the timber trade.

At first sight the timber trade appears to be independent of the state. However, the manner in which the state allowed the plundering of the commonly owned forests for private profit makes it clear that state support and protection was essential for its existence. While Arunachal's forest department controlled the supply of permits to cut down trees, these permits 'were issued with such frequency and under such a framework of political patronage that community control over forests remained at best a minor irritant for the traders, whether from indigenous tribal groups or from outside the State' (Harriss-White *et al.* 2009: 537). Some indigenous traders invested surpluses in establishing local sawmills, plywood factories and the transportation business.

Arunachal's horticultural estates have been created by powerful local elites through enclosing the commons. The tea gardens are the exception here. Most agricultural investment has the distinctive characteristic of 'land grabbing' for rent rather than that of productive investment. Most of the Brahmaputra littorals and the low-lying valley land have been acquired for leasing out to migrant tenants. Political restrictions on land sales, community controls over land transfer, lack of suitable land in the mountainous areas, and urbanisation, all contribute to the increase in local demand for land. Rents from land put to non-agricultural use are often substantial, particularly in villages near roadsides or urban centres. Even when non-agricultural surplus is being invested in agriculture, there are severe environmental and social limits to the degree to which such investments can enhance agricultural productivity.

The peasantry has been integrated into the market economy as petty producers to the extent that even in the remotest hilly areas of the state, independent peasant households cannot reproduce themselves without interacting with markets of one kind or other. The commercialisation of the needs-based local economies has happened rapidly, but the processes of dispossession normally associated with such commercialisation occur very unevenly. There are few instances from the 2007 village field research where the classic processes of differentiation, marginalisation, pauperisation and proletarianisation are clearly visible. By and large, commercialisation and capitalist transformation has proceeded without significant differentiation and de-peasantisation. Institutional heterogeneity and complexity in community control over land and forests, laws blocking transfer of land to non-indigenous populations, relatively low population density and the relative importance of the non-agrarian surplus for the accumulating classes are among the factors responsible for this idiosyncratic transformation.

The state and institutional diversity

The diversity of production and exchange relations is deeply entrenched in the local politics of accumulation. The region known as Arunachal Pradesh today was not directly administered during the colonial period, and the postcolonial Indian state faced significant challenges in establishing and consolidating its rule over the region (known as the North-East Frontier Agency or NEFA) which was inhabited by numerous micro-nationalities. The vulnerabilities of the Indian state were further exposed during the Indo-China war in 1962.[16] Along with building military infrastructure and consolidating strategic control over the region, the establishment of civil administration in the hitherto un-administered region was among the key challenges faced by the Indian state. The Nehru–Elwin policy[17] had earlier established a framework for administrative control that favoured a gradual integration of the pre-existing social and political structures of the tribes with the local administration. In an effort to strengthen and consolidate its control over this border region, the Indian state tried to co-opt chiefs and other tribal representatives. It recognised indigenous institutions such as tribal councils and community laws.[18] This framework of political governance had several implications for Arunachal's economic transformation (Mishra 2013).

First, it created a whole framework of ethnicised governance, where civil rule was replaced by a rule of difference based on collective ethnic identities. Second, the state (and particularly the military administration) played an important role in establishing the basic infrastructure for the creation of a market economy: from bringing goods and labour from outside into the interior regions of the state, to building markets and shopping centres, and incentivising businessmen to settle down in various towns and administrative centres.[19] The emergence of a

Agrarian relations and diversity in Arunachal 77

local contractor politician class, which used its connections with the local administration to extract rents in various forms (from renting out agricultural land, houses and business licences to rent-seeking in the state apparatus), further consolidated this ethnicised governance. As representatives of their respective ethnic groups, these politicians and businessmen were engaged in a politics of negotiation not only with the government (both central and state), but also among themselves. Since the state remained the prime mover of the economy through the substantial inflow of resources from the centre to the state[20] either as aid or as loans, a key objective of local elites has been to capture the resources of the state (both political and economic). The ability to represent their respective ethnic groups has been vitally important for elites in their bargaining for and extracting rents from the state (and from others). Thus, over time, the politics of ethnic difference has become the hallmark of Arunachal's social, economic and political life. In the co-evolution of ethnic politics and the local economy, institutional diversity is neither a relic of the past, nor may it be expected to be gradually transcended in a process of institutional convergence. Institutional diversity facilitates the accumulation strategies of the local elites and is often defended as part of tribal rights and privileges. Institutional ambiguity and fuzziness, moreover, are not simply manifestations of the inadequacies or inefficiencies of a weak state; they create the necessary institutional space for the accumulation strategies of the rentier classes. While the coexistence of market and non-market institutions has been recognised as a significant dimension of India's 'socially regulated' capitalism (Harriss-White 2003; Harriss-White *et al.* 2014), the distinctiveness of the trajectory taken by Arunachal is the active role the state has played in forging this institutional diversity. However, the state was not the sole transformative force. The extraordinary ethnic diversity in the region together with powerful indigenous institutions of local governance have also contributed to this trajectory. It is thus the three-way interaction of state politics with ethnic institutional diversity and capitalist dynamics that has given Arunachal's ongoing transformation and its distinctive regional character.

One of the ways in which the state and markets have interacted with, and changed, the ethnic landscape of the region pertains to property rights over crucial livelihood resources (such as land and forests). Depending on resource endowments and the community's particular history, its rules may be well defined or ambiguous and negotiable, strictly or loosely applied. But the state-induced move towards the modernisation and integration of these local economies with those of the border regions and of the Indian nation itself led to significant alterations in the way property rights were created, destroyed or rearranged to suit the demands of changing local economic and political contexts. This was far from a straightforward destruction of pre-capitalist property relations and its replacement by private property. On the contrary, ethnically inflected property rights were protected through policies such as restrictions on land transfers and on the mobility of labour, and massive reservations in jobs, government contracts and business licences. By these means people were given a strong vested interest in ethnic identities (Harriss-White *et al.* 2013).

78 *D.K. Mishra*

Capital did not enter Arunachal Pradesh in search of raw materials, labour or markets. It entered this border state to strengthen state power. The interests of capital, for a considerable period at least, remained subservient to the interests of the state. The resulting capitalist trajectory has many distinct features (Rao 1995), including commercialisation without de-peasantisation; the emergence of a rentier class within and outside agriculture; and elements of neo-bondage in landlord–migrant tenant contracts. The ecological specificities of this mountain region have also shaped its transition by, for example, limiting the extent to which increasing agricultural productivity and wage work could be used for surplus appropriation and accumulation by the neo-landlord class in specific regions. This is a capitalist transition marked by diversity, unevenness and discontinuities of myriad kinds, in a context where diversity does not necessarily mean the incompleteness of capitalist transition, but becomes the defining characteristic of the transition itself.

Concluding observations

It is beyond doubt that capitalism has made deep and uneven inroads into the rural economy of Arunachal Pradesh. Moreover, the evidence presented here clearly shows that its transition to capitalism has not resulted in institutional convergence. Institutional adaptation, continuity and hybridity are as integral to the emergence of the market economy as are processes that create new institutions and destroy old. The reasons behind the persistence of such institutional diversity are complex, but the role of the state in creating and sustaining it cannot be overlooked. This diversity is not simply a relic of the past, nor is it the unfinished business of capital. In part at least, it is the result of the deliberate policy choices made by the Indian state as part of its developmentalist intervention in a weakly integrated border region (Mishra 2013; Harriss-White *et al.* 2013).

Given the general diversity of Indian agriculture, the dimensions of regionally embedded agrarian transformations need to be incorporated into the narrative of agrarian development. A regionally differentiated understanding of the agrarian transition leads to the conclusion that while capitalist agriculture is firmly in place in many regions of India, in large parts of eastern, northeastern and central India dominated by tribal populations, the classic agrarian question is far from resolved.

The 'classic agrarian question' as formulated by Byres and others consists of three problematics: accumulation, production and politics (Akram-Lodhi 1998; Byres 1996). Bernstein's argument about the delinking of accumulation in agriculture and non-agriculture – such that agriculture no longer has to be squeezed of labour and financial resources to bring about industrialisation as it develops towards capitalism – may be correct to an extent at the macro level.[21] However, the increasingly manifest agrarian dimension of financial globalisation limits his idea that the agrarian question is irrelevant (Ghosh 2010). In the specific regional trajectories of agrarian capitalism, the agricultural transition needs to be investigated in two ways. First, in terms of the extent to which the agricultural surplus determines the regional trajectories of capitalist development; second, in terms of the complex ways in which agrarian relations are being reconfigured and transformed under global capitalism. In this context, the changing production relations in Arunachal Pradesh constitute a complex and multi-layered transition to capitalism, in which institutional diversity based on identity economics of a particular type is at the core of the transformation process. The physical, cultural, political and economic specificities of Arunachal Pradesh play important roles in its agrarian transition.

Notes

1 This paper draws upon collaborative research undertaken by the author with Barbara Harriss-White and Vandana Upadhyay. Some of the arguments presented here have been discussed at greater length in Harriss-White *et al.* (2009) and in Mishra (2013). Special thanks are due to Barbara Harriss-White, Judith Heyer, Elisabetta Basile and David Gellner for insightful comments on earlier drafts.
2 The village chiefs had special privileges such as shares from produce, free labour services of the villagers, etc. Surpluses generated were generally redistributed through rituals, feasts and festivals (Mishra 1979).
3 For many years the Jhum Land Regulations, 1947 to 1948, which did recognise, to some extent, the rights of the tribes practising shifting cultivation, remained the only legal framework governing access to cultivable land. More recently, the Arunachal Pradesh (Land Settlement and Record) Act 2000 was passed with a view to conducting a cadastral survey of land in the state.
4 On the basis of a micro study, Mishra (2002) has reported that in case of privately owned land the rights of use, occupancy and inheritance are generally enjoyed by the owners, but the right to transfer is often conditional. In some cases *'limited transfer rights'* (i.e. temporary transfer rights under mortgage, use rights without inheritance rights, etc.) and *'preferential transfer rights'* (i.e. transfer within family, clan or tribe) were found, along with unconditional rights, to alienate. The specificity of the emerging private property regime lies not only in its institutional basis but also in the changing dimensions of collective ownership.
5 Other than Nagaland, all other hilly states in northeast India have a lower average size of holdings than Arunachal Pradesh.
6 There are inherent difficulties in trying to understand the agrarian structure in the hilly regions through an analysis of distribution of operational holdings from the Agricultural Census. First of all, in the non-land record states such as Arunachal Pradesh, 'the data is collected through sample survey following household enquiry approach in 20% of villages in each block. In these selected villages, all the operational holdings are enumerated following household enquiry approach.' Thus the data from the Agricultural Census are actually based on sampling. Second, given the state of land records, there are no data on ownership holdings. Finally, the agricultural land in the state ranges from land with steep slopes to fertile, plains valleys and often 'size-class of holdings' conveys little about the actual size or nature of farm operations.
7 West Kameng district is characterised by a higher degree of occupational diversification of the workforce, lower cropping intensity and lower yield rate for most crops in comparison with state averages. The four study villages were Nyukmadung (I), Chug (II), Khaso (III) and Shera (IV). In all the study villages, the Buddhist Monpas were the dominant tribe.

80   *D.K. Mishra*

8 In our field survey in areas of wet rice cultivation, we came across a number of ways in which the un-freedom of migrant tenants and labourers manifested itself. First of all, many among the migrants in agriculture do not have the Inner Line Permit (ILP) that is required for citizens from other parts of India to enter Arunachal Pradesh. In some cases, landlords and employers keep the ILPs of tenants and workers (and their family members) as security. The family of the tenants live in huts built on land owned by the landlords and their unpaid labour in the fields is assumed to be part of the tenant's labour contribution. They also depend upon the landlords for other resources such as firewood, house-building materials, etc. Some, though not all, landlords restrict the tenant's and his family members' right to seek employment elsewhere. Most tenants are indebted to their landlords. Interest is charged on all loans in cash, and charges on account of any inputs supplied by the landlords are added to the dues to be paid by the tenants. The tenants usually receive their share of output only after deducting all such dues. Apart from these, the threat of violence and occasional 'eviction drives' by powerful non-state groups add to the insecurities of tenants.

9 The NSS 59th round data provide ample evidence to support our claim; see Harriss-White *et al.* (2009). However, Salam (2007) in a study of peasant households has attempted to research the extent of capitalist production relations in rural Arunachal Pradesh and has found evidence for the coexistence of different dimensions of capitalist agriculture at the farm/household level. This evidence goes against our argument here.

10 In 2009/2010 the total production of horticultural crops reached nearly 214,645 metric tonnes per annum and the total area under horticulture was 83,402 hectares. Of this, fruits were responsible for 162,303 metric tonnes and 68,937 hectares. Among the major horticultural crops in the state are citrus, pineapple, banana and apple.

11 We did not find instances of agricultural households diversifying into non-farm activities by using agricultural surpluses. The most common pathways to non-farm employment were through government services, contract work distributed through ethnicised political patronage and, for a limited period, through timber trade.

12 For example, in four villages with clear private ownership rights over land no land market operates and in many others land sales were reported to be sporadic.

13 In the three villages in East Siang district, close to the town of Pasighat, where the sale of output is more frequent than in other villages, the dominant form of labour organisation, other than family labour, is tenant rather than wage labour. Otherwise long-term, tied labour contracts with outside labour (in many cases illegal foreign migrant labour) seem to be the dominant mode of labour contract for many of the tribal landowners.

14 Forms of bondage such as slavery were prevalent in pre-independence Arunachal Pradesh, and sometimes inter-tribe relations were marked by relations of dependence and hierarchy. Early anthropologists, for example, have described the Sulungs, now called Puroiks, as a 'slave tribe' (Deori 1982). However, the tribal economy was not dependent upon the labour of the slaves alone (Sikdar 1982: 16).

15 In certain villages in Tawang district, where agricultural production continues to be largely for subsistence, there are, however, early signs of differentiation. A stratum of local rural society has started working on road and other construction activities, mainly for local tribal contractors and against wage advances. At present this is confined to non-agricultural seasons and is viewed by those concerned more as a livelihood supplement than as entry to the non-farm labour force to which it is likely to be a prelude. But their increasing dependence on wage advances to meet consumption requirements, combined with declining productivity in agriculture, could lead towards their proletarianisation.

16 Along with the military setbacks, the ambivalent attitude of the local population towards the Chinese army necessitated a rethinking on the administrative front. P.N.

Agrarian relations and diversity in Arunachal 81

Luthra, who was an adviser to the Governor of Assam (who administered NEFA in the 1950s), wrote in 1969:

> The administrative aim of security is a vital one against the back-drop of Chinese threat from across the northern frontier of the Agency. The people are joining in increasing numbers the Home Guards, the Police and the armed forces.... Their contribution to security is a part of the defence system of our country.
>
> (Luthra 1993: 32)

17 The most precise articulation of the Nehru-Elwin policy is found in the Foreword written by Nehru to Elwin's book, *A Philosophy for NEFA* in 1958:

> Development in various ways there has to be, such as communications, medical facilities, education and better agriculture. These avenues of development should, however, be pursued within the broad framework of the following five fundamental principles:(1) People should develop along the lines of their own genius and we should avoid imposing anything on them. We should try to encourage in every way their own traditional arts and culture. (2) Tribal rights in land and forests should be respected. (3) We should try to train and build up a team of their own people to do work of administration and development. Some technical personnel from outside will, no doubt, be needed, especially in the beginning. But we should avoid introducing too many outsiders into tribal territory. (4) We should not over-administer these areas or over-whelm them with multiplicity of schemes. We should rather work through, and not in rivalry to, their own social and cultural institutions. (5) We should judge results, not by statistics or the amount of money spent, but by the quality of human character that is evolved.
>
> (Elwin 1958/1999)

18 It is however important to remember that the purpose of consolidation of administration was to ultimately impose the supremacy of the state over the local institutions of the tribes. There are many instances to demonstrate that in order to consolidate its control and legitimacy over the northeastern border region, the Indian state used force and emergency powers. However, it is important to understand that tribal institutions and community laws were also followed, at least as a legitimising device. This was in direct contrast with experience elsewhere in the country, particularly in the tribal-dominated regions of central and eastern India, where heavy industries, hydropower projects and other state-funded development projects displaced and marginalised tribal communities, and the pauperisation of the tribal peasantry resulted in the gradual disintegration of the agrarian economies.

19 Interview with traders in Bomdila, Tawang and Pashighat markets, September to October 2007 and October 2010.

20 The federal structure of India allows for preferential treatment of some states designated as special category states, for which 90 per cent of Plan assistance from the central government is given as grants, and 10 per cent as loans (unlike other states which get 30 per cent grant and 70 per cent loan). As per the recommendations of the Twelfth Finance Commission that the Centre should give only grants, and leave it to the states to raise loans, this formula is restricted to centrally sponsored schemes and external aid. At present there are 11 special category states in India: Arunachal Pradesh, Assam, Himachal Pradesh, Jammu and Kashmir, Manipur, Meghalaya, Mizoram, Nagaland, Tripura, Sikkim and Uttarakhand.

21 See Bernstein (1996, 2004, 2006) and for a discussion on the bypassing and/or resolution of the 'agrarian question of capital'; also Lerche (2010, 2011, 2013) for a discussion in the Indian context.

82 *D.K. Mishra*

References

Akram-Lodhi, A.H. (1998) 'The agrarian question, past and present', *Journal of Peasant Studies*, 25(4): 134–149.

Ambagudia, J. (2010) 'Tribal rights, dispossession and the State in Orissa', *Economic and Political Weekly*, 45(33): 60–67.

Basole, A. and Basu, D. (2011) 'Relations of production and modes of surplus extraction in India: Part-I-Agriculture', *Economic and Political Weekly*, 46(14): 43–58.

Bernstein, H. (1996) 'Agrarian questions then and now', *Journal of Peasant Studies*, 24(1): 22–59.

—— (2004) 'Changing before our very eyes, agrarian questions and the politics of land in capitalism today', *Journal of Agrarian Change*, 4(1–2): 190–225.

—— (2006) 'Is there an agrarian question in the 21st century?', *Canadian Journal of Development Studies*, 27(4): 449–460.

Bhalla, G. S. and Singh, G. (2012) *Economic Liberalisation and Indian Agriculture: A District-level Study*, New Delhi: Sage.

Bordoloi, B.N. (1998) 'Tribal land tenure system and land alienation in northeast India', in S.N. Mishra (ed.) *Antiquity to Modernity in Tribal India, Vol.III*, New Delhi: Inter-India.

Byres, T.J. (1996) *Capitalism from Above and Capitalism from Below: An Essay in Comparative Political Economy*, London: Macmillan.

Das, G. (1995) *Tribes of Arunachal Pradesh in Transition*, New Delhi: Vikas.

Deori, R.K. (1982) *The Sulungs*, Shillong: Government of Arunachal Pradesh, Department of Research.

Dutta, P.C. (2003) *Tribal Chieftanship*, Itanagar and New Delhi: Himalayan Publishers.

Elwin, V. (1958/1999) *A Philosophy for NEFA*, Itanagar: Directorate of Research, Arunachal Pradesh.

Ghosh, J. (2010) 'The unnatural coupling: food and global finance', *Journal of Agrarian Change*, 10(1): 72–86.

Harriss-White, B. (2003) *India Working: Essays in Economy and Society*, Cambridge: Cambridge University Press.

—— (2011) 'Local capitalism: agri-business in Northern Tamil Nadu, 1973–2011', *Work in progress paper 1*, Oxford University, School of Interdisciplinary Area Studies, Contemporary South Asian Studies Programme.

—— (2012) 'Capitalism and the common man', *Agrarian South: Journal of Political Economy*, 1 (2): 109–160.

Harriss-White, B., Mishra, D.K. and Upadhyay, V. (2009) 'Institutional diversity and capitalist transformation in rural Arunachal Pradesh', *QEH Working Paper No. 179*, Oxford University, Department of International Development.

Harriss-White, B., Prakash, A. and Mishra D.K. (2013) 'Globalization, economic citizenship and India's inclusive developmentalism', in Subrata K. Mitra (ed.) *Citizenship as Cultural Flow: Structure, Agency and Power*, Heidelberg: Springer: 187–210.

Harriss-White, B. with Basile, E., Dixit, A., Joddar, P., Prakash, A. and Vidyarthee, K. (2014) *Dalits and Adivasis in India's Business Economy: Three Essays and an Atlas*, New Delhi: Three Essays Press.

Lerche, J. (2010) 'From "rural labour" to "classes of labour": class fragmentation, caste and class struggle at the bottom of the Indian labour hierarchy', in B. Harriss-White and J. Heyer (eds) *The Comparative Political Economy of Development*, London: Routledge.

Agrarian relations and diversity in Arunachal 83

—— (2011) 'Agrarian crisis and agrarian questions in India', *Journal of Agrarian Change*, 11(1): 104–118.

—— (2013) 'The agrarian question in neoliberal India: agrarian transition bypassed?', *Journal of Agrarian Change*, 13(3): 382–404.

Luthra, P.N. (1993) *Constitutional and Administrative Growth of Arunachal Pradesh* (first published 1971).

Mishra, Deepak K. (2001) 'Political economy of agrarian change in Arunachal', *Man and Development*, 23(3): 40–50.

—— (2002) 'Agrarian structure and labour-use patterns in rural Arunachal Pradesh: a case study', *Arunachal University Research Journal*, 5(2): 31–56.

—— (2006) 'Institutional specificities and agrarian transformation in Arunachal Pradesh: changing realities and emerging challenges', *Indian Journal of Agricultural Economics*, 61(3): 314–327.

—— (2007) *Rural Non-farm Employment in Arunachal Pradesh: Growth, Composition and Determinants*, National Labour Institute Research Studies Series No. 075/2007, V.V. Giri National Labour Institute, Noida.

—— (2013) 'Developing the border: The State and the political economy of development in Arunachal Pradesh', in David N. Gellner (ed.) *Borderland Lives in Northern South Asia*, Durham, NC, and London: Duke University Press: 141–162.

Misra, B.P. (1979) 'Kirata Karyokinesis: mode of production in tribal communities of North East India', in A.N. Das and V. Nilkanth (eds) *Agrarian Relations in India*, New Delhi: Manohar: 51–81.

Pandey, B.B., Duarah, D.K. and Sarkar, N. (eds) (1999) *Tribal Village Councils of Arunachal Pradesh*, Itanagar: Government of Arunachal Pradesh, Directorate of Research.

Rao, R.S. (1995) *Towards Understanding Semi-feudal Semi-colonial Society*, Hyderabad: Perspective.

Roy Burman, B.K. (2002) 'Traditional self-governing institutions among the hill tribal population groups of north east India', in Atul Goswami (ed.) *Traditional Self-Governing Institutions among the Hill Tribes of North East India*, New Delhi: Akansha.

Roy, N.C. and Kuri, P.K. (2001) *Land Reforms in Arunachal Pradesh*, New Delhi: Classical Publishing House.

Salam, M.A. (2007) *Agricultural Transformation in North-East India: With Special Reference to Arunachal Pradesh*, New Delhi: Mittal.

Sikdar, S. (1982) 'Tribalism vs. colonialism: British capitalistic intervention and transformation of primitive economy of Arunachal Pradesh in the nineteenth century'. *Social Scientist*, 10(12): 15–31.

5 First transaction, multiple dimensions

The changing terms of commodity exchange in a regulated agricultural market in Madhya Pradesh

Mekhala Krishnamurthy[1]

Introduction

> *Uchit mūlya. Sahi taul. Nagad bhugtan.*
> A fair price. Accurate weight. Cash payment.

This trinity of terms was often repeated during fieldwork conversations with the local functionaries in charge of managing activities in Harda Mandi, a regulated primary agricultural market in the central Indian state of Madhya Pradesh. Indeed, this was a *mandi* motto of sorts, a regulatory recitation, listing the basic conditions of exchange a farmer has a right to expect when he or she brings agricultural produce for sale into the market yard.

In their reiteration of these principles, the present-day market functionaries in Madhya Pradesh echo a long history of policy prescription that has taken the view that the establishment of 'properly' regulated markets can confer 'an immense boon on the cultivating classes of India' and must therefore be 'an essential part of any ordered plan of agricultural development in the country' (Royal Commission on Agriculture in India 1928: 289). It is an article of faith that has been enshrined in both colonial and postcolonial state-level marketing acts, notifying regulated market yards under the management of locally constituted market committees (better known as Agricultural Produce Marketing Committees (APMCs) or simply as Mandi Committees).[2] Over time, although with considerable variation in speed and scale across Indian states, these regulated primary markets, estimated at over 7500 in number[3] and typically located in small market towns and commercial centres, have become the most important sites for state regulation of the critical 'first transaction' between the producer and the first buyer of his or her produce. It is here that a fair price to the farmer, for an accurately weighed lot, paid for in cash on the spot has assumed its place as a fundamental objective of regulation. Unsurprisingly, in practice, each element apart and taken together, this has all too often proved to be an exceedingly elusive objective. The reasons for this not only lie in the highly varied and differentiated conditions of marketing across diverse agrarian regions and commodity systems at any given time. They also need to be traced in historically shifting conceptions as to what constitute 'legitimate' or 'illegimate' transactions and practices in marketing in the first place, and how these relate dynamically to the changing composition, economic roles and social relations of the different actors that shape particular agricultural commodity markets over periods of time (Thompson 1971; Harriss-White 1996b).

This chapter explores critical changes in the terms of the first transaction as these have been expressed and experienced over the past 30 years by farmers, traders, labourers, and market functionaries involved in making and managing a regulated primary market in Madhya Pradesh. The centre of action is Harda Mandi, a notified market yard overseen by an Agricultural Produce Marketing Committee (APMC) located in Harda, a small but bustling market town with a population of around 74,000 (Census 2011) and the administrative headquarters of an agriculturally productive district by the same name. The core material presented here is based on ethnographic fieldwork conducted between November 2008 and April 2010, and is drawn from sustained observation, in-depth interviews and immersion in the everyday activities and seasonal dynamics during two consecutive marketing years (four post-harvest seasons altogether) for soybean and wheat, the two main crops grown in Harda and sold in its mandi.

It does not take long for a fieldworker to realise, however, that the significance of contemporary movements in agricultural commodity markets cannot be properly understood without analysing their linkages and relations to the wider political economy, and to particular agroecological contexts, regional histories, technological developments, processes of reform, and to complex and conjunctural changes over time. As this chapter will try to show, these interactions are vital to the study of regulation and to a theoretically grounded and empirically rigorous understanding of the possibilities, limitations and very real and diverse effects of specific regulatory actions intended to define and discipline transactions inside and outside the market yard. This is especially important in the current context in India where state-regulated agricultural markets are at the heart of politically charged and volatile debates, with high-profile calls for their reform and even outright removal, as well as agitated and anxious rallies to their defence.

The ethnographic research from which this chapter emerges has drawn inspiration and instruction from the field economics of Barbara Harriss-White and her extraordinarily productive engagement with the diversity, dynamism and institutional complexity of India's agricultural markets. Sustained over four decades, beginning with initial investigations in the wholesale markets of Punjab (1974), her deepest and most prolific studies grew and multiplied with long-term field research in Tamil Nadu (1984, 1996a, 2010) and West Bengal (2008), penetrating the intricate networks and myriad activities within the food grains sector and across a variety of agricultural commodity systems in these regions and subregions. It has yielded a body of work that is so substantial in and of itself that when immersed in its scope and detail it is easy to forget how rare and unique Barbara Harriss-White's contribution remains in illuminating the political economy of agricultural markets in contemporary India. Her approach to the

86   *M. Krishnamurthy*

study of regulation, which is one of the most consistently and creatively explored themes, worked and reworked in her writings in a way that does not exogenise or reduce different elements and forces in action all at once, has been of particular relevance to this chapter (1996b). She develops an analytical framework, moreover, that enables one to study how law is defined through social interaction, and to sense and specify the ways in which power is expressed and enforced at every point in the marketing process, often in the most routine everyday practices (1996b, 1999).

In the sections that follow, I will attempt to illustrate this through a close study of the first transaction in Harda Mandi. In doing so, the chapter pivots around two critical interventions in the recent history of this regulated market. The first dates back to the early 1980s and describes state-directed action to abolish a layer of commission agents and reorganise the market, moving from a credit-linked system defined by long-term relationships between farmers and their commission agents to direct cash payments made by traders to farmers in the state-regulated market yard. The second narrates a turn-of-the-century initiative to install an electronic weighbridge and replace manual weighing of farmers' produce. The decision to focus on these two elements of exchange, namely weight and payment, means that vital aspects, such as price, are left for consideration elsewhere. However, it is also the case that the prominence of price in economic research on markets often makes invisible these other crucial (and related) aspects of market transactions and their critical roles in the structure, practice and experience of exchange in primary agricultural markets. Indeed, as we shall see, changes in the modes of payment and techniques of weighing not only influence market relations and outcomes in significant and diverse ways; they also serve as sensitive indices of the shifting balance of power in agricultural markets as a result of political and economic dynamics well beyond the market yard.

The 'c' in transaction: cash, credit and commissions

In order to understand why 'cash payment' has come to be a central tenet of the first transaction, one has to identify what it is defined against. Cash payment refers to the immediacy, completeness and independence of the transaction: payments made to farmers in the market yard must be made directly by the buyer, paid up fully and on the spot, without any commission charged and without any linkage to credit that may have been advanced to the seller. It is here that the 'c' stands for 'challenging', as the interlinkage between credit and commodity marketing has long posed one of the most tightly reinforced constraints to the regulation of rural markets.

Interlocked transactions, where sales of post-harvest produce are tied to credit advances, are a well-documented feature of India's agricultural markets (Bardhan and Rudra 1978; Bardhan 1980; Basu 1983; Bhaduri 1986; Harriss-White 1996a; 2010). Such transactions, moreover, have not only been reported between farmers and moneylender traders in village- and town-based sites *outside* the regulated market yard, but have also defined exchange *inside* the mandi system, in states where sales are arranged through specialised commission agents, commonly known as *kacha arhatiyas*, who charge a commission as a fee for service and are a critical source of credit to farmers, with whom they typically maintain long-term relationships to ensure regular, post-harvest arrivals (Jodhka 1995; Gupta 1997; Gill 2004).

If one had walked into Harda Mandi in 1980, one would have witnessed a market full of *kacha arhatiyas*, with around 35 to 40 commission agents lining the market yard, which was then a small, three-acre, mud compound. The many small commission agents served primarily as intermediaries between farmers and a handful of four or five large buyers. On one side of the transaction, the *arhatiyas* were responsible for auctioning the produce for a fixed commission and disbursing loans to cultivators at various times during the year, advanced against claims to the post-harvest crop. On the other, the rotations of commodity capital and the time-lag in payments further along the commodity chain led to a reliance on small commission agents to spot finance producers and keep the produce moving through the mandi. It was a system, moreover, that over the years had become central to the management of mandi processes: the *kacha arhatiyas* conducted the auctions, organised market infrastructure and managed labour. It was also a system that was well known for its repertoire of malpractices and modes of pressure and control. Beyond the commission, which was officially 1 per cent, but commonly reported to be higher, *arhatiyas* charged interest on credit, made deductions on immediate cash payments, and frequently delayed providing the required amounts to farmers, who were typically old customers and regular debtors bound to particular *arhatiyas*. The few state-sanctioned functionaries present barely made an impression, working out of a small room rented from a trader, and keeping records of transactions over which they had virtually no control. The APMC, which was officially notified in 1969, was responsible for running the yard only on paper, while the mandi, popularly known as the *adda*, literally a 'den' of commission agents and traders, was a market in private hands.

By 1983, however, Harda Mandi looked dramatically different. The old *adda* had been uprooted and the market yard was moved across the road into a large but undeveloped 65-acre plot owned by the state. Around the same time, the *kacha arhatiyas*, the commission agents who had organised the old mandi, were suspended. Instead, licensed buyers were now made to participate in an open-outcry auction run by a state-appointed auctioneer and had to make full and direct payments in cash to farmers, with a fine charged for delays over 24 hours. No commission was to be deducted from any seller and all lots brought for sale in the auction would be sold to the highest bidder. By the time I began fieldwork in 2008, this system had been in place for 25 years; credit and commissions between farmers and traders in the mandi were firmly a feature of the past.

Outside the world of agricultural marketing in Madhya Pradesh, the abolition of the *kachi arhat pratha* in this state is a little-known reform. For those who witnessed and experienced it in places like Harda, it was often described as

88 *M. Krishnamurthy*

nothing short of *krantikari*, a revolution. It was also an act described as sudden, forceful and irreversible. A closer look, however, reveals the more gradual, conjunctural and contingent aspects of this change, the multiple and interconnected factors at work, and the diverse effects that unfolded.

The political calculus

The impetus for the abolition of the *kachi arhat pratha* in Madhya Pradesh in the early 1980s came from a high-powered political decision by the State Government, then under the Congress Party. A young and rising political leader, Digvijay Singh, who would himself become the Chief Minister a decade later, was Minister for Agriculture at this time and is widely credited for pushing through the orders. In an interview conducted in Delhi during my research, Digvijay Singh described the political reasoning behind the state's action. First, the elimination of the *arhatiyas* was presented as an attack on local traders, who were considered a loyal base of the main opposition, Bharatiya Janata Party (BJP), often called the '*bania* party' in MP.[4] Second, the abolition was publicly justified as an act intended to 'liberate the *kisan*' from the clutches of commission agents, a move that it was hoped would help the Congress expand its own rather narrow social and political base by reaching out to a potentially much larger constituency, i. e. the state's farmers.[5] Here, it is important to note that this was not in response to the demands of the farmers themselves, whose ties to the *arhatiyas* for credit silenced, at least in public, their objections to the exploitation they experienced at the hands of the commission agents in the market yard.[6] Third, Digvijay Singh stressed that mandi governance needed to be overhauled and brought under tighter control by the state if it was to capture a greater share of market fees from the agricultural produce being exchanged in the mandis. The abolition of the *arhat pratha*, therefore, was a critical step towards trying to wrest the mandi from local control and to stem evasion of revenue due to the state.

Administrative action

On the ground, across the market towns of Madhya Pradesh, the implementation of the State Government's policy was never going to be easy. Each mandi presented different challenges arising from its particular local context, including different agricultural conditions, trading and credit systems, and local political dynamics. In Harda, the removal of the *arhatiyas* was enforced in conjunction with the physical relocation of the mandi yard. In a response familiar to market sites across the country, both actions were severely resisted by the *arhatiyas* and traders. In the months before, traders had tried to stall the relocation, filing court cases and arguing that the new yard was inadequately equipped. On the day the commission system was dissolved, the traders went on strike, refusing to buy from farmers under the new conditions. But they faced swift and concerted action. The Mandi Committee, which was controlled by the oldest and largest

Terms of commodity exchange in MP 89

trading firm in Harda, was dissolved and replaced by a state officer-in-charge. In addition, the District Collector was asked to personally manage the transition. He did so by instructing government agencies to buy all the produce until traders called off the strike. He also made sure that weighing scales, which were otherwise owned by the *arhatiyas*, were bought or rented until permanent arrangements could be made. Farmers present on the day recall that the Collector stayed on late into the night, reassuring them that their produce would be sold. Once the dust had settled, those who experienced the event could sense that there was no going back.

No amount of infrastructure or administrative oversight, however, could have substituted for the informal production credit that farmers had been borrowing against the post-harvest sales of their produce through commission agents, whether inside or outside the mandi. Indeed, we know from field research in other states of regulated market yards, such as those in Tiruvannamalai in Tamil Nadu (B. Harriss 1981) or Burdwan in West Bengal (Harriss-White 2008), that have spent long years in disuse, quite literally gathering weeds, while tied commodity exchange took place in busy sites outside these notified premises. And yet, in Harda, it is clear that farmers who had previously sold their post-harvest produce through *arhatiyas* in the mandi did not move their sales outside the yard once commission agents were evicted. Instead, they moved over to transact in the new mandi yard, now selling directly to traders in the open auction and for payments made in cash. How did this delinking come about?

The changing dynamics of production: canal and crops

The answer seems to spring from a critical conjucture in the early 1980s when the abolition of the commission agents and the reorganisation of the mandi coincided with two other major interventions that came together to significantly change agricultural production and marketing in Harda. The first was the arrival of canal irrigation as a result of the Tawa Dam built on the longest tributary of the Narmada. The Tawa Canal irrigated a large part of Hoshangabad district, including Harda, which was then its westernmost *tehsil*, located at the tail-end of the Tawa Command Area. By the mid-1980s, Harda began to benefit from extensive expansion in irrigation and, with it, the possibility of taking two crops, leading to greater levels of productivity and income for the district's farmers.[7] The second was the introduction of a new cash crop, soybean, which from the mid-1970s was being actively promoted as the key agent of Madhya Pradesh's Yellow Revolution. To encourage its expansion, strong market linkages were developed for this protein-rich, export-oriented oilseed, both by the government (as part of the National Oilseeds Mission) and by regional (mainly Marwari) entrepreneurs, who were busy setting up soybean processing units in and around the commercial centre of Indore (Kumar 2009).

In Harda, soybean, a short-duration *kharif* crop, was seen as an excellent substitute for the long-duration cotton that farmers had been cultivating before the advent of the canal, making way later in the new agricultural cycle for a second *rabi* crop of irrigated wheat. Soybean appears to have played a particular role in enabling the delinking of credit and commodity marketing: as a short-duration crop it was considerably less input- and labour-intensive when compared to the long-duration cotton that it replaced. Moreover, further along the chain, payments from soybean processors to traders in the mandi also moved quickly, making immediate cash payments to farmers more viable. In contrast, cotton was well known for longer time-lags in payments across the trading and processing chain all the way through to farmers, who seldom received full payment immediately after sales.

At the same time, there were new demands on farmers as they tried to mobilise financial resources to invest in improving the quality of their fields and farm equipment, as well as meeting the increases in household consumption that accompanied the growth in production. Here, it is important to note that Harda stands out for its relatively large landholdings, which are double the size on average of those in the rest of the state (4.43 ha in Harda to 2.02 ha in MP). Furthermore, Harda is remarkable for the fact that small and marginal farmers (below 2 ha) comprise only 37 per cent of landowners in the district, an almost exact inversion from the rest of Madhya Pradesh, where 68 per cent of all farmers own such small and marginal parcels of land.[8] The sizeable number of medium and large landowners were particularly quick to follow the public investment in irrigation with private investments in agricultural production, including buying new land whenever possible. In interviews retracing this period they explained that they did this by managing multiple sources of informal credit, both in the village and from different segments of the town bazaar. For the majority of farmers, agricultural credit from banks was inaccessible at the time, a situation that was only widely reported to have changed with the availability of Kisan Credit Cards (KCCs), especially from the mid-2000s. What is clear, however, is that the mandi had ceased to be a key source of credit for farmers soon after the elimination of the *kacha arhatiyas* and, even when farmers did draw upon established relationships with specific firms, the loans were not linked to the sale of their crop. In fact, this kind of borrowing was no longer an option because, within a matter of a few years of the action in 1983, the mandi itself had changed.

The exit and entry of arhatiyas *and traders: the changing character of buyers*

With the mandi no longer issuing *kachi arhat* licences, the numerous *kacha arhatiyas* were now officially out of business. For a few years, the old *arhatiyas* tried to make the transition. Some continued to provide credit and retrieve grain off the record, but without the security of the formal commission that bound farmers to their firms, most discovered that in the new direct, open auction system they no longer had assured access to the grain and the risks of lending were too high. One such *arhatiya*, who closed his shop in the mid-1980s, described the loss of a few lakhs when his farmer-customers chose to treat the

Terms of commodity exchange in MP 91

abolition as a virtual 'loan-waiver'. Of the 35 to 40 *kacha arhatiyas* in the old mandi, a mere six or seven survived the transition to the new market, which favoured those who had greater access to capital and well-developed commercial networks, trading ties and agro-processing concerns. Most of the old *arhatiyas* struggled for a few years before shutting shop and exiting the mandi. Some entered the bazaar as retailers, while the larger landholders among them turned their attention towards supervising cultivation. A further few experienced declines in their fortunes and became *munims* (accountants) for larger trading firms. Around the same time, between the late 1980s and early 1990s, a new crop of traders took up licences to try their hand in the new mandi. These young traders, most of whom were from the dominant *bania* castes of Agarwals, Jains and Maheshwaris, some of whom emerged from the ranks of *munims* of old and established firms, now quickly began pursuing commercial connections, especially in the soybean trade. In addition, two Gujjars set up small *dal* mills, a Sikh transporter ventured his hand at wheat trading, and two Telis from the same extended family applied for mandi licences, linking their well-established small grain aggregation businesses with minor positions in the wholesale market.

Credit advances to cultivators were no longer a prominent feature of mandi transactions in what became known as a *nagad* or 'cash' mandi, where the new traders had little interest in dispensing credit against unsecured grain, but instead rotated available cash in frequent buying, stocking and trading activities. Moreover, while delays in payment did not disappear overnight, in the absence of credit ties and regular contact between farmers and traders, stalling on the part of cash-strapped firms was less and less likely to be tolerated by farmers. During my fieldwork, an old firm notorious for over-leveraging itself was temporarily barred from the auction by the Mandi Secretary when farmers complained about having to wait overnight for their cash.

Interestingly, the same issue also arose when the State Government started large-scale procurement of wheat directly from farmers in 2008. In order to make available a high minimum support price (MSP) topped up by an MP state 'bonus', mandi regulations had to be waived and farmers had to accept payments by cheque and subsequently electronic bank transfers, typically waiting for a week or so for the money to be credited to their accounts. This caused problems for cash-strapped farmers, especially in the immediate post-harvest period when there are numerous accounts to be settled on and off the farm. For some this meant short-term borrowing until the payment came through, while in the yard a few farmers opted to sell part of their produce to traders for cash, even as the government agencies started to arrange for a fixed amount to be paid by bearer cheque (Krishnamurthy 2012). Even small changes in the timing of payments, then, are highly consequential for farming households.

Cheque payments generated two further observations. Once the cash constraint had been met, many farmers said they preferred cheque payments, and the direct deposit system introduced in the 2011 wheat season, because they didn't have to worry about theft, which was otherwise a constant concern when carrying such large sums of cash on their person, no matter how inventively they

92   *M. Krishnamurthy*

disguised and distributed the wads of money. Second, since farmers didn't have cash immediately in hand, local retailers were quick to note that they didn't stop to make the usual volume of purchases from the bazaar, often returning home with an empty tractor trolley after selling wheat to the state during the procurement season.

Cultivation, credit and commodity markets in comparative perspective

Stepping back, if we place this major change in primary transactions in Harda Mandi in comparative perspective, two key points become more evident. First, the relationships between cultivation, agricultural credit and commodity marketing are critical to the structure of primary markets. Second, there is nothing automatic or formulaic about how these respond and adapt to the presence of regulated markets. Such important interactions, therefore, need to be studied in specific regional, commodity and regulatory contexts.

For instance, the experience in West Bengal during a period of impressive agricultural growth demonstrates that strides in agricultural production do not in and of themselves loosen interlinked markets. In fact, in this case, it was quite the opposite. Here, where markets have been left largely unregulated by the state (but are deeply socially regulated), the webs of credit and debt managed by agents to control paddy supplies were further tightened in a system of rice markets that squeezed the mass of petty producers and petty commodity traders, and expanded the margins of a small, oligopolistic section of agro-commercial capitalists as agricultural production grew (Harriss-White 2008). In a very different context, in the agriculturally advanced Green Revolution granaries of Punjab and Haryana, the ties that bind farmers and commission agents remain strong and are reaffirmed by state regulation. In these north Indian markets, *arhatiyas* not only continue to function as an integral part of mandi organisation, but commission agents have emerged as a powerful political lobby, drawing upon their status as the dominant source of informal credit to farmers and their essential role in day-to-day operations and transactional processes in the mandi to ensure that private and public procurement is routed through them (Gill 2004; Damodaran 2000; 2010). In contrast, in Harda, improvements in agricultural production *coincided* with the implementation of this important market reform in the early 1980s, enabling at least a significant proportion of producers to delink their marketing activities from their credit relations, while eliminating a layer of intermediaries, who might have otherwise strengthened their control over mandi operations until they appeared, like the *arhatiyas* in Punjab, indispensable to the smooth functioning of the local market and inimical to its reform. Importantly, it was also the elimination of credit-linked commission agents in the 1980s in Madhya Pradesh that later enabled the State Government in the 2000s to experiment with and expand both corporate procurement channels and public grain procurement programmes, generating a range of sites and systems to buy directly from farmers, which both undermined and affirmed the state-run mandi system in different ways (Krishnamurthy 2011).

Finally, the local *sabzi* (vegetable) mandi in Harda provides an interesting contrast, a coda to the question of commission agents. Here, 25 years later, in 2009, a virtually identical set of actions, discharged with equal administrative zeal to relocate and regulate the local vegetable and fruit market, failed to deliver similar results to those achieved in the grain market earlier. In the absence of concomitant changes in production and credit in this market for perishable produce, the *arhatiyas*, temporarily evicted, returned to run the mandi within a fortnight, as state-appointed auctioneers and mandi staff, accustomed to managing soybean and wheat sales, ran out of time and temper in running the multiple simultaneous auctions required to rapidly clear the fresh produce each morning. Within a matter of days, credit advanced and commissions deducted, from both sides, from farmers, as well as from local retailers and numerous poor, daily vendors, on and off the book, resumed to structure transactions in this mandi. Moreover, the APMC now levied a formal 2 per cent market fee and allowed a 4 per cent commission to be deducted from the buyers, a move that hit the numerous small, landless, daily vendors, most of whom, in sharp contrast to the traders in the grain mandi, were among the poorest participants in the fresh produce market.

Two different conditions of intermediation, then, prevail and persist in two different markets situated within the same yard in Harda, and tell distinct tales about the interactions among cultivation, credit and the regulation of commodity markets. The commission, however, is only one aspect of the marketing process. Let us now return to the main soybean and wheat mandi in Harda and turn our attention to another critical element at work in the market yard.

Weights, measures and the balance of power in the mandi

Given all the talk about liberating farmers from the interlocked clutches of *arhatiyas* and their exploitative practices, I was rather surprised to hear farmers in Harda insist that the decade following the eviction of the old commission agents actually marked a deterioration in the conduct of key mandi processes. As they explained, farmers who experienced the transition from the *adda* to APMC discovered that while they may have been freed from tied transactions and the costs of commissions, they had also lost the individual attention, common courtesy, frequent contact and, on occasion, personal protection that had come along with their status as *grahaks* or customers of their respective *arhatiyas*. At the same time, in the new trading mandi, their produce – now untied to credit – was more attractive than ever before, and by all accounts the brazen mistreatment of producers in the market yard only became more evident. Weight-related malpractices were especially rife during this period, basic infrastructure in the new yard was dismal, additional charges were unofficially extracted, and incidents of farmers being verbally abused and even physically manhandled were common. The right to 'accurate weight' must have seemed like a distant and demoralising promise.

It is against this backdrop that the installation of an electronic weighbridge in 1999 is seen as a turning point in Harda Mandi. This weighbridge, the first to be put in place to weigh farmers' produce in a mandi yard in MP, completely changed weighing dynamics, transforming the experience of what is widely considered to be one of the most important and conflict-ridden activities in mandi life. In Harda, this was the site where farmers had suffered all manner of theft, from tampered weights, purposefully spilled grain, and even entire bags stolen from underneath them. These acts, both subtle and audacious, were commited by male *hammals* (porters/head load workers) and female *soopda walis*, who were sweepers employed by the traders to collect the spilled produce, retaining a proportion as their payment. As one old labourer evocatively recalled, the *soopda walis* were skilled and would 'fan the grain on the market floor with their hands the way a peacock spreads its feathers'. In the meantime, farmers, who came to the traders' shops after the auction, had to wait, one at a time, as all their produce was heaped separately, then bagged and individually weighed, as a basis for the calculation of the final weight by the *taulauti*, the trader's weighman, who worked the manual, three-legged scale, balancing it adeptly with his foot.

The electronic weighbridge, popularly called the *dharam kata*, 'the honest weighing scale', changed the whole process. Now, farmers drive their tractors on to the weighing platform twice, first full and then empty, and are given a printed receipt by the mandi-appointed weighbridge operator. For this, they pay a one-time fee of Rs.10. In between the two weights, they deposit their produce in a common heap at the trader's godown. Increasingly these days, this is done by activating a hydraulic pump that raises the trolley to empty out its contents in a matter of minutes, further avoiding any labour charges for offloading their produce. They no longer need to wait to supervise the time-consuming process of bagging or for the round of manual weighing to ensure that each bag is accurately filled and ready for stacking. That and all other tasks associated with the heap are now solely the concern of the trader. Most importantly, if grain is stolen after it is heaped on the ground, it now goes missing not from the farmer's final weight, but from the trader's account. Soon after the arrival of the weighbridge, the *soopda walis* disappeared and grain theft became much harder to pull off for the *hammals*, who had previously been able to augment their wages in cash with small but significant quantities of produce that they had helped steal, with the full knowledge of traders, under the old manual system.

For mandi labourers, the installation of the electronic weighbridge was a measure of a significant change in the economic status of farmers and in the volume of their produce, which not long ago came into town in bullock carts and not on tractor-trolleys. But it also coincided with a trend towards the consolidation of mandi trade in the hands of fewer, larger traders, which meant uneven access to work for those attached to small and medium-sized trading firms.[9] In response to these changes, in 2008, the hammals went on strike and achieved a significant increase of Rs.2 per bag (quintal), but this paled when compared to the doubling of the prices of both wheat and soybean between 2005 and 2010, pushing up commodity prices by well over Rs.600–800 per quintal during this period. In the aftermath of the rise in rates, in order to reduce labour costs, larger traders also did away with manual weighing before dispatch to onward buyers, relying on electronic weighbridges at the point of delivery as well.

The tipping point

In contrast to the elimination of the commission agents in the early 1980s, the installation of the electronic weighbridge in Harda Mandi in the late 1990s was achieved by a farmer-led campaign. In this case, there was no larger state-wide initiative or pressure from above to change prevailing weighing practices and the local mandi staff were highly doubtful that such a system could work. In fact, they worried that using a single weighbridge rather than spreading out weighing among the different traders' shops would create tractor jams, fights and delays in the market yard. Unsurprisingly, traders also vehemently opposed the weighbridge, protesting that it would be misused by farmers, who could now add additional weights to their full trolleys, pushing up the weight and causing the buyer serious losses. They did not mention, of course, the lucrative loopholes that they knew would be lost with the end of manual weighing.

It was a group of activist farmers associated with the local chapter of the Bharatiya Kisan Sangh (BKS) and another local farmers' organisation called the Kisan Panchayat (KP) that led the demands for an electronic weighbridge to be installed in Harda Mandi. The young, educated leader of the KP, a 90-acre Jat farmer with an M.Sc. in Agriculture, spearheaded the campaign and is credited by all parties in the mandi for seeing it through to implementation. He did so by convincing a doubtful District Collector to order a one-month field trial to see whether it could work. During this time he personally supervised implementation at the weighbridge, repeatedly explaining the new process, and intervening whenever disputes erupted, both among anxious farmers and between farmers and traders, who were verifying the weights by using the original, manual method. As a result of these efforts, the trial period was extended, and soon this became the sole, permanent system of weighing for tractor trolleys in Harda Mandi.

The fight for the electronic weighbridge is still thought of as the mandi's *maha yudh*, its 'greatest battle'. Beyond transforming the dynamics of weighing and waiting, however, it is also seen as marking a shift in the way in which farmers were treated more generally in the market yard. In 2000, the young Jat leader, still fresh from his weighbridge victory, was elected by farmers as the Chairman of the Mandi Committee in the first direct elections for this post held in mandis across MP.[10] Up until this point, the Chairman had always been nominated from among the members of the Committee, and previous heads had been close associates of the largest trading firm. For Harda's farmers this was the first time an independent *kisan neta*, or farmer leader, took on this role. Over the next decade, under him and then later another Jat Chairman, as well as a newly appointed and dynamic Mandi Secretary, a whole series of measures were taken to upgrade the infrastructure for farmers in the yard, including covered sheds, a rest house, water coolers and fans on the platforms, paid for by the income from mandi fees.

Some of the small changes in the reorganisation of services are easy to miss, but reflect larger shifts at work. For instance, the water coolers replaced the old water carriers, who came from a family of Brahmins who had been associated for generations with one of the oldest Marwari trading firms. For their services, they used to be paid in fistfuls of produce, liberally lifted without permission from farmers' carts and trolleys. Anything but insignificant, these are the micro-manifestations of market power in practice. As one of the most seasoned mandi functionaries once advised me:

> If you want to know how strong farmers are in a market, look first at the mandi floor. If grain is scattered all around, spilled and swept up, as farmers scramble to secure their loads, you know that the farmers are weak. In Harda today, if you try to flick uncompensated grain, a fight is certain to erupt. It is a sign that farmers are *haavi* – 'dominant' – in the mandi.

Power in grain markets, then, is sometimes quite literally grounded in the mandi yard. Its roots, however, are likely to lie outside, as new political seeds are sometimes sown along with the new crops that take hold in the fields.

Weight and vigilance

This was certainly the case in Harda where, for all its significant effects, the installation and functioning of the electronic weighbridge in the mandi at the turn of the century was a consequence not a catalyst of the changing balance of power in the agricultural market. This, in turn, was closely connected to political movements taking place in Harda town and countryside, and in particular to the growing assertiveness of a certain caste of cultivators who have already featured prominently in our story: the Jats.

Among the four major landowning agricultural castes in Harda – the Gujjars, Rajputs, Jats and Bishnoes, all of whom are recorded to have travelled from Marwar and settled in these parts around 200 to 250 years ago – the Jats, while relatively small in numbers, have been the most aggressive buyers of land.[11] Their rising political clout in Harda, however, is much more recent and is usually dated to 1993, and the election of Harda's first Jat Member of the State Legislative Assembly (MLA), a man who subsequently held on to this seat for four consecutive terms, most recently re-elected in 2008.[12] As a young, Indore-returned aspirant in the early 1990s, the future leader had used the mandi as a key site for his early political activities, launching a series of protests against various malpractices committed by traders. Recounting his dramatic trajectory in politics, old mandi people remembered him during the dry days of cotton cultivation, waiting as a young boy for a few hundred rupees from his family's *arhatiya* in the old *adda*. Now, after the coming of the canal, in the new soybean and wheat mandi, he publicly took on the traders as part of his political campaign. By the time the fight for the weighbridge was underway, therefore, the mandi had already started to become an active site of political mobilisation. Moreover, the two vocal farmers' organisations during this period, the BKS and the KP, were also led by Jat activists, and both took inspiration from and tried to

Terms of commodity exchange in MP   97

forge links with the popular Jat farmer leader Mahendra Singh Tikait and the much larger farmers' movement in Uttar Pradesh.

For the majority of farmers who sell their produce in Harda Mandi, conversations about the Jats provoked deeply ambivalent responses. On the one hand, they are widely viewed as hot-headed and aggressive, known for bullying other farmers to claim space on the auction platforms, causing trouble by muscling ahead to the weighbridge, and using their political connections to cut the queue and deposit their grain out of turn during government wheat procurement (Krishnamurthy 2012). On the other hand, most farmers acknowledge that the Jats are just the sort of vigilant and mobilising force required in a physical market, and that their attitude and activism has forced changes in the conduct towards all farmers in the mandi, especially when it has led to major changes in market practice, such as the use of the electronic weighbridge.

Conclusions

This chapter has explored the changing terms of the first transaction between farmers and traders over the past three decades in a regulated agricultural market in the central Indian state of Madhya Pradesh. It has focused in particular on two critical elements of transactional life in a primary market, modes of payment and techniques of weighing, and illustrated, through ethnographic attention to these elements in action, the diverse and interrelated causes and consequences which unfolded as changes in specific market practices were introduced, resisted, enforced and experienced by different actors on the ground.

Given the very weak record of state-regulated markets in enforcing the central conditions of the critical first point of exchange between farmers and commission agents and traders operating in local market sites across states and commodity systems (Harriss-White 1996b), the experiences of Harda Mandi certainly provide cause for optimism about the possibilities of securing significant improvements in performance, especially from the perspective of farmer-sellers in the market yard. However, since our approach to these interventions, whether it was the elimination of commission agents or the installation of the electronic weighbridge, was conceptually relational and grounded in the specific political, economic and social contexts within which markets are shaped and operate, we were also able to grasp the deeply conjunctural and contingent character of changing market practices and outcomes. Here, three points are worth briefly emphasising.

First, changes in agricultural markets and their regulation cannot be analysed without understanding the structures and dynamics of agricultural production, and in particular the relationships among cultivation, credit and marketing in different commodity systems. In Harda, for instance, the expansion of canal irrigation, the spread of soybean, and the political and administrative action against commission agents came together to dislodge the *kacha arhatiyas* and reorganise the market for food grains and oil seeds, with specific effects on market composition and character. Second, while this was an especially productive

98 *M. Krishnamurthy*

conjuncture, we also saw the *disjunctures* within and between market practices at any given time. Indeed, it was following the successful eviction of commission agents and the delinking of credit and post-harvest sales in the mandi that the 'liberated farmers' reported a deterioration in weighing practices and grain theft, where anonymity brought improvements of one kind (open auction, immediate cash payments) but, in the absence of greater vigilance, also gave rise to greater exploitation of another kind (weight-related malpractices). It was over 15 years after the end of the commission-based system that farmer-activists campaigned for an electronic weighbridge in the mandi. This leads to the third point: changing market practice, such as modes of payment and techniques of weighing, not only affect outcomes in diverse and consequential ways, they are also particularly sensitive indices of the changing balance of power in agricultural markets, which manifest themselves in a range of economic and political actions inside and outside the market yard.

Any agenda to 'reform' agricultural markets therefore requires a deep reading of the grounding and giving way of relations over time. As Barbara Harriss-White concluded in her detailed study of the regulation of agricultural markets in the mid-1990s, quoting Bernard Schaffer, this is in fact its central challenge:

> There is no lack of political will, but a scatter and conflict of wills, inconvenient for some, not for others.... But reform is not just a question of removing impediments once they have been listed by a 'methodologist.' Reform means indicating just where the interests are grounded, where the lines of opposition are drawn, the pain and guilt felt and hidden.
>
> (Harriss-White 1996b)

Nearly 20 years later, this is a reminder that deserves repetition and pushes the boundaries of existing approaches to policy making and regulation in rapidly changing agricultural markets in India today. In order to break ground, however, we need to first engage much more closely with actually existing markets in diverse contexts, and try to better grasp the challenges and possibilities of reforming them where they matter most.

Notes

1 My thanks to the participants at the conference, 'Capitalism and Development in the 21st Century' held at Oxford University in July 2012, where a version of this paper was first presented. Subsequent revisions have been greatly strengthened by the careful reading and critical feedback of Barbara Harriss-White and Judith Heyer, for which I am most grateful. All inadequacies remain my own.
2 As Barbara Harriss-White has pointed out, this model can be traced to the largely unimplemented ideas reigning in unruly wheat and meat markets in early twentieth-century Britain, transplanted into India via Lord Linlithgow, who, having presided over an effort to set in order the 'legal chaos' in the urban underbelly of the metropole was shortly thereafter appointed to chair the Royal Commission and its deliberations on how to regulate the vast and varied rural markets of the colony (B. Harriss 1984: 72).

3 Data on the number of regulated markets is from the National Council of State Agricultural Marketing Boards (COSAMB): www.cosamb.org/markets.html.
4 On the socio-economic base of political dynamics in Madhya Pradesh, see Gupta (2005), especially the upper-class support base, comprising brahmins and *banias*, of the BJP in the state. See also Jaffrelot (2008).
5 Expanding the Congress's narrow and contracting social base in MP was an important aspect of Digvijay Singh's political practice. As James Manor, writing about Singh's term as Chief Minister in the 1990s observes, as a politician he was very conscious of the need to 'promote renewal and political regeneration'. For Singh, a Rajput, therefore, actively reaching out to the state's OBCs, *Dalits* and Scheduled Tribes (ST) communities was an important political imperative (Manor 2010: 202). Although the abolition of the *kachi arhat* pre-dates his period as Chief Minister, the broadening of the social base, which was clearly an important part of Digvijay Singh's approach to political work, is also evident earlier in his career.
6 Interestingly, research conducted in Tiruppur's regulated market in the late 1970s found that it was precisely this dependence upon commission agents' banking activities that emasculated the protests of farmers' organisations seeking to curb their malpractices and evict them from the market yard (B. Harriss 1981).
7 Today, the net irrigated area in Harda is recorded at 76 per cent, making it one of the most highly irrigated districts in Madhya Pradesh, a state which contains 20 per cent of the country's drylands and where average irrigation coverage is under 30 per cent, the majority of which is from well- and tubewell-driven groundwater extraction (Vijay Shankar 2005).
8 Data on distribution of landholdings are from the Agricultural Census website: http://agcensus.nic.in/.
9 Krishnamurthy (2013) describes the changing dynamics of mandi trade in Harda between 1990 and 2010.
10 Strictly speaking, although few farmers made a point of it, the post was won by his mother in a reserved election.
11 The late nineteenth-century Narmada Valley came under the *malguzari* system of land settlement, introduced by the British in 1860 across the newly created Central Provinces. Under this settlement, the *malguzars* (the revenue farmers of the former Maratha system) were given full proprietary rights over most of the land, upon which revenue was then collected solely from this class at a reduced rate. By the mid-twentieth century, with the abolition of the *malguzari* system, land was increasingly transferred from the vast tracts and differentiated tenancy arrangements to individual ownership, dominated by these four caste groups, among which the Jats and Bishnoes are known for their relatively larger landholdings.
12 After 20 years as the MLA, he finally lost his seat in the 2013 state legislative assembly elections.

References

Bardhan, Pranab (1980) 'Interlocking factor markets and agrarian development: a review of issues', *Oxford Economic Papers*, 32(1): 82–98.
Bardhan, Pranab and Rudra, Ashok (1978) 'Interlinkage of land, labour and credit relations: an analysis of village survey data in East India', *Economic and Political Weekly*, 13(6/7): 367–384.
Basu, Kaushik (1983) 'The emergence of isolation and interlinkage in rural markets', *Oxford Economic Papers*, 35(2): 262–280.
Bhaduri, Amit (1986) 'Forced commerce and agrarian growth', *World Development*, 14(2): 267–272.

100 M. Krishnamurthy

Damodaran, Harish (2000) 'Grain market still under sway of commission agents', *The Hindu Business Line*, 12 May, www.thehindubusinessline.in/2000/05/12/stories/071203ya.htm (accessed 25 April 2013).

—— (2010) 'Why cash is king in grain market', *The Hindu Business Line*, 16 March, www.thehindubusinessline.in/2010/03/16/stories/2010031651330800.htm (accessed 25 April 2013).

Elliott, Charles A. (1867) *Report on the Land Revenue Settlement of the District of Hoshungabad, Central Provinces*, Allahabad: Government Press, North Western Provinces.

Gill, Anita (2004) 'Interlinked agrarian credit markets: case study of Punjab', *Economic and Political Weekly*, 39(33): 3741–3751.

Government of Madhya Pradesh (2009) *Madhya Pradesh Krishi Upaj Mandi Adhiniyam, 1972*, Diglot Edition, Indore.

Gupta, Khadija Ansari (1997) *Ardhat and Ardhatdari: A Sociographical Study of Agricultural Marketing in Small Towns*, Delhi: Kalinga Publications.

Gupta, Shaibal (2005) 'Socio-economic base of political dynamics in MP', *Economic and Political Weekly*, 40(48): 5093–5100.

Harriss, Barbara (1974) 'The role of Punjab wheat markets as growth centres', *The Geographical Journal*, 140(1): 52–71.

—— (1981) *Transitional Trade and Rural Development: The Nature and Role of Agricultural Trade in a South Indian District*, New Delhi: Vikas Publishing House.

—— (1984) *State and Market: State Intervention in Agricultural Exchange in a Dry Region of Tamil Nadu, South India*, New Delhi: Concept Publishing Company.

Harriss-White, Barbara (1996a) *A Political Economy of Agricultural Markets in South India: Masters of the Countryside*, New Delhi: Sage Publications.

—— (1996b) 'Order ... Order ... agrocommercial microstructures and the State – the experience of regulation', in Burton Stein and Sanjay Subrahmanyam (eds) *Institutions and Economic Change in South Asia*, Delhi: Oxford University Press.

—— (1999) 'Power in peasant markets', in Barbara Harriss-White (ed.) *Agricultural Markets From Theory to Practice: Field Experience in Developing Countries*, Basingstoke: Macmillan.

—— (2008) *Rural Commercial Capital: Agricultural Markets in West Bengal*, Oxford: Oxford University Press.

—— (2010) 'Local capitalism and the foodgrains economy in northern Tamil Nadu, 1973–2010', Working Paper, Chennai: Madras Institute for Development Studies (MIDS).

Jaffrelot, Christophe (2008) 'The uneven plebeianisation of Madhya Pradesh politics', *Seminar*, 591 (November).

Jodhka, Surinder S. (1995) 'Who borrows? Who lends? Changing structure of informal credit in rural Haryana', *Economic and Political Weekly*, 30(39): A123–132.

Krishnamurthy, Mekhala (2011) *Harda Mandi: Experiencing Change in an Agricultural Market in Central India* (1980–2010), unpublished Ph.D. thesis, University College London.

Krishnamurthy, Mekhala (2012) 'States of wheat: the changing dynamics of public procurement in Madhya Pradesh', *Economic and Political Weekly*, 47(52): 72–83.

—— (2013) 'Margins and mindsets: enterprise, opportunity and exclusion in a market town in Madhya Pradesh', in Nandini Gooptu (ed.) *Enterprise Culture in Neoliberal India*, London: Routledge.

Kumar, Richa (2009) *The Yellow Revolution in Malwa: Alternative Arenas of Struggle and the Cultural Politics of Development*, unpublished Ph.D. dissertation, Massachusetts Institute of Technology (MIT), Cambridge, MA.

Manor, James (2010) 'Beyond clientalism: Digvijay Singh's participatory, pro-poor strategy in Madhya Pradesh', in Pamela Price and Arild Engelsen Ruud (eds) *Power and Influence in India: Bosses, Lords and Captains*, New Delhi: Routledge.

Royal Commission on Agriculture in India (1928) *Report: Royal Commission on Agriculture in India*, Calcutta: Government of India, Central Publication Branch.

Sarkar, Suman (1989) 'A theory of multistratum competition for primary agricultural markets of less developed countries', paper presented at the International Society of Agricultural Economics Conference, Athens.

Thompson, E.P. (1971) 'The moral economy of the English crowd in the eighteenth century', *Past and Present*, 50: 76–136.

Vijay Shankar, P.S. (2005) 'Four decades of agricultural development in MP', *Economic and Political Weekly*, 40(48): 5014–5024.

6 The political economy of microfinance and marginalised groups

Implications of alternative institutional strategies

D. Narasimha Reddy[1]

Introduction

Since Independence, improving access to institutional credit for poor and tiny producers has been a persistent challenge faced by successive governments in India. The 1990s saw financial liberalisation in the form of the deregulation of interest rates and an increase in profit seeking. In this context new initiatives like self-help based microcredit started to emerge in different parts of the country in the late 1980s and 1990s. The evolution of microcredit institutions, including commercial microcredit, has clear footprints derived from national and sub-national specificities, and shows that alternative institutions appropriate for the provision of affordable credit to poor and small borrowers can evolve even in a pervasive profit-seeking atmosphere. This chapter, in analysing alternative institutional forms of microfinance in India with specific reference to Andhra Pradesh (AP), examines first the record of appropriate agencies for lending to the poor, and then the implications of commercial microfinance as an agency for inclusive finance. The introduction is followed by an account of bank-linked self-help groups in AP. The third section analyses the emergence and performance of commercial microfinance institutions (MFIs). The fourth section looks at the search for regulatory mechanisms. The final section concludes.

It was the search for an institutional alternative to the mainstream banking system that resulted in innovative approaches to microcredit which involved providing loans to self-help groups of 10 to 20 members. In most cases these were all-women groups.

The emergence of group-based lending in India coincided with the spread of the neoliberal agenda across the globe. Meeting the credit needs of the poor was part of the well-being strategy of the state which could be turned to political advantage if nurtured properly. In contrast, private financial enterprise saw the gap in provision as a huge opportunity for profitable exploitation. The result was the birth of microfinance with two diametrically opposed and often conflicting objectives. The group-based approach has taken two distinct identities described in different ways by different authors, here termed 'for-profit' and 'not-for-profit'.

Microfinance and marginalised groups 103

The very nomenclature used speaks volumes about the difference in the nature of their functioning and well-being outcomes. The 'for-profit' approach is commercially oriented with a minimalist package of financial services. Cost recovery, a profit margin and financial sustainability mark its neoliberal orientation. It emphasises that markets can work for finance for the poor as well, and this assumes a kind of hegemonic position in the development agenda (Kabeer 2005). In contrast, the 'not-for-profit' approach is socially oriented, often donor subsidised or state sponsored, with a wider agenda than mere provision of financial services.

Self-help group–bank linkage

The self-help group–bank linkage (SHG–BL) model has evolved as the 'not-for-profit' approach in India, while 'Grameen-type' private MFIs represent the 'for-profit' approach. In this section, we will trace briefly the conditions under which SHG–BL-based microfinance institutions have emerged, their rapid growth, and the diversity of functions assumed by them, with particular reference to AP.

The SHG–BL model of microfinance is unique to India (Basu and Srivastava 2005) and has been well documented (e.g. Shenoy 2002; CGAP 2007; Shylendra 2006; SERP 2012). The National Bank for Agriculture and Rural Development (NABARD), a government-owned apex finance institution, launched SHG–BL in 1992, acting as a catalyst for the development of SHGs, initially primarily as thrift societies, and later, through training and capacity building, as societies eligible for access to bank credit.

Initially, SHGs were promoted in association with NGOs. The State of AP had a unique advantage here. The 1993 South Asia Association for Regional Cooperation (SAARC) meeting in Dhaka set out an ambitious agenda to eradicate poverty in the region by 2002. As part of the strategy, a pilot South Asia Poverty Alleviation Programme (SAPAP) was launched with the assistance of the United Nations Development Programme (UNDP) in 20 mandals in three districts in AP in 1993. The thrust of the SAPAP was the formation of women's SHGs with the objectives of the promotion of thrift, social mobilisation and empowerment. The SAPAP lasted until 2000. By then the state, under the Chief Ministership of Chandrababu Naidu, had achieved a reputation of being a leading reform state receptive to the World Bank's policies and programmes of structural adjustment. The World Bank saw the SAPAP-based SHG model as having the potential to wean the poor from targeted credit, and also to get the poor into habits of saving and commercial borrowing. It provided a loan and helped create the AP State-sponsored agency, the Society for the Elimination of Rural Poverty (SERP), which took over SHG–BL development in 2000. AP served as a training and testing ground for the faster spread of SHG–BL which has emerged as the institutional basis not only for extending credit to the poor but also for anchoring a number of programmes aimed at empowering women and increasing the well-being of the poor.

By the late 1990s SHG–BL had emerged as a model of microfinance unique to India. The 'Grameen-type' for-profit private MFIs were miniscule in comparison (Basu and Srivastava 2005). There was evidence that the majority of SHG

104 D.N. Reddy

members were from the poorest groups, and the promoting NGOs found that the benefits of the SHGs went beyond microfinance, including the empowerment of women. The vast network of rural bank branches, otherwise unable to reach the poor, was able to provide finance through SHGs. NABARD's role in refinancing banks through subsidised loans, and the RBI's guidelines treating lending to SHGs as 'priority sector lending', helped the substantial progress of SHG–BL, especially in the southern states (Basu and Srivastava 2005). By the end of March 2010, there were 6.95 million bank-linked SHGs in the country of which 13.65 per cent were in AP. The total bank loans advanced to these SHGs stood at Rs.280,400 million, of which AP accounted for about 23 per cent.

SHG–BL: the AP model

SHG–BL in AP has recorded a distinct and rapid growth path with the active support of the state government working through SERP. SERP manages a comprehensive set of poverty alleviation programmes. There is a three-tier structure with all the SHGs in a village forming a village organisation (VO), all VOs in a mandal/block forming a Mandal Samakhya (MS), and all MSs in a district forming a Zilla Samakhya (ZS). The fundamental idea behind the programme is that the credit needs of the poor can be met and sustained if addressed in combination with their livelihood and social security concerns. Although credit to poor households is a priority, SHG activities under SERP cover as many as 18 areas which include food security, health and nutrition, dairying, collective procurement and marketing, micro-insurance and social security.

SHG formation in AP increased from 277,000 in 2000 to 1.06 million in 2011/2012, an average annual rate of growth of about 22 per cent (SERP 2012). The 1.06 million SHGs in 2011/2012 were organised into 38,821 VOs and 1098 MSs. These SHGs generate considerable *internal resources* through their own savings and the interest thereon which becomes the 'corpus'. They also get grants provided by the state government to each of the MSs which go into the Community Investment Fund (CIF).

The total savings of these SHGs increased from Rs.9529 million in 2003/2004 to Rs.36,575 million in 2011/2012, an average annual rate of growth of about 30 per cent. The total 'corpus' reached Rs.53,335 million by the end of 2011/2012. The SHGs also have access to the CIF from which MSs provide loans to VOs which in turn extend loans to SHGs. The interest on CIF loans is 12 per cent, and of this the SHGs are allowed to retain 3 per cent, and the VOs another 3 per cent, to meet their maintenance expenditure. The remaining 6 per cent goes to MSs.

Bank linkage and bank credit

It normally takes about one year for an SHG to acquire the capacity to manage and access bank credit. Training plays a critical role. During the past decade, 30 to 40 per cent of the SHGs have been able to access bank credit. Annual bank

Microfinance and marginalised groups 105

credit to SHGs increased significantly from Rs.1734 million in 2000/2001, the year of formation of SERP, to Rs.79,416 million by the end of 2011/2012 (SERP 2012). A better indicator is the credit per group, which increased from about Rs.17,000 to Rs.222,000. The availability of credit per member increased from less than Rs.2000 to over Rs.22,000. The cumulative credit-to-savings ratio also increased substantially from about two in 2003/2004 to almost 12 in 2011/2012. On the supply side, the increase was due to the growing confidence of the banks in the SHGs based on their high repayment rate, and on the demand side it was due to the link to productive activities like agriculture, and allied activities like dairy, petty trade and to an extent also to increased payments for private education and health. The latter period also saw the entry of the MFIs which provided multiple lending even to bank-linked SHGs.

Banks provide credit to SHGs at the priority sector lending rate (PLR) of about 9 per cent. The state government introduced a direct interest subsidy to SHG members in 2004 under the '*Pavala Vaddi* Scheme', which pays 3 per cent interest. The difference between the PLR and 3 per cent, the state subsidy, is directly credited to SHG borrowers who repay their loan instalments regularly. Beginning with a modest amount of about Rs.500 per group in 2004/2005, the interest subsidy increased to Rs.4512 per group in 2011/2012.

As pointed out earlier, besides accessing institutional credit at regulated or subsidised interest rates, the SHGs with the assistance of SERP also undertake economic and social security-related activities such as providing land access to members, improving agricultural practices through the Community Managed Sustainable Agriculture (CMSA) programme, promoting dairying by establishing a network of milk-chilling plants and training SHG members in milk production and collection, introducing collective agricultural commodity marketing, extending micro-insurance to members' families in collaboration with the Life Insurance Corporation (LIC), and disbursing pensions under the National Social Assistance Scheme (NSAS).

What the SHG–BL model in AP demonstrates is that community-based organisations with adequate training and motivation are not only sustainable as institutions providing low-cost credit to the poor and marginalised, but also have the potential to undertake a wide range of mutually reinforcing activities that enable better utilisation of credit, besides meeting the contingent needs of these communities. There have been similar successes with the SHG–BL model in Tamil Nadu and Karnataka, and a panchayat-linked SHG–BL model in Kerala. In March 2001, 71 per cent of the bank-linked SHGs in the country were from the four southern states (NABARD 2008: 80). The model also seemed to be progressing well even in Bihar (Tiwari 2010).

MFIs in AP

This section deals with the 'transformation' of socially oriented thrift and credit institutions into profit-seeking MFIs which brought into prominence the issue of oversight and regulation of MFIs with particular reference to AP. In spite of the

106 *D.N. Reddy*

positive record of not-for-profit SHG–BL as the dominant model of microfinance in states like AP, there have been concerted global efforts to depict SHG–BL as financially unviable and unsustainable. The costs and subsidies involved in promoting SHG–BL have been exaggerated, and it is argued that unless these costs are recovered and higher rates of interest charged, credit provision under SHG–BL will become unsustainable.[2] There are simultaneously pressures on the government to create space for new, independent MFIs (Basu and Srivastava 2005).

These pressures can be traced to the celebration of microfinance through MFIs as the panacea for addressing problems of poverty and underdevelopment at the 1997 Microcredit Summit organised by the Consultative Group to Assist the Poorest (CGAP). The consensus at the Summit was in favour of extending credit to 100 million of the world's poorest families by the year 2005, seeing 'microcredit/microenterprises as the panacea' for addressing structural problems of poverty and underdevelopment. The CGAP, while promoting microfinance as a powerful tool to fight poverty, maintained that only with commercial capital could demand for financial services among the poor be fully met and that microfinance would only realise its potential if integrated into a country's mainstream financial system (Copestake 2007).

The neoliberal campaign for microfinance to be profitable and only then sustainable has been persistent. The designation of 2005 as the UN International Year of Microcredit with an emphasis on sustainable microfinance served as a signal for global financial interests to project MFI as the model to be emulated across the globe. A huge euphoria was built around this approach. The following excerpt from UN Secretary General Kofi Annan's inaugural speech was quoted everywhere: '[S]ustainable access to microfinance helps alleviate poverty by generating income, creating jobs, allowing children to go to school, enabling family to obtain healthcare and empowering people to make the choices that best serve their needs.'

MFI transformation in AP

The promotion of for-profit private MFIs as the answer to the sustainability of microfinance had its impact on Indian microcredit. Inspired by the support provided by global financial interests, some of the not-for-profit credit societies transformed themselves into for-profit MFIs. The methods adopted, the pace of progress, and the outcomes arising from this transformation created a public furore.

Here we focus on the process whereby not-for-profit microcredit societies were transformed into for-profit MFIs with particular reference to four large MFIs in AP, and the business leap achieved by them, particularly after 2005. The main source for this section is the graphic and incisive analysis of the transformation by Sriram (2010). Before we analyse the four specific cases, a brief description of the formal status of 'not-for-profit' and 'for-profit' institutions and the methods adopted to move from the former to the latter are in order.

Microfinance and marginalised groups 107

Almost all 'not-for-profit' credit societies started with donor funds which were intended to benefit the poor. The not-for-profit societies were registered as 'charitable trusts or societies' for 'public purpose' with donor money for the 'larger social good'. There is no room for 'residual claims' by the organisers of the society either on current income (no dividends) or on liquidation proceeds. When the promoters of a not-for-profit charitable society decide to transform it into a 'for-profit' commercial non-bank financial company (NBFC), the problem is that the transfer of capital from the society to the NBFC is not legally permitted. Furthermore, the new NBFC requires a minimum of Rs.20 million for registration. The method adopted to solve the problem is to create a number of Mutual Benefit Trusts (MBTs), which can legally invest for profit, by making members of the credit societies members of MBTs, by lending or donating a society's funds to these members to invest in MBTs, and then getting the MBTs to invest in the newly floated NBFC.

Table 6.1 shows the phenomenal growth in the clientele of India's top 11 MFIs between 2005 and 2009. By 2009, AP, which was in the forefront in not-for-profit SHG–BL, was also at the top of the table in the case of private MFIs. Out of the top 11 private MFIs in India, five were promoted from AP. The top three MFIs in outreach in India were also based in the state. Most of these top MFIs started as public purpose not-for-profit societies. Here, we present briefly the transformation process of four MFIs from AP. These four are also the MFIs which experienced the highest growth across the country. Their growth is shown in Table 6.2.

SHARE Microfinance Ltd (SML)

The Society for Helping and Awakening the Rural Poor through Education (SHARE) was registered as a 'public purpose' society in 1989, when it started operating in two districts of AP. In 1999, it was rechristened SHARE Microfinance Limited (SML) and registered as an NBFC. By the end of March 2002, SML had expanded to 13 districts of the state with a cumulative loan disbursement of Rs.1084.7 million and a recovery rate of 100 per cent (Ray 2005). In 2002, SML

Table: 6.1 Growth of active borrowers in India's top 11 MFIs, 2005 to 2009

State of origin	Number of active clients (lakhs)	
	2009	*Added since 2005*
1 Andhra Pradesh (5 MFIs in India's top 11)	142.70	120.2
2 West Bengal (1 MFI in India's top 11)	23.01	21.5
3 Tamil Nadu (2 MFIs in India's top 11)	16.61	15.7
4 Karnataka (1 MFI in India's top 11)	17.93	15.6
5 Orissa (1 MFI in India's top 11)	3.06	1.8
All top 11 MFIs	200.00	175.0

Source: www.mixmarket.org as in Ramesh (2010a).

108   *D.N. Reddy*

Table: 6.2 Growth of active borrowers in top four MFIs of AP origin, 2002 to 2009

Name of MFI	Date of establishment	Number of clients (lakhs)			CAGR 2005–2009
		2002	2005	2009	
1 SKS (All India No. 1 in Outreach)	1 January 1997	0.11	1.18	57.95	118.57
2 Spandana Spoorty Financial Ltd (All India No. 2 in Outreach)	1 January 1998	0.34	7.23	36.63	79.43
3 SHARE Microfin Ltd (All India No. 3 in Outreach)	1 January 1999	1.32	8.17	23.57	43.37
4 Asmitha Microfin Ltd	1 January 2002	1.28	3.90	13.40	47.37

Source: www.mixmarket.org as in Ramesh (2010b).

floated two Mutually Aided Cooperative Societies (MACS). The 'residue', meaning the resources of the public purpose society originally floated as SHARE, was given as a grant to members and transferred through members as the share capital of SML. In 2003/2004, SML provided loans to 4000 members of their MACS at the rate of Rs.1000 each, and got them to invest the entire amount, Rs.40 million, in SML, the NBFC. By 2005/2006, the share capital of SML was Rs.200 million, but the number of shareholders had fallen to 3000. By 2006/2007, the promoter family's shares had reached 57 per cent, and another 40 per cent of the shares were owned by an investment company wholly owned by the family. The total number of shareholders had dwindled to 68 (Sriram 2010). In 2007/2008, the salary of the Managing Director (MD) (a member of the family) was Rs.22.9 million per annum. The following year it was increased to Rs.80.8 million, i.e. 15 per cent of total personnel costs (Sriram 2010).

Asmitha Microfinance Ltd

Asmitha was promoted by the same family that controlled SML. In 2003/2004 the share capital was Rs.20 million, and it had 59 shareholders. In 2006/2007 the salary of the MD (the wife of the MD of SML) was fixed at Rs.3.4 million. The following year the MD's salary was raised to Rs.35 million and accounted for roughly 11 per cent of total personnel costs. A daughter was also made a full-time Director at an annual salary of Rs.2.4 million (Sriram 2005).

Spandana Spoorthy Innovative Financials (SSIF)

'Spandana' was registered in 1998 as a public purpose 'not-for-profit' society (Sriram 2005). By 2003 it had decided to go private and it provided a grant of Rs.1000 to each of its 20,000 members who it then got to invest in its for-profit

Microfinance and marginalised groups 109

MBT. SSIF was registered as an NBFC with investment transferred from the MBT, and it obtained a 'transformation loan' from the public sector Small Industries Development Bank of India (SIDBI). It also received securitisation investment from the ICICI Bank. By 2007 the MBT shares had been picked up by the 'family promoters' and the MD's salary was Rs.3.6 million per annum. This was raised to Rs.8.9 million the following year.

SKS Microfinance Ltd

Swayam Krushi Sangham (SKS) was registered in 1997 as a not-for-profit public purpose society with a declaration: 'Our purpose is to eradicate poverty. We do that by providing financial services to the poor and by using our channel to provide goods and services that the poor need.' In 2003 it applied for registration as an NBFC under the name SKS Microfinance Ltd and in 2005 it obtained a licence for operation as an NBFC. SKS had donated Rs.20.5 million to society members and got them to float five MBTs. By 2006 the portfolios of these five MBTs had increased to Rs.780 million. The entire sum was transferred to SKS. SIDBI also extended loans to SKS. The MD did not take any salary but in 2007 he allotted himself shares valued at Rs.16 million which he sold for Rs.166 million after 18 months. In 2009 he allotted himself shares at substantially below the market value of Rs.49.7 each, and after three months he sold these at a market price of Rs.636 each, netting a total of Rs.550 million. By 2010, SKS Microfinance Ltd had emerged as one of the leading MFIs in the country with an estimated 5.8 million clients. Garnering attention in the right financial circles, including obtaining the 2006 TIME Magazine award for Hundred Global Achievers for the MD, SKS was the first MFI in India to go for public issue. The issue was oversubscribed 13 times. Investors included Morgan Stanley, J.P. Morgan and George Soros's Quantum Fund.

There was political turmoil in the state in 2006 on the issue of unethical practices of MFIs (see below). In spite of SML being at the centre of this, there was continued unashamed amassing of wealth both in 2006 and the years immediately following. The hegemony of global finance capital aggressively promoting profits at the 'bottom of the pyramid', the anxiety of public agencies like SIDBI and even the RBI to see MFIs as agents of 'financial inclusion' of the poor, and the growing clout of some of the MFIs in political circles, drove the growth of MFIs, regardless of client complaints on the nature of the practices they followed. At the same time as MFIs were busy distancing themselves from their self-appointed social mission and turning to the pursuit of economic returns at the expense of poor clients, bilateral and multilateral agencies and development finance institutions were shifting from grants to more commercially oriented funding to microfinance.[3] After another major crisis in MFI lending in AP in 2010 and in spite of serious concerns raised by borrowers and the state government, the RBI, concerned about 'the specific needs of (the) microfinance sector', permitted MFIs in 2011 to increase external commercial borrowing to $10 million in a financial year (Nair 2012).

110   D.N. Reddy

Nefarious practices of MFIs

The period of surge in membership and expansion of lending also saw the beginning of widespread protests against MFI practices. The methods adopted in the transformation of 'not-for-profit' public purpose societies into 'for-profit' companies shown above demonstrate their unethical underpinnings. The MFIs in AP had benefited from the pre-existing SHGs which had been nurtured on the basis of state support. Thirty per cent of the clients of SML overlapped with the membership of government-supported SHGs (Sriram 2006). Rapid scaling up was the MFI thrust. There were clear confessions of multiple lending by MFIs to shared Joint Liability Groups (JLGs) and clients (Ramesh 2010b). Spreading resources across clients without sufficient vetting of their needs and capacity to repay led to coercive methods of recovery that resulted in public outrage.

The rapid growth of MFIs in AP was accompanied by growing grievances from borrowers. The first major wave of grievances caught media attention in March 2006 and culminated in widespread public protests and government intervention (Shylendra 2006). The Collector of Krishna district ordered the suspension of operations of about 50 branches of four leading MFIs, two of which had been labelled 'Bellwhether MFIs of India' (Sriram 2006). Complaints related mainly to three issues:

1   Exorbitant interest and other concealed charges.
2   Unethical and coercive methods of recovery.
3   Poaching of members of SHG–BL programmes (NALSAR 2011; Ramesh 2010b).

First, the rate of interest has been one of the critical issues in lending to the poor. MFIs use group lending to reduce transaction costs, but not interest rates. On the contrary, interest rates shown as 'flat rates' of about 15 per cent effectively worked out at 35 to 50 per cent. MFIs also collected membership fees, bank charges, documentation charges, loan security amounts, insurance charges and, in some cases, deposits without interest. Fines were often levied if repayment was delayed even by a day.

Second, unethical ways of recovering loans were the cause of resort to extreme measures such as suicide by some borrowers. Loans were often combined with insurance, and insurance charges were recovered from loans but the policy papers were retained by MFIs. The 'nominee' in the policy was shown as the MFI, not the MFI borrower, or the borrower's family members. Many members and their families were kept in the dark about the insurance. In cases where members died, the insured amount was recovered by the MFIs and not passed on to the bereaved family. Although theoretically MFIs lend without collateral, in most cases blank promissory notes or blank white papers with the signature of the borrowers were retained by MFIs. If the loan amount was high, land title deeds or house-site pattas were retained by MFI branches. Further, there was extensive documentation of wide-ranging coercive practices of loan recovery (Ramesh 2010b). The methods

Microfinance and marginalised groups 111

included the use of abusive language, criminal trespass, kidnapping, wrongful confinement, criminal intimidation and the assault of women.

The third set of undesirable practices resorted to by MFIs included poaching SHG–BL members and multiple lending, resulting in debt traps for poor borrowers (Sriram 2006; Ramesh 2010b). For instance, it was found that 40 per cent of mature members and 31 per cent of new members of SHARE were also members of government-sponsored SHGs (Kabeer 2005). In some villages the SHG–BL became passive with the advent of MFIs. Most MFI clients were saddled with multiple loans. Many of the loans were used to repay the loan of another MFI. Members were often caught up in a vicious debt trap due to these multiple loans (GoAP 2006).

There were a number of investigations into these practices. A Coordination Committee was formed in 2006 at the behest of the AP state government with representatives of the RBI, MFIs, banks and the state government. A code of conduct for MFIs proposed by the Sa-Dhan, the agency representing MFIs, was agreed upon. The code included a self-imposed cap of 15 to 20 per cent on interest rates and self-regulation of MFI practices. It was also decided that the MFIs would return house pattas and blank signed bond papers to clients. It was agreed to undertake a detailed inquiry into the functioning of some of the MFIs in the state.

The events of 2006 should have acted as a warning signal to MFIs, but there were contradictory signals from the powers that mattered at the national level. Except for deputing an officer to represent it on the Coordination Committee, the RBI did not initiate any inquiry into NBFC-MFIs (Sriram 2011). There were strong signals from the Central Finance Ministry not to interfere with MFIs. For instance, in November 2006, P. Chidambaram, the then Finance Minister of the Government of India, observed: 'The cost of delivering credit through micro-finance route involves cost. We need to educate people on microfinance in order to make them understand the model.' He went on to add that the government's role in regulating the microfinance segment would be minimal. 'The MFI Act would make only minimal regulation of microfinance activity. The regulation would be focused only on those taking public deposits' (*The Hindu*, 6 November 2006). In 2008, when NABARD appointed a committee on financial inclusion, the Rangarajan Committee, there was a major opportunity to make a proper assessment of developments in microcredit and provide a road-map for healthy microcredit expansion. However, the Rangarajan Committee (NABARD 2008) appeared to be totally oblivious to the developments in the MFI sector highlighted by the 2006 crisis in AP. It pronounced a death sentence to the expansion of SHG–BL by concluding that the financial support provided by NABARD and the Ministry of Rural Development was not sustainable (NABARD 2008: 79–80). The Committee was guilty of total insensitivity to the public revulsion at the practices on which MFIs themselves had agreed to have a code of conduct, and instead joined the global lobby in celebrating the virtues of microfinance. It observed that MFIs could play a significant role in facilitating inclusion since they were

112   D.N. Reddy

uniquely positioned in reaching out to the rural poor! It went on to say that MFIs had 'greater understanding of the rural poor', 'greater acceptability amongst rural poor' and 'have flexibility in operations providing a level of *comfort* to their clientele' (NABARD 2008: 87–89, emphasis added). It recommended a separate category – of NBFCs, Microfinance (NBFC-MFI), provision of equity support by NABARD, Securities and Exchange Board of India (SEBI) permission for the use of venture capital funds in MFIs, and tax concessions to the extent of 40 per cent of profits of MFIs in excluded districts (NABARD 2008: 89). The language and the tenor of these recommendations echo the views of the MFI representative on the Committee.

In the euphoria of support from global financial institutions and determined policy signals from the highest levels in India, the MFIs in AP threw all caution to the winds, left the code of conduct in cold storage and resorted to aggressive expansion by whatever means they could muster. Growth of MFIs in the state continued unabated. By 2010, there was another wave of suicides by MFI borrowers and a return to a focus on all the earlier malpractices of MFIs which would have been contained had the code of conduct been enforced.

From regulatory failure to regulatory capture

One of the major reasons for periodic turmoil in the commercial microfinance sector is the neglect of proper oversight or regulation. In 1999, when the first efforts were made to evolve a regulatory framework for microcredit by appointing a Task Force (NABARD 1999), whatever microcredit existed was dominated by the SHG–BL programme, and commercial microfinance was miniscule. There were three types of institutions to which banks awarded loans for on-lending. These were public purpose credit societies registered as not-for-profit cooperatives, NBFCs and NGO-microfinance institutions. The NBFCs, which currently dominate commercial microfinance, were yet to show their colours.

The Task Force assumed that cooperatives were regulated under the concerned legislation, and NBFCs by the RBI. It focused on NGO-microfinance institutions, and recommended the promotion of a self-regulating organisation (SRO) for them. The Task Force did not provide any framework that would help in regulating commercial MFIs. Furthermore, one of the casual recommendations that bank loans to MFIs should be treated as 'priority sector lending' (PSL) benefited commercial MFIs immensely (Sane and Thomas 2013).

It was not until the 2006 crisis in AP that the question of how to handle the irregularities of the activities of commercial MFIs was raised again. In 2006, when the Krishna District Collector received complaints from borrowers of MFIs, he had only one law which came close to regulating lenders with usurious interest rates, and that was the Money Lenders' Regulation Act. The MFIs protested that the state government had no authority to take action against them since they were NBFCs regulated by the RBI. Given that there was virtually no RBI regulatory mechanism for NBFC-MFIs even in 2011, the following observation of an RBI Committee is nothing short of astounding:

Microfinance and marginalised groups 113

[W]hile it may be true that perhaps in the past the Reserve Bank did not regulate this sector as vigorously as it should have done, with the lessons which have been learnt, there is no reason why it should not adequately regulate this sector in the future.

(RBI 2011: 48–49)

In the context of a regulatory void the government of AP came out with the AP Microfinance Institutions (Regulation of Money Lenders) Act 2010. The basic premise of AP was that the operations of MFIs were reminiscent of money-lending activities with usurious rates of interest, coercive debt collection practices and mis-selling of microcredit products (GoAP 2011). The contention of AP was that activities similar to moneylending were constitutionally the domain of state regulation, and hence it went ahead with the legislation to regulate MFIs. However, the Malegam Committee appointed by the RBI (2011) took a proactive view in favour of MFIs stating that *if* regulations recommended by it were implemented, and *if* MFIs honoured commitments made under the code of conduct, 'a new dawn will emerge for the microfinance sector and *the need for state intervention will no longer exist*' (RBI 2011: P54, emphasis added). The Committee's recommendations placed significant emphasis on prudential norms for MFIs, and addressed the problem of systemic failure due to MFI risk. The basic difference between the regulatory approach of the RBI Committee and that of the AP government was that while the former was overly concerned about the *prudential* risk, the latter was concerned about the *lack of protection* for small borrowers. The AP experience shows that MFIs are too small to be a source of systemic risk and what is important is *protection* of the small borrower (Sahoo *et al.* 2012). A central government initiative to bring about national legislation also aims at taking the regulation of MFIs out of the purview of the state. The Microfinance Institutions (Development and Regulation) Bill was introduced in 2007 as a consequence of the developments in AP in 2006, but the Bill lapsed due to the dissolution of the Lok Sabha in 2009. The Bill was reintroduced with some modifications in 2012. The Bill is biased in favour of MFIs, and against state intervention, and instead of bringing in the moneylender element it sees MFIs as 'the extended arms of banks and financial services' (Sahoo *et al.* 2012).

Not surprisingly the MFI sector is comfortable with the Bill. In fact the share value of the only listed MFI, SKS, which had been dwindling for several months, rose on the day the Bill was introduced in Parliament.

The government of AP raised a number of serious concerns arising out of the nature of the proposals in the Bill (GoAP 2011). Among its objections were, first, that it found the description of MFIs as 'extended arms of the banks' fallacious taking into consideration the lending practices, interest rates and recovery practices of banks which are radically different from MFIs. Allowing MFIs to accept deposits and other privileges would amount to making them banks through the 'back door' without any corresponding responsibilities. Second, Section 42 of the Bill says that none of the activities of the MFIs shall be categorised as 'moneylending', thereby taking the MFIs out of the purview of

114   *D.N. Reddy*

moneylenders' regulation. The Bill should have treated MFIs as involved in moneylending activities and brought them under the ambit of moneylending regulation. Third, allowing MFIs to collect the savings of the poor, which so far MFIs have not been allowed to do, would be extending a special dispensation to these institutions instead of bringing them under regulation.

It was not only the government of AP that raised objections to the Bill. The then Union Rural Development Minister, Jairam Ramesh, observed that 'the Bill, as currently drafted, will have adverse impact on the SHG movement in India' (*The Hindu*, 15 April 2012). A former Governor of the RBI cautioned that

> RBI does not have the organizational presence in the rural areas where the MFI activity is concentrated. In my view, the RBI may be unnecessarily exposed to serious reputational risks. In any case, it will be initially imposs-ible for the RBI to conduct its regulation and supervisory functions in rural areas without full cooperation of the state governments.
>
> (Y.V. Reddy 2011)

One of the unique aspects of lending to the poor is the political risk. The pro-posal of the Bill to consider MFIs as an 'extended arm of banking' and extend the facility of MFIs to taking deposits from low-income households would threaten the savings of large numbers of the poor in the case of bankruptcy of an MFI. This would certainly call for political action in the form of bailing out poor savers in the event of an MFI collapse.

Concluding observations

We may reflect on why and how AP emerged as a leading state in the growth of the SHG movement to begin with, and, closely on the heels of this, the MFIs. In 1991, the Government of India, at the behest of the World Bank, launched its struc-tural adjustment programme (SAP) along with a set of safety net programmes to soften the adverse impact of reforms on the poor. With the coalition government at the centre, and state governments belonging to different political parties, the cen-tre's power to push reforms at the state level was limited. In AP, Chandrababu Naidu, who became Chief Minister in 1995, was desperate to establish his creden-tials as a leader, and to mobilise resources to shore up state finances which were in a poor state. In 1995/1996 the AP government ushered in an agenda of economic reforms under the AP Economic Restructuring Project (APERP). The mother of all reforms under APERP was 'fiscal reform' which envisioned that the government would make a shift from being a promoter and regulator to a facilitator. This involved reducing the fiscal involvement of the state in the economy and the welfare of the people, leaving them to market-driven incentives.

Putting the poor on to thrift-based credit linked to banks was part of the reform agenda. The Chandrababu Naidu government realised the political potential of SHGs and facilitated their rapid expansion through the expansion of credit and other programmes. The Congress government which succeeded Chandrababu

Microfinance and marginalised groups 115

Naidu's in 2004 went one step further in launching the 'pavala vaddi' programme (see above).

The availability of SHGs on which they could piggy-back, and more importantly the global donor and microfinance intermediaries which saw huge opportunities for profits at the bottom of the pyramid, brought about the rapid expansion of MFIs, along with politically explosive practices of usurious interest rates and extortionate recovery practices. The MFIs were also seen as a liability for the expansion of the SHG movement which was important politically at the state level. While the Congress Party in AP had to intervene to regulate MFIs, Chandrababu Naidu directed his criticism at the centre, saying: 'the encouragement given by Congress President Sonia Gandhi and AICC General Secretary Rahul Gandhi had given scope for the MFIs to continue their activities unabated' (*The Hindu*, 28 October 2010).

MFIs and the poor

The real politics lie in the rise of finance capital and the politics of protecting the poor as a political constituency. The entry of MFIs into India came with the strong armour of arguments that MFI interest rates were not high compared to those of informal sources like moneylenders, and that sustainable microfinance was possible through cost recovery. While SHGs in the bank-linkage programme are managed largely by members themselves, the high costs of MFIs are due to extra personnel like loan officers for business expansion, recovery agents for coercive collection, high salaries of MDs, etc.

The argument that MFI interest rates are not high compared to credit card interest rates, or those of moneylenders, or comparable MFIs in countries like Mexico, and that 'the burgeoning volume of money pouring through international microfinance investment funds is coming mainly from *investors who are not willing to accept higher risks or lower returns for the sake of social objectives*' (Rosenberg *et al.* 2009, emphasis added), is a clear argument in favour of the free play of predatory market capitalism. The range of about 30 to 50 per cent effective interest rates charged by large MFIs cannot be considered 'fair' by any standards. Another question is: should institutions with high cost structures deal with the poor who are borrowing mostly for basic needs? Should the concern shown for the sustainability of commercial microfinance blind one to the question of survival of the poor without getting into debt traps?

There are two major problems in MFIs lending to the poor: a moral problem and a problem of political risk. First, it is immoral to allow MFIs to borrow from banks at low rates of interest and to permit on-lending to the poor at high rates of interest to meet basic needs. Second, there is a huge political risk which works both against the political parties in power and the MFIs profiting from the poor. The poor have rights as citizens to mobilise for better provision of basic needs by the state. Exposing them to the hazards of high interest loans associated with coercive methods of recovery is a power keg that could explode, jeopardising the loan portfolio of MFIs (there is ample evidence of that from the AP

116 D.N. Reddy

experience) and also putting the political fortunes of parties in power at stake. Therefore, it is desirable that MFIs desist from entering the arena of lending to the poor particularly for 'non-income-generating activities' and that political parties pursue policies that not only ensure effective regulation of MFIs but also strengthen institutions like the SHG–BL in their multiple roles as institutions of the poor.

Notes

1 An earlier version of this paper were presented at the MIDS-ICSSR National Seminar on 'Indian Economy in Transition: Prospects, Issues and Concerns', Madras Institute of Development Studies, Chennai, 10–11 February 2011. The author is grateful for comments of the participants in the seminar, namely Judith Heyer, Barbara Harris-White and Y.V. Reddy. The usual disclaimers apply. The help of C.P. Nagi Reddy of SERP in securing material on the progress of SHG–BL in AP is gratefully acknowledged.
2 There are fundamental differences in the cost structure between MFIs and the SHG–BL. For instance, accepting the data provided by the MFIs, the High Powered Committee of the RBI arrives at an estimate of 12.39 per cent of the loan portfolio as the 'total internal cost' of an MFI (RBI 2011). And, if the external cost of funds borrowed even at a minimum rate of 10.20 per cent is added, it comes to about 23 per cent, a rate below which an MFI would incur loss. These high costs of MFIs are due to staff, overheads and coverage for loan losses, all of which do not exist in the SHG–BL model which is operated almost entirely on a self-help basis.
3 Between January 2007 and March 2009 14 deals worth $230 million were struck by Indian MFIs (Nair 2012: 37).

References

Basu, Priya and Srivatsava, Pradeep (2005) 'Exploring possibilities in microfinance and rural credit access to the poor in India', *Economic and Political Weekly*, 40(17): 1747–1755.
CGAP (2007) 'Sustainability of self-help groups in India: two analyses', *Occasional Paper No. 12*, CGAP, August.
—— (2010) 'Andhra Pradesh 2010: global implications of the crisis in Indian microfinance', *Focus Note No. 67*, November.
Copestake, J. (2007) 'Mainstreaming microfinance: social performance, management or mission drift?', *World Development*, 35(10): 1721–1738.
GoAP (2006) *Enquiry Report of Dr. V.P. Jauhari, Special Chief Secretary into the Issue Relating to the Closure of Microfinance Companies in Krishna District*, Hyderabad: Government of AP.
—— (2011) *Government of AP's Submission Before the RBI Sub-Committee of the Central Board of Directors to Study Issues and Concerns in MFI Sector*, Hyderabad: Government of AP.
Kabeer, N. (2005) 'Is microfinance a "magic bullet" for women's empowerment? Analysis of findings from South Asia', *Economic and Political Weekly*, 40(44–45): 4709–4718.
NABARD (1999) *Report of the Task Force on Microfinance*, Mumbai: NABARD.
—— (2008) *Report of the Committee on Financial Inclusion*, Mumbai: NABARD, January.

Microfinance and marginalised groups 117

—— (2009) *The Status of Microfinance in India 2008–09*, Mumbai: NABARD.

Nair, T.S. (2012) 'Financing of Indian microfinance: experience and implications', *Economic and Political Weekly*, 47(25): 33–40.

NALSAR (2011) *A Study of Microfinance Institutions in Andhra Pradesh*, a study conducted for SERP by NALSAR University students, Hyderabad: NALSAR University of Law.

Ramesh, S. Arunachalam (2010a) *It is Easy to Confess Today but why did MFIs Engage in Such (Over) Lending in the First Place?*, blog posted on 10 November.

—— (2010b) *Candid Unheard Voice of Indian Microfinance*, a series of bulletins posted on the net by Ramesh S. Arunachalam, November.

Ray, Nandita (2005) *Alternative Banking for Rural Women: The NGO Experience: Some Issues of Upscaling*, Ph.D. thesis submitted to Dr B.R. Ambedkar Open University, Hyderabad.

RBI (2011) *Report of the Sub-Committee of the Central Board of Directors of Reserve Bank of India to Study Issues and Concerns in the MFI Sector*, Mumbai: RBI, January.

Reddy, Y.V. (2011) 'Microfinance industry in India: some thoughts', *Economic and Political Weekly*, 41: 46–49.

Rosenberg, Richard, Gonzalez, Adrian and Narain, Sushma (2009) 'The new moneylenders: are the poor being exploited by high microcredit interest rates?', *Occasional Paper No. 15*, CGAP, February.

Sane, Renuka and Thomas, Susan (2013) 'Regulating microfinance institutions', *Economic and Political Weekly*, 48(5): 59–67.

SERP (2012) *Society for Elimination of Rural Poverty: Indira Kranthi Patham*, Hyderabad: SERP.

Sahoo, M., Sane, Renuka and Thomas, Susan (2012) 'How is financial regulation different for micro finance?', *IGIDR Working Paper No. WP-2012–005*, Mumbai.

Shenoy, Suchitra (2002) *Macro–Micro Linkages: Microfinance and Social Mobilisation in Andhra Pradesh*, Hyderabad: SERP.

Shylendra, H.S. (2006) 'Microfinance institutions in Andhra Pradesh: crisis and diagnosis', *Economic and Political Weekly*, 41(20): 1959–1963.

Sriram, M.S. (2005) 'Expanding financial services access to the poor: the transformation of SPANDANA', *IIM – A Working Paper Series 2003–04*.

—— (2006) 'Microcredit in India: microsharks', *The Economist* (London), 19 August: 62–63.

—— (2010) 'Commercialisation of microfinance in India: a discussion on the emperor's apparel', *Economic and Political Weekly*, 45(24): 65–73.

—— (2011) 'Microfinance industry in India: more thoughts', *Economic and Political Weekly*, 46(50): 110–111.

Tiwari, M. (2010) 'Didi of Rural Bihar: real agent of change?', *Economic and Political Weekly*, 45(33): 27–30.

7 Labour in contemporary south India

Isabelle Guérin, G. Venkatasubramanian and Sébastien Michiels*

Introduction

This chapter is greatly inspired by Barbara Harriss-White's work on the social regulation of the Indian labour landscape.[1] Harriss-White's renewed approach to political economics and her intensive field research have shown the extent to which social institutions such as caste, class, gender, age, space, religion and the state affect property rights and transfers, production processes and labour. Her micro-studies highlight processes overlooked by large-scale surveys, showing that markets, just like scarcity, are historical and social institutionalised processes. She examines the reproduction and evolution of power relationships, and how these are shaped by and constitutive of larger socioeconomic and political dynamics. This is by no means a deterministic form of reasoning: she discusses the distinctive ways in which institutions evolve, interact and mutually reinforce one another according to local circumstances and the historical period. Our goal has been to adopt such an approach in our work. This draws on fieldwork from villages in Tamil Nadu from over the past ten years to examine how labour interrelates with social and political structures, and how it interacts with other forms of institutions, especially credit. We also consider how variable levels of access to a variety of resources can have a wide range of impacts. We evaluate the specific characteristics and the diversity of local effects, considering phenomena that may escape large-scale surveys, while taking the micro-level as indicative of broader structural dynamics.

Employment structures in rural India have changed significantly over recent decades. It is well known that agriculture has been steadily declining in terms of GDP share and employment rates. In 2009/2010, only 51.8 per cent of workers worked in agriculture, in contrast to 81.6 per cent in 1983, despite the fact that most of the population still lives in so-called rural areas. The decline of agricultural labour has so far not been compensated by growing or prosperous industrial employment. Rural workers, whether landless or marginal farmers, survive by combining several sources of livelihood. This is a complex, often precarious process, devoid of any form of social protection. The latest NSSO data indicate that employment informalisation continues to rise, with 93 per cent of the workforce belonging to the informal economy (Government of India 2012).

Labour in contemporary south India 119

Social differentiation is no longer solely determined by landownership and the form of agriculture practised. Traditional categories such as 'poor peasant', 'middle peasant' and 'rich peasant' have become obsolete (Shah and Harriss-White 2011). As Bernstein and Lerche argue, the concept of 'classes of labour', defined as all those 'who now depend – directly and indirectly – on the sale of their labour power for their own daily reproduction' (Bernstein 2010: 111) offers a useful framework for analysing the 'fluidity of labour relations for workers of rural origin' (Lerche 2010: 66).

Contemporary labour in the countryside is highly dynamic: workers regularly switch occupations, employment status and places of work, either over their life-times or on a seasonal basis. Circular migration has always been a practice, but it is on the rise (Srivastava 2012). There are an estimated 50 million seasonal migrants in India (Breman 2011: 7). Labour is also extremely segmented and fragmented (Harriss-White 2003; Lerche 2010). Scheduled Castes and Sched-uled Tribes still face considerable discrimination and remain specialised in the most precarious and degrading jobs. They are twice as likely to carry out casual agricultural labour and to be poor (Harriss-White and Gooptu 2001). They account for the bulk of bonded labourers (Srivastava 2005; Breman *et al.* 2009). Compared to others with the same education levels and occupation, they are paid less and their working conditions are poorer (Thorat and Newman 2010). Gender is also an important source of segregation and discrimination: women are far more likely to carry out agricultural work, to work from home, to have casual contracts and to receive low wages (Harriss-White 2003; Harriss-White and Gooptu 2001; Srivastava 2012). Life cycle position also counts: not only are many Indian children and elderly people forced to work, but employers discrimi-nate against them (Harriss-White 2010a).

Against this general background, this chapter draws on a micro-level analysis of several villages in coastal/central Tamil Nadu to highlight broader trends which we believe are key to the future of Indian labour. The micro-level analysis confirms some general trends while highlighting a variety of situations and pro-cesses that do not emerge at the macro level.

The first trend is the increasing importance of non-farm employment in rural areas: it is now a fundamental part of rural household income, much of it remain-ing precarious and without any form of social protection. Another trend relates to the segmentation and fragmentation of labour along various lines, such as caste, class, gender and space. Although there is nothing new in this, two fea-tures of contemporary labour markets deserve to be noted.

First, we observe a growing differentiation among Dalits, within local areas and also between locations. While some local labour markets are nothing other than new forms of bondage, others allow Dalits to achieve some form of upward mobility. The latter is partly related to the increasing importance of small towns. This trend has facilitated new forms of short-distance, individual and intermediary-free labour circulation, and allowed for greater political engage-ment in villages, which in turn has facilitated access to government programmes. At the same time, neo-bondage relationships persist, and remain mostly a Dalit

120   *I. Guérin* et al.

phenomenon. Beyond individual and household-specific trajectories, this diversity is closely related to specific village patterns. The micro-level analysis highlights the variety of village economies, which in turn result from diverse and interrelated factors. Agro-ecological conditions, proximity to industrial centres or small towns, financial markets, social and political structures (land concentration, caste interdependence, political mobilization, etc.) give rise to a wide diversity of social, economic and political dynamics and a wide diversity of modes of integration into the global economy.

Second, segmentation along gender lines seems to be on the rise. Non-farm employment opportunities are mostly a male preserve, while agricultural labour is increasingly female. We also observe that the wage gap between men and women is increasing. It seems that women are systematic losers in the changing labour landscape.

Third, we suggest that our understanding of labour is inseparable from consumption. Labourers switch between multiple forms of employment, positions, places and sectors of work (Picherit 2012). We argue that labourers' movements are influenced by the opportunities available to them, their social relationships – which still affect labour access – and the rising cost of education, social and religious rituals, and consumer goods. Even as caste and class are still constitutive of individual and collective identities, we believe that increasing access to consumption is also a major factor in the transformation of social statuses.

Data and context

This chapter draws on a collection of cases studies conducted over the past ten years in coastal/central Tamil Nadu by a team at the French Institute of Pondicherry. It is well known that human development indicators in Tamil Nadu are better than in most Indian states, although average indicators conceal considerable regional disparities. The increasing importance of non-agricultural income resulting from industrialisation and a variety of social policies has clearly contributed to this (Harriss-White and Colatei 2004; Vijayabaskar *et al.* 2004). Various micro-studies have confirmed these broad trends. Although pockets of poverty remain, and new forms of servitude have emerged (Guérin *et al.* 2009; Guérin and Venkatasubramanian 2009; Roesch *et al.* 2009), various recent micro-studies drawing on longitudinal data have highlighted Dalits' relative upward social mobility (Djurfeldt *et al.* 2008; Harriss *et al.* 2010, 2013; Heyer 2012).[2] Such micro-studies confirm that social change has been driven by the shift to non-farming labour due to migration, local industrialization, and social policies. Our own observations largely confirm these broad trends, while highlighting significant disparities between and among villages.

The villages studied cover a very small part of Tamil Nadu – around 20 villages located in Villupuram and Cuddalore district, known as the former south-Arcot region. We started field work in 2003 with a focus on bonded labour – seasonal migrants who migrate for six to eight months per year to brick kilns or sugar cane fields. These labour arrangements can be found in a number of

Labour in contemporary south India 121

Dalit settlements in both districts. Over time we extended our fieldwork to other villages, with the idea of including different types of local economies to capture more of the diversity of labour and financial markets. In 2010 we undertook a household survey comprising ten villages in a contiguous zone at the border of the two districts, the main purpose of which was to quantify the diversity of labour and financial arrangements at the household level. This zone illustrates very distinct trends. One can find pockets of bonded labour migrants, but also "post-agrarian" villages, where Dalits enjoy relative autonomy and have experienced relative social mobility over the last decades.

In this area, agriculture continues to be a dynamic industry. The Pennaiyar river from which many irrigation canals are derived crosses both districts. The most common crops in Tamil Nadu are found. Rice and sugarcane are grown in the irrigated area. Cashew nuts are grown in the driest zone. Three towns in this area (Cuddalore, 173,000 inhabitants in 2011), Neyveli (106,000 inhabitants) and Panruti (56,000 inhabitants) have very strong economies. The area also exemplifies an increasingly common geographical feature of rural India: smaller towns as opposed to megacities are an increasing source of urban growth (Denis and Marius-Gnanou (2011). The surveyed area is ten to thirty kilometres from the three towns above, and lies along either side of the road linking Cuddalore and Salem. The household survey was carried out in March 2010, with 405 households surveyed. Within the chosen area, households and villages were randomly selected, with a stratified sample based on caste at the household level and location at the village level (water availability and quality of infrastructure).

The industrial town of Neyveli dates from the 1960s, when a state-run lignite mine and a thermal power station were constructed. Workers in both state enterprises still live on site in purpose-built housing, enjoying considerable privileges. However there are also many small-scale subcontracting industries on the site, which hire local workers and migrants. A few kilometers away, the coastal town of Cuddalore is also highly industrialised. While it has long specialised in fishing, it now also embraces large scale agribusinesses such as sugar cane and cashew nut processing, and pharmaceutical and petrochemical industries. Panruti is twenty kilometers away. It is one of the district's commercial centres and an export market. Panruti is a big player in the cashew and jackfruit export business. The local non-farm labour market is thus highly dynamic, and goes far beyond agriculture.

Vanniyars and Paraiyars are the two major population groups in the region as a whole. Vanniyars are a farming caste with a low ritual rank, classified as Most Backward Classes, but they are a dominant caste from the perspective of Srinivas (1987) in this region. In the villages we studied, as with many in coastal/central Tamil Nadu, they control much of the land and are politically dominant (Trouillet 2009). There are also a few Gramanis, Navithars, Nattars, Kulalars and Asarais, who occupy a similar position in the caste hierarchy. Paraiyars are one of the three major Dalit communities in Tamil Nadu. They are particularly well established in the north of the state (Arun 2009). A few Arunthathiyars also rank among the Dalits. As in many other northeast Tamil Nadu villages, conflict

122   *I. Guérin* et al.

often breaks out between Vanniyars and Paraiyars (Arun 2009; Pandian 2013; Trouillet 2009) over a variety of issues including the use of common land, temple management, religious ritual organisation, local politics and access to government schemes and resources. The upper castes of the local hierarchy are Mudaliyars, Naidus, Reddiyars and Settus, and account for only a small proportion of the village population. As has been observed in other parts of Tamil Nadu (Djurfeldt *et al.* 2008; Harriss *et al.* 2010; Heyer 2012), many of the upper castes have mostly moved away from the villages in recent decades to nearby towns, adopting urban jobs and lifestyles. Their dominance has greatly declined but is by no means a thing of the past. Christians and Muslims are a minority in the area.

Non-farm labour and the precariat

The first major observation is the importance of non-farm – and precarious – labour. Most households combine different occupations in different places. According to our 2010 data, only 12.1 per cent of all households live off agriculture alone. The percentage of households living only from non-farm labour is similar (15.3 per cent) but significantly higher for upper castes (41.8 per cent as opposed to 9.9 and 10.3 per cent for Dalits and middle castes).

With the exception of a few upper-caste households who earn a living only from self-employment, juggling employment statuses (wage/self-employment) is the norm. Dalits stand out in this regard: one-third depend entirely on casual labour (as opposed to 10.3 per cent and 4.5 per cent for middle and upper castes).

Diversity of livelihood is associated with great vulnerability of labour. While low labour status used to be agricultural, we are now dealing with a large diversity of low-status jobs outside agriculture, mostly in construction, transport, markets, services (mostly security guards) and local industries. Even if wages – nominal and probably real[3] – have increased significantly over the past decade, non-farm labour remains irregular and outside any form of formal regulation.

Formal employment remains an exception. Our survey shows that irrespective of caste, there is a very small percentage of retirement benefits, which confirms the virtual absence of a retirement system. A tiny minority of present jobs include bonuses (6.2 per cent), health insurance (1.9 per cent) and pensions (4.4 per cent). Employment remains mostly informal. A significant number of labourers declare themselves as 'regular employees' but this is not related to any sort of formal protection. They describe themselves as 'regular' because there is some continuity in terms of tasks undertaken and employer. Coolie work by contrast is inherently unstable, both in terms of the task carried out and period of employment. The vast majority of regular employees have no written contract. Working time is determined by mutual agreement between the supervisor and the employee, and can be broken off at any time due to an unexpected production decline or conflicts between supervisors and workers.

'Casual labour' as a category incorporates a whole spectrum of situations and levels of financial insecurity, involving a trade-off of sorts (although labourers

Labour in contemporary south India   123

don't necessarily have much choice) between wages, how hard the work is, and how secure and regular the employment is. It is interesting to compare coolie labour work with neo-bondage. Coolie labour includes activities such as building work and work as a builder's assistant, driver or loader/unloader at the market. Wages have risen sharply in recent years, there are decent six- to eight-hour working days, and acceptable working conditions (although without any social protection, as noted above). In the area under study, neo-bondage activities include cane cutting and brick moulding. These labour arrangements are characterised by very long days (12 to 16 hours), extremely low wages (four to six times lower hourly wages than for coolies), restricted freedom, and harassment in exchange for a 'guarantee' of six to eight months of employment. Until the debt involved is repaid, borrowers are forced to work, but are also confident of having a job, and aware of the possibility of receiving lump sums of cash.[4]

Juggling occupations, recruiters/employers, farm and non-farm labour is a matter of risk diversification (and access to other resources, as we shall see later). But it is also a matter of identity, in particular with regard to the combination of farm and non-farm labour. The rise of non-farm labour does not necessarily translate into a willingness to abandon agriculture. This is particularly the case for upper castes, as mentioned above. Cultivating land is also a strong element in the social competition that engages Vanniyars ('middle castes') and Paraiyars (Dalits). For Dalits and middle castes, land and agriculture continue to play a central role, both in terms of occupation – money from non-farm labour is partly invested in land – and in terms of identity.

The social fragmentation of labour

Caste and class

An interesting feature of our survey is that Dalit household incomes are, on average, similar to non-Dalit.[5] This however should be nuanced for three reasons. First of all, there are still considerable disparities in terms of assets. Dalits have only half the total assets of non-Dalits, i.e. land, housing, agricultural equipment, vehicles and durable consumer goods. Second, Dalits receive similar incomes because Dalit women especially work more than others: while household size is roughly similar regardless of caste, there is almost one more job on average per Dalit household as compared to upper castes,[6] and this is entirely due to women's labour.[7]

Third, the nature of labour also differs. Dalits are more often casual labourers. Moreover, Dalit households have more migrants, they migrate further, for shorter periods, and more often for casual labour. In terms of the type of work carried out, the job market remains highly segmented along caste lines, including for the youth. Although educational disparities are declining, most Dalits and some middle castes spend most of their time carrying out unskilled manual labour. This includes mining in Neyveli, pharmaceutical company packaging work, assembly-line work in the automobile industry, loading and unloading in

124   *I. Guérin* et al.

sugar mills, Cuddalore harbour or Panruti markets, as well as hulling and drying cashew nuts in local industries in Cuddalore or Neyveli, Cuddalore harbour or Panruti markets. Non-Dalits, and especially upper castes, work in the same industries but more often as graduates in management and leadership positions.

The fragmentation of labour markets is also reflected in the caste of employers and in recruitment methods: one rarely recruits someone who is higher up in the caste hierarchy.[8] Labour fragmentation also contributes to substantial differences in wages earned. Except for daily wage labourers, upper castes are significantly better paid. A high-caste self-employed farmer earns 52 per cent more than a Dalit – this relates to the size of the landholdings but also, in all likelihood, to productivity (Harriss-White and Janakarajan 2004). The income/wage gap is 26 per cent for the self-employed, and 40 per cent for regular labourers.

In line with evidence all over India (Prakash 2010), starting and running a business remain the preserve of upper castes. In the surveyed area, 31.7 per cent of upper castes run an independent business against 12.2 per cent for middle castes and 6 per cent for Dalits. Multivariate analysis shows that caste (and gender) are very strong determinants of self-employment, while formal education has no influence (Guérin *et al.* 2013).

The relative upward mobility of Dalits, illustrated by the fact that Dalit incomes are not significantly lower than non-Dalit, is associated with increasing internal differentiation: the Gini index for assets and income is greater among Dalits than among the total population. Successful Dalits often work as labour intermediaries (especially in the brick kiln and cane-cutting industries), civil servants (teachers, white collar workers, etc.) or as moneylenders, which is often a secondary occupation for the previous two categories.

Gender

Important differences also emerge along the lines of gender, which in turn vary according to caste. Women's participation rates vary greatly according to caste: 35.2 per cent of Dalit women above age 14 do not work, as opposed to 50.2 per cent for middle castes and 62.9 per cent for upper castes. Caste differentiation also significantly influences the nature of work. Dalit and middle-caste women are mostly agricultural coolies. Upper-caste women work as agricultural coolies but also as self-employed (28.6 per cent of upper-caste working women are self-employed against 4.7 per cent for Dalits and 3.4 per cent for middle castes). Forms of self-employment for women include small businesses (mostly grocery shops, fruit and vegetable stalls, cheap jewellery sales, running telephone booths), tailoring and weaving. Very few women have access to regular employment regardless of caste, including the younger generation. By contrast they are the main NREGA[9] users (around 90 per cent, in line with observations elsewhere in Tamil Nadu) (Kannan and Jain 2013: 53). About one-third of households have access to NREGA, with no significant differences between castes. Annual earnings represent only a meagre share of family income (around 5 per cent on average), but a higher share of women's income (20 per cent on average).

These findings reflect two wider trends throughout India. First, they reflect the feminisation of casual agricultural labour, which has been observed over the past few decades (da Corta and Venkateshwarlu 1999; Marius-Gnanou 1993). NSSO data from 2004 to 2005 indicate that for India as a whole, 72.5 per cent of all female workers were in agriculture, as opposed to 48.9 per cent of male workers.

The growth of agricultural labour is in steady decline other than among women rural workers (Srivastava 2012). Compared to men, women have benefited very little from the general improvement in employment opportunities as pointed out by Heyer (2012). It is mostly men who engage in non-farm labour and regular labour. At the same time, the gender gap for agriculture wages is increasing. In the surveyed area, in 2004 women were paid around half of what men were paid (Rs.35 to 45 for one day of harvest against Rs.80 for men). In 2012, they were paid only just over one-third (Rs.120 for women against Rs.350 for men). Second, our findings indicate that the employment rate of women declines with caste – the higher the caste, the less women work (Harriss-White and Gooptu 2001; Heyer 2014). This confirms the low status of women's labour.

Are women less likely to work than before, as has been observed elsewhere in India in recent years (Chowdhury 2011)? If this is the case, is it a regression, as many observers argue, or is it instead a breakthrough given that women's work is very often very hard, poorly paid and low status, especially for Dalits (Heyer 2014)? Does NREGA substitute for other sources of employment, or is it a supplement? These questions should be the subject of future research.

The spatial fragmentation of labour

The fragmentation of labour is also spatial, in the sense that location can influence workers' opportunities (Harriss-White 2003). Even with a higher-quality transport infrastructure, and much improved information circulation than ten years ago – most households, and most household members now have mobile phones – location remains a strong barrier.

In our surveyed area three categories of settlements may be distinguished. The first category includes 'migrant settlements', which have specialised over time in specific channels of seasonal migration, brick moulding or sugar cane harvesting. Take the example of Kamaraj Nagar settlement: around 90 per cent of the households – men, women and some of the children – go every year to brick kilns located 200 to 300 km away, in Kancheepuram district, or in the Red Hills areas, a Chennai suburb. Not only is the village deserted for six to seven months of the year, but it is badly maintained. Rocks, wasteland and swampy areas give an impression of neglect. The houses are all very rudimentary. Out of 45 houses, three are constructed of brick, and these all belong to labour intermediaries. A makeshift temple has been built recently. There is also a small shop selling basic necessities, but it is often poorly stocked and is closed throughout the migration period. In another hamlet, most Dalits also circulate for six to eight

126   *I. Guérin* et al.

months per year, for sugar cane harvesting. The hamlet is located in a wet zone – while most brick kiln migrants come from dry areas – but farmers have shifted to less labour-intensive crops such as trees, and workers have no other choice than to migrate.

The second category of village is the 'semi-agrarian settlement'. These are located in wet areas with large-scale agriculture where there is a high level of caste interdependence. Most major landowners, all of whom are high caste, increasingly combine agricultural and non-agricultural incomes, but still farm the land and live in the village, such that some vestiges of the old attached labour system remain. For instance, in Mananthavizntha Puthur village, which lies on the edge of a large reservoir, there are two major landowners who own between 70 and 100 acres, although given the complexity of intra-family transactions and official ceilings on land property it is often difficult to ascertain the exact size of major landowners' properties. The first landowner lives in the US and a permanent hired manager takes care of the farm. The second landowner is still in the village and has five attached Dalit families, three from the same village, and two from far away who live in the cowshed. There are also around 20 medium-sized farmers from upper and middle castes who hire out labour but whose household members, mainly women, may also work in their own fields. Few Dalits have land, as is often the case in irrigated areas. They lease land, work as agricultural coolies and combine this work with non-farm urban labour, be this on a daily basis or over a few days, weeks or months depending on the distance and the available opportunities.

The third category includes 'peri-urban settlements' in the sense that most men come and go to and from nearby towns – the port, the industrial town of Neyveli or the small town of Panruti described above.[10] It is in peri-urban villages that the process of ongoing social change is the most visible: the long-standing contrast between the basic housing of the Dalit settlements and the relative luxury of the *ur* is fading away. The relative upward mobility of Dalits is frequently brought up in informal daily discussions in the village: non-Dalits often comment that it is now in the 'colony' (Dalit settlement) that money is to be found. Most Dalit settlements in the peri-urban villages studied here have their own temples. These are not confined to a small statue sheltered by a hut, as observed in many Dalit hamlets, but they are cement buildings, some of which are quite comparable to non-Dalit temples. In one of these hamlets, a Dalit man has built a marriage hall and rents it out to all castes. He offers special rates to non-Dalits so that they come, including upper castes. The simple fact that they agree to hold their ceremonies in the same places as Dalits is noteworthy.

Eco-type systems and infrastructure accessibility play a key role in shaping diverse village patterns: migrant villages are mostly in dry areas, or in wet villages that have moved into non-labour-intensive crops; peri-urban villages are those that are close to towns or industrial centres, while agrarian villages have access to water. These 'physical' determinants are key in shaping identities, social hierarchies, and spatial and social mobility circuits. The spatial fragmentation of labour is inseparable from other forms of fragmentation, and from the persistence of interlinked transactions and interlinked markets. There is a wide literature on interlinked transactions, most of which associates linked transactions with agrarian settings, landlordism and traditional resources such as labour, land, credit and possibly water.[11] The interlinked transactions we observed are much more diverse, both with regard to the profile of gatekeepers and to the nature of resources involved.

Access to credit remains a central – and probably growing – concern. Without exception, all the households live on debt, and we estimate that outstanding debt on average represents one year of household income (including for Dalits). Households borrow to make ends meet, to cope with shocks – health, death, job loss – to fund social and religious rituals and sometimes to buy consumer-durable items or invest in housing. In the three categories of villages discussed above, credit markets clearly differ. In migrant villages, migrants are highly dependent on job brokers, because wage advances determine access to other loan sources and serve as a form of guarantee. In peri-urban villages by contrast, cash is very easily available. Almost every day, mobile lenders come to offer their services on doorsteps. There are also many options in the nearby cities and places of work: in Panruti, for instance, there are around 150 pawnbrokers. There are up to several microcredit organisations in every Dalit settlement, which compete and offer either group or individual loans. These are rarely used for income-generating activities, but allow households to juggle, repay other debts and maintain their creditworthiness. Dalits also frequently lend to each other. In agrarian villages, there are also several options such as loans from farmers, mobile lenders, pawnbrokers in neighbouring cities, and microcredit NGOs.

Credit and labour arrangements are thus strongly interrelated. Employers and recruiters may lend money, but, most importantly, local labour and credit markets depend on one another. While some lenders also offer jobs, the vast majority provide complementary services. Additional services also include 'access to information', primarily regarding public programmes and administrative procedures, as well as 'political support' for facilitating access to public programmes, obtaining administrative certificates, and negotiating with the police or courts. This brings us to another form of strategic resource: social policies and government programmes.

Social policies and local politics

As various scholars have pointed out (Heyer 2012; Djurfeldt *et al.* 2008; Harriss *et al.* 2010), social policies have greatly contributed to improving the situation of Dalits. Our case study is no exception. The contrast between migrant and peri-urban Dalit settlements is clearly linked to differing access to social policies and government benefits. Bonded labour migrants have very poor access to such services in the field of education, subsidised housing or access to NREGA, compared to labourers from peri-urban villages. It is also interesting to consider the ways in which the labouring poor obtain access to government schemes. These processes are both shaped by and constitutive of local social and political

128 *I. Guérin* et al.

structures. It is well known that the implementation of government programmes is undemocratic and carried out through patronage, clientelism and gatekeeping relationships (Harriss-White 2003; Harriss-White and Janakarajan 2004). Decentralisation processes and the use of NGOs expected to facilitate direct relationships with citizens have instead served to create additional intermediaries (Pattenden 2011; Picherit 2012). Although gatekeeping seems to be a very common barrier, the profile of gatekeepers and the way they articulate within local power structures may vary significantly. Again, our case studies highlight a diversity of patterns.

In the villages studied here, landlordism has declined, but not entirely disappeared, especially in wet villages. Even when landowners have given up agriculture and live in cities, they very often maintain ties to their villages through moneylending, which in turn allows them to maintain political control over their native village.

In migrant settlements, the state seems to be invisible: no tar road; the 'electricity-for-all' scheme has never taken off – the few connections are private; a water tank has been erected only after years of negotiations. Apart from a programme of land distribution in the 1960s, the families declare that they have never benefited from anything and one feels a certain fatalism: 'The politicians are not interested in us, they are afraid that we will not vote since we are migrants', they tell us. The NGOs are also absent and the reason is probably the same: how to ensure continuity with a migrant population? A few self-help groups (SHGs) (groups entitled to microcredit) were formed in the early 2000s, but quickly collapsed. The few available resources are channelled through labour intermediaries. Echoing Picherit's observations on job brokers in construction in Andhra Pradesh (Picherit 2012), the well-established labour intermediaries are all involved in politics, either through alliances or direct party representatives. They have over time become key figures in village life, with respect to job opportunities, conflict settlement and politics. Their role is to help workers take advantage of the few rights they have in the village.

In peri-urban colonies by contrast, where a significant proportion of non-farm labour takes place locally, access to labour does not require any intermediary and access to government schemes seems to be much easier. Regarding employment, workers have their own networks and access to information. Most of them now have mobile phones, which considerably facilitate direct contact with employers. With regard to government schemes, access is also based on local bonds of allegiance but these seem to be more diverse and Dalits themselves act as intermediaries for their caste fellows. A few individuals still play a key role in transmitting information and 'helping', but it seems that most of them are Dalits.

Local politics are instrumental. The peri-urban hamlets studied here are at the heart of the 'Vanniyar belt' where the Paattali Makkal Katchi (PMK), a regional party created by and for the Vanniyars, has had a decisive influence on politics since the 1990s. Dalits are also very active politically. For each political party, Dalits have their own leader, which is far from being the case elsewhere. The *ur* and the dalit settlement have their own meetings. In Panruti constituency, the

Labour in contemporary south India 129

MLA is a Dalit who has held office for around 15 years. This political power has probably facilitated access to government programmes. Dalits' relative political power in the study area is inseparable from their relative economic strength, and both factors are probably mutually reinforcing. Non-farm employment outside the village has greatly facilitated Dalits' independence from dominant groups in the village. The fact that many employment opportunities are close to the villages, and that migration is still limited in comparison to what we have observed in other Dalit settlements in the region, facilitates the anchoring of Dalits in everyday village life and their political strength.

Labour and consumption

Consumption in rural south India is still under-researched (Cavalcante 2009), despite the fact, we would argue, that it is one of the keys to the future of the Indian countryside, both with regard to the agrarian transition and to labour. In the villages studied here, whether for agricultural wages or sharecropping, payments in kind have become very rare. The costs of education and health keep on growing. A culture of consumerism is also emerging, stimulated by mass advertising campaigns (largely through television) (Kapadia 2002), and facilitated by urbanisation – not because of the rural exodus but rather through circular migration. The persistence of hierarchy as an organising principle does not exclude evolutions and aspirations for change, including among the most marginalised.

Labour migration and circulation probably play a major role. Working in Chennai, the capital, is highly valued, partly because it is a way of buying 'modern' items, such as the latest models of mobile phones that are not found in Cuddalore or Villupuram. An increasing number of households aspire to acquire motorbikes, household appliances, ready-made clothing, etc. Social and religious rituals, especially weddings, may require lump sums of one to several years of household earnings.

Even without longitudinal data, we may reasonably assume that spending on education and ceremonies has increased considerably over recent decades. For Dalits in particular, in the area studied here, investing in education is relatively new. It is also likely that the nature and amount of expenses for ceremonies have changed. Villagers testify that 15 years ago ceremonies took place at home. Now most events take place in a marriage hall, with professional photography and video recordings. As Karin Kapadia (1996) observed in another region of Tamil Nadu, the practice of dowry has become widespread and prices are constantly increasing. The basis is gold, the price of which has kept on increasing over the last decade. It is now usual to include a motorbike as part of the dowry as well.

In many villages in the studied area, Dalits want to finance their own temples and festivals to assert their independence from higher castes, and some are able to do so, as we have seen. Young men play an active role in this process, taking most of the regular jobs. Their salaries and aspirations are key to consumer good acquisition. Young Dalits, for instance, all wear Western clothes such as blue jeans and shirts. They are often the ones who encourage their parents to invest in

130 *I. Guérin* et al.

housing, arguing that their status as regular workers calls for better housing. Women, despite having a limited income over which they have little control, are not entirely excluded from this process. NREGA income and microcredit are partly used to meet women-specific consumption needs.

According to our 2010 survey, access to durable consumer goods has risen sharply in recent years. Mobile phones have entirely democratised (almost 95 per cent of households have at least one mobile phone). Other goods such as motorbikes, cooking gas and televisions are unevenly distributed and have spread more rapidly among middle and upper castes, but Dalits are not excluded. For instance, 45.2 per cent of Dalit households own a motorbike, against 63.7 per cent for middle castes and 64.2 per cent for upper castes. Some 27.6 per cent of Dalit household use cooking gas, against 45.2 per cent for middle castes and 70.2 per cent for upper castes. Some of these goods (televisions and cooking gas) come under free distribution programmes, but this is not the case for motorbikes.

Consumerist behaviours vary greatly in intensity and nature. They show a desire to integrate into global society – for instance, through durable goods – while probably helping to strengthen caste identity when they occur through social and religious rituals. 'Consumerism' is itself a problematic concept – should we see motorbikes or gold (a fundamental component of marriage costs) as consumption or as productive assets? The consumer market is also highly segmented – the working poor and Dalits do not consume in the same way as landowners, employees and upper castes.

With regard to gold, for instance, the working poor – including Dalits – buy small amounts in small shops located in neighbouring towns, while the upper classes and upper castes go to Pondicherry or Chennai to more luxurious shops with a much wider choice of design. Upper castes often make fun of Dalits, saying that they buy motorbikes but don't know how to drive. Motorbikes which are hardly used because petrol is too expensive may be seen parked in front of Dalit houses. The same goes for grinders and televisions due to a lack of electricity.

Caste and class – the position in labour relations – remain key in building identities. However, given the increasing role that consumption will play in the coming years in rural settings, one can also wonder what will be the consequences of these consumption patterns on social identities, with the probable emergence of a combination of various and perhaps conflicting senses of belonging. These are issues for future research.

We suggest that growing access to consumption and the desire to consume – be it consumer durables, ceremonies or education expenses – are both shaped by and constitutive of ongoing changes. This desire to consume is a clear incentive as regards employment strategies. In many cases, people decide to spend, borrow and then deploy various strategies to repay their debts.

Conclusion

Our case study shows that old hierarchies persist in the midst of the changes that India has undergone over the past decades. Non-farm employment is now

Labour in contemporary south India 131

a fundamental part of rural household income while being a male preserve, agricultural labour being in large part female. On average the situation of Dalits is improving, but high levels of inequality and discrimination persist, albeit with strong regional and local variations. Our data suggest changing regional inequalities and migration patterns: seasonal migration flows characterised by poor working conditions coexist with commuting patterns to nearby towns and industrial centres that allow some form of upward mobility for Dalits. Not only do peri-urban villages benefit from increasing employment opportunities, but they also enjoy better credit opportunities and have much easier access to public schemes. Seasonal migrants by contrast are very often excluded from local development programmes and welfare schemes. In other words, some migration flows reflect and reinforce pre-existing inequalities, while others iron out inequalities. The National Commission for the Unorganised Sector's detailed report on the Indian labour landscape identified migrants as one of the most vulnerable segments within the workforce (NCEUS 2007: 97). Today in India, there are probably increasing numbers of circular migrants who remain invisible to policy makers and politicians, and who are excluded from mainstream society (Breman 2010: 18–20; Kannan and Breman 2013).

Our analysis also confirms a trend that has been widely observed throughout India: the emergence of a new form of precariat. This goes far beyond daily agricultural labor to a huge range of activities outside agriculture. These new forms of casual labor are temporary and irregular, and where there is regularity, it often comes at a very high price – bondage. These forms of casual labour often demand moving from one job to another, with no rights, security or any great degree of promotional prospects. Social benefits, where they exist, remain a State prerogative: employers are relieved of any responsibility (Kannan and Breman 2013; Vijayabaskar 2011).

Rural/urban boundaries have moreover become blurred. Beyond the usual dichotomy between cities and the countryside, there are increasing differences between villages. Harriss *et al.* (2012) used the term 'rural urbanism' for an emerging trend in south Tamil Nadu, where agriculture has declined significantly and local industrialisation is on the rise. Beyond this particular case, and Tamil Nadu for that matter, there is growing evidence of the blurring of rural and urban categories: the concept of 'rural labour' now has little meaning given the very high mobility of workers (Lerche 2010), some industries are locating to more rural settings (Ghani *et al.* 2012), and many small towns are developing independently from large urban centres (Mukhopadhyay *et al.* 2012).

All this calls for a re-evaluation of spatial categories (Mukhopadhyay *et al.* 2012), for a rethink of the issue of agrarian transition, and for a consideration of new forms of accumulation and redistribution stemming from the mobility of labour and capital. The very detailed and innovative work of Barbara Harriss-White on the emergence of new forms of accumulation in rural India in the 1980s and 1990s (Harriss-White 1996) needs to return to the top of the agenda.

132 *I. Guérin* et al.

Notes

* The fieldwork that this chapter is based on was carried out between 2004 and 2013 within the *Labour, Finance and Social Dynamics* research programme of the French Institute of Pondicherry. The latest fieldwork has been supported by the RUME and the IOW research projects funded by the French National Agency for Research (ANR). Special thanks are due to Barbara Harriss-White and Judith Heyer for insightful comments on earlier drafts.

1 Among many references, see e.g. Harriss-White (1996, 2003, 2010a, 2010b; also Harriss 1981).

2 Around 2010 Harriss, Jeyaranjan and Nagaraj revisited two villages which Gilbert Slater studied in 1916, followed by different teams on subsequent occasions over the century (Harriss *et al.* 2010; 2012). Djurfeldt and colleagues studied Dalit and non-Dalit social mobility between 1979 and 2004 in six villages in the former Tiruchiparalli district (central Tamil Nadu). Heyer collected longitudinal data from 1981 to the present on Dalit working and living conditions in villages in the Tiruppur region (westernTamil Nadu).

3 It is difficult to evaluate changes in real wages insofar as official inflation rates do not take certain critical goods into account, such as gold, the price of which has dramatically increased over recent years, and which plays a key social role. Increasing levels of subsidised food available per household are taken into account in the CPIAL.

4 For more details on the working conditions of neo-bonded labourers, see Guérin (2013).

5 Average household annual incomes are around Rs.77,000 (median Rs.68,000). There are no significant differences between castes.

6 The figure is 3.7 on average for Dalit, 3.3 for middle-caste, and 2.8 for upper-caste households.

7 The number of female occupations per household is 1.6 for Dalits, 1.1 for middle castes and 0.9 for upper castes. There is no significant difference in terms of number of male occupations.

8 We don't have the space to elaborate here, but our quantitative data are extremely clear on this.

9 The National Rural Employment Guarantee Act aims to guarantee livelihood security in rural areas by providing at least 100 days of guaranteed wage employment in a financial year to every household whose adult members volunteer to do unskilled manual work.

10 The village structure seems quite similar to the description given by Harriss *et al.* (2012) in south Tamil Nadu.

11 For a review, see e.g. Srivastava (1989).

References

Arun, J. (2009) 'From stigma to self-assertion: paraiyars and the symbolism of the parai drum', *Contributions to Indian Sociology*, 41(1): 81–104.

Bernstein, H. (2010) *Class Dynamics of Agrarian Change*, Blackpoint, Nova Scotia, and Sterling, VA: Fernwood Publishing and Kumarian Press.

Breman, J. (2011) *Outcast Labour in Asia, Circulation and Informalisation of the Workforce at the Bottom of the Economy*, New Delhi: Oxford University Press.

Breman, Jan, Guérin, Isabelle and Prakash, Aseem (eds) (2009) *India's Unfree Workforce of Bondage Old and New*, New Delhi: Oxford University Press.

Cavalcante, M. (2009) 'Income-based estimates vs consumption-based estimates of poverty: evidence from rural Tamil Nadu after liberalization', in E. Basile and I. Mukhopadhyay (eds) *The Changing Identity of Rural India: A Socio-historical Analysis*, London/New-York/Delhi: Anthem Press: 113–150.

Chowdhury, S. (2011) 'Employment in India: what does the latest data show?', *Economic and Political Weekly*, 46(32): 23–26.

da Corta, L. and Venkateshwarlu, D. (1999) 'Unfree relations and the feminization of agricultural labour in Andhra Pradesh', in T.J. Byres, K. Kapadia and J. Lerche (eds) *Rural Labour Relations in India*, New Delhi: India Research Press: 71–139.

Denis, E. and Marius-Gnanou, K. (2011) 'Toward a better appraisal of urbanization in India, a fresh look at the landscape of morphological agglomerates', *Cybergeo*, 569: 1–32.

Djurfeldt, G., Athreya, V., Jayakumar, N., Lindberg, S., Rajagopal, A. and Vidyasagar, R. (2008) 'Agrarian change and social mobility in Tamil Nadu', *Economic and Political Weekly*, 43(45): 50–61.

Ghani, E., Goswami, A.G. and Kerr, W.R. (2012) 'Is India's manufacturing sector moving away from cities?, *Working Paper No 17992*, National Bureau of Economic Research, Cambridge, MA.

Government of India (2012) *Informal Sector and Conditions of Employment in India, NSS 66th Round (July 2009–June 2010)*, New Delhi: National Sample Survey Office, National Statistical Organisation, Ministry of Statistics & Programme Implementation.

Guérin, I. (2013) 'Bonded labour, agrarian change and capitalism: emerging patterns in South-India', *Journal of Agrarian Change*, 13(3): 405–423.

Guérin, I. and Venkatasubramanian, G. (2009) 'Corridors of migration and chains of dependence: brick kiln moulders in Tamil Nadu', in J. Breman, I. Guérin and A. Prakash (eds) *India's Unfree Workforce, Old and New Practices of Labour Bondage*, New Delhi: Oxford University Press: 170–197.

Guérin, I., d'Espallier, B. and Venkatasubramanian, G. (2013) 'Why does microfinance fail in rural south-India? The social regulation of self-employment', *CEB Working Paper No. 13/034*.

Guérin, I., Bhukhut, A., Marius-Gnanou, K. and Venkatasubramanian, G. (2009) 'Neobondage, seasonal migration and job brokers: cane cutters in Tamil Nadu', in J. Breman, I. Guérin and A. Prakash (eds) *India's Unfree Workforce, Old and New Practices of Labour Bondage*, New Delhi: Oxford University Press: 233–258.

Harriss, B. (1981) *Transitional Trade and Rural Development*, Delhi: Vikas Publishing House.

Harriss, J., Jeyaranjan, J. and Nagaraj, K. (2010) 'Land, labour and caste politics in rural Tamil Nadu in the twentieth century, Iruvelpattu 1916–2008', *Economic and Political Weekly*, 45(31): 47–61.

—— (2012) 'Rural urbanism in Tamil Nadu: notes on a "Slater Village": Gangaikondan, 1916–2012', *Review of Agrarian Studies*, 2(2), www.ras.org.in/rural_urbanism_in_tamil_nadu.

Harriss-White, B. (1996) *A Political Economy of Agricultural Markets in South India: Masters of the Countryside*, New Delhi: Sage.

—— (2003) *India Working, Essays on Society and Economy*, Cambridge: Cambridge University Press.

—— (2010a) 'Work and wellbeing in informal economies: the regulative roles of institutions of identity and the State', *World Development*, 38(2):170–183.

—— (2010b) 'Globalisation the financial crisis and petty commodity production in India's socially regulated informal economy', *Global Labour Journal*, 1(1): 152–177.

Harriss-White, B. and Colatei, D. (2004) 'Rural credit and the collateral question', in B. Harriss-White and S. Janakarajan (eds) *Rural India Facing the 21st Century, Essays on Long Term Change and Recent Development Policy*, London: Anthem Press: 252–283.

Harriss-White, B. and Gooptu, N. (2001) 'Mapping India's world of unorganised labour', *Socialist Register*, 37: 89–118.

134   *I. Guérin* et al.

Harriss-White, B. and Heyer, J. (eds) (2010) *The Comparative Political Economy of Development: Africa and South Asia*, London: Routledge.

Harriss-White, B. and Janakarajan, S. (eds) (2004) *Rural India Facing the 21st Century, Essays on Long Term Change and Recent Development Policy*, London: Anthem Press.

Heyer, J. (2012) 'Social policy and labour standards: a South Indian case study', *Global Labour Journal*, 3(1): 118–142.

—— (2014) 'Dalit women becoming "housewives": lessons from the Tiruppur region 1981/2 to 2008/9', in C. Still (ed.) *Mobility or Marginalisation: Dalits in Neo-Liberal India*, New Delhi: Routledge.

Kannan, K.P. and Breman, J. (eds) (2013) *The Long Road to Social Security*, New Delhi: Oxford University Press.

Kannan, K.P. and V. Jain (2013) 'Historical initiative, limited by design and implementation: a national overview of the implementation of the NREGA', in K.P. Kannan and J. Breman (eds) *The Long Road to Social Security*, New Delhi: Oxford University Press: 33–80.

Kapadia, K. (1996) *Siva and Her Sisters. Gender, Caste and Class in Rural South India*, New Delhi: Oxford University Press.

—— (2002) 'Translocal modernities and transformations of gender and caste', in K. Kapadia (ed.) *The Violence of Development. The Politics of Identity, Gender and Social Inequalities in India*, New Delhi: Kali for Women: 142–182.

Lerche, J. (2010) 'From "rural labour" to "classes of labour": class fragmentation, caste and caste struggle at the bottom of the Indian labour hierarchy', in B. Harriss-White and J. Heyer (eds) *The Comparative Political Economy of Development: Africa and South Asia*, London: Routledge: 64–85.

Marius-Gnanou, K. (1993) 'Socio-economic impact of the Green Revolution on Tamil rural society: the example of Pondicherry area', *Pondy Papers in Social Sciences*, Pondicherry: Institut Français de Pondichéry, no. 11.

Mukhopadhyay, P., Denis, E. and Zérah, M.H. (2012) 'Subaltern urbanization in India', http://f.hypotheses.org/wp-content/blogs.dir/489/files/2013/01/Subaltern_Urbanisation_in_India_EPW2012.pdf: 52–62.

National Commission for Enterprises in the Unorganised Sector (2007) *Report on Conditions of Work and Promotion of Livelihoods in the Unorganised Sector*, New Delhi: NCEUS.

Pandian, M.S.S. (2013) 'Caste in Tamil Nadu: II. Slipping hegemony of intermediate castes', *Economic and Political Weekly*, 48(4): 1–13.

Pattenden, J. (2011) 'Gatekeeping as accumulation and domination: decentralisation and class relations in rural South India', *Journal of Agrarian Change*, 11(2): 164–194.

Picherit, D. (2012) 'When manual labourers go back to their village: labour migration and protection in rural South India', *Global Labour Journal*, 3(1): 143–162.

Prakash, A. (2010) 'Dalit entrepreneurs in middle India', in B. Harriss-White and J. Heyer (eds) *The Comparative Political Economy of Development: Africa and South Asia*, London: Routledge: 291–317.

Roesch, M., Venkatasubramanian, G. and Guérin, I. (2009) 'Bonded labour in the rice mills: fate or opportunity?', in J. Breman, I. Guérin and A. Prakash (eds) *India's Unfree Workforce, Old and New Practices of Labour Bondage*, New Delhi: Oxford University Press: 284–311.

Shah, A. and Harriss-White, B. (2011) 'Resurrecting scholarship on agrarian transformations', *Economic and Political Weekly*, 46(39): 13–18.

Srinivas, M.N. (1987) *The Dominant Caste and Other Essays*, New Delhi: Oxford University Press.

Srivastava, R.S. (1989) 'Interlinked modes of exploitation in Indian agriculture during transition: a case study', *Journal of Peasant Studies*, 16(4): 493–522.

—— (2005) 'Bonded abour in India: its incidence and pattern', ILO Working Paper, Declaration/WP/43.

—— (2012) 'Changing employment conditions of the Indian workforce and implications for decent work', *Global Labour Journal*, 3(1): 118–142.

Thorat, S.K. and Newman, N. (2010) *Blocked by Caste, Economic Discrimination in Modern India*, New-Delhi: Oxford University Press.

Trouillet, P.-Y. (2009) 'Violences et spatialités du sacrifice hindou en Inde du Sud', *Cahiers de Géographie du Québec*, 53(150): 317–334.

Vijayabaskar, M. (2011) 'Global crises, welfare provision and coping strategies of labour in Tiruppur', *Economic and Political Weekly*, 46(22): 38–45.

Vijayabaskar, M., Swaminathan, P., Anandhi, S. and Balagopal, G. (2004) 'Human development in Tamil Nadu: examining linkages', *Economic and Political Weekly*, 39(8): 797–806.

8 Emerging spatio-technical regimes of accumulation in the globalising south and implications for labour

M. Vijayabaskar

Introduction

In this chapter, I focus on the processes through which technology shapes labour regimes and the embedding of technology practices in the political economy of state policy. Through this exercise, I hope to contribute to a relatively less recognised domain of Professor Barbara Harriss-White's (BHW) work which resonates with her lifelong attempts to reveal the politics of apparently neutral institutions like markets and technologies. After working on the politics of technological change and consequent impacts in agriculture in the 1970s, in two recent papers she once again focuses explicitly on technology and its politics in development (2005; 2009). This chapter attempts to engage with her insights to shed light on the relationship between technology and the emergence of specific kinds of labour regimes in the textile region of Tiruppur and Coimbatore, southern India that has witnessed large-scale diffusion of new technologies. In analysing the politics of technological change, I emphasise its links with the spatiality of accumulation, a domain that has been central to BHW's work. My attempt draws upon 'field economics', a methodological device that has enabled BHW to deploy her theoretical categories rooted in political economy to illuminate the micro-politics of development processes in ways seldom emulated.

There is a growing recognition in the literature of the political enmeshing of scientific and technological practices. Recent studies of market institutions, artefacts and technological practices such as use of standards, communication and financial technologies make visible their non-neutrality and the politics that guide their choice, design and use (MacKenzie 2009; Preda 2008; Licoppe 2008). Furthermore, there has been a deepening of our understanding of what constitutes technology through an emphasis on the need to take on board the various elements that enable the functioning of a particular technology (Geels 2004). The study of the relationship between technology and socio-economic development however has become an unfashionable concern. This trend is far removed from discussions of development in the 1970s and 1980s when the role of technology and its appropriateness in different contexts received prime attention (e.g. Stewart 1977; Sen 1975). Not only have such concerns of appropriateness declined but so have important concerns about the distributional implications of new technologies not

Accumulation in the globalising south 137

only between labour and capital, but also between segments of labour – between the skilled and the less skilled, and across other recognised markers of labour market segmentation like gender and caste. How does the introduction of a technique within a regional production arrangement shape labour regimes? Do efficient technologies in terms of competitiveness in global markets influence labour markets in ways that are detrimental to labour? How do new technologies interact with regimes of social reproduction to generate specific regimes of labour control and use? In this chapter, I address these questions by looking at how the diffusion of new technologies is enabled and accompanied by critical shifts in spatio-production relations. I also highlight how policy shifts directed at improving productivity and competitiveness have been critical to the diffusion of particular technologies in the textile sector in post-reform India. As the chapter shows, despite spinning, weaving and clothing segments being located in the same region and being subject to similar policy and market imperatives, each segment has witnessed the emergence of distinct spatio-technical regimes of labour control and use. This distinction, I go on to argue, is primarily shaped by the technological specifities of each of the segments mediated by market imperatives.

In the following section, I develop the category 'spatio-technical regime' by linking two strands of BHW's work: the politics of technology and the spatiality of accumulation. Understanding how the diffusion of new technologies effect changes in spatial organisation and accompanying labour practices is a line of enquiry that expands her work. I then go on to show how her incorporation of the politics of markets in shaping use and outcomes is an important analytical link between policy reforms and the outcomes of diffusion of new technologies. To illustrate this argument, I briefly describe the politics of policy shifts in the textile sector that have incentivised the introduction of certain technologies. Next, I map the changes in socio-technical arrangements in the spinning, weaving and clothing segments in the districts of Coimbatore and Tiruppur. By comparing socio-technical arrangements across different market segments, I highlight the mediation of product markets in shaping new production arrangements. The final section works these observations towards conceptualising the role of technology in late industrialising regions.

Spatiality and technological change: extending BHW's conceptualisation of the politics of technology

It is widely acknowledged that mainstream economic theory has failed to come up with an adequate perspective to capture the gamut of relationships between technology and economic development (Faulkner *et al.* 2010). Marxist political economy, evolutionary and institutional economics have provided more useful frameworks to develop a systemic approach to studying technological change. In her attempts to address the failure of mainstream economic theory, BHW draws upon and develops an understanding of technology put forward by Frances Stewart (1977). To begin with, there is a clear move away from the treatment of technology as an isolated technique used to transform inputs into outputs, the

138   M. Vijayabaskar

choice being guided by its price which is in turn determined by relative factor prices. Stewart contends that technologies have to be viewed as a complex system of multiple relationships between tools and the institutional arrangements in which they are deployed. This is best captured in BHW's synthesis of her treatment (Harriss-White 2011: 94, emphasis added):

> '[T]echnology is a package and each technique is designed to be operated within a particular technological system'. The elements of the system … include information/knowledge (pp. 2–3); the organisation of production – which affects capacity utilisation and management as well as upstream and downstream linkages between techniques (pp. 4, 61–66, 194); and the distribution of incomes – which shapes markets for the products of technology and which determines the opportunity cost of labour, which in turn affects technological productivity (pp. 66–74). They also include infrastructure for communications, banking and insurance (p. 81); local scientific and engineering capabilities; legal and administrative institutions; managerial capacities; and last but not least an appropriately skilled labour force (pp. 8, 74) with social services and associated infrastructure (p. 7).

The diffusion of new techniques may therefore require an overhauling of the earlier institutional arrangements to ensure that they work efficiently. Reiterating the strength of Stewart's conceptualisation, recent work in science and technology studies (STS) also highlights the systemic nature of technological use and change (Geels 2004). The deployment of a new technology is made possible through effecting a number of changes to the larger social 'eco-system' in which the technique is deployed. BHW, in pointing out the significance of such a conceptualisation, identifies some limitations of Stewart's approach. Two of her observations in this regard are pertinent here. First, Stewart's perspective does not account for the imperative of capital accumulation and how that shapes the way in which technologies are deployed. Of particular relevance is the role of the state and the institutional crucibles in which markets function. In her study of the commercialisation of paddy processing, BHW highlights the politics of promotion of new technologies by the state, and the process by which markets work to dispossess low-caste women of their traditional livelihoods (2005). As the state assigns a greater role for markets in resource allocation, compulsions of the market are likely to drive both the choice of technology adaptation and the way in which it is deployed even more strongly within a particular production arrangement. Second, in her critique of the innovation systems approach, BHW points out that the framework completely obscures the agency of labour.

To these limitations, I would like to add one more. The relationships are theorised in aspatial terms despite a growing recognition of the relationship between social space and technologies. Although the strong links between technological change and spatial configurations are not a dominant theme in either technology studies or studies on spatial aspects of social change, there are a few insightful studies that locate themselves in the interstices of urban geography and technology studies (Furlong 2011; Hommels 2005; Coutard and Guy 2007; Truffer 2008). In one of her more important works, BHW develops a framework for examining processes of capital accumulation in the informal economy by incorporating spatial relations (2003). Dispersed through the book, but with an explicit focus in a chapter entitled 'Space and synergy' (pp. 200–238), she delineates the modes through which capital accumulation constitutes and makes use of spatial and social relations in small-town India. She deals at length with the processes through which capital draws upon social institutions like gender and caste, with their attendant spatial manifestations, to further the process of surplus extraction (pp. 25–41).

Such intersections of institutions of social reproduction such as the household, caste and gender with institutions of capital accumulation that generate certain spatial arrangements constitute an important terrain of analysis. New technologies may shape the domains of both production and social reproduction even as their mode of deployment in specific spaces is conditioned by region-specific institutions, as indicated earlier. Importantly, as labour process analyses reveal, relations of power shape the direction and nature of changes to the production system associated with the introduction of new technologies (Knights and Willmott 1988). Combining the insights derived from the politics of technological change with the spatiality of accumulation can be a productive exercise for analysing how new technologies allow for the rise of certain spatio-technical regimes that generate patterns of inclusion and exclusion, across space and across social groups.

By mapping changes in spatio-technical regimes in the textile and clothing sector, I highlight how the spatial transformations enabled through the use of new technologies shape the lives of the labouring poor. The account of the working of three different segments of textile and clothing production in the Tiruppur-Coimbatore region also reveals the politics of markets in shaping the use of specific technologies and consequent labour market outcomes. This exercise is based on fieldwork conducted in the region over three phases since the mid-1990s. The first two phases involved worker surveys and case studies of firms drawn from a typology of firms framed in terms of their relation to the market and buyers in the knitwear value chain (Vijayabaskar 2001). The final phase conducted in 2008/2009, in addition to a survey of 300 workers and detailed interviews of select firms in the knitwear segment, also included lengthy open-ended interviews with 30 workers in the weaving segment, 20 workers in the spinning segment, and another five ex-workers in the spinning sector. This was supplemented by interviews with trade union officials, owners/managers of four spinning mills and five power loom units, key office-bearers of producer associations, officials of the Textiles Ministry and members of civil society organisations working in the area.

Policy shifts in the Indian textile industry

The textile industry has been one of the most regulated manufacturing sectors in postcolonial India. As a sector subjected to de-industrialisation by colonial policies, a key sector for non-farm employment for the less skilled and a producer of wage goods, state regulation in the initial decades of planned industrialisation

140   *M. Vijayabaskar*

had to address its survival and growth which it did through a slew of policy measures. The hand loom industry, large sections of which were decimated by colonial policies, was seen to require protection from the technologically more efficient mill sector to ensure the livelihoods of millions of weaver families. Mills were not allowed to produce certain kinds of fabric that could be produced on hand looms. Clothing was reserved for the small-scale sector due to its role in employment generation for the less skilled who faced substantial barriers to entry into modern manufacturing. Mills were mandated to produce a certain proportion of yarn for hand looms which was then provided at subsidised rates. The policy of ensuring both employment for the less skilled and cheap clothing for the poor continued until the mid-1980s when the Textile Policy of 1985 sought to reorient the priorities of the sector.[1] This was a period of early liberalisation that pre-dated the more intensive measures introduced after 1991 when deregulation was seen as a step towards improving the efficiency of resource utilisation by allowing a greater role for market signals.

By then the state was no longer able to regulate the large-scale diffusion of power loom technologies that not only produced cloth efficiently at low scales but importantly employed more informal and cheap labour than the formal mill sector. The mill sector was the site of considerable labour mobilisation that provided access to secure employment, internal career paths and social security to large sections of the workforce. The 1985 Textile Policy document identified excessive state regulation as a key factor undermining the competitiveness of the mill sector in relation to the power loom sector. Emphasis was placed on the production of cheap cloth through the use of more productive technologies (Srinivasulu 1996). Importantly, there was also a political shift away from the employment and social welfare objectives that had guided policy up until then.[2] Mills were allowed to expand their capacities at the same time as power looms were allowed to expand. This allowed the splitting up of composite mills into large-scale spinning mills, a segment that continued to operate at high economies of scale, and a highly diffused small-scale power loom sector operating in the informal economy with obvious implications for labour welfare. This policy shift is argued to have facilitated the modernisation of spinning mills and the growth of exports of cotton yarn witnessed since.

The shift in priorities, building competitiveness in global markets with little regard for the quality or quantity of employment, was further strengthened with the New Textile Policy of 2000. Clothing that had been reserved for the small-scale sector until then was de-reserved to encourage exports, as reservation was seen to inhibit investments in new technologies. In fact, the first objective of the new textile policy was to 'Facilitate the Textile Industry to attain and sustain a pre-eminent global standing in the manufacture and export of clothing'.[3] Spinning mills, despite having been modernised on account of the post-1985 Textile Policy, were still seen to have not invested adequately in frontier technologies. Power looms too were using outdated technologies and required investment to improve the competitiveness of the clothing industry that needed quality fabrics. The Technology Upgradation Fund (TUF) was initiated in 1999 with the aim of

Accumulation in the globalising south 141

providing subsidised capital for the industry to upgrade its processes and products. However, despite pronouncements on the employment promotion aspects of the industry, there was no explicit policy directed at enhancing the quality or quantity of employment in the sector. Gradually, the policy thrust moved away from directly targeting the labour market. Instead, state policy reflected the overall assumption that increasing growth, through improving competitiveness in the global market and the diffusion of frontier technologies, would indirectly expand employment. The implications of such policy-induced technological shifts for labour in the spinning sector are addressed in the following section.

Technological change and labour regimes in the cotton-spinning sector

The state of Tamil Nadu accounts for more than 65 per cent of cotton-spinning units in the country (National Skill Development Corporation n.d.: 12). The Coimbatore region has not only been the major centre of spinning in the state but is also home to vibrant weaving and clothing segments. The spinning sector in Coimbatore has a long history of unionisation and labour mobilisation which also led to labour mobilisation in downstream segments of the value chain (Chari 2004). The institutionalisation of a collective bargaining arrangement in the textile industry in Coimbatore since the mid-1950s has been seen as a success story in managing labour relations in segments of the industry (Patil 1983). It led to improved working conditions for labour such as permanent employment, social security and a clear internal career path. It also enabled a process of rationalisation and modernisation of machinery with minimum retrenchment. However, the expansion of the power loom sector was also substantially aided by segments of the formal mill sector that began to outsource its weaving to the power loom sector in response to labour mobilisations (Srinivasulu 1996). There was large-scale closure of spinning mills beginning in the 1980s, which was associated with retrenchment and job losses.[4]

Along with the TUF which provided subsidised loans, the GOI also launched the 'cotton technology mission' to enhance research and development directed at improving productivity and the quality of cotton. Further, separate tax incentives were offered for export-oriented production and infrastructure for export production was created through the establishment of apparel parks. While reforms were thus introduced explicitly in the domain of product markets, labour market reforms were introduced through stealth (Jenkins 2004). The state allowed regressive labour practices and interpretations of existing laws rather than formally modifying the legal framework governing labour. The textile industry has over the years witnessed an undermining of labour mobilisation and the institutionalisation of collective bargaining in Coimbatore and elsewhere.[5] The TUF scheme also provided subsidised loans for units introducing a voluntary retirement scheme for their workforces as a part of the overall restructuring of production.

The above policy moves enabled the rapid upgradation of technology in the spinning sector marked by high levels of automation and improvements in the quality of output and the speed of processing. Automation in material handling, cleaning of raw cotton, faster spinning and lower monitoring of spinning processes through movement from ring spinning into open-end rotor spinning and air-jet spinning are some of the key process improvements that the industry has witnessed in recent years.[6] These technological changes have served to meet a major market demand – the need for improved quality even as it allowed for less time for the conversion of raw cotton fibre into yarn and expanding the varieties of yarn. The introduction of new technologies, while enabling a move into production of a much wider range of cotton yarn (in terms of number of counts), and improved quality, has also had an impact on the organisation of production.

To begin with, automation has led to reduced demand for labour. It was estimated in an earlier study that with new technologies firms could generate the same output with only 15 per cent of the labour utilised under traditional technologies (Datta 1999: L42). The labour requirement will have fallen further since. In addition, quality control that used to rely on the experience of workers is now taken care of through automated technologies. Workers can be deployed on the shop floor with minimum training as the computerised control machines address problems of coordination, monitoring and control with few demands on labour. Automation has also made work less physically demanding and this is held to have enabled the entry of women in large numbers into this segment of the value chain. Finally, higher end jobs like supervision, programming and some aspects of quality control require more training backed by educational qualifications, unlike in the past when operators could move on to supervisory positions with adequate on-the-job experience.

Since the older spinning mills have closed down, the new technologies have been deployed in mills that have come up recently in a different spatial milieu. Coimbatore city has hardly seen a new mill in the past decade. Similarly, the four spinning mills that accounted for the bulk of formal employment in Tiruppur town in the 1980s have all closed down. On the other hand, mills have come up in villages located at a radius of about 60 to 80 km from Coimbatore. Another cluster of new mills have come up in Dindigul district which is reputed to have the largest spindlage in the state after the old Coimbatore district[7] (interview with Dr Selvaraju, South Indian Mills Association, 13 March 2009). The move to villages was designed primarily to take advantage of lower land costs and tax concessions for setting up units in 'backward areas'.[8] The spread of electricity to rural areas in the state as well as improvements in transport and communications facilitated this shift. The location away from centres of traditional labour mobilisation reinforced the ability of capital to engage labour under regressive working conditions. Unlike in the past when the workforce was essentially male, and drawn from urban areas, these mills draw the bulk of their labour from rural areas, young women in particular, some from nearby villages, more from distant villages. The South India Spinners Association highlights this feminisation of the labour force on its website by pointing out that not only are their member mills located in rural and backward regions, but they also contribute to women's empowerment by largely employing rural women (http://sispa.in/ (accessed 14 May 2012)).

Accumulation in the globalising south   143

This ruralisation on the one hand, and feminization on the other, has been accompanied by important changes in modes of recruitment and working conditions. The higher capital costs of the new technologies make it more important for mills to run at near-full capacity to recover their costs. While women workers can be recruited at lower wages, it is not easy for local women to commute to work in night shifts. Many spinning mills in the region have resolved this problem by recruiting women from distant villages and housing them in dormitories or hostels within the factory premises. These women are employed as apprentices (under the Apprenticeship Act) in an informal and illegal agreement whereby they are required to work for a minimum of two to three years (SOMO-ICN 2011), with the promise of a lump sum when the term comes to an end. In addition to deductions made for their stay and food, they are paid a token amount (Rs.1000 to Rs.1500 per month in 2008). These workers come from poor and low-caste households, and their average age is about 17 to 19. Parents send their daughters to work under such a scheme in the hope that the lump sum given at the end of the work period may be used to pay dowry for their daughters' weddings.

This scheme, termed the 'sumangali thittam' ('bride scheme'), has been rightly seen by activists and civil society organisations as neo-bondage (SOMO-ICN 2011). Once recruited, the workers are not allowed to leave the hostel premises except under special circumstances. Entrance to the hostels is barred to outsiders. Employers cite this as one important reason parents permit their daughters to work in their factories. This paternalist control through spatial exclusion however also serves the purpose of undermining the possibility of worker mobilisation. The spatial arrangement makes it extremely difficult for unions to mobilise workers. This is an example in which the deployment of new techniques in production draws upon local institutions of reproduction to forge specific spatial regimes of control.

What I would like to stress is the fact that the deployment of these particular new technologies has enabled a low-road techno-spatial regime of capital accumulation even as productivity and quality of output has improved. This has been reinforced by policy practices that pay little attention to ways in which labour laws are practised, which in turn has been made possible by virtue of the decline in institutions of collective mobilisation in the segment. It has also been reinforced by the larger politics of market demand that requires better quality standards and faster production at lower costs. Such conditions undermine the possibility of deploying technologies in ways that may be more beneficial to labour in terms of both quality of work and employment.

In the following section I focus on the relationship between production organisation and diffusion of new technologies in the weaving sector.

Weaving

As one travels through the villages in Coimbatore and Tiruppur districts, it is difficult to miss the loud clacking sounds from power loom units. These two districts, along with the neighbouring district of Erode, account for more than 56

144   *M. Vijayabaskar*

per cent of the total number of power looms in the state (Manivannan *et al.* 2012). While there are some power loom clusters in urban centres where several large units are located in close spatial proximity, several thousands of power loom units are dispersed on farms over large parts of the rural landscape. These have emerged as a major source of non-farm income for rural households, especially since the introduction of the Textile Policy of 1985. The spatial spread has largely been made possible by the ease with which power loom technologies may be used and the scale economies of weaving technology. It has also been facilitated by developments in transport and communication, and the longer history of rural electrification in the region. The organisation of this industry is based on a classic putting-out system with traders providing raw material and paying on a piece-rate basis for output. The diffusion of technologies of weaving spans a wide range, from the sophisticated shuttle-less looms catering to quality markets, export and domestic, to the regular fly-shuttle looms that produce low-end coarse fabric for the mass domestic market. While the new technologies tend to be housed predominantly in the larger units in urban power loom clusters, the shuttle loom dominates the rural landscape. Its diffusion into small and marginal farmers' lives has been made possible by virtue of the fact that its operation is simple and can be undertaken with little training. Many of the units are family run, with the husband, wife and at times the children providing the bulk of labour requirements. If the capacity of the unit is more than the minimum, the family may hire an additional worker or two to take care of alternate 12-hour shifts. In addition to units relying predominantly on household labour, there has also been an increase in the number of larger rural power loom units, housing anywhere between 20 and 60 looms (De Neve and Carswell 2011: 14). Hired workers are invariably male, drawn from the same or nearby villages. In the case of larger units, families from other districts in the state are brought to the premises and housed in small sheds close to the unit, but quite far from nearby towns. Women members of migrant families alternate between taking care of the reproductive needs of their families and doing productive work like cone winding in the unit.

While power loom technology has enabled the entry of less skilled workers, their participation implies poorer working conditions and terms of employment than were available in mill weaving earlier. Power loom workers are employed on a temporary basis, paid an average of Rs.150 per 12-hour shift (in 2008/2009),[9] and are not eligible for any social security or employment protection benefits. Furthermore, workers are often recruited by the offer of an advance. De Neve and Carswell observe that more than 80 per cent of the workers in power loom units in a village near Tiruppur had taken advances (2011: 16). Trade union activists concur that neo-bondage is difficult to resist given the spatially dispersed nature of production and the poverty of households supplying labour. Power loom labour is increasingly drawn from among Dalit youth, especially those who have attended school for less than five years, who are often pushed into this work due to household indebtedness.

There are important differences between the practices of tying labour or neo-bondage that are prevalent in both spinning and weaving segments. In the case of female workers under the 'sumangali scheme' in the spinning sector, labour is tied through payments only on completion of a minimum period. In the case of male workers in power looms, tying takes place through a system of advances at the time of recruitment. This divergence may also indicate that even as specific technological requirements shape gender and spatially based labour requirements, gender and space also shapes labour control strategies across the two segments. The two distinct arrangements also pose distinct constraints for labour mobilisation. The spatial diffusion and small-scale nature of weaving activity and tying of labour undermines collective action in the weaving sector, unlike the constraints of spatial exclusion confronted by labour in the spinning segment.

In the following section, I turn my attention to the production of cotton knitwear. Here, I highlight how two important characteristics of global garment markets, namely time and quality, are critical to both the nature of technologies employed and the way in which the techniques are enmeshed in production arrangements to shape conditions of work. I begin with production for export markets in the knitwear cluster. The export market for Tiruppur garment producers has witnessed rapid changes in the past decade or so, particularly since 2005 with the expiry of the Multi-Fibre Agreement (MFA). Two aspects of this change stand out. First, there has been a growing emphasis on quality across all aspects of the production process which has warranted the introduction of new automated technologies in all segments of the garment export chain. Buyers playing a crucial role increasingly insist on tying knitwear orders to the installation or use of specific kinds of machines. The second important change in the market concerns time. Typical of post-Fordist accumulation regimes, market demand is increasingly shaped by fashion trends that are subject to shorter and shorter cycles. Some brands like Zara, for instance, have as many as eight to 12 cycles over a year. Furthermore, wholesalers and retailers also seek to cut down costs by holding smaller inventories and placing orders closer to the start of the fashion cycle. Since the mid-1990s, exporters in Tiruppur report a one-third decline in the time period given to deliver their output to the buyers. Such shorter turnaround times, apart from warranting certain changes in techniques deployed, also direct the organisation of production in specific ways.

Segmented global markets for clothing and shaping of local production regimes

With the expiry of the quota regime and the removal of reservation of knitwear production for the small-scale sector, Tiruppur's garment exporters have diversified their output profile from largely low-volume semi-fashion segments to mass-market segments consisting of large volumes of standard products that do not fetch the same value per piece as the low-volume segment. Leading exporters house production for the two segments in separate units. Cutting, machining and trimming (CMT) operations, common to both segments, are the most labour-intensive and least subject to automation of the processes involved.

In the mid-1990s, when workers in a firm had gone on strike in protest against installation of computerised cutting machines, the firm was forced to give up the idea. By 2009 most medium to large units had installed computerised cutting machines and specialised units offering cutting operations had come up. The introduction of the cutting machine has come about as part of a wholesale move to use advanced imported technologies in all segments of garment production. Quality-conscious markets had gained greater agency in shaping the technological regime. Labour had become less powerful as an agent influencing the choice of technology. While basic garments require at most two sewing operations, namely chainlock and overlock, semi-fashion garments require additional sewing operations such as flatlock, button holing and fixing, and sewing of embellishments. The wide range of garments produced warrants an ability to use different sewing machines capable of producing a range of sewing operations even on a single garment. There has been a growing division of labour between different kinds of sewing like overlock, flatlock and chainlock. However, since the order lots for the semi-fashion segment tend to be small, firms prefer to rely at least partially on multi-skilled tailors who can undertake all the required sewing operations.

With the diversification in the export market, there have been some changes in the spatial organisation of production. While the high-end and semi-fashion segments continue to be produced in factories close to Tiruppur town, the mass-market segment does not require the same amount of skill for tailoring or cutting operations. Since the order sizes are large, firms find it profitable to set up these factories in nearby villages on cheaper land with production organised along regular assembly lines. In such cases a large share of labour tends to be drawn from among young women in the villages. Wages tend to be lower, but more importantly exporters find this labour force more 'reliable'. The majority of the workers are recruited directly by the firm. The longer turnaround times for this segment allow a relatively less rigorous work schedule which in turn makes it feasible even for married women to combine household work with factory work. In units catering to the mass markets run by large exporters, firms also resort to housing long-distance workers in dormitories close to the factories to exert greater control over their work time. Instances of such garment factories located in rural areas resorting to 'sumangali'-type employment schemes are also reported (SOMO-ICN 2011).

At the other end, in semi-fashion and quality-sensitive segments, there are periodic shortages of labour, particularly skilled labour, and a tighter labour market. The emphasis on low turnaround times, and the predominance of small orders in the output profile, pushes firms towards what may be termed 'just-in-time' recruitment of labour. Firms, especially subcontracting firms, find it more profitable to rely on a pool of casual labour that may be drawn upon as and when orders are procured, and shed when there is less production. Under such conditions firms rely on a network of labour contractors even for core operations like sewing. Labour contractors have become important labour market intermediaries in this segment over the past decade (De Neve 2012), enabling firms to

Accumulation in the globalising south   147

rely on employment flexibility to keep costs down. Greater demands on quality also warrant a close monitoring of the work process, a function that has emerged as critical to the labour contractor's role. The low turnaround time also implies an intensification of the work process, with workers routinely forced to work overtime to meet shipment deadlines. This has reduced the prospects of employing women workers in these units. In general, women account for a smaller proportion of this mobile workforce than in units catering to mass markets in nearby villages.

A key technology mediating between producers, contractors and workers is the mobile phone. Producers have a set of phone numbers of contractors that they rely upon to access labour as soon as it is required. Otherwise, the shorter production runs would have forced firms to rely on a captive pool of labour, retaining a 'bench' within the firm to make sure that labour was available as soon as the orders came in. Contractors also rely extensively on cell phones to mobilise workers. Of late, migrant workers have also been drawn from distant regions in central and eastern India, through labour contractors who are also often workers themselves. Incremental additions to the labour force are often made through current migrant workers calling upon their contacts in their native villages. Such networks of labour access and deployment have become more effective over such distant spaces with the advent of the mobile phone. Importantly, by reducing the transaction costs of recruiting workers almost on a per-order basis, the mobile phone has made viable a highly flexible production arrangement.

The following section focuses on 'waste' generated by the quality standards of global markets which in turn generate a new regime of production that draws upon labour and materials excluded from production for high-end markets.

The domestic market as a 'backyard' for export manufacturing

Along with the growth in exports, there has been an expansion of the domestic market both in terms of product profile and penetration into newer markets. This process has been accentuated by the need for export manufacturers to offload materials on to the domestic market to cut down on costs and risk. Given the high-quality requirements of export manufacture, manufacturing for the export market generates a substantial amount of rejected goods that are used to cater for this segment. The market for clothing produced from using rejected material from the export market is a segment that owes its existence to the need for export manufacturers to have a 'backyard'. The rejected yarn or fabric is sold to small household units dispersed throughout the region for the production of 'backyard' clothing. The sector also generates 'waste' fabric left over after trimming that expands with increases in production. It is said that the annual market turnover for goods belonging to this segment reached nearly Rs.400 crores in as early as 2001/2002.[10]

A large informal sector producing low-end clothing of various kinds for the domestic market using secondhand machines, reject material and labour that is

148 *M. Vijayabaskar*

less skilled and also less well paid has emerged in the slums of Tiruppur. Informal estimates suggest that by 2008/2009 the slums in Tiruppur were home to more than 2500 small-scale or household-based units catering for the new value chain. Such production is however not confined to the slums in the town, but is dispersed in the nearby villages as well. The units compete primarily on the basis of low costs. Use of subsidised family labour and household premises constitute two major means of cost reduction. Firms of this type are sustained solely on the basis of the surge in exports that generates 'wastes' and the accompanying emphasis on quality which in turn generates 'rejects'. Workers in these units are either those who have worked in export units earlier but have not been able to continue because of ill health or inability to work long hours. Alternatively, they tend to be women workers who find it difficult to work in factories due to household responsibilities. Often they draw upon the labour of other household members like older men and women, and younger children. Although they are less skilled compared to those employed in the export factories, the less stringent demands on quality and time allow such a regime to emerge. Production for the upper end of the domestic market is organised on lines very similar to the mass segments of the export market, in large units in rural areas employing female labour.

We thus observe a clear segmentation in the nature of technological and spatial arrangements between production for different kinds of markets. These are associated with different labour market outcomes and socio-economic inequalities. Market characteristics play an important role in how technologies shape work and labour-use practices. In turn, market segmentation is driven by the structure of demand generated through income inequalities (Yanagisawa 2010). Market segmentation is thus a deeply political phenomenon driven by uneven distribution of incomes and macro-policy shifts that privileges growth over equity to the detriment of labour.

Technology and labour under late industrialisation

In the preceding sections, I have tried to indicate how despite being located in the same region and constituting segments within a single sector, markets and technologies have shaped the emergence of distinct spatio-technical regimes of accumulation across spinning, weaving and different segments of clothing production. Diffusion of technologies enables different spatial arrangements of production and such spatial arrangements are critical to the rise of specific forms of labour control. The cases also highlight how demands of distinct market segments enable distinct spatio-technical regimes. While these relations are played out at the micro level, formal and informal policy shifts at the national level in the domain of both product and factor markets have incentivised the introduction of a set of technologies on the one hand, and undermined the efficacy of agency of labour on the other. Under such conditions, technologies that have propelled the Indian textile industry to improve its competitiveness in the global market have also produced regressive work and employment regimes. New technologies, labour regimes and spatial

Accumulation in the globalising south 149

arrangements have undermined the ability of labour to resist or fashion alternate production regimes. While policy shifts that undermined institutions of collective bargaining are critical to the production of such spatio-technical regimes, no less important are the imperatives of the global market such as cost, quality and time.

The decline in demand for labour in the spinning sector reflects a larger global trend in manufacturing. As Bhaduri points out, low employment elasticities are a feature of frontier technologies in the manufacturing sector (2010). Large segments of labour are excluded from employment in these sectors and hence excluded from the prospects of gaining a share of the surplus generated (2010: 28–30). Clearly, lack of employment generation is of particular concern in countries like India seeking to take a advantage of the 'demographic dividend' made possible by a growing potential labour force. But policy making in India and other low-income or late industrialising regions appears to completely sidestep this issue, presuming that increases in economic growth are sufficient to generate trickle-down effects for labour. The fact that employment generation has declined during a phase of labour market deregulation clearly indicates that the solution to creating jobs does not lie in dismantling institutions regulating labour markets.

This chapter also draws attention to spatial and technological factors that shape the quality of employment generated in high-growth sectors. A combination of spatial, sectoral and labour market re-regulation premised on creating appropriate incentives for private investments and on increasing global competitiveness has allowed for the generation of a new spatiality of accumulation that undermines both quality of employment and traditional modes of labour mobilisation. Capital's ability to appropriate new rural spaces and their accompanying institutions of social reproduction allows for the emergence of distinct labour regimes even as there is an overarching tendency towards the generation of low-quality work and employment.

How do we understand this lack of attention in policy circuits? Structural explanations like labour share becoming a cost rather than a source of demand with the emphasis on export markets and policy shifts that undermine institutions of labour mobilisation as discussed above are clearly important. Sum (2009) also offers an explanation based on the hegemonic rise of 'competitiveness' as a key discursive instrument that shapes policy making. This hegemony implies that policy makers are constantly engaged in responding to measures and indices of competitiveness. Cluster development has become a key arena for the exercise of 'competitiveness'-related policy measures with several standardised strategies circulating within policy circuits to address the lack of competitiveness. This hegemony tends to undermine the ability to perceive and act on other aspects of development, labour market implications being one among several areas of neglect. The launch of the TUF without paying attention to how the new technologies may shape labour markets is a case in point. So is the policy thrust on identifying clusters with potential to compete, identifying gaps in this potential, and acting to address these gaps, with scant regard for the embeddedness of the cluster in locale-specific institutions. However, this is not

150 M. Vijayabaskar

to deny the political logic of economic shifts that opens up spaces for the ascendance of such discursive practices. By recognising how technological specifities shape regimes of labour control at the local level, and how policy shifts at the national level incentivise the introduction of specific technologies, this chapter has sought to highlight the importance of engaging simultaneously with larger policy changes and the control regimes they generate at the micro level to articulate alternate models of production under globalising conditions.

Notes

1 Although there were suggestions for the replacement of hand looms with power looms by certain government-appointed committees earlier, this shift became visible only with the 1985 textile policy (Niranjana and Vinayan 2001).
2 'It differed from other textile policies with the shift in emphasis from employment potential to that of enhancing productivity' (Niranjana and Vinayan 2001: 114).
3 http://texmin.nic.in/policy/policy_2000.pdf (accessed 9 February 2013).
4 This also happened in other major centres of textile production in the country like Mumbai and Ahmedabad (Breman 2004; D'Monte 2002).
5 See Valsan (2012) for a note on the decline in trade union activity in the Coimbatore spinning sector.
6 Information on technological changes in the spinning sector and consequent changes in labour requirements described in this section is drawn from interviews with spinning mill owners, managers and trade union members associated with the sector in 2008/2009.
7 The new Tiruppur district was carved out of Coimbatore and parts of Erode district in 2009.
8 Interestingly. Ghani *et al.* (2012) point to the growing ruralisation of formal manufacturing firms in the country as a whole over the past decade.
9 Which is higher than the wages paid to entry-level workers under the 'sumangali scheme' and unskilled labour in the clothing factories by about Rs.50 and Rs.40 respectively, but much lower than the wages for agricultural work and skilled work in the garment factories (Rs.200 and above).
10 www.thehindubusinessline.in/2002/07/08/stories/2002070800871300.htm (accessed 14 March 2013).

References

Bhaduri, A. (2010) *Essays in the Reconstruction of Political Economy*, New Delhi: Aakar Books.
Breman, J. (2004) *The Making and Unmaking of an Industrial Working Class: Sliding Down the Labour Hierarchy in Ahmedabad, India*, New Delhi: Oxford University Press.
Chari, S. (2004) *Fraternal Capital: Peasant-Workers, Self-Made Men, and Globalization in Provincial India*, Stanford, CA: Stanford University Press.
Coutard, O. and Guy, S. (2007) 'STS and the city: politics and practices of hope', *Science Technology and Human Values*, 32(6): 713–734.
D'Monte, D. (2002) *Ripping the Fabric: The Decline of Mumbai and its Mills*, New Delhi: Oxford University Press.
Datta, R.C. (1999) 'New technology and textile workers', *Economic and Political Weekly*, 34(39): L41–44.

De Neve, G. (2012) 'Fordism, flexible specialisation and CSR: how Indian garment workers critique neoliberal labour regimes', *Ethnography*, published online 22 November, http://eth.sagepub.com/content/early/2012/11/22/1466138112463801.

De Neve, G. and Carswell, G. (2011) 'From field to factory: tracing transformations in bonded labour in the Tiruppur region, Tamil Nadu', *Manchester Papers in Political Economy, Working Paper No. 1*, Centre for the Study of Political Economy, University of Manchester.

Faulkner, P., Lawson, C. and Runde, J. (2010) 'Theorising technology', *Cambridge Journal of Economics*, 34(1): 1–16.

Furlong, F. (2011) 'Small technologies, big change: rethinking infrastructure through STS and geography', *Progress in Human Geography*, 35(4): 460–482.

Geels, F.W. (2004) 'From sectoral systems of innovation to socio-technical systems: insights about dynamics and change from sociology and institutional theory', *Research Policy*, 33(6–7): 897–920.

Ghani, E., Goswami, A.G. and Kerr, W.R. (2012) 'Is India's manufacturing sector moving away from cities?', *Harvard Business School Working Paper 12–090*.

Harriss-White, B. (2003) *India Working: Essays on Economy and Society*, Cambridge: Cambridge University Press.

—— (2005) 'Commercialisation, commodification and gender relations in post-harvest systems for rice in South Asia', *Economic and Political Weekly*, 40(25): 2530–2542.

—— (2011) 'Revisiting "technology and underdevelopment": climate change, politics and the "D" of solar energy technology in contemporary India', in Valpy Fitzgerald, Judith Heyer and Rosemary Thorp (eds) *Overcoming the Persistence of Inequality and Poverty*, Basingstoke: Palgrave Macmillan, 92–126.

Harriss-White, B., Rohra, S. and Singh, N. (2009) 'Political architecture of India's technology system for solar energy', *Economic and Political Weekly*, 44(47): 49–60.

Hommels, A. (2005) 'Studying obduracy in the city: toward a productive fusion between technology studies and urban studies', *Science, Technology and Human Values*, 30(3): 323–351.

Jenkins, R. (2004) 'Labour policy and the second generation of economic reform in India', *India Review*, 3(4): 333–363.

Knights, D. and Willmott, H. (eds) (1988) *New Technology and the Labour Process*, London: Macmillan.

Licoppe, C. (2008) 'Understanding and reframing the electronic consumption experience: the interactional ambiguities of mediated coordination', in Trevor Pinch and Richard Swedberg (eds) *Living in a Material World: Economic Sociology Meets Science and Technology*, Cambridge, MA: MIT Press: 317–340.

MacKenzie, D. (2009) *Material Markets: How Economic Agents Are Constructed*, Oxford: Oxford University Press.

Manivannan, L., Mangalam, S. Chandrakumar and Suresh, G. (2012) 'A study on production and marketing of powerloom products with special reference to select clusters in Tamilnadu, India', *European Journal of Social Sciences*, 28(2): 293–305.

National Skill Development Corporation (n.d.) *Human Resource and Skill Requirements in the Textile Industry 2022: A Report*, New Delhi: National Skill Development Corporation.

Niranjana, Seemanthini and Vinayan, Soumya (2001) *Report on Growth and Prospects of the Handloom Industry*, study commissioned by the Planning Commission, http://planningcommission.nic.in/reports/sereport/ser/stdy_hndloom.pdf (downloaded on 10 March 2013).

152 M. Vijayabaskar

Patil, B.R. (1983) 'Collective bargaining practices in textile and non-textile industries in *Coimbatore*', project report submitted to the Indian Institute of Management Bangalore, October (unpublished).

Preda, A. (2008) 'Technology, agency and financial price data', in Trevor Pinch and Richard Swedberg (eds) *Living in a Material World: Economic Sociology Meets Science and Technology*, Cambridge, MA: MIT Press: 217–252.

Sen, A. (1975) *Employment, Technology and Development*, Oxford: Clarendon Press.

SOMO-ICN (2011) 'Captured by cotton: exploited Dalit girls produce garments in India for European and US markets', report prepared by SOMO (Centre for Research on Multinational Corporations) and ICN (India Committee of the Netherlands).

Srinivasulu, K. (1996) '1985 Textile Policy and handloom industry: policy, promises and performance', *Economic and Political Weekly*, 31(49): 3198–3206.

Stewart, F. (1977) *Technology and Underdevelopment*, London: Macmillan.

Sum, Ngai-Ling (2009) 'The production of hegemonic policy discourses: "competitiveness" as a knowledge brand and its (re-)contextualizations', *Critical Policy Studies*, 3(2): 184–203.

Truffer, B. (2008) 'Society, technology and region: contributions from the social study of technology to economic geography', *Environment and Planning A*, 40(4): 966–985.

Valsan, Binoy (2012) 'When working class ruled Coimbatore', *Times of India*, 2 May, http://articles.timesofindia.indiatimes.com/2012–05–02/coimbatore/31537493_1_cambodia-mills-kaleeswara-spindle-capacity (accessed on 12 March 2013).

Vijayabaskar, M. (2001) *Industrial Formation under Conditions of Flexible Accumulation: The Case of a Global Knitwear Node in Southern India*, unpublished Ph.D. dissertation, Centre for Development Studies, Jawaharlal Nehru University, New Delhi.

Weiss, C. and Jequier, N. (1984) *Technology, Finance, and Development: An Analysis of the World Bank as a Technological Institution*, Lexington: Lexington Books.

Yanagisawa, H. (2010) 'Growth of small-scale industries and changes in consumption patterns in South India 1910s–50s', in Douglas E. Haynes *et al.* (eds) *Towards a History of Consumption in South Asia*, New Delhi: Oxford University Press: 51–75.

9 Commodification, capitalism and crisis

Umar Salam

Introduction

Commodification – the process by which a thing or activity is transformed into a commodity for the purposes of exchange in a market – is, according to Barbara Harriss-White, 'the dominant process underlying the transformation of life in all societies' (in Leys and Harriss-White 2012). It is a recurring subject throughout her work, from the commercialisation of food production in Indian rice markets (Harriss-White 2005; 2011) to the pauperisation of petty production and the commodification of domestic labour (Harriss-White 2006; 2010a), to her work on the political economy of climate change and the trading of carbon emissions (Harriss-White 2008). Influenced by her work, I consider in this chapter three key ways through which commodification and the dynamics of capitalist development are interrelated – the dialectics of commodification, the politics of markets and the unity of opposites.

Commodification has always been at the heart of the study of capitalist development. It is, after all, with the 'analysis of a commodity' that Marx famously begins *Capital*.[1] Capitalism is driven by commodification, by the need to subject more and more things to commodified production, because without commodification ultimately there can be no (capitalist) accumulation. Commodification is self-generating, in the sense that capitalist production has a tendency to commodify also the factors of production – as Sraffa says, 'capitalism is the production of commodities by means of commodities' (Sraffa 1960) – and also in that the competitive pressure of capitalism will always drive firms to 'expand markets and to occupy non-market spheres' (Leys 2001).

Like capitalism itself, commodification, in both theory and practice, has always been associated with crisis; but recent events and the debates generated by them have returned this association to a central position (see e.g. Fraser 2011a). One such argument is that, first, the crisis in which capitalism finds itself today is not unitary in nature, but multiple – economic, ecological, social, political, even moral – and that, moreover, these multiple dimensions, though qualitatively distinct, would seem to be interrelated and impossible to understand in isolation from one another. Second, commodification, albeit in very different forms, is an essential part in each of these multiple dimensions of crisis, either

154   *U. Salam*

directly, as when a process of commodification has itself created crisis, or indirectly, when our understandings of crisis have come to be represented predominantly in terms of commodification. For instance, if the start of the banking crisis is attributed to the deregulation of the financial services industry and the emergence of markets for certain securitised financial products, such as those derived from sub-prime mortgages, then we can see this in terms of the commodification of debt and of risk. The environmental crisis, on the other hand, reflects a different sort of commodification, in which our attempts to gauge the scale of the crisis or even respond to it have come to be seen in commodified or marketised terms, such as the cost–benefit analysis of the 2006 Stern Report[2] or the trading of carbon emissions; in effect, the commodification of licensing to cause future environmental damage. As a result, a problem which is fundamentally political has been recast as an economic one, a collective action problem in which some form of market mechanism, expected to provide the mobilisation necessary today to prevent catastrophe in the future, has conspicuously failed to deliver. A third category of example would be the commodification of various forms of social labour, domestic, reproductive[3] or 'care' which were previously provided within the household or other non-market spaces. The introduction of markets or market mechanisms has, in various ways, redefined these social relationships and in so doing given rise to a host of ethical questions regarding the destructive effects of capitalism and the market on society (Katz 2001; Bakker and Silvey 2008).

One could claim, on the basis of these and other examples, that commodification – the introduction of markets into areas or problems which were previously organised or understood along non-market principles – should be seen fundamentally in terms of social and political change. On this view, the various forms of crisis we are currently experiencing are the overall product of simultaneous processes of commodification across many spheres. As such, we could look to commodification as a conceptual device broad enough to describe the multiple dimensions of capitalist crisis yet specific enough that their essential qualities are not obscured. But immediately we encounter a formidable theoretical challenge. Should we think of commodification as a single phenomenon steadily encroaching in different ways upon the uncommodified world, or as multiple phenomena which may be working with or against each other? If commodification entails a change in the social and political relations of those who produce and exchange a thing, then how on earth do we describe the dynamics of these changes when so many different aspects of our lives are being commodified at once? How do we characterise the impact of commodification on the intersections between, for instance, class, gender, race or other social categories or relations? Does commodification in one area always lead to commodification in others or are there competing forces at work here? How does one resist commodification?

If we are to respond to these difficult questions we will need to have a considerably more nuanced picture of how commodification contributes to the dynamics of capitalist development. This is where, I believe, Barbara Harriss-White's work is particularly helpful, in that it manages, on the one hand, to develop a range of

Commodification, capitalism and crisis   155

practical theoretical principles which may be applied to any process of commodification, but, on the other, being informed by such detailed and original empirical work, to recognise the specific features – the essence, or as Harriss-White would say, 'the quiddity' – of the particular processes themselves. In this chapter, I want to consider how certain key themes that inform Harriss-White's work on the Indian political economy may be used to construct a framework of three interrelated levels through which we might usefully analyse commodification.

The first of these levels is based on the fundamental observation that any process of commodification involves a *transformation* of the thing that is being produced, consumed and exchanged, and hence a contradiction between the uncommodified and commodified forms. The nature of this contradiction, such as that between Marx's use-value and exchange-value, for instance, or Polanyi's idea of fictitious and non-fictitious commodities, is essential to the dynamics of commodification which, in different ways, Marx and Polanyi both represent in terms of a dialectic. But this sort of approach is primarily concerned with *what* the effects are of a process of commodification which has already taken place (or is in the midst of doing so). However, of no less importance are the questions of *how* the details of that process came to be and *why* they took the form they did. In other words, if a commodity is to be traded in a market, what are the ways in which that market is created and regulated, connected to other markets, and in what ways do different agents in that market relate to one another? How does one describe the politics of markets which underlie commodification? This, I would argue, is where Harriss-White's work is so valuable in understanding the detail, techniques and the strategic moves which are used to direct various commodification processes. Lastly, I would like to suggest that a rigid demarcation between the commodified and uncommodified spheres may be a false dichotomy. It is not just that commodification is generally incomplete, and that the commodified and uncommodified coexist; it is rather that the relationship between the two is, in many cases, an indispensable part of any substantive analysis. It is this 'unity of opposites' that forms the third level of my analytic framework. In some cases the commodified realm directly exploits the uncommodified, as in the reliance of private laboratories on publicly available research, or the bailing out by the state of failing banks. One of Harriss-White's most interesting contributions has been to describe, in various South Asian contexts, the emergence or persistence of non-commodified social structures which arise not in spite of or alongside the commodification of the formal economy, but are in fact integrally co-dependent with it and which are stable or at least not easily broken down. My argument here is that the logical endpoint of commodification is not the commodification of everything. Instead the contradictions of commodification seem to generate their own complex dynamics which paradoxically may limit or constrain capitalist development.

On mainstream economics

After three decades of unprecedented market triumphalism in most Western economies, commodification extends deeper and wider than ever before: into the provision of public services (Leys 2001; Huws 2003); the organisation of various forms of (previously uncommodified) social labour (Fraser 2011a; Katz 2001) (such as care, domestic or even reproductive labour); and into the ways in which we develop, disseminate and utilise knowledge and information, especially scientific knowledge (Jessop 2000). The language of the market saturates much of public discourse, including the practice of a large part of the social sciences, and even the functionings of the state may be said to resemble a marketplace, in which political decision making is itself a product (Leys and Harriss-White 2012).

Yet, despite the ubiquity of commodification, mainstream economics, concerned as it is with the properties and behaviour of commodities themselves, would seem to lack an adequate language to describe those non-market qualities which are swept away by the process of commodification. Standard neoclassical assumptions, namely: that commodities are homogeneous and discrete; rivalrous and at least partially excludable; that property rights are attributable and externalities simply do not hold for those things – land, labour, money, knowledge, culture, health – which provide the most important examples of commodification as the source of social and political change. Moreover, the utilitarian criterion of market efficiency may be applied only after commodification has taken place and market relations are in force, but it is in precisely this process that we are most interested. Mainstream economics fails to capture the changes that result from the imposition of market structures because it has no way of adequately describing the non-market interactions that precede them.

However, mainstream economics is important for an understanding of commodification not because it provides a description of it (it does not) but because one cannot explain the extent to which commodification has taken place without appreciating how ideas from mainstream economics – rational choice theory, human capital theory, new institutional economics – have penetrated so deeply into public discourse. Such ideas have facilitated and legitimised commodification and extended the purpose of economic enquiry beyond that of offering a satisfactory formula for the allocation of material goods, rather as a framework for the representation of all human behaviour, in which the study of incentives and responses to those incentives is the sole empirical foundation (Mankiw 2009). It offers what Foucault (2008) called a 'principle of intelligibility' of the social world, and, at the same time, a form of 'permanent economic tribunal' according to which the state may be held to account to the demands and criteria of the market. The extension of what Gary Becker (1992) called the 'economic way of life' to all aspects of human behaviour, the colonisation (Fine 2001) by rational choice methods of so much of social science, amounts to a set of very strong and contestable claims about what markets do and do not do. These claims include that commodification does not change the nature of the thing being commodified, that money does not corrupt, that market relations do not crowd out non-market forms or create perverse incentives (Sandel 2012). In a sense, the starting point for a study of commodification is exactly a rejection of these assumptions and a systematic attempt to study the consequences. In this vein, I propose that we reflect on three levels of analysis through which we might consider commodification in political economy terms.

1 Dialectics of commodification

The first level of analysis is driven by the question of *what* is the fundamental difference between commodified and uncommodified forms. This question lies at the centre of dialectical interpretations of the dynamics of capitalist transformation of both Marx and Polanyi.

For Marx, commodification reveals a contradiction between *use-value*, a qualitative property manifested only through use or consumption, and *exchange-value*, the quantitative measure conferred upon a commodity through exchange.[4] When labour itself is commodified, Marx's contradiction manifests itself as an 'estrangement' between the worker and the object of his labour, which then stands in opposition to him as an 'alien power' (Marx and Engels 1844, 2011: 83–84). The value relation between commodities no longer has any connection with their material properties, and social relations between human beings become conceived of primarily in terms of objects. For Marx, the commodification of labour was an essential and corrosive part of capitalism, alienating man from humanity, and substituting the capacity to appreciate worth with the ability to calculate price. The objectification of labour, the sale of labour power as a commodity to the capitalist, creates the object of labour as something alien to the worker (ibid.).

Commodities become fetishified, the value relation between the labour which produced them having 'no connection' with their physical properties (Marx and Engels 1888; 2004: 222). From this contradiction comes reification in which social relations between human beings become conceived of in terms of objects (Marx 1867; 1992: 77–78). Commodification, fetishification, alienation and reification are then, for Marx, a set of interrelated processes in which social and political relations are reconfigured. Distinctive aspects of capitalism, such as private property, follow logically as consequences not causes of alienated labour, 'just as the gods are *fundamentally* not the cause but the product of confusions of human reason' (Marx and Engels 1844; 2011: 91).

For Polanyi, on the other hand, a crucial contradiction emerges between *capitalist* commodities, namely those commodities produced in a labour process subject to capitalist competition, and *fictitious* commodities which, though they are commodities insofar as they may be bought or sold, are not actually produced for that purpose, nor is their production subject to the competitive pressures of the market (Polanyi 2001; see also Jessop 2007). Polanyi's further distinctive view of the formal (market) economy as opposed to the substantive economy, 'submerged in social relationships' (Polanyi 2001: 46) in which exchange may be market, reciprocal or redistributive, leads to an understanding of commodification as a reorganisation of society, in which traditional norms are subordinated before the 'satanic mills' of the market (Polanyi 2001). Whereas Marx's focus was on labour,[5] for Polanyi the three principal fictitious commodities were land, labour and money, and while Marx's dynamics of social change depend on class struggle and ideology, Polanyi's idea of the 'Double Movement' is a reaction of society at large against the 'disembedding' effects of commodification.[6] The

158   *U. Salam*

great weakness of Polanyi's account is that so little is said about the mechanism by which the Double Movement is meant to arrive, beyond the idea of a struggle between proponents of marketisation and those of social protection. Moreover, the concept of a fictitious commodity carries with it a sense of 'original condition', of pre-market socially embedded norms, such as trust and reciprocity, as being inherently more desirable than that of market exchange. But the problem with that position is that it is somewhat blind to questions of domination, seeing only the type of domination that can come through marketisation, and implicitly assuming that non-market structures do not lead to domination. Resistance then, for Polanyi, is simply resistance to marketisation, nothing more. On the other hand, Polanyi's view of the crisis of his time, to which the *Great Transformation* is a response, is genuinely holistic. Polanyi attaches as much weight to the despoliation of nature as he does to the outcomes of financial collapse or the ruptures in the social fabric.

Marx and Polanyi share the key insight that commodification is not only (or even primarily) about the ways in which goods are produced, consumed and exchanged but rather about the ways in which both the nature of and relations between those who produce, consume and exchange those goods are transformed. However, Polanyi gives little indication as to the mechanism by which the Double Movement would take place. Orthodox Marxism, on the other hand, gives an ontological privilege to the commodification of labour relations but does not register, at least not to the same degree, those other elements of commodification which we would like to address.

Accounts such as those of Marx and Polanyi present grand narratives of the ways in which commodification leads to social and political change, how the transformation to market-based modes of production and exchange results in further changes in the relations between those who now participate in markets. What they do not do is give a detailed analysis of *how* these markets are organised, nor even how they arise in the first place. And yet these questions of how commodification takes the forms that it does are in a sense prior to those regarding its consequences. We need to know how political opposition to the creation of markets is overcome, what changes need to occur and what conditions need to be met for commodification to take place. We need to understand how the structure of those markets which arise out of commodification reflects the underlying political economy and how questions of power enter into the operations of markets.

2 The politics of markets

The second level of analysis, then, concerns the politics of markets and the very specific questions of power relations between those who participate in them. These questions are of paramount importance in Harriss-White's work and in certain other authors whom she regularly references. One such author is Colin Leys and his concept of 'market-driven politics', the idea that governments no longer manage their own economies, let alone aim to implement some

Commodification, capitalism and crisis 159

democratically achieved consensus. Instead, politics is increasingly driven by the need to satisfy various (often transnational) market forces. Commodification is an essential vehicle for market-driven politics and, for it to be achieved, a range of administrative and legislative procedures must be implemented and often a well-entrenched degree of political opposition overcome. Leys, writing on the commodification of public services (especially health care and public service television), has described in detail the techniques and strategies that are typically deployed to this end. A sequence of moves is involved, including the systematic devaluation of the public provision of services, the incentivisation of private sector involvement through state-underwritten capital investment and the coordinated rebranding in the public consciousness of former services as commodities (Leys 2001; 2008).

Another important author is Gordon White, whose four-point typology of the politics of markets (1993) is an invaluable starting point for articulating the ways in which power enters into the creation, regulation and operation of markets. White's classification of the politics of markets has four categories: (1) the politics of *state involvement* encompassing both direct participation (when the state itself is an actor in the market) and regulation (which can mean direct intervention but is also used to refer to the background institutions (e.g. property rights, licensing laws, regulation of money)); (2) the politics of *market organisation* which governs the various ways in which actors in markets collaborate, cooperate and compete with one another (e.g. formal association, networks and hierarchies); (3) the politics of *market structures* referring to the patterning of market exchange by pre-existing asymmetries of power deriving from social and political structures and material differences; (4) the politics of *embeddedness* which raises the vital question of how power relations in markets are affected by the social and cultural norms shared by participants in the market.

One context in which Harriss-White applies the typology is to the politics of technology markets in renewable energy in India (Harriss-White 2008). In this work, the commodification of energy is seen to have complex and unhelpful consequences for the capacity of the state to devise and implement coherent energy policy. Harriss-White also reveals the extent to which the interests of capital are enmeshed with the political structures underlying these markets. In particular, technological development (for instance, solar energy) is seen to be politically constrained where those constraints reflect relative positions of power within markets. As Hobsbawm says, 'It is often assumed that an economy of private enterprise has an automatic bias towards innovation, but this is not so. It has a bias only towards profit' (1969: 40).

However, while the systematic study of the politics of markets must surely be an indispensable component of any analysis of commodification, there is an important aspect which still has to be addressed. In distinguishing between a commodified realm in which social, political and economic relations are organised along market lines and an uncommodified realm in which alternative modes of production and exchange are possible, we should not be drawn into thinking of the two as independent of or exclusive to one another, nor should we see

160 *U. Salam*

commodification as an inevitable and unidirectional process steadily taking over the whole of the uncommodified realm. In fact, commodified and uncommodified structures typically coexist, locked into complex, often exploitative relationships which may well be stable and resistant, at least to some extent, to further commodification. In this sense, the logical end-point of commodification may not be the commodification of everything.[7] We need to understand how the commodified and uncommodified are in fact a 'unity of opposites'.[8]

3 The unity of opposites – commodified and uncommodified

The final level of the analytic framework presented here is to investigate the relationship between the commodified and the uncommodified. We see this sort of relationship in various contexts. The privatisation of public services is generally a piecemeal affair, with private firms keen to cherry-pick those parts of the service that are most profitable and easiest to run, leaving the state with the responsibility for those areas that are less readily commodifiable and which may well remain uncommodified. In such cases, the private sector also looks to the state to underwrite the risk involved to capital, further entrenching the relationship between the commodified and uncommodified. While the coexistence of public and private alternatives may lead, as Leys observes (2001: 85), to a situation in which the public provision is systematically devalued, and also to a cultural change in which the workforce is remotivated and redefined in market terms, it still remains the case that the private sector depends for its profitability very much on the exploitation of various uncommodified structures, such as the investment made by the state in infrastructure or training. In a similar way, the commodification of knowledge through patenting and the extension of intellectual property legislation depends crucially on the vast repository of publicly available scientific knowledge, the common heritage of mankind (Salam 1989). And in a rather different way, the current international banking crisis, and the dysfunctionality of the markets in which debt has been commodified, are inextricably bound up with the political, 'uncommodified' questions of what these debts mean to sovereign states, firms and individuals. The point in each case is that what drives the dynamics of the system as a whole is not only the internal logic of the commodified sector but the interaction between it and the uncommodified. The contradiction between the two is very much a unity of opposites.

Harriss-White's work details the complexity of this relationship in numerous, diverse contexts. In her work on the Indian informal economy, for example, she describes how the global commodification of money leads to 'labour trapped, more intensely commodified in the "space of flows" connecting the metropolises and less commodified and even increasingly decommodified in the "space of places" in which most of the population is embedded' (Harriss-White 2010a; 2010b). The resulting process of 'informalisation' creates an informal economy, in which the distinction between state and market is blurred at the local level, while the informal economy itself is regulated by a host of non-state means: family ties; repeated, interlocking contracts and networks; trust, reputation; and

Commodification, capitalism and crisis 161

private protection forces (Harriss-White 2003: 74–75). Despite the rapid economic growth India has experienced in the formal sector in recent years there is no evidence whatsoever that the informal economy is diminishing as a result. In fact the reverse seems to be the case (ibid.).

These themes, and especially the mechanisms that govern the interaction between the commodified and uncommodified, continue in her work on poverty and capitalism, petty production and the commodification of domestic labour. Harriss-White describes how pauperised petty production, again apparently outside the ambit of state regulation, 'may not be a precapitalist relic in the course of being eradicated but may actually be intrinsic to state-regulated capitalism and incorporated by it' (Harriss-White 2006: 1242). Petty production is intertwined with state-regulated commercial capitalism, through a system of money advances from commercial firms, which are themselves regulated and protected by the state. Survival for the small firms is only possible through the 'super-exploitation' of family labour. The commodification of this domestic labour also provokes complex and difficult questions regarding the ways in which social structures such as gender, class or caste impact upon capitalist development. Harriss-White's work on the commodification of rice production in West Bengal, Tamil Nadu, Bangladesh and the Punjab (Harriss-White 2011) looks in particular at the question of gender and shows how capitalist production can under certain conditions coexist alongside petty commodity production, in which the economies of scale available to the capitalist producer are offset by the exploitation of unwaged women's labour in the realm of petty production. This finding contrasts with Huws' (2003) argument which predicts 'waves of commodification' in advanced capitalist societies, the crucial difference being the low returns to labour in developing countries.

A further example of how we might locate Harriss-White's work within the analytic framework presented in this chapter is provided by the role of the intermediate classes in modern-day India. Drawing on the work of Mushtaq Khan (2000; 2005) on the fragmented clientelist nature of Indian politics, an argument is made that primitive accumulation does indeed coexist with capitalist accumulation and is closely linked to the politics of the intermediate classes (Harriss-White 2003). Far from being in decay, the intermediate classes are 'fighting back' and show a resilience to modernised capitalist development unanticipated by earlier theorists such as Kalecki (1972) or Jha (1980) (Harriss-White 2003: 71). What Harriss-White's work illustrates so well is that pre-capitalist social structures not only persist but in fact are integrally connected with the path of capitalist development. The result is a pattern of rent-seeking (against the state) and 'primitive accumulation' that goes against the developmental trajectory that many social theorists have predicted. Liberalisation undermines the intermediate classes (Harriss-White and McCartney 2000) but does not abolish them.

In a different way, one could argue that the intermediate classes, despite lacking a materially based class identity, are at least partially defined in relation to another form of commodification, namely that of political stability. The model of fragmented clientelism is a form of market in which political influence,

162   *U. Salam*

whether in the form of votes, lobbying or the threat of strikes, demonstrations or violence, have become products which may be exchanged for transfers or rent-seeking opportunities. As such, it is wrong to expect class formation and commodification to be simply related. The intermediate classes arise and persist in opposition to commodification (by the capitalist classes) and yet are themselves also defined by it (through the commodification of political stability).

On the commodification of knowledge

Commodification, as we have seen, is *the* dominant driving force behind capitalist development. Nowhere has this been more apparent than in the commodification of knowledge and in particular in the emergence, over the past 20 years or so, of the concept of the 'knowledge economy'. Indeed, the World Development Report 1998–1999 argued that knowledge *was* development and that development strategies should be aimed towards 'building a knowledge economy'. Various themes have emerged, which are now global orthodoxies among policy makers: that 'knowledge', however defined, is the key driver of economic growth; that 'human capital' or 'intangible capital' are a country's most precious resources; that education, especially higher education, and academic research should be reconceived in terms of the generation of that capital; that 'building knowledge infrastructure' and establishing appropriate institutional arrangements, systems of innovation and liberal trade regimes, for instance, will lead to the effective dissemination and economic exploitation of knowledge. As corollaries, debates on intellectual property, deregulation or privatisation of education, and the trading of information of various kinds are more immediate and interrelated than ever.

Knowledge and the dialectics of commodification

Insofar as one can address the commodification of knowledge in a Marxian or Polanyian vein, one can make the argument (as Bob Jessop (2000; 2007) has done) that knowledge has the status of a fictitious commodity, in line with Polanyi's classic treatments of land, labour and money, and that accumulation and subsumption also apply, *pace* Marx. In this way, Jessop is able to draw an analagous dialectic presentation from the contradictions between different stages of commodification (2007).

The first of these stages is that of a *'non-commodity'*; that is to say when knowledge exists as an intellectual commons, circulating more or less freely through reciprocal exchange and produced largely under non-market conditions. The second, that of a *'simple fictitious commodity'*, is that at which these intellectual commons have been enclosed by some non-market mechanism, some form of primitive accumulation, so that they may be regarded as private property and to be exchanged within a market. This is analogous to Polanyi's own treatment of the enclosure movement[9] in *The Great Transformation*. Primitive accumulation of this kind may be via the appropriation of indigenous, tribal or

Commodification, capitalism and crisis 163

peasant knowledge and its transcription without compensation, as in bio-piracy; the separation of intellectual labour from control over the means of production of knowledge; the 'creeping extension' of copyright into broader forms of property right and the accompanying erosion of public interest (see e.g. Drahos and Braithwaite 2002; Robins and Webster 2004; Shiva 1997). The third stage is when intellectual labour has formally been subjected to and subsumed under capitalist exploitation and transformed into immaterial goods and services; in this case knowledge may be considered a *'fictitious commodity'* as with labour power. The fourth and final stage, that of *'fictive commodity'*, is when the revenue streams generated by intellectual labour are formally protected by intellectual property rights, enabling 'technological rents' to accrue to the holders of those rights and facilitating the abstract exchange of these rights and the establishment of derivative transactions and secondary markets upon them. These rents are the price the market pays for the use of knowledge as a commodity and are in direct analogy to wages, the price the market pays for the use of labour; (tenancy) rents, the price the market pays for the use of land; and interest, the price the market pays for the use of money. There is a contradiction between the continual pressure to innovate and the continual need to protect rents. In other words, the reflexivity and generalisability of knowledge create an intrinsically unstable system in which there is an in-built tendency to seek to decommodify knowledge inputs, and so to minimise costs, while commodifying outputs and hence maximising profits.

Knowledge and the politics of markets

In an analogous way to that in which Leys describes the essential pre-conditions for the commodification of public services, one can also seek to characterise the reorganisation of society that is necessary for the commodification of knowledge to take place. There are at least three crucial aspects: the *codification* of knowledge, in which knowledge is detached from manual labour and the minds of workers and relocated in formal, exchangeable products and services; the *disembedding* of knowledge from its social roots, through which the primary code governing its use becomes one of profit, rather than 'truth', 'need' or 'beauty'; and the expansion of the *market* as a means of circulation and redistribution of knowledge ahead of previously existing reciprocal relationships between and within specific economic units, such as the household.

By way of a topical example, the marketisation of higher education in the West typically involves just this pattern of strategic moves and political tactics. In transforming education from a universal welfare entitlement to a private investment in human capital and then to a full consumer-driven system, the university is first reconceived within a wider economic system, such as a system of innovation which will place particular demands for particular output; further market-oriented criteria are introduced to assess performance, accompanied by a shift towards private sector and corporate managerialism, with traditional, democratic governance structures downplayed; and finally the

164 *U. Salam*

creeping introduction of privatisation, through student loans, tuition fees and other means of ownership.

The commodification of knowledge is also richly illustrative of Gordon White's politics of markets typology, described previously. Any step towards marketisation inevitably involves the politics of state involvement, since so much of the knowledge production infrastructure (public universities, military research labs, etc.) falls under state control. Questions of regulation are raised, for instance, in the course of negotiations over intellectual property rights, while the politics of association are relevant to a discussion of rent-seeking in techno- logy markets, for instance, when Schumpeterian rents become monopoly rents (Khan 2000). Finally, the politics of embeddedness manifest themselves in a multitude of ways, not least in academia itself where academic capitalism and commodification threatens the very ethos of research (Collini 2012).

Knowledge and the unity of opposites

In some ways, the distinctive feature Harriss-White describes regarding the simultaneous coexistence of commodified and uncommodified social structures (with regard to the commodification of labour) is even more in evidence with the commodification of knowledge. This is ultimately because intellectual property rights can only be asserted to a limited degree and because publicly available knowledge will always be of great importance. Any realm of capitalised com- modified knowledge production will necessarily be immersed in a host of uncommodified relationships. The extent to which the commodified sphere is able to exploit the uncommodified is the part of the picture that is up for political contestation. On the other hand, it is also the case that knowledge necessarily involves both public and private characteristics. The production of pure scient- ific research, for instance, often cited as a global public good, is typically fraught with secretive competition whereas, conversely, the output of public education results in major private gains for individual students. Similarly, while one might very well wish to demarcate services provided by the state from those provided by the market, one cannot so easily distinguish their output nor the reverse impact of that output on the state's provision of services. Indeed, in a more general sense, the state itself, especially in a democracy, is subject to market influence of many kinds. Conversely, just as there is no state without markets, there is no market without states. Every market is created and to some extent regulated by the state (or by states). Finally, dualisms of this kind, which are unhelpful at the national level, are completely inappropriate at the international level where there is, of course, no global state. It is precisely because one cannot separate market and state that the *politics of markets* becomes so important.

Knowledge and Indian political economy

There are few developing countries that have had a more significant engagement with the knowledge economy discourse than India. The World Bank has for

Commodification, capitalism and crisis 165

some time argued that India holds certain advantages over other developing countries. According to the Bank, large numbers of English speakers, concentrations of particular skills, macro-economic stability, and a relatively dynamic private sector make India particularly well placed to take 'advantage of the knowledge revolution' (Dahlman and Utz 2005). With the establishment in 2006 of the National Knowledge Commission, the Indian government had set out explicitly to adopt *'a knowledge-oriented paradigm of development'* which *'would enable India to leverage the demographic advantage'* of its vast population of young people. Such an initiative was merely a formal reflection of a process that was already well underway, and which had, over at least the two preceding decades, been steadily revolutionising the education system and creating an increasingly significant 'knowledge sector', built around ICT and biotechnology.

As the economy liberalised, the view of knowledge as a key avenue of economic exploitation strengthened, and an explosion of commodified knowledge services resulted (Agarwal 2006).

Perhaps nowhere are the effects of commodification more clearly illustrated than through the expansion of privatised higher education in India. In 1983 there were 120 universities, rising to 367 in 2006 and to 567 by 2012, with the vast majority of that increase being in the private sector. These new universities, though accorded charitable status, are 'de facto profit-oriented commercial establishments ... inimical to the national interest' (Anandakrishnan 2007). Among the various criticisms made of the new universities are the narrowness of their curricula; the lack of adequate mechanisms for regulation, quality control and governance; and the inconsistent and occasionally extremely poor level of education provided. All of these criticisms are, in some shape or form, reflections of the question of 'what' knowledge is being provided, and of the particular pitfalls that may beset a market-oriented provision of that knowledge. But, at another level, the existence and nature of the new universities reveals a further question of 'how' this particular form of commodification came to be, to which the answer is through a complex combination of changing socio-economic circumstances in the classes who are driving demand for and consumption of higher education, and certain political repositionings, at state, national and international levels, that accompany the creation and regulation of markets for such products. Finally, as has been noted before, the intrinsically simultaneously private and public characteristics of education as a knowledge commodity/public good ensure that this phenomenon is not well understood through the binary lens of commodified/uncommodified but, instead, is in many ways a unity of opposites.

Conclusion

This chapter began by emphasising the multi-dimensional nature of the global capitalist crisis we are currently facing, and by observing that commodification, in a variety of ways, is central to almost every aspect of it. Seeking a single theoretical framework in which to simultaneously conceptualise these different dimensions may be neither necessary nor possible, but this should not lead us to narrowly privilege or isolate one dimension over any other. This is why commodification, as an analytical device, may be useful, as it directly concerns the social and political consequences which follow a transition to a market-oriented mode of behaviour, whichever context that may be in. I have argued that there are three key levels at which one should interrogate a process of commodification. First, there is the question that Marx and Polanyi ask, which is *what* is fundamentally altered by commodification, and what effects this has on those involved in that transformation. Second, there are the political questions of *how* a process of commodification takes place. There is nothing neutral or natural about markets, or their absence. It is imperative that we understand the nitty-gritty of how marketisation takes place and in whose interest it does so, and how the operations of markets reflect the underlying political economy of those who create, regulate and participate in them. Finally, there is the highly complex question of the relationship between the commodified capitalist realm and the uncommodified. I have suggested that seeing this relationship as a stark binary is a mistake, that as Harriss-White's work shows, there is typically not only a necessary coexistence, but that the two are intertwined often in an exploitative form. As such, the question of resistance to commodification is less a futile enquiry of how to put the genie back in the bottle and more a question of how to bolster and defend social structures to minimise the potential for exploitation in the relationship between the commodified and the uncommodified. There are, of course, alternative points of view. Niall Ferguson used his Reith Lectures in 2012 (Ferguson 2012) to argue a Hayekian position that markets solved problems of information in a way that no other system could, and that marketisation should be welcomed and regulation feared. There is also the undeniable fact that we do seem to be moving towards an ever more commodified world and that the counter-movements, such as they are, are fractured and outgunned. In the light of these difficulties, I conclude that Harriss-White's work is not just an incisive analysis of our times but a call-to-arms, a rallying cry for resistance.

Notes

1

> The wealth of those societies in which the capitalist mode of production prevails, presents itself as 'an immense accumulation of commodities,' its unit being a single commodity. Our investigation must therefore begin with the analysis of a commodity.
>
> (Marx 1867, 1922: ch. 1)

2 http://webarchive.nationalarchives.gov.uk/+/http:/www.hm-treasury.gov.uk/sternreview_index.htm.
3 Such as the practice of commercial surrogacy, legalised in India in 2002 and now estimated to involve over 1000 clinics and to be worth in excess of $2 billion per annum (Dasgupta and Dasgupta 2014).
4 A thing may, of course, have use-value without being a commodity (such as air) but to be a commodity (and therefore to be exchanged) requires both a use-value, or else it would not be purchased, and an exchange-value, or else it would not be produced.

Commodification, capitalism and crisis 167

5 Marx writes on the commodity character of money – the 'universal whore, the universal pander between men and nations' – in the *Economic and Philosophical Manuscripts* and also, extensively, in *Capital*, Volume 1. In the same volume, he also explicitly mentions the productive power of nature and of virgin land.
6 In recent work, Nancy Fraser (2011b) has extended Polanyi's idea of fictitious commodification in a feminist direction and postulates a 'triple movement' in which the three competing poles of marketisation, social protection and emancipation generate the dynamics of social and political struggle. Her account, incorporating as it does an explicit challenge to forms of domination, overcomes some of the shortcomings in Polanyi's work while retaining many of its original and distinctive features.
7 Leys and Harriss-White (2012) argue, on the other hand, that the logic of commodification is further commodification. But it would seem (see the next section) that the 'equilibrium' point which commodification may ultimately reach is a mixture of the commodified and the uncommodified.
8 'The recognition (discovery) of the contradictory, *mutually exclusive*, opposite tendencies in *all* phenomena and processes of nature *(including* mind and society)' (Lenin 1958).
9 Polanyi (2001: 37) in which he famously describes the seventeenth-century enclosure movement as a 'revolution of the rich against the poor'.

References

Agarwal, P. (2006) *Higher Education in India: Need for a Strategic Paradigm Shift and Framework for Action*, New Delhi: ICRIER New Delhi.
Anandakrishnan, M. (2007) 'Critique of Knowledge Commission', *Economic and Political Weekly*, 42(7): 557–560.
Bakker, I. and Silvey, R. (eds) (2008) *Beyond States and Markets: The Challenges of Social Reproduction*, Oxford: Routledge.
Becker, G. (1992) *The Economic Way of Looking at Life*, Nobel Prize Lecture, available at http://home.uchicago.edu/~gbecker/Nobel/nobellecture.
Collini, S. (2012) *What are Universities for?*, London: Penguin.
Dahlman, C. and Utz, A. (2005) *India and the Knowledge Economy: Leveraging Strengths and Opportunities*, Washington, DC: World Bank.
Dasgupta, S. and Dasgupta, S. (2014) *Globalization and Transnational Surrogacy in India: Outsourcing Life*, Plymouth, MA: Lexington Books.
Drahos, P. and Braithwaite, J. (2002) *Information Feudalism: Who Owns the Knowledge Economy?*, London: Earthscan.
Ferguson, N. (2012) *The Darwinian Economy* – Lecture 2/4, the Reith Lectures, available at www.bbc.co.uk/programmes/b01jmxqp/features/transcript.
Fine, B. (2001) *Social Capital versus Social Theory*, London: Routledge.
Foucault, M. (2008) *The Birth of Biopolitics: Lectures at the College de France 1978–9*, London: Palgrave Macmillan.
Fraser, N. (2011a) *Between Marketization and Social Protection: Ambivalences of Feminism in the Context of Capitalist Crisis* (unpublished), http://sms.cam.ac.uk/media/1117457.
—— (2011b) 'A Polanyian feminism? Re-reading The Great Transformation in the 21st century', *Humanitas Lecture*, University of Cambridge, March, www.crassh.cam.ac.uk/events/1534/.
Gupta, N. (2005) *International Trends in Private Higher Education and the Indian Scenario*, Berkeley: University of California.

168 U. Salam

Harriss-White, B. (2005) 'Commercialisation, commodification and gender relations in post-harvest systems for rice in South Asia', *Economic and Political Weekly*, 40(25): 2530–2542.

—— (2006) 'Poverty and capitalism', *Economic and Political Weekly*, 3(4): 1241–1246.

—— (2008) 'Market politics and climate change', *Development*, 51(3): 350–358.

—— (2010a) 'Globalization, the financial crisis and petty production in India's socially regulated informal economy', *Global Labour Journal*, 1(1): 152–177.

—— (2010b) 'Work and wellbeing in informal economies: the regulative roles of institutions of identity and the State', *World Development*, 38(2): 170–183.

—— (2011) 'Commodification and masculinisation in post-harvest systems for rice in South Asia', in *Du grain à moudre. Genre, développement rural et alimentation*, (dir.) C. Verschuur: 59–99. Actes des colloques genre et développement. Berne: DDC-Commission nationale suisse pour l'UNESCO; Genève: IHEID, http://graduateinstitute.ch/webdav/site/genre/shared/Genre_docs/Actes_2010/Actes_2010_HarrissWhite.pdf.

—— (2012) 'Capitalism and the common man – four decades of development in Africa and South Asia', *Work in Progress Paper 2, Oxford University CSASP*, www.southasia.ox.ac.uk/__data/assets/pdf_file/0004/39424/bhwpcp12.pdf.

Harriss-White, B. and McCartney, M. (2000) 'The "intermediate regime" and "intermediate classes" revisited: a critical political economy of Indian economic development from 1980 to Hindutva', *QEH Working Paper 34*, Oxford University.

Hayek, F. (1936) *Economics and Knowledge*, Presidential address delivered before the London Economic Club, 10 November 1936, available at www.virtualschool.edu/mon/Economics/HayekEconomicsAndKnowledge.html.

—— (1945) 'The use of knowledge in society', *American Economic Review*, 35(4): 519–530, www.virtualschool.edu/mon/Economics/HayekUseOfKnowledge.html.

Hirshmann, A. (1982) *Shifting Involvements: Private Interest and Public Action*, Princeton, NJ: Princeton University Press.

Hobsbawm, E.J. (1969) *Industry and Empire from 1750 to the Present Day*, London: Penguin.

Huws, U. (2003) *The Making of a Cyberteriat*, London: Merlin.

Jessop, B. (2000) 'The State and the contradictions of the knowledge-driven economy', in J.R. Bryson, P.W. Daniels, N.D. Henry and J. Pollard (eds) *Knowledge, Space, Economy*, London: Routledge.

—— (2007) 'Knowledge as a fictitious commodity: insights and limits of a Polanyian perspective', in Ayse Bugra and Kaan Agartan (eds) *Reading Karl Polanyi for the Twenty-First Century: Market Economy as Political Project*, Basingstoke: Palgrave.

Jha, P. (1980) *The Political Economy of Stagnation*, New Delhi: Oxford University Press.

Kalecki, M. (1972) *Essays on the Economic Growth of the Socialist and Mixed Economies*, London: Unwin.

Katz, C. (2001) 'On the grounds of globalization: a topography for feminist political engagement', *Signs* (Chicago): 1213–1234.

Khan, M. (2000) 'Class, clientelism and communal politics in Bangladesh', in K.N. Panikkar, T.J. Byres and U. Patnaik (eds) *The Making of History: Essays Presented to Irfan Habib*, Delhi: Tulika: 572–606.

—— (2005) 'Markets, states and democracy: patron–client networks and the case for democracy in developing countries', *Democratization*, 12(5): 704–724.

Lenin, V.I. (1958) 'On the question of dialectics', *Collected Works, Vol. 38*, Moscow: Progress.

Commodification, capitalism and crisis 169

Leys, C. (2001) *Market Driven Politics: Neoliberal Democracy and the Public Interest*, London: Verso.
—— (2008) *Total Capitalism: Market Politics, Market State*, London: Merlin Press.
Leys, C. and Harriss-White, B. (2012) 'Commodification: the essence of our time', Open Democracy, www.opendemocracy.net/ourkingdom/colin-leys-barbara-harriss-white/commodification-essence-of-our-time.
Mankiw, G. (2009) *Macroeconomics*, NewYork: Worth Publishers.
Marginson, S. (2007) 'The public/private divide in higher education', *Higher Education*, 53: 307–333.
Marx, K. (1867, 1992) *Capital: Volume I*, London: Penguin.
Marx, K. and Engels, F. (1888, 2004) *The Communist Manifesto*, London: Penguin.
—— (1844, 2011) *Economic and Philosophical Manuscripts*, London: Wilder.
North, D. (1990) *Institutions, Institutional Change and Economic Performance*, Cambridge: Cambridge University Press.
OECD (1996) *The Knowledge Based Economy*, Paris: OECD.
Peters, M. (2003) 'Classical political economy and the role of universities in the new knowledge economy', *Globalisation, Societies and Education*, 1(2): 153–168.
—— (2004) 'Education and ideologies of the knowledge economy: Europe and the politics of emulation', *Social Work*, 2(2): 160–172.
—— (2005) 'Knowledge networks', in Michael A. Peters and Tina Besley, *Building Knowledge Cultures: Education and Development in the Age of Knowledge Capitalism*, Lanham, MD, and Oxford: Rowman & Littlefield.
Polanyi, K. (2001) *The Great Transformation*, Boston, MA: Beacon.
Read, R. (2011) 'There are no such things as "commodities": a research note', *Journal of Philosophical Economics*, 4(2): 93–104.
Robins, K. and Webster, F. (2004) 'The long history of the information revolution', in F. Webster (ed.) *Information History Reader*, London: Routledge.
Salam, A. (1989) *Ideals and Realities*, Singapore: World Scientific Publications.
Samuelson, P. (1947) *Foundations of Economic Analysis*, Cambridge, MA: Harvard University Press.
Sandel, M. (2012) *What Money Can't Buy*, London: Alan Lane/Penguin.
Shiva, V. (1997) *Biopiracy: The Plunder of Nature and Knowledge*, Boston, MA: South End Press.
Smith, A. (1776) *The Wealth of Nations*, London: Penguin.
Sraffa, P. (1960) *Production of Commodities by Means of Commodities*, Cambridge: Cambridge University Press.
Stern Report on the Economics of Climate Change (2006) UK HM Treasury, http://webarchive.nationalarchives.gov.uk/+/www.hm-treasury.gov.uk/sternreview_summary.htm.
White, G. (1993) 'Towards a political analysis of markets', *IDS Bulletin*, 24(3): 4–11.
World Bank (1998a) *World Development Report: Knowledge For Development*, Oxford: Oxford University Press.
—— (2002) *Constructing Knowledge Societies*, Washington, DC: World Bank.
—— (2008) *Building Knowledge Economies: Advanced Strategies for Development*, Washington, DC: World Bank.

10 A heterodox analysis of capitalism

Insights from a market town in South India after the Green Revolution[1]

Elisabetta Basile[2]

1 Introduction

The 'purely' capitalist economy in which all social relations are money relations and individuals are rational and optimising beings is only found in mainstream textbooks. Despite predictions about institutional and economic convergence, capitalist countries do not converge towards a unique model, and a great variety of production structures, socio-economic relations and patterns of spatial distribution of resources coexists and persists.

The evidence of the varieties of capitalism undermines the interpretive power of mainstream economic theory showing that innovative theoretical tools are needed to address development and change in 'real world' economies. This chapter contributes to this analytical endeavour by proposing a 'heterodox' framework based on a combination of Marxist and institutionalist propositions in which the impact of institutions upon human behaviour is conceptualised as a key to explore variety.

The chapter is organised as follows. I introduce the Marxist/Institutionalist framework in section 2, and review its contribution to the analysis of capitalism in section 3. In section 4, I apply the Marxist/Institutionalist framework to the analysis of Arni, a market town in South India which has been widely researched over four decades. Section 5 concludes.

2 Introducing the Marxist/Institutionalist framework

The complexity of contemporary capitalism is largely unpredicted by economic theory. Power structures and institutions inherited from the pre-capitalist past are not being dissolved by capitalism. They intertwine with capitalist production relations, giving birth to multiple modes of inequality and to a variety of socio-economic organisations and patterns of change. As a consequence, capitalist societies and economies are highly diversified and conflict-ridden.

Economic theory lacks suitable tools to address this complexity. Neoclassical economics is inadequate to explore variety and conflicts with its focus on equilibrium and uniformity. Other approaches such as Marxism and Institutionalism, which explicitly address conflict and change, provide only partial insights.

A heterodox analysis of capitalism   171

Marxism reveals the commoditisation of the labour force and capital/labour conflict as the main features of the capitalist economy, but does not account for the interplay between individual behaviour and institutions that lead to the variety of socio-economic structures. Institutionalism has a powerful agency theory, which explains how individual behaviour influences institutions and how institutions influence individual behaviour (then solving the agency/structure problem), but misses the centrality of capital/labour conflicts.

This theoretical impasse may be overcome with an analytical framework in which Marxist and Institutionalist propositions are combined to address inequalities and conflicts, different patterns of individual behaviour and the varieties of organisational forms (Basile 2011). The combination of the two approaches is a methodological rather than a theoretical exercise, whose originality lies in the way in which concepts and propositions are organised in a single framework which is intended as a guide for empirical analysis.

The literature on the Marxist/Institutionalist dialogue shows that, while the approaches broadly converge in their analysis of capitalism, two major areas of divergence exist: class analysis and agency theory. Accordingly, the analysis of change differs. On the Marxist side, change is seen as a process determined by capital/labour conflicts, while on the Institutionalist side, change is taken to be an evolutionary and cumulative process driven by the two-way interplay between individuals and institutions. Yet, as the literature (e.g. Dugger and Sherman 2000; Cullenberg 2000) shows, these discrepancies do not prevent the Marxist/ Institutionalist dialogue. Analytical connections exist between 'New Marxism' (i.e. Marx's theory adapted and integrated with the contribution of critical Marxists, from Gramsci and Althusser, to Resnick and Wolff, and Wright) and 'Old Institutionalism' (i.e. the Institutionalist framework built on Veblen's critique of the micro-foundations of mainstream economics).

New Marxism and Old Institutionalism are compatible and coherent, and the initial discrepancies are largely reduced. Confronting unpredicted developments of capitalism, and building on the concept of overdetermination,[3] Marxism has overcome its determinist view of history and has been led to acknowledge the complexity of class structure and labour commoditisation. Institutionalism has been led by the recovery of its Veblenian roots to the conceptualisation of capitalism as a conflicting socio-economic system, in which institutions are power tools that shape individual desires and aims.

A Marxist/Institutionalist 'synthesis' is theoretically feasible and enhances the interpretive power of the 'heterodox' framework. The feasibility of this framework is best observed in relation to the way in which the theoretical weaknesses of Marxism and Institutionalism are dealt with. The main solution I propose is to introduce into the framework Veblen's theory of agency (Veblen 1919) which, rejecting any form of determination of human behaviour, points to the influence of institutions and their two-way interplay with individuals. The employment relation is taken to be the major trait of capitalism and the conflicts of vested interests the major driving force. Class and class interests and stratifications are explicitly considered in this framework and class interests are included among vested interests.

172 *E. Basile*

As an institution, class influences individuals, being at the same time an outcome of social intercourse. Moreover, class stratifications intertwine with other forms of social stratification. While the primacy of class conflicts may not be explicitly acknowledged, the Institutionalist view of capitalism is not inconsistent with it.

2.1 The Marxist/Institutionalist framework

The aim of the Marxist/Institutionalist framework is to provide the conceptual tools to interpret and explain the processes leading to growth and change in contemporary 'real world' economies. The framework proposes a theoretical representation of the main socio-economic relations of the capitalist economy – from human agency to socio-economic change – which are described by means of concepts borrowed from New Marxism and Old (Veblenian) Institutionalism.

The framework consists of 15 propositions for three levels of analysis: the nature of the capitalist economy, its working, and its change.

The capitalist economy and society

Proposition 1: The capitalist economy and society and the market
The capitalist economy and society is the social formation produced by the capitalist mode of production. Markets and commodity production are pervasive. The vast majority of goods and services are produced for the market (including the labour force).

Proposition 2: Capital accumulation and the commoditisation of the labour force
Capitalist production requires accumulation to enlarge the scale of production, and to enhance growth and employment. In turn, accumulation requires the commoditisation of the labour force. Multiple forms of commoditisation of the labour force exist according to the features of employers and employees, and to the patterns in which commoditisation occurs.[4]

Proposition 3: Social stratification
Capitalist society is unequal and stratified. Modes of inequality and forms of stratification vary among and within countries. Several modes of inequality co-exist – in relation to wealth and income, gender, religion, ethnicity – producing a complex network of social stratification that takes economic and non-economic forms. Among all modes of inequality, the one between the capitalist class and the working class pertaining to the control of the means of production is specific to the capitalist economy, as are those specific to capitalism class conflicts over the access to resources and over the appropriation of labour effort.

Proposition 4: Class relations and class conflicts
Capitalist class structure is complex owing to the persistence of pre-capitalist residuals and the variety of social institutions and formal/informal rules influencing individual rights and powers. The main classes are the capitalist class – which includes the individuals who control the production process and commoditise the workers – and the class of subaltern workers – which includes the individuals who do not have control over their labour power, over their means of production and over the product of their labour. Capitalists exploit workers, excluding them from access to resources and appropriating their labour effort.[5]

Proposition 5: Middle classes
In between the capitalist class and the class of subaltern workers, there are the middle classes. Middle classes exist due to the complexity of class structure. They consist of individuals with contradictory class locations, who are at the same time employees and employers or, alternatively, who are neither employers nor employees.[6]

The working of the capitalist economy and society

Proposition 6: Agency
Individuals are not rational optimising beings; rationality is simply not possible, due to uncertainty and to the limits of the human brain. Individual behaviour is socially determined by means of institutions – formal and informal social rules – in which shared habits of thought are embodied.[7]

Proposition 7: Agency and structure
Institutions provide the cognitive framework for human action. They constrain and enable human behaviour and, being the by-products of human society, are influenced by it. Institutions influence individuals and individuals influence institutions: between them there is a 'reconstitutive causation'.[8]

Proposition 8: Power and institutions
Owing to the reconstitutive causation between individuals and institutions, institutions may constitute and reconstitute individual aims and desires. They may also be created – or transformed – in order to embody specific cognitive frameworks functional to established or emerging interests. Then, they may be used to enhance the power of individuals and groups.

174   E. Basile

Proposition 9: Agency and class
Class is not an agent, but it is made up of agents. Agents in a class may acquire class-consciousness and participate in the process of class formation on the basis of their class identity. Class identity is the outcome of the relationships with the means of production and is articulated on the basis of culture – construed as ethnicity, caste, gender and religion.

Proposition 10: Structure and superstructure
The capitalist economy and society consists of an economic structure *(i.e. relations of production and forces of production) and a* superstructure *(i.e. ideas and institutions). No primacy is given to economic structure over superstructure: economic structure influences the superstructure and is influenced by it in a two-way causation. Thus, production relations are determined by productive forces, ideas, institutions, and by the past history of production relations, while productive forces are determined by production relations, ideas, institutions, and by the past history of productive forces.*[9]

Proposition 11: Ideology and hegemony
The capitalist class exerts a hegemonic (economic and non-economic) dominance over the subaltern class, obtaining its consensus by means of ideology and of an institutional framework in which the hegemony is negotiated between the classes. Production relations and ideology constitute the 'historical bloc' that enforces the hegemony of the dominant class, ensuring social stability.[10]

Change and growth of the capitalist economy and society

Proposition 12: Evolutionary change
Capitalist change is an evolutionary process in which nothing is given and unchangeable. Economy and society change through an adaptive process in which every step may be explained on the basis of the previous one. The fittest institutions and individuals prevail. No laws of motion govern the outcomes and change never has a final term.[11]

Proposition 13: The institutional embeddedness of capitalist change
History and culture matter. As the institutional framework is the outcome of the relations between human beings and the external environment, institutions are specific to any historical and geographical context. Change is then path dependent and historically specific.

Proposition 14: The necessary impurities

Real world economies diverge from the model of the 'purely' capitalist economy in which all social relations are expressed in market terms. This is due to the persistence of institutions and structures of the previous modes of production which are not dissolved by capitalism. These are 'impurities' that are 'necessary' to the workings of the capitalist system.[12]

Proposition 15: Conflicts and change

The capitalist economy and society is characterised by a variety of conflicts that impact at many levels and interact. They are determined by different modes of inequality. Among them, class conflicts play a key role in the development of the capitalist economy, both in the short and in the long run. They influence the development of the forces of production, including the introduction of technical change, determining the material conditions for production and the standards of living.

2.2 The heterodox framework and the analysis of capitalism

The heterodox framework improves our understanding of the nature and workings of contemporary capitalist economies. It provides the tools to explore the variety of organisational and institutional forms and to account for the several modes of inequality that cross capitalist society: variety is the consequence of the institutional embeddedness of growth and change, while capitalist production relations are at the origin of class inequality, which accompanies non-class modes of inequality, reinforcing them.

The framework constitutes a significant improvement in comparison with other heterodox approaches such as the Social Structures of Accumulation theory (Kotz *et al.* 1994) and the Regulation School theory (Aglietta 1979) that have been successfully employed to address the developments of capitalism in the second half of the twentieth century, exploring long-term change at the macroeconomic level, as in the case of the periodisation of long waves in USA and in other industrialised countries and of the analysis of the Fordist crisis and the post-Fordist transition. Yet, despite this success, which largely accounts for their high reputation in the 1980s and 1990s, they appear to be inadequate for exploring the working of macro-dynamics at micro level with the aim of assessing the changes in individual behaviour.

The Marxist/Institutionalist framework that I propose has many qualities. First, it relies on Veblen's theory of agency, rejecting the idea of rational optimising behaviour, and solves the agency/structure problem conceptualising the 'reconstitutive causation' between individuals and institutions. Second, it acknowledges the primacy of class and class conflicts as a major driver of growth and change. Third, it rejects all forms of determinism, interpreting change as an evolutionary process influenced by past history and culture.

176 *E. Basile*

3 Capitalist development in Arni town

I argue that the Marxist/Institutionalist framework is suitable for the analysis of capitalism in India. India's society is deeply influenced by institutions rooted in culture and history – pre-capitalist residuals not dissolved by the spreading of the capitalist mode of production – which give birth to a complex social stratification impacting upon class identity and class-consciousness. Moreover, social and cultural institutions produce ideologies that have a direct impact on individual aims and behaviour, influencing capital/labour relations.

To show how the 'heterodox' framework improves our understanding of capitalist change, I apply the conceptual categories of the Marxist/Institutionalist framework to the analysis of the economy and society of Arni, a rural market town in South India. The town has been widely researched over four decades and rich empirical material has been produced that can be employed to interpret its process of growth and change.[13]

Arni's variety of capitalism

Arni town is located in a semi-arid rice-growing district in northern Tamil Nadu (TN).[14] When the Green Revolution (GR) was introduced at the end of the 1960s, Arni was a small-sized market town specialising in agro-food trade and processing, and in the production of silk saris. Since then, the town and its district have undergone a process of change which has had a deep impact on its economy and society. This change is documented in three major surveys of the town and its district that have assessed the progress and problems related to the introduction of the new GR varieties (1973 survey) and their impacts on the non-farm economy (1983 survey), and the changes induced by economic liberalisation (1993 survey). I rely on the survey data to begin my assessment of the variety of capitalism emerging in Arni following the GR.[15] My aim is to explore the development of capitalism in the town, focusing on the changing composition of businesses and on the pattern of integration of economic activity.

From the 1970s until the mid-1990s Arni's economy expanded constantly at a very high rate, both in terms of the number of businesses and their economic range (Tables 10.1 and 10.2). The growth was not uniform across sectors and decades. As measured by the number of businesses, agricultural products (other than rice), rice and farm inputs showed the lowest rate of growth, while the production of silk saris increased greatly over the period, particularly in the first decade. A notable rate of growth was also observed for trade (both retail and wholesale), particularly in the second decade. In contrast, the dynamics of gross output showed the high growth of agricultural products and wholesale and retail trade, while rice stagnated and silk decreased in the second decade.

The main characteristic of Arni's change was diversification. The growth in the number and size of businesses mirrored the change in the economic weight of sectors and in their mix. While in each round the town seemed to specialise, the specialisation changed over time. In 1973 the main activity was rice; in 1983

Table 10.1 Private firms in Arni

Business	1973 (1)	1983 (1)	1993 (1)	1973–1983 (2)	1983–1993 (2)	1973–1993 (2)	1973–1983 (3)	1983–1993 (3)	1973–1993 (3)
1 Rice and paddy	62	121	159	95.2	31.4	156.5	6.9	2.8	4.8
2 Agricultural products	96	139	254	44.8	82.7	164.6	3.8	6.2	5.0
3 Foods	439	564	1371	28.5	143.1	212.3	2.5	9.3	5.9
4 Farm inputs	13	28	32	115.4	14.3	146.2	8.0	1.3	4.6
5 Silk products	62	243	345	291.9	42.0	456.5	14.6	3.6	9.0
6 General merchants	150	232	373	54.7	60.8	148.7	4.5	4.9	4.7
7 Fuel and energy retailers	12	18	59	50.0	227.8	391.7	4.1	12.6	8.3
8 Transport repairs and services	191	321	623	68.1	94.1	226.2	5.3	6.9	6.1
9 Other repairs and services	87	121	152	39.1	25.6	74.7	3.4	2.3	2.8
10 Money and financial services	87	121	152	39.1	25.6	74.7	3.4	2.3	2.8
Total	1194	1923	3562	61.1	85.2	198.3	4.9	6.4	5.6

Source: Census of Arni's business economy (Arni surveys – 1973, 1983, 1993).

Notes
1 No. of units.
2 Rate of growth over the period (%).
3 Average annual rate of growth (%).
* In 1993 1141 weavers have been censused in addition to 345 silk businesses. For reason of comparability of the data across the years, the 1141 weavers have not been considered in computing the rate of growth.

Table 10.2 Gross output in the Arni samples

Business	1973	1983	1993	1973/1983	1983/1993	1973/1993			
	(1)	*(2)*	*(1)*	*(2)*	*(1)*	*(2)*	*(3)*	*(3)*	*(3)*
1 Rice and paddy	53.284	40.2	99.880	31.4	57.324	3.0	6.5	−5.4	0.4
2 Agricultural products	3.678	2.8	227	0.1	1348.802	70.0	−24.3	138.4	34.3
3 Foods	17.515	13.2	23.702	7.5	43.328	2.2	3.1	6.2	4.6
4 Farm inputs	5.101	3.9	9.267	2.9	37.733	2.0	6.2	15.1	10.5
5 Silk products	23.803	18.0	83.338	26.2	196.510	10.2	13.3	9.0	11.1
6 General merchants	22.005	16.6	44.962	14.1	144.109	7.5	7.4	12.4	9.9
7 Fuel and energy retailers	2.639	2.0	29.601	9.3	34.971	1.8	27.3	1.7	13.8
8 Transport repairs and services	227	0.2	619	0.2	35.570	1.8	10.5	50.0	28.7
9 Other repairs and services	3.086	2.3	4.195	1.3	16.652	0.9	3.1	14.8	8.8
10 Money and financial services	1.062	0.8	22.346	7.0	12.584	0.7	35.6	−5.6	13.2
Total	132.400	100.0	318.137	100.0	1927.583	100.0	9.2	19.7	14.3

Source: Sample data (Arni surveys – 1993, 1983, 1973).

Notes
1 Thousand Rs. (Prices 1993).
2 Distribution over total (%).
3 Average annual rate of growth (%).

A heterodox analysis of capitalism   179

Arni was a silk town; and in 1993 wholesale and retail trade dominated. Moreover, economic diversification meant not only the coexistence of different sectors, both in manufacturing and trade, but also the coexistence of firms engaged both in retail and wholesale trade.

In addition, the pattern of economic integration of Arni's businesses was very varied. While there is evidence of an overall increase, systematic changes could be observed over the decades in the origin of raw materials and the destination of goods.[16] The importance of local sources had decreased in comparison to sources outside TN.

The survey data also show that the local area was the most relevant origin of finance for Arni's businesses and that its role increased over the years. The bulk of finance came from the family and from individual/family savings. In addition, the role of the finance sector was significant (but decreasing over the period).

Major conclusions about the variety of capitalism following the GR may be drawn from the evidence provided by the Arni surveys for the period 1973 to 1993. First, Arni's economy was composed of two broad segments. In the first, production relied largely upon local raw materials and sold partly to its hinterland and partly to other centres in TN. The second segment used raw materials from distant sources and sold to distant markets. A few sectors – rice and silk, but also agricultural products – were integrated into the global economy. They represented the bulk of Arni's economy in terms of gross output. The remaining sectors produced and sold in the town for local use.

Second, despite the fact that part of its economy was globally integrated, Arni had many features of a 'local economic system' which relied increasingly on its local area. Not only was a significant segment of its economy locally integrated with respect to the source of its inputs and the destination of its output, but also the sources of capital were increasingly local.

A major confirmation of Arni's local economic integration comes from the surveys of the surrounding villages (Harriss-White and Janakarajan 2004). Following the GR, the town and the villages underwent an interlinked process of change. Economic diversification was extensive, involving both agriculture and non-farm activities. The development of non-farm activities in the villages has been one of the major trends since the 1980s and influenced the structure of employment and the distribution of assets (Jayaraj 2004). There is evidence (Harriss-White *et al.* 2004) that some of the workforce in the non-farm economy was engaged in non-farm activities in the villages, while another part was increasingly providing the workforce for the growth of trade and manufacturing activities in Arni. Srinivasan (2010), on the basis of detailed field research on Arni and two villages in its hinterland, also reports that a large number of workers commute between the town and the local area, being involved in several types of casual work.

Third, Arni continued to be a market town. While the first two surveys stress the growth of silk manufacturing as a major harbinger of change in the town, the final survey shows that there was a clear reversal: in the 1990s Arni was again a market town, with ever-diversifying patterns of integration. Silk sari production

180   *E. Basile*

was still a leading activity, but by no means the most important one, as the town grew to play a major role as a wholesale centre.

Class structure and class relations

Interesting insights into Arni's social and class structure are found in the studies of the silk sector, which represents a major component of Arni's business economy. Field evidence from more than ten years (Nagaraj *et al.* 1996; Roman 2004; 2008) shows that Arni's silk sector was organised as an industrial district[17] in which a large number of production units coexist, specialising in all phases of silk hand loom weaving, from the sale of raw materials, to twisting and dyeing, to the production of weaving tools and the sale of saris. Owing to geographical concentration, firms can internalise external economies, cutting transaction costs in production and marketing, and engaging in joint action to increase collective efficiency.

Arni's silk district also had a territorial dimension, the town showing an increasing economic and territorial interdependence with the villages. Since the GR, both have undergone a major change which had an impact on the distribution of resources among sectors and through space. The town extracted resources from the villages, relying on them for the reproduction of the labour force. Agricultural workers left agriculture to feed the growth of the silk economy in the town, while the growth in the number of weaving units in the villages extracted labour from agriculture to produce goods that were sold in the town and exported from it. Consumption and production linkages in the area strengthened, consolidating the hierarchical relations between Arni and the villages.

Production was informally organised, being based on a form of putting-out system in which intermediaries, master-weavers and silk merchants (*maligais*) controlled the production process. They occupied different roles: master-weavers were directly involved in production, while *maligais* were involved in trade. Yet, the two roles often overlapped in the same person, and the overlapping increased with the spreading of the putting-out system that progressively eliminated the manufacturer role of the master-weavers and enlarged the role of *maligais* in production. *Maligais* and master-weavers used to buy weaving tools, raw silk and the *zari* to supply to the weavers, together with instructions on colours and designs. They also collected and sold the saris.

The social structure was complex. There were two types of master-weavers: (1) small-scale master-weavers, who were usually weavers themselves and needed the intermediation of large-scale master-weavers and *maligais* to operate in the market; and (2) large-scale master-weavers who controlled a large number of looms and were the operators on the market. There were also several types of weavers. While only a small number of weavers were independent, the vast majority were dependent on *maligais* and master-weavers for credit, tools and equipment. Both independent and dependent weavers owned their own looms and formed units of production usually located in their household premises, employing household members as assistants. By contrast, wage weavers did not own their own looms but worked on looms owned by *maligais* or master-weavers. Finally, a small number of weavers worked in cooperative societies.

Weavers were 'dependent' workers and were progressively deprived of entrepreneurial functions, even when entering social production relations as 'independent' agents. Entrepreneurial activity was in the hands of master-weavers and *maligais* who controlled the entire economics of silk, from the organisation of production to the marketing of the output, also providing liquidity to the weavers. They were the agents who ensured that the district as a whole enjoyed *economies of scope*, i.e. economies that derive from the flexible and multi-task use of resources.

Master-weavers and *maligais* were crucial for the viability of Arni's silk economy, being in charge of the introduction of new technologies and types of product, and of the discovery of new market outlets. They were similar to the 'versatile integrators' who, according to Becattini (1990), made a success of industrial districts in the Third Italy. They ensured that Arni's production structure adapted to market signals and changes, enhancing competitiveness. They performed a 'plural' role that involved their class as a whole.

Arni's silk industrial district contained master-weavers and *maligais* who were a component of the capitalist class, and weavers and other dependent workers who were part of the class of subaltern workers. These were two segmented classes which were composed of groups of individuals differing in their origins and their trajectories of class formation, but showing internally a basic social and economic homogeneity. They represented the antagonistic classes of Arni's silk capitalism and were major actors in Arni's class dialectics. The *maligai* fraction derived from agricultural merchants and moneylenders who in the changes induced by the GR started to diversify their economic activity by investing in silk production. The master-weaver component was the outcome of social differentiation among the weaving castes. In spite of different origins and trajectories of class formation, the two capitalist segments gave birth to a single class of agents with shared interests, values and lifestyles. In addition, weavers and other dependent workers, the subaltern segmented class, also had different origins and different trajectories of class formation. The evidence showed that only a small proportion of the weavers came from weaving castes, and they were mainly located in the town (Nagaraj *et al.* 1996). The other major segment of the subaltern class was made up of helpers and assistants: unpaid family workers, mainly women and children. In between, there were small-scale master-weavers who still wove and had only a small number of looms. They had a contradictory class location and their positions in social production relations depended on their ideological perception of their class interests and aspirations, and on their linkages with the capitalist class.

The social stratification of subaltern workers was complex and highly hierarchical. Class, caste and gender modes of inequality interacted, while labour trajectories also depended on personal and family features. The evidence seemed to suggest little permeability between the strata of weavers and helpers (Roman 2004). Women very rarely became fully fledged weavers but remained helpers indefinitely, often even after marriage.

182   E. Basile

Several forms of commoditisation were found: from the wage labour of dependent weavers and wage weavers and self-employment of independent weavers, to subcontracted wage labour, children's and women's wage labour, and the bonded labour of helpers and assistants. Independent weavers had the formal status of self-employment, yet they lacked autonomy in decision making: they were dependent labour in disguise. Dependent weavers, helpers and the other segments of subaltern workers were a 'dependent' labour force; yet they had no formal written contracts and no provisions for social security. They were paid on the basis of the number of woven saris produced per year and their wages were usually a little above the poverty line (Nagaraj *et al.* 1996).

There were major obstacles to upward mobility. To become fully fledged weavers it was necessary to go through a long period of apprenticeship, and it was necessary to have the 'right' gender and caste characteristics. An individual needed to buy her/his loom in order to become an independent weaver and would incur other debts to buy another loom, initiating the rise toward the status of master-weaver. This explains why a large number of helpers and weavers were kept in a condition of subordination.

Social structure was also segmented along caste lines.[18] As in other cases in South India (De Neve 2005), weaving and non-weaving castes coexisted in Arni's weaving industry. Caste segmentation was particularly significant in relation to the learning process and upward mobility.

Caste connections were the key to learning opportunities. In traditional weaving castes children started learning from their parents, while in non-traditional weaving castes they needed to find a different way to enter the sector. As Roman (2004) shows, caste-based and neighbourhood-based relations created the trust that was necessary to be accepted as an apprentice and to start the learning process.

Caste influenced upward mobility too (Roman 2008). The mobility from assistant to fully fledged weaver depended on the caste and trust characteristics of the assistant. Master-weavers were mainly from traditional weaving castes. Caste origin was also relevant for *maligais*. As this segment of the capitalist class usually developed from trade rather than from weaving, weaving castes were scarcely represented among *maligais*.

Thus, in Arni's silk economy, caste was a *regulative* factor of social production relations and it performed its regulatory function interacting with class. Caste affiliations influenced both access to the weaving profession and upward mobility within the sector. In so doing, they formed a segmentation within the two broad classes of capitalists and subaltern workers, creating new non-class hierarchies within each segment. In this sense, caste segmentation increased the non-permeability of Arni's social structure, hindering mobility from one class to another.

Caste and capital's hegemony

The regulative role of caste is further illuminated by the survey of the organisation of Arni's civil society that I carried out at the end of the 1990s. Building on Gramsci (1975), I have taken civil society – non-state associations – as the sphere in which class and non-class interests are expressed and represented. Then, assuming that the organisation of civil society reveals the intertwining of class and non-class interests, I have explored the influence of civil society on social production relations.[19]

From the surveys important insights emerge on the rich interplay between Arni's economy and society.

First, in the town there existed an associational order governing the production process representing capital and labour's interests. Owing to the joint action of 'big' business associations which were overt associations of capital, and locally dominant caste associations, the representation of capital was strong. By contrast, labour was systematically under-represented, being aggregated in caste associations, mainly in the SC and MBC categories, and in petty trade and small business associations.

Second, the state was a central component of Arni's collective life. Despite economic liberalisation, the state's role in providing infrastructure and in supporting effective demand was strong and the aim of the associations was to enter into political relationships with the state in order to negotiate particularistic interests. Formal interest representation was widely recognised as a necessary condition for entering into political relationships with the state.

Third, caste representation was strong in formal caste associations but also in small business and professional associations, unions and political parties, particularly for SCs. Caste and caste-based associations exhibited two fields of action: an internal field, with the aim of self-regulation, and an external field, with the aim of lobbying and bargaining with the state. They regulated internal relationships by defining a widely accepted behavioural code and by providing several forms of social support for the weakest members. Since some caste associations were also occupational groups, internal self-regulation became a major organising factor for the economy.

Castes also involved themselves in political exchanges with the state. The most common attempt took the form of lobbying to obtain a lower caste status which would entitle their members to more beneficial treatment by the state. Other forms ranged from requesting recognition for the public importance of specific activities, to seeking protection from police harassment, to asking for improved access to public employment. As *representatives* and *intermediaries* of particularistic interests, they determined members' interests, negotiated agreements on members' behalf, and enforced the agreements on their members.

Arni's civil society showed features of societal corporatism (Schmitter 1974; Cawson 1985): (1) the associational order emerged under the pressure of social groups (and not of the state); (2) it was composed of interest associations which were involved in the production process; and (3) their aim was to regulate social relationships and to enhance economic growth. Membership in associations was a necessary condition for participating in political relationships, while non-participation implied exclusion from political exchange and often also from entry into economic activity. Accordingly, the degree of voluntariness was low, and decreased as the value of economic interests increased.

184   *E. Basile*

Arni's corporatism was meant to promote economic growth. The survey shows that this aim was pursued in three major ways. First, the social function of (trade and business) associations was to limit inter-firm conflicts and capital/labour conflicts promoting social stability, which, creating a favourable environment for decision making, was in itself a factor conducive to growth. Second, associations regulated the relations between Arni's economy and the state: the state was an important source of demand, and associations ensured that state procurement orders were distributed among producers without conflicts. Third, the social regulation of the economy reduced risk and enhanced investment.

As an institution and an ideology, caste was the major pillar of Arni's corporatism. Since the political-economic organisation of wage labour and other types of 'dependent' labour on the basis of non-class criteria substituted for the formal representation of workers in trade unions, non-class (caste and petty business) associations combined to undermine the class-consciousness of the lower strata of Arni's society, playing a major ideological role in Arni's production relations. Paradoxically, by undermining class-consciousness and by fracturing the unity of the working class, caste enhanced social cohesion. Moreover, it provided the ideological instruments limiting the perception of the quasi-compulsory nature of the associational order, ensuring a 'voluntary' consensus in favour of the hegemony of the dominant classes, and promoting the 'voluntary' participation of subaltern classes in organised civil society. Finally, caste-based associations gave birth to an institutional structure that influenced capitalist growth, creating the cross-class social environment in which capital's hegemony was negotiated and workers' 'spontaneous' consensus on it gained.

4 From theory to applied research

In proposing a Marxist/Institutionalist framework for the analysis of contemporary capitalism, I am led by three major beliefs. First, the aim of applied socio-economic research on capitalism is to explain the processes of change and growth in the real world. Empirical evidence has a primacy over theoretical rigour and cannot be adapted to fit abstract theoretical models; on the contrary, it is the theory that needs to be adapted to explore the variety of social structures observed in the contemporary world economy. Second, applied research on capitalism requires a theoretical background, without which it cannot identify the forces behind the processes of growth and change, ending up with only a descriptive analysis of the existing situation. Third, social theory is itself a social construction and is produced in a specific socio-economic context. A major task for applied analysts is to understand the interpretive power of the theoretical frameworks that support their empirical research, and when and how adaptations or improvements are necessary in order to explain the evidence.

The Marxist/Institutionalist framework presented in section 3 is the outcome of these beliefs. It is eclectic in many senses. It relies on Marxism and Institutionalism. It includes concepts and propositions borrowed from several Marxist and Institutionalist theories joined in their rebuff of rational/optimising behaviour. It has been built 'empirically', selecting the theoretical contributions on the basis of their power to explain the evidence. It is suitable for the assessment of the variety of organisational forms and social structures in contemporary capitalism, for its straightforward representation of the working of the capitalist economy, conceptualising individual agency and social intercourse by means of a few basic propositions.

Relying on the rich body of evidence collected over four decades, I have applied the Marxist/Institutionalist framework to the analysis of Arni's capitalist development in section 4. The outcome of this exercise is a comprehensive assessment of the change and growth in the town, which underlines aspects and processes, such as the evolutionary nature of capitalist change and the role of caste, that would be missed with a mainstream approach or only partially explored with Marxism and Institutionalism taken individually. Throwing new light on capitalist development, this exercise shows how the 'heterodox' framework contributes to the understanding of capitalism in the real world.

Evolutionary change

Field evidence suggests that Arni has undergone a remarkable process of change and growth that has impacted upon its socio-economic structure and upon that of the district in which is located. Taking into account the overall change, I have interpreted the post-GR transformation as a process leading to the formation of a 'local system' which it is globally integrated. By using this concept, I have suggested that the change in Arni has to be assessed jointly with the change in the district, while economic processes such as production and exchange, and social processes such as employment and consumption, need to be taken into account equally when exploring the forces driving change.

Post-GR change has involved a whole range of activities in the town, changing the structure of its economy across the decades. While in the 1970s Arni was a market town, in the 1980s silk production became the leading sector, and in the 1990s the town was again a market town dominated by wholesale and retail trade. The use of Marxist/Institutionalist concepts shows that the crisis of the silk economy in the 1990s was *not* a failure of capitalist development and the increasing importance of trade was *not* a form of involution along the road to industrialisation. Since capitalist change is an evolutionary process, the starting situation at any stage is the outcome of previous changes and every next step is causally determined by the previous one. Accordingly, Arni's post-GR change needs to be interpreted as made up of steps which are the joint outcome of path dependency and of the local/global integration of the economy and society.

Class structure

In post-GR Arni, class structure differed widely from that of the 'purely' capitalist economy. However, as the Marxist/Institutionalist interpretation of the class structure in the silk sector has shown, it had distinctive capitalist features. Despite the

186 E. Basile

remarkable complexity, due to segmentation along class and caste lines, and to the presence of individuals with a contradictory class location, workers were commoditised by capitalists and commoditisation took a plurality of forms.

The complexity of class structure was *not* an indicator of incomplete capitalist transition, as the segmented capitalist class and the class of individuals with contradictory class locations were *not* 'intermediate classes' (i.e. classes in between the two ends of the capitalist transition: feudalism and capitalism). They were the form taken by the capitalist classes when capitalist production relations intertwined with social stratifications rooted in culture and history. Similarly, the segmented class of subaltern workers was the working class of the capitalist economy: the multiple forms of commoditisation were the outcome of the interplay among the multiple modes of stratification crossing Arni's society. Accordingly, there was nothing 'intermediate' in Arni's economy. The town was *not* in the transition to capitalism: its high rate of growth and its increasing local/global integration showed that the capitalist transition had long been concluded, while the change following the GR had been occurring *within* the capitalist mode of production.

The role of caste

The survey of Arni's civil society provides evidence of the influence of caste on social production relations. The Marxist/Institutionalist analysis shows that the conventional Marxist analysis of caste (Sharma 1994; Shah 2002), that sees it as a 'false consciousness' (which manipulates the perception workers have of their position in production relations) and as a pre-capitalist residual that capitalism will dissolve, did not fully accord with the evidence. By contrast, caste was a major regulating factor in Arni's economy and society, playing a twofold role as an ideology and an institution.

The Marxist/Institutionalist reading of civil society's organisation in Arni shows that caste was the ideological cement that kept together the segments of the capitalist and subaltern classes, creating the institutional structure through which subaltern workers were led to accept the moral and intellectual leadership of capitalists. Caste was *not* a 'pre-capitalist residual' to be dissolved by capitalist development; because of its role in ensuring social stability and in enhancing capital's hegemony, it appeared as a 'necessary impurity' that supported a historically specific 'variety' of capitalism in which class and non-class relations intertwined. Caste associations – the 'materialisation' of caste ideology – were necessary as non-class mediators of class interests in order to limit capital/labour and capital/capital conflicts. As an institution and an ideology, caste undermined the unity of the working class, endorsing the 'alliance' between capital and labour.

Notes

1 This chapter relies on the theoretical and empirical analysis presented in Basile (2013; 2011). I am grateful to Barbara Harriss-White, Judith Heyer and the participants to the Conference on *Capitalism and Development in the 21st Century* (University of Oxford, July 2012) for their comments on an earlier draft.

2 Department of Economics and Law, University of Rome 'La Sapienza', elisabetta. basile@uniroma1.it.
3 The concept of overdetermination refers to the idea that any single observed effect is the outcome of multiple contradictions occurring into the political, economic and ideological spheres, which cannot be reduced to an expression of a single contradiction. Similarly, a complex structured social totality cannot be reduced to the aggregation of its independently constituted parts (Althusser 1967: 173–177).
4 The existence of multiple forms of commoditisation has been theorised by van der Linden (2008), who distinguishes between 'autonomous' commoditisation (when the carrier of labour power is also its possessor) and 'heteronomous' commoditisation (when the carrier of labour power is not its possessor).
5 Following Wright (2005), I conceptualise class conflicts by means of a concept of 'exploitation', in which exploiters and exploited are compared in terms of access to resources and living standards.
6 The concept of 'contradictory class location' is borrowed from Wright (2005).
7 This proposition relies on Veblen's theory of agency.
8 The concept of 'reconstitutive causation' has been introduced by Hodgson (2004).
9 I build on the conceptualisation of the two-way interplay between structure and superstructure proposed by Gramsci (1975).
10 Gramsci's theory of hegemony (1975) provides the background of this proposition.
11 This proposition relies on Veblen's view of change as an evolutionary (Darwinian) process without a final term.
12 The concept of 'necessary impurities' has been elaborated by Hodgson (2001) to refer to social relations which cannot be explained in pure market terms.
13 Barbara Harriss-White began her empirical research on Arni in 1973. Over the years a number of her students and collaborators have worked on the town, which has become a workshop for testing theories of rural and urban development. Some recent contributions are collected in a volume in which several aspects of Arni's capitalist development are analysed (Harriss-White forthcoming).
14 The town is located on the banks of the Kamandala Naaga river and is 132 km away from Chennai and 60 km from Tiruvannamalai. The state highways SH-4 and SH-132 are the main roads connecting Arni to other urban centres in Tamil Nadu, while the main railway station (Katpadi) is 45 km away. The town had a population of 33,000 in 1971, which increased to 54,900 in 1991 and to 60,800 in 2001.
15 The Arni surveys provide information on the number of firms in each sector and on the features of the firms. For each survey, the data come from a 6 per cent random sample drawn from the census of firms directly compiled by Harriss-White and her assistants (Harriss-White 2009).
16 For details on this aspect, see Basile (2011: tables 7 and 8).
17 Defined as a geographical concentration of firms embedded in a community and involved in interdependent production processes, in which the labour process is flexible (Becattini 1990; Becattini et al. 2009).
18 Members of 15 castes and sub-castes, and people from the major religions, such as Hindus, Jains, Christians and Muslims, all live together in Arni. While SCs represent about 15 per cent of Arni's population, the main caste groups are Veera Saiva Chettiars, Acaris, Karuneekars, Senguntha Mudaliars, Saurashtrians, Naidus, Ahadudaiyan Mudaliars and Vanniar Chettiars, among the BCs, and Vanniars, Barbers, Odeyars, and Yadavas, among the MBCs. For details see Basile (2011: ch. 12).
19 I interviewed 66 associations, classified in four groups – philanthropic, business and professional, social, and political – according to their reported sphere of activity. I analysed the interviews focusing on: aims, impact on the production process and economic stability, and degree of voluntariness in membership (Basile 2011: ch. 12).

188   *E. Basile*

References

Aglietta, M. (1979) *A Theory of Capitalist Regulation: The US Experience*, London and New York: New Left Books.

Althusser, L. (1967) 'Contraddizione e surdeterminazione', in L. Althusser *Per Marx*, Rome: Editori Riuniti: 69–108 [original in French, 1965].

Basile, E. (2011) *A Marxist/Institutionalist Analysis of Rural Capitalism in South India, The Case of a Tamil Market Town After the Green Revolution*, D.Phil. thesis, Oxford University.

—— (2013) *Capitalist Development in India's Informal Economy*, London: Routledge.

Becattini, G. (1990) 'The Marshallian industrial district as a socio-economic notion', in F. Pyke, G. Becattini and W. Sengenberger (eds) *Industrial Districts and Inter-Firm Co-operation in Italy*, International Institute for Labour Studies, ILO, Geneva: 37–51.

—— (1997) *Il Bruco e la Farfalla: Prato nel Mondo che Cambia*, 1954–1993, Florence: Le Monnier.

Becattini, G., Bellandi, M. and De Propis, L. (eds) (2009) *A Handbook of Industrial Districts*, Cheltenham (UK), and Northampton (USA): Edward Elgar.

Cawson, A. (1985) 'Varieties of corporatism: the importance of the meso-level of interest intermediation', in A. Cawson (ed.) *Organised Interests and the State, Studies in Meso-Corporatism*, London: Sage: 1–21.

Cullenberg, S. (2000) 'Old Institutionalism, New Marxism', in R. Pollin (ed.) *Capitalism, Socialism and Radical Political Economy, Essays in Honour of Howard Sherman*, Cheltenham: Edward Elgar: 81–102.

De Neve, G. (2005) *The Everyday Politics of Labour, Working Lives in India's Informal Economy*, New Delhi: Social Science Press.

Dugger, W.M. and Sherman, H.J. (2000) *Reclaiming Evolution, A Dialogue Between Marxism and Institutionalism on Social Change*, London: Routledge.

Gramsci, A. (1975) *Quaderni del Carcere*, 4 vols, edited by V. Gerratana, Torino: Einaudi.

Harriss-White, B. (2009) 'A small town in South India: long-term urban studies and three decades of revisits', paper for the International Conference on Market Town, Market Society, Informal Economy, Contemporary South Asian Studies Programme, Oxford University, June.

—— (ed.) (forthcoming) *Middle India and Urban-Rural Development: Four Decades of Change in Tamil Nadu*, New Delhi: Springer.

Harriss-White, B. and Janakarajan, S. (2004) *Rural India Facing the 21st Century. Essays on Long Term Village Change and Recent Development Policy*, London: Anthem Press.

Harriss-White, B., Janakarajan, S. and Colatei, D. (2004) 'Introduction: heavy agriculture and light industry in South Indian villages', in B. Harriss-White and S. Janakarajan (eds) *Rural India Facing the 21st Century, Essays on Long Term Village Change and Recent Development Policy*, London: Anthem Press: 3–46.

Hodgson, G.M. (2001) *How Economics Forgot History, The Problem of Historical Specificity in Social Science*, London: Routledge.

—— (2004) *The Evolution of Institutional Economics: Agency, Structure and Darwinism in American Institutionalism*, London: Routledge.

Jayaraj, D. (2004) 'Social institutions and the structural transformation of the non-farm economy', in B. Harriss-White and S. Janakarajan (eds) *Rural India Facing the 21st Century, Essays on Long Term Village Change and Recent Development Policy*, London: Anthem Press: 175–191.

A heterodox analysis of capitalism 189

Kotz, D.M. (1994) 'The regulation theory and the social structure of accumulation approach', in D.M. Kotz, T. McDonough and M. Reich (eds) *Social Structures of Accumulation: The Political Economy of Growth and Crisis*, Cambridge: Cambridge University Press.

Kotz, D.M., McDonough, T. and Reich, M. (eds) (1994) *Social Structures of Accumulation: The Political Economy of Growth and Crisis*, Cambridge: Cambridge University Press.

Nagaraj, K., Janakarajan, S., Jayaraj, D. and Harriss-White, B. (1996) 'Sociological aspects of silk weaving in Arni and its environs', paper for the *Workshop on Adjustment and Development*, Madras Institute of Development Studies, Chennai.

Roman, C. (2004) *Skills and Silks: Learning to Work in the Informal Sector*, M.Phil. thesis, Oxford University.

—— (2008) *Learning and Innovation in Clusters: Case Studies from Indian Silk Industry*, D.Phil. thesis, Oxford University.

Schmitter, Ph.C. (1974) 'Still the century of corporatism?', *Review of Politics*, 36(1): 85–131.

Shah, G. (2002) 'Introduction: caste and democratic politics in India', in G. Shah (ed.) *Caste and Democratic Politics in India*, New Delhi: Permanent Black: 1–31.

Sharma, K.L. (1994) 'Introduction: some reflections on caste and class in India', in K.L. Sharma (ed.) *Caste and Class in India*, Jaipur and New Delhi: Rawat Publications: 1–17.

Srinivasan, M.V. (2010) *Segmentation of Urban Labour Markets in India: A Case Study of Arni, Tamil Nadu*, Ph.D. thesis, Jawarhalal Nehru University.

van Der Linden, M. (2008) *Workers of the World. Essays toward a Global Labor History*, Leiden, and Boston, MA: Brill.

Veblen, T. (1919) *The Place of Science in Modern Civilisation and Other Essays*, New York: Huebsch.

Wright, E.O. (2005) 'Foundations of a neo-Marxist class analysis', in E.O. Wright (ed.) *Approaches to Class Analysis*, Cambridge: Cambridge University Press: 1–26.

11 Money laundering and capital flight

Kannan Srinivasan[1]

Introduction

India's capitalism is incompletely described when the account does not include the laundering of wealth: its concealment in other business, including its flight from India's jurisdiction in order to separate the surplus extracted from the gaze of labour.[2] Although the customary understanding of money laundering is 'the process of concealing the origins of money obtained illegally by passing it through a complex sequence of banking transfers or commercial transactions' (OED 2002), I suggest it might be more usefully defined as the concealment of assets acquired *legally or illegally*, intended for personal consumption or beneficial heirs (whether the purpose is benevolent or otherwise).

I will try here to show[3] that the flight of Indian capital is one of three significant manifestations of the exercise of coercive authority: these being the extraction of the surplus; the movement of such wealth out of the Indian jurisdiction, and the culture of silence about extraction and flight, both in India and abroad. These are little discussed I suggest, because at a certain point economics stopped acknowledging coercion as a significant motive for the acts of societies and states.

All over the world, funds flow constantly between different businesses. The illegal is easily concealed in the legal, as when individuals hide legally earned income, transferring it abroad by arrangement with traders who misprice trade; or when corporations hide it by internal transfer pricing between subsidiaries or related companies. Tax evasion must be conducted by laundering money. Yet this category is generally absent from all discussion, perhaps because it is the wealthy and powerful who benefit from such silence. Money laundering also includes what is earned in business *that is entirely illegal everywhere*, such as trafficking in minors, women, narcotics or extortion.[4]

At one time, former sovereigns were exiled so that their subjects would forget that they had once ruled and the social surplus could be the more easily extracted.[5] This exile anticipated the contemporary movement of wealth away from the site of extraction, such as the surplus created by the land and labour of rural Orissa to a zone of recreation like Kensington in London. This displacement

Money laundering and capital flight 191

enforces an amnesia whereby we forget what we have once known as to where such wealth originated. Such obfuscation better enables the most significant laundering of money, tax evasion in weak jurisdictions, and capital flight from them, both generally excluded from the category of money laundering, but as I have suggested, incorrectly so. Indeed, subordinate jurisdictions may be so powerless that they lack the authority or confidence to even offer their own legal definition, or to attempt resistance to the departure of wealth from their borders, even as they are crippled by the outcome.

When the concealment of income from taxation authorities in Nigeria by over-invoicing payments to suppliers in London in order to bank those funds in the Channel Islands is *not* called money laundering, while money paid by a hawala dealer in Kochi to the relatives of a labourer in Abu Dhabi *is* (McCulloch and Pickering 2005), this merely follows the arbitrary definition of crime by dominant jurisdictions. That definition serves to legitimise the flight of capital from the subordinate jurisdiction and to develop a policy towards crime that assists the ceaseless expansion of the predatory sovereignty of the strongest states in the international system.

Colonial origins

The separation of wealth from its origin in labour is evident in *colonial drain* (Bagchi 2005; Banerjee 1990; Habib 2006; Patnaik 2002). Dadabhai Naoroji (Naoroji 1901) employed the term to identify the transfer of surplus from India by employing Indian revenues granted by the Dewani of Bengal in 1765 to buy textiles in India. These were then sold in England thereby constituting an unrequited trade in that no money flowed from Great Britain to pay for cloth sold there. In the second stage, Indian revenues were used to buy opium sold locally in China with profits remitted to Britain. Finally, Indian revenues paid for the subjugation of India by armed force (termed the 'Home Charges'), as well as numerous other activities deemed related to the 'Defence of India' (which meant British interests in India and included expenses to do with Suez or the Mediterranean Fleet (Palme Dutt 1940)), and for the development of the oilfields operated by Anglo Persians in the Middle East and the policing of the entire Empire by Indian men in arms (Srinivasan and Gangoli 2005). The opaque official accounts of this cross-border transfer of funds served to disguise what was really tribute.

Such concealment was subsequently adopted by managing agencies that were accused of cheating British investors when they did so. Accounts of such nature also provided useful terms of reference for the multinationals that succeeded them, and for the flight capitalists of today. For instance, Finlay Muir in Calcutta was appointed agent of Champdany Jute at the very incorporation of that firm in 1873, receiving a 5 per cent commission on sales irrespective of profit. In the following two decades, during which Champdany performed poorly, this arrangement suited Finlay Muir but not Champdany's shareholders. In 1893 a complainant alleged:

192   K. Srinivasan

> [T]here is no public confidence in your management ... you have a double interest in your undertakings and ... your interests as shareholders are largely subordinated to your interests as managers, agents and financiers. The way in which the Champdany company has been managed has made it the laughing stock of the business community.
>
> (Misra 2000)

Shareholders sued the company in the Scottish courts in 1895, two of the plaints addressing themselves to the high interest rates Champdany was forced to pay on loans from Finlay Muir that had been arranged without the consent of shareholders. Yet, despite such lawsuits, and despite the fact that between 1897 and 1900 the management paid no dividend to Champdany shareholders, it paid Finlay Muir a fee of £41,000 in 1900, a substantial sum at the time. Harrison & Crossfield, one of the other two large managing agencies, charged the plantation companies it managed for secretarial services as well as commissions on buying and selling irrespective of profit or loss (Jones and Wale 1998).

Very similar charges to these were made in relation to Indian firms following Independence suggesting a continuity of practice. Concealment of this kind occurred not just in relation to imperial or colonial possessions but also in relation to those parts of a larger informal empire, including countries such as Brazil, Egypt and Argentina, where the interests of British investors could overpower local and nominal sovereigns. For instance, Brazil accumulated sterling balances by 1947 of £68 million, small in comparison to India, yet 45 per cent of total Brazilian foreign debt and 50 per cent of Brazilian imports. In the case of cotton alone, Brazil lost at least £70 million by accumulating such balances and purchasing inflated British assets with them (Abreu 1990). These cases illustrate the point that dependent countries' elites may identify with the strong and negotiate unattractive arrangements for their own states, enabling capital flight.

Money laundering today

I shall now try to give some idea of how money is siphoned out of public sector contracts, how laundering services are solicited in India today, and how laundered wealth is managed outside the original jurisdiction in which it was earned. My research has shown that the most important institutions that aid all varieties of money laundering today are not back-alley hawala merchants, but the main money-centre banks, respectable law partnerships and accounting firms, with the support of the Western states in which they originate.

Laundered funds often originate in legitimate business, such as any manufacturing or trading activity that seeks to evade the taxes levied on earnings by governments. It is such funds that are the bulk of the business of laundering money, and of global unreported or misreported flows. The concealment has long been conducted by European and American private banks that serve the very wealthy from all over the world with personal attention, and in absolute secrecy. The 'banques privees' of Switzerland became known between the two World Wars

Money laundering and capital flight   193

as the home of flight capital from other parts of Europe, and Wall Street served that same purpose for flight capital from France (Helleiner 1994; 2005).

Since then, this has become an important aspect of the City of London's business too, although nominally located in the Channel Islands or Overseas Territories. Money from business entirely illegal in every jurisdiction, such as the trade in narcotics, or the traffic in persons, is laundered identically through such tax havens.

Significant Indian money laundering and capital flight originates in corrupt government contracts. Let us look at a couple of examples from my research on how these work. In the first case my informant B explained to me how his earlier employer, a law firm, organized the kickbacks for a contract for an important new port. The contractor was a European multinational. The provision for arbitration in the event of cost escalations concealed a secret understanding to allow the multinational super-profits at the expense of the public sector port trust, and ultimately the Indian taxpayer. Enormous escalations in cost were claimed. In an elaborate charade, the port trust pronounced these to be completely unacceptable. The foreign contractor, seemingly enraged, referred the matter to arbitration by a panel composed of retired High Court and Supreme Court judges. The law firm had meanwhile, for the purpose of arbitration, set up a Potemkin village of a firm, comprising two associates who formed a bogus firm in partnership. This bogus firm was set up at the old chambers of the real law firm. A nameplate of the fictitious firm was set up at this office for a fortnight. The original firm appeared in the arbitration for the foreign multinational, and its bogus firm associates for the port trust, and the latter bungled the case. Without this elaborate procedure, cost escalations would have been challenged by the Annual Report of the Comptroller and Auditor General of India (CAG), which would have written what are called audit paras about negligence, to be placed on the floor of Parliament, and provide fodder for attack by the Opposition. With this mechanism of rigged arbitration, hundreds of such agreements went through unnoticed every year.

One might also get a feel for such transactions by looking at Indian Navy procurement. The Soviet Union supplied the Indian armed forces with technology and equipment, beginning in the 1950s. Its factories were very widely dispersed: a ship assembled in Vladivostok might require engineered supplies from various Soviet states in Europe and Asia. When the USSR broke up, obtaining spare parts required an intimate knowledge of the different factories, excellent technical Russian, negotiating skills and of course incorruptibility, if the Ministry of Defence was not to be exploited by agents who now assumed a powerful role.[6] My informant, a retired Rear Admiral, attempted to ensure that procurement be undertaken competitively by government negotiating teams travelling abroad, or by offering tenders to the very large number of high-quality Indian engineering firms in both the public and private sector who could undertake the work. He failed. The deals which went through were generally conducted through intermediaries in London[7] or New York,[8] perhaps owing to the proximity of private banks that facilitate the concealment of the money made.

194   *K. Srinivasan*

The third case shows how laundering services are solicited. I first met private banker C through my lawyer informant B. In 1994, when he began freelancing with C, B was operating out of the chambers of his old firm, developing his own clients. People who he would meet either at work or on the Bombay social scene who did not have assets abroad, or who had assets poorly concealed and inefficiently deployed in terms of preservation of value for the long term, he would introduce to C, and she would pass on commissions. His networks developed, in Bombay, in Delhi, in Dubai and in London. Today he is celebrated for the elegant parties he hosts and the retreats and seminars he organizes for international businessmen seeking Indian connections.

C had been an airline 'stewardess', as it was then termed, and was good at dealing with people, and it was this that enabled her to build relationships and cultivate clients which led to her becoming a private banker. She looked after South Asia and the Middle East for a UK private bank nominally located in the Channel Islands but actually run from the City of London. It was also a subsidiary of one of the most respected investment banks. Channel Islands trusts, she claimed, were much safer than Swiss accounts, their mechanisms being far more sophisticated. She dealt with a lot of arms deals.

She asked me for contacts, businessmen and other Indian wealthy people who wanted to keep wealth abroad out of the reach of taxation as well as currency depreciation. She was not like some private bankers who will only deal with very large amounts. For her, $300,000 in cash or liquid assets was an acceptable minimum from a client to whom she could offer something worthwhile. She could give an assurance of absolute secrecy, and absolute safety, such that no government or other authority, no wife, no business partner, no rival, could get at the funds of the client. Five years after I last saw her she was killed when her farmhouse in Tuscany was blown up. Her death was little discussed in Mumbai, although a London colleague had at the time remarked on her involvement in a sensational arms deal, which must have meant that a reasonable number of people in more than one country knew about it.

Many countries from which there is capital flight, whether Russia, Pakistan, Nigeria or India, are *weak* jurisdictions,[9] in even the nominally egalitarian enforcement of law, and therefore weak in resisting the ability of the powerful to export their wealth. But weak jurisdictions that provide extraordinary returns may also be an uncertain store of value. Political movements or changes of government may challenge the settled order, as in the Philippines or Indonesia, or Pakistan or Chile. The arbitrariness that has appropriated the value created by others makes them a poor home for the long-term residence of surplus. Recipient states receive the benefit of such capital without having had to assist in its creation, generally offering no tax at the point of entry. The destination economies of the US and the UK, the tax havens connected with them, and neutral countries such as Switzerland and Austria, are the most attractive both for the physical residence of flight capitalists and for their wealth.

The City of London

UK-connected jurisdictions dominate international tax-avoiding fund flows, and are of great importance both to the UK and to the US. There are two categories of these: the Crown Dependencies[10] and the Overseas Territories.[11] The UK, the Overseas Territories and the Crown Dependencies form one undivided realm, which is distinct from the other states of which Her Majesty The Queen is monarch (UK Government 2012). The Crown Dependencies, where a unique system of taxation and secrecy in regard to non-residents is guaranteed by law, were inherited by the Sovereign as successor to the Dukes of Normandy. The UK Parliament has authority to legislate for them, but chooses not to do so. The Queen acts on matters concerning them on the advice of her ministers acting in their capacities as Privy Councillors. This formula of nominal independence permits the UK to employ the Crown Dependencies to mop up international funds while maintaining the fiction of being at arm's length from them.

The Overseas Territories are more evidently administered by the government:

> As a matter of constitutional law the UK Parliament has unlimited power to legislate for the Territories.... Governors or Commissioners are appointed by Her Majesty The Queen on the advice of Her Ministers in the UK, and in general have responsibility for external affairs, defence, internal security (including the police) and the appointment, discipline and removal of public officers.
>
> (UK Government 2012)

Following a public campaign,[12] the Labour government in 1998 commissioned an official report on issues of concern in the administration of trusts in the Channel Islands. This report, the Edwards Report (UK Government 1998), was eager to find excuses for the sort of money that finds its way to the Channel Islands. Thus:

> [I]t may have nothing to do with crime in any generally recognised sense but be illegal within the extreme laws of some repressive regime.
>
> (Part I, ch. 14)

Further, the Report recorded unquestioningly the statement of accountants in the Channel Islands who had never heard of requests from abroad for information concerning tax evasion, or indeed of any tax-evading money. This contrasts with what Assistant District Attorney John Moscow prosecuting BCCI (the Bank of Credit and Commerce International) said in relation to Jersey's compliance with international requests for assistance:

> It is unseemly that these British dependencies should be acting as havens for transactions that would not even be protected by Swiss bank secrecy laws.[13]

No similar campaigns have been undertaken regarding the 'Overseas Territories' Anguilla, Bermuda, British Virgin Islands, Cayman Islands, Gibraltar, Turks and Caicos Islands, all former colonies where a Governor or other executive authority is accountable to the UK government. Nevertheless, in 2009, suddenly frightened that some criminal scandal might devolve responsibility to the UK, the government entrusted Michael Foot, a former Bank of England official with a fresh study (UK Government 2009) dealing with both the proximate Dependencies and the far flung Overseas Territories. He turned for assistance to Deloitte Touche, an accounting firm specializing in tax avoidance (which to the unworldly may be seen to constitute a conflict of interest). Foot makes evident the importance of these Overseas Territories. The Cayman Islands are the world's leading centre for hedge funds.[14] Bermuda is the third-largest reinsurance centre in the world and the second-largest originator of insurance business, with firms based there writing a significant part of UK and US insurance. They wrote 30 per cent of the 2008 premium at Lloyds of London, worth £5.4 billion. The British Virgin Islands are the leading home for International Business Corporations (IBCs), corporations located in a jurisdiction untaxed on the condition that they conduct their entire business elsewhere, and permitted to issue bearer share certificates making their real or 'beneficial' owners practically untraceable.

The Crown Dependencies and Overseas Territories together provided net financing to UK banks of $257 billion as of June 2009. The UK has always been a net recipient of funds from these offshore jurisdictions. The Foot Report acknowledges the UK to be a tax haven: accordingly (p. 21), it considers the 'net financing position for "competitor" jurisdictions', defined as Switzerland, Ireland and Luxembourg.[15] Lest there be any doubt as to the peculiar attraction of the Dependencies and Territories, Foot cites the consultants Deloitte Touche as concluding that they were:

> distinguished within the developed world by differentiating themselves from the international consensus, sometimes through tax rates but more often through the absence or near absence of certain forms of taxation.
>
> (p. 34)

The UK Parliament's Justice Committee's Report (UK Government 2010) is characterized by a similar remoteness from any concern about the laundering of money and accordingly also seeks to maintain the fiction of independence for the Crown Dependencies. As Jack Straw, the Labour Home Secretary, pointed out, UK government policy is generally not to intervene merely because a financial or other crime had been committed in the Dependencies:

> You have to be very careful about exercising [the power to intervene on the ground of good government] and it will be known that I have had representations in respect of certain criminal proceedings ... and I have declined to intervene in those, as far as I am concerned, on good grounds.[16]

Money laundering and capital flight 197

Happily mesmerized, the Committee agreed (UK Government 2010: 18). That really has been the end of any UK government policy to police these possessions of the Queen.

Burke's claim that plundering India would corrupt Britain (Burke 1789, 1870)[17] is perhaps still a valid concern today.

The UK government and the City see flows of returning capital flight to India as an extension of the work of the City, much of it passing through Mauritius:

> The UK has become the biggest foreign investor in India, according to ... the Commonwealth Business Council ... when investments made by UK companies through Mauritius, the British Virgin Islands and Cyprus were included it outstripped the US as the leading investor with more than £8billion.[18]

Given this, it is curious that UK official statistics in the annual Pink Book, for instance, do not consider it worthwhile to record London–Mauritius capital transactions. The Reserve Bank of India tells us that Mauritius is the largest *direct* investor into India accounting for over $8.142 billion out of $23.474 billion of foreign direct investment (FDI) in 2012 (Reserve Bank 2012). What is such FDI? The official definition is offered in the *Balance of Payments Manual* (Reserve Bank 2013):

> [I]t is considered as an (*sic*) FDI if the non-resident acquires shares in a company other than by way of acquisition from the stock market, *i.e.*, through initial public offerings (IPO) or through private arrangements (including private placements) in line with the requirements laid down in Schedule 1 of FEMA Notification No. 20 dated May 3, 2005.

So what passes for foreign investment in India need not be any greenfield venture, nor bring in technology or expertise; it can be the acquisition *outside* the stock market of shares in Indian firms, ideal for Indians operating through a front.

Foreign institutional investors brought in $17 billion, often again routed through Mauritius in the form of participatory notes (PNs) issued to holders whose names are kept secret from any Indian regulatory agency, including the Reserve Bank and the Securities and Exchange Board. To the Reserve Bank's expressed concern (Reserve Bank 2009)[19] the Government of India's response has been that there is no need to worry because foreign institutions must themselves know. Should any Indian agency need to, it can always ask.

Could these investment flows from Mauritius really originate there? The Norwegian Commission on Capital Flight (Government of Norway 2009) has pointed out that:

> [L]ocal representatives are passive front persons.... This means that the capital in reality is administered by people who do not live in Mauritius.

Global business companies (GBCs) registered in Mauritius are exempt from preparing an annual report, annual return of funds held and invested, or any statement of profit and loss; nor need there ever be any official inspection; nor need any corporate documents be held on record. Such GBCs can be set up in 48 hours. Although the Mauritius Financial Services Commission can take action if a company is used to launder money, since GBCs are immune from inspection the possibility of detecting wrongdoing is slight. A request from a foreign government for assistance must be processed within three years, within which time the foreign investor may well have vanished.

Given the general public concern in India, the government was compelled to issue a White Paper (Government of India 2012). This sees money laundering as a vindication of the official policy of amnesty and finds proof in the nature of direct investment:

> 2.8 Has Money transferred abroad illicitly returned?... FDI statistics perhaps point to this fact. As per data released by the Department of Industrial Policy and Promotion (DIPP) ... the two topmost sources of the cumulative inflows from April 2000 to March 2011 are Mauritius (41.80 per cent) and Singapore (9.17 per cent).

Further, the earlier contention that PNs need not be laundered money has now been abandoned:

> Investment in the Indian Stock Market through PNs is another way in which the black money generated by Indians is re-invested in India.... The ultimate beneficiaries/investors through the PN Route can be Indians and the source of their investment may be black money.
>
> (Government of India 2012: 17)

Wall Street

It is not just Asian economies' official investments in US instruments (such as US Treasury securities and corporate stocks and bonds) that have helped America finance its current account deficit. Laundered funds have also played a part.[20]

Of the $3.86 trillion of foreign inflows into the US at the end of 2012 (US BEA 2013), deposits in US banks and financial institutions by foreign residents and banks and securities brokers amounted to $3.63 trillion. However, another important government report shows official and private holdings of US Treasury securities by foreign residents and banks (US Federal Reserve Bank 2013: 20, table K) were $5.57 trillion, 34 per cent of total outstanding Treasury securities. Of course, China and Japan as important government investors of their own liquid overseas assets are the largest.

But it is also worth noting that Belgium, Luxembourg, Switzerland, Hong Kong and the Caymans are very significant; as are Belgium, Luxembourg, the

Money laundering and capital flight 199

UK, Ireland, Switzerland, and Caribbean financial centres in the case of foreign private holdings of US corporate and other bonds and equities.

Investment flows into the US from these financial centres ought to be a matter of concern because a large amount of their holdings are in the form of *bearer* securities, Treasury securities, long-term and short-term debt and equities, where the identity of the owner is entirely unknown to not just the US government but even unrecorded by anyone save his or her nominee, lawyer or accountant. Those who invest in such bearer instruments are attracted above all by the matching US assurance that non-resident investors may buy them, and thereby keep their identity secret. Mere *possession* of such an instrument constitutes the title of ownership.[21]

Another reason that so much money flows into the US from tax havens which assure anonymity is because US taxes that would otherwise be withheld at source by the Internal Revenue Service (IRS) on earnings from portfolio investments[22] and bank deposits[23] were in 1984 exempted for non-resident foreigners by the US Treasury. Immediately a flood of international anonymous investment flooded into the US, and thereafter in the past three decades these enormous flows have comfortably financed the large trade deficits. The business economist Lawrence Hunter claimed the portfolio-interest exemption:

> (section 871(h)) is perhaps the greatest single example of Congress's attempt to attract offshore investment.
>
> (Hunter 2002: 3)

He characterized this policy as being:

> perhaps the purest example of enlightened self-interest and realism in attracting foreign capital ... analysts generally believe that this provision has attracted somewhat over $1 trillion in foreign capital to the United States.
>
> (Hunter 2002: 3–4)

What is true of the portfolio-interest exemption benefits is equally true of the benefits assured by the exemption on taxes withheld at source for bank deposits. Such investors often pay no taxes anywhere. This means that the world's tax-avoiding, corrupt and criminal money finds in the US as in the UK a welcome so warm that it renders absurd any claim by their governments to be resisting the laundering of money, since their external economic policies are directed to just that purpose. I suggest that this mopping up of the wealth of the world is concealed in euphemism and silence by today's democracies and strong states.

David Hume's price specie flow mechanism for adjustment[24] formed the basis of one view of the nature of equilibrium in international trade. This view of the nature of equilibrium represented an inherent challenge to the labour theory of value. That is why it *necessarily* led to Jevons' insistence that such a self-adjusting mechanism could dispense with the labour theory of value, since value varied constantly with every transaction (Jevons 1866). Jevons believed that value depended on marginal utility, which he saw as determined by taste, or the market, from time to time.

Once labour was no longer seen as a source of value, free capital flows became the new dogma, since the self-adjusting equilibrium would, it was believed, arrive at the best outcome, substituting for political choice (even if this is in fact deeply political). It is sometimes argued by those such as Hunter (cited earlier) or IMF officials such as Rojas-Suarez (Rojas Suarez 1991) that such flight may be a matter of the optimum deployment of capital, and in any case cannot be checked by government fiat. That is the official view today of OECD governments and the Bretton Woods institutions (although periodic crises encourage episodes of self-doubt).

Locke and others had seen the fruits of man's labour as value. Yet, as long as the work of each labourer was in any sense unique, commodities in the modern sense could not exist, and the labourer retained some autonomy; neither value in use nor value in exchange offered a satisfying basis for valuing labour. It was only when large amounts of identical commodities could be manufactured and exchanged for money, and the role of each labourer could be reduced to a person-ality virtually interchangeable with all others, that the leading exponent of classical political economy, Marx, could deploy both use-value and exchange-value to offer a modern definition of value itself. Today, the ultimate stage in the process he iden-tified has been reached. Through instruments of great financial sophistication that have been developed, and policies to support them that have been developed, the entire wealth of a country can now vanish in a few days. It is this very environment that enables the concealment and flight of wealth from any jurisdiction.

The labour theory of value compels us to remember that the wealth that has appeared magically as stock in Wall Street or the education of a future genera-tion at Harrow is actually the labour of a Dhanbad worker.

Trade mispricing

As the instances of rigged cost escalations, fake arbitrations, weapons deals and private banking would suggest, systematic trade mispricing has undoubtedly been an important mechanism for organizing capital flight out of India. Zdanow-icz and others estimated that several billions of dollars were laundered annually through Indian trade. They developed a global price matrix and analysed every single India–US import and export transaction for the years 1993 to 1995, to estimate abnormal pricing and the magnitude of consequent capital flight (Zdanowicz *et al.* 1996). In the most recent year studied (1995), capital flight from India to the US effected through the mispricing of trade between the two countries was estimated as amounting to up to $5.58 billion. Were this maximum figure in the range to hold true for other countries with which India trades today, Indian money laundering through trade would exceed $50 billion annually. I say this guardedly. By examining trade data we can see how likely it is that there is capital flight. I am not confident about precise estimates as to how much.

Money laundering and capital flight   201

Epstein and others (Epstein 2005) have made serious estimates of flight from several countries. But the most comprehensive recent studies of flight from different countries based on trade data as well as other methodologies have been produced by Global Financial Integrity of Washington, DC. Kar (2010) estimates India's annual outflows at $16 billion and total outflow since Independence at nearly half a trillion dollars ($462 billion). This would seem to further indicate that wealth tends to be laundered outside the jurisdiction in which it is generated. Kar did not find (ibid.: 20–31) that inflation or expectation of inflation based on imprudent government policies induced capital flight. The wealthy steadily took their money out following Independence; and, when it became easier to take it out because of the absence of exchange control, they took it out faster.

Keynes, White, on setting up the WB and the IMF

What countries do to each other was the concern of Keynes and the American official Harry Dexter White who at the end of the Second World War worked to design the World Bank and the International Monetary Fund. But their ideas were quite different. White, whose secret provision of information to the Soviet Union has been confirmed by the Venona Transcripts (Craig 2004), attempted to right colonial injustice, prevent the exclusion of the Soviet Union, and set up significantly multilateral arrangements employing the authority of the US to check that of Britain. Keynes on the other hand wanted to build a US–UK condominium with London as a great global centre for finance. It was Keynes who prevailed.

By 1936 White had developed a strategy for restraining incoming capital flight from other countries into the US by imposing 100 per cent reserve requirements on incoming bank deposits (meaning that for each dollar of such a deposit lent out another should be kept in reserve, discouraging the soliciting of such funds by raising the cost of acquiring them) and taxing the foreign depositors themselves (Boughton 2002: 9–10). Horsefield's official history of the International Monetary Fund reproduces White's design of the IMF in his Plan of April 1942 (Horsefield 1969: 37–96). Moreover, regarding flight capital, White proposed that each country should agree first not to accept or permit deposits or investments from any member country except with the permission of that country (Horsefield 1969: 44).

Keynes' own proposal of 11 February 1942 for an International Currency (or Clearing) Union (Horsefield 1969: 3–18) sets out so clearly to ensure an Anglo-American condominium to rule the world that White's altruism shines by contrast. Keynes' Anglo-American condominium would have exercised a veto over any or all other countries in combination for the first five years (p. 3). This was, he said, 'an attempt to recover the advantages which were enjoyed in the nineteenth century'. In his memorandum to the US delegation he proposed that it should be set up by the US 'and its possessions (*sic*)' and the UK and the British Commonwealth (p. 15). His design anticipated that Britain would control a voting bloc that would include its Dominions and Empire:

202   K. Srinivasan

> [T]he great advantage [with this arrangement is] that the United States and the United Kingdom ... could settle the charter and the main details of the new body without being subjected to the delays and confused counsels of an international conference.
>
> (p. 15)

A system such as he had in mind would preserve 'the historical continuity of the sterling area in the same form and with the same absence of restraint as heretofore' (Horsefield 1969: 17). While both Keynes and White wanted restraint on the movement of capital, Keynes feared above all a flight of capital from a weakened Britain to the US and therefore appealed to a common transatlantic culture. His strategy required the continued subordination of the Empire, that Latin America be discounted and that the Soviet Union be entirely excluded. He sought to ensure that the Empire would be a voting bloc for the future world order, enforced by an alliance with the US on equal terms so that each would have an Empire to rule post-war.

The limited common perspective that united Keynes and White against the view of Wall Street led them both to discourage capital flight. But since the 1980s even that has been discarded. The very coercive authority that White had wanted to vest in states to resist flight is now employed by the Fund and Bank to *encourage* it.

The acceptance of coercion versus silence

The fact that coercive flight is not ordinarily investigated arises not just from the nature of the discussion in political economy, but a failure to observe, itself a form of coercion, and an agreement not to see. Bourdieu (1987: 194–195; Bourdieu and Haacke 1994) speaks of 'common knowledge', 'everyone knows', as preventing any serious discussion, for what passes for debate is actually a set of coded instructions. This language of power universalizes a particular set of interests that are claimed to be the interests of all, even though they only represent those of a tiny elite. Euphemism is understood in Bombay where the threat of violence is explicit at the time of extraction of value from labour, and the subsequent unstated threat ensures the good behaviour of the journalist, and therefore the opacity of all public record. This is evident in the absence of public discussion about the source of Indian or Russian wealth now in London, or in the City's business of private banking. So many around the world have been impoverished and their land and water ruined; perhaps we might ask not only whether a surplus was extracted, but where it has gone.

Notes

1 I am indebted to the New York Public Library for access to its collections; and especially to Jay Barksdale who has enabled me to do my research and writing at the splendid Wertheim Study.

Money laundering and capital flight 203

2 It is because Barbara Harriss-White has been curious about the real lives of people that she has found important and original explanations. When we met through Jairus Banaji she invited me to join them on a proposed study on corporate governance and capital flight. Sadly this study never obtained funding. Her willingness to look outside convention has been an inspiration. I shall discuss our original project, namely the cross-border flow of capital from the city in which I was born and grew up, now Mumbai, to the UK and the US.

3 I have earlier argued that there has been too little examination of international private banking (Srinivasan 1995); and that the laundering of Indian wealth by sending it abroad is enabled both by India's pusillanimity and by the rapacity of the West (Srinivasan 2007).

4 The latest manifestation of such concealment is internet pornography, i.e. the traffic in images of persons by means of their transfer to the internet and sale there, enabling a physical separation from the ultimate buyer that renders those exploited even more powerless just as those who exploit them are even less accountable.

5 Examples include the removal of Wajid Ali Shah, last King of Avadh, to Matiaburj outside Calcutta, the removal of the Mogul Emperor to Burma, and the removal of the King of Burma to Ratnagiri.

6 A piston rod, for instance, that had cost Rs.626 two years earlier thereafter cost Rs.98,420 if bought through the government's favoured middleman, and a 'valve cover seat ring' bought earlier for Rs.436, in two years, cost Rs.7539. Some items have been inflated by as much as 5000 per cent (personal communication from my informant, the senior officer of flag rank dealing with logistics at the time).

7 Even when suppliers were important Russian equipment manufacturers such as the Baltic Shipyard, the invoices were still routed through firms such as M/s GS Rughani in London.

8 A deal from Kiev for spares for the Kamov-28 helicopter was a tripartite one which included the happily named Banking Investment Saving Insurance Corporation, registered in the US.

9 Capital flight occurs in advanced Western states such as the UK, but very differently: governments may permit legal tax avoidance by the rich, such as allowing concessions for non-residents or Jersey subjects; yet occasional capital flight does not arise from complete helplessness, since the UK and the US, for instance, have long had policies in force that have enabled them to finance their trade deficits with predictably consistent net capital flows; by contrast, in weak states, flight is a long tradition arising from the collapse of state authority.

10 Jersey, Guernsey and the Isle of Man.

11 Anguilla, Bermuda, British Antarctic Territory, British Indian Ocean Territory, Cayman Islands; Sovereign Base Areas of Akrotiri and Dhekelia in Cyprus, Falkland Islands, Gibraltar, Montserrat, Pitcairn, Henderson, Ducie and Oeno Islands (commonly known as the Pitcairn Islands), St Helena, Ascension and Tristan da Cunha; South Georgia and the South Sandwich Islands, Turks and Caicos Islands, and Virgin Islands (commonly known as the British Virgin Islands). It goes without saying that some of these Territories are not tax havens.

12 Led by John Christensen of Tax Justice Network, Austin Mitchell MP for Great Grimsby and Professor Prem Sikka, Professor of Accounting, University of Essex.

13 Assistant District Attorney John Moscow, quoted in the *Observer*, 22 September 1996, p. 19, cited in *Submissions to the Clothier Committee Jersey's Review Panel on Machinery of Government*, 26 June 2000, http://visar.csustan.edu/aaba/Jerseyclothier.html.

14 Just one building, Ugland House in the Caymans, was the sole registered office of 18,857 companies as of March 2008 through its only tenant, the law firm of Maples and Calder (Report to the Chairman and Ranking Member, Committee on Finance, US Senate, US Government Accountability Office (GAO 08 = 778)), www.gao.gov/new.iterms.d08778.pdf (downloaded 10 December 2011).

204 *K. Srinivasan*

15 These fluctuate sharply; those from Switzerland have consistently been positive ($8.4 billion at end-June 2009, down considerably from $137 billion at end-2007); those from Ireland have been negative for the UK; and those from Luxembourg have varied considerably.

16 House of Commons Justice Committee – Eighth Report Crown Dependencies Q 17, oral evidence on The Work of the Ministry of Justice, 7 October 2008, HC 1076i, publications.parliament.uk/pa/cm200910/cmselect/cmjust/56/5606.htm (downloaded 11 February 2014).

17

> We dread the operation of money. Do we not know that there are many men who wait, and who indeed hardly wait, the event of this prosecution, to let loose all the corrupt wealth of India, acquired by the oppression of that country, for the corruption of all the liberties of this, and to fill the Parliament with men who are now the object of its indignation? To-day the Commons of Great Britain prosecute the delinquents of India: to-morrow the delinquents of India may be the Commons of Great Britain.

18 www.ft.com/cms/s/0/e208a9f0–479a-11dd-93ca-000077b07658,dwp_uuid=a6dfcf08–9c79–11da-8762–0000779e2340.html (downloaded 29 July 2008).

19

> One concern … which has been debated is the investment through the participatory note (PN) route by FIIs. The Government is of the opinion that as FIIs maintain records of identity of the entity they issue PNs to and SEBI can obtain this information…. Further, PNs can be issued or transferred only to persons who are regulated by an appropriate foreign regulatory authority. The Reserve Bank's concern is that as PNs are tradable instruments overseas, this could lead to multi-layering which will make it difficult to identify the ultimate holders of PNs.
>
> (Reserve Bank 2009: 356–357)

20 Raymond Baker (2005), and www.gfintegrity.org, (downloaded 27 January 2014), long the leading international authority, has been my guru in understanding not just US policies and data, but so much about this entire issue.

21

> Another problem in country attribution is that many U.S. securities are issued directly abroad, with settlement and custody occurring at international central securities depositories (ICSD)…. Among the ten countries with the largest holdings of US securities on the most recent survey, five – Belgium, the Cayman Islands, Luxembourg, Switzerland, and the United Kingdom – are financial centers in which substantial amounts of securities owned by residents of other countries are managed or held in custody. If securities are issued in bearer, or unregistered, form, the owners of such securities do not need to make themselves known, and typically little or no information is available about them.
>
> (Federal Reserve Bank 2013: 10)

22 (Section 871(h)) Internal Revenue Code United States Internal Revenue Service.

23 (871(i)(2)(A)) Internal Revenue Code United States Internal Revenue Service.

24 It is, says Hume, 'the low price of labour in every nation' that enables poorer states to undersell the richer in all foreign markets (Hume 1758: 136). Even as the lowest prices ensured the greatest earnings from trade, national currencies thereafter appreciate as trade remittances increase, raising prices and making each country with increasing trade remittances and an appreciating currency less competitive. This *prices–trade–currency value–public expenditure–price inflation/deflation* equilibrium was, argued Hume, entirely self-correcting, since equilibrium must always be restored on its own – 'prices adjust until supply equals demand'. This claim about international trade was thereafter applied to the flow of capital.

References

Abreu, Marcelo de Paiva (1990) 'Brazil as a creditor: sterling balances, 1940–52', *The Economic History Review*, 43(3): 450–469.

Bagchi, Amiya Kumar (2002a) 'The other side of foreign investment by imperial powers', *Economic & Political Weekly*, 37(23): 2229–2238.

—— (2002b) 'The problem of colonialism in classical political economy: analysis, epistemological breaks and mystification', *Centre for Development Economics/Delhi School of Economics Occasional Paper 1*, March.

—— (2005) *Perilous Passage: Mankind and the Global Ascendancy of Capital*, Lanham, MD: Rowman & Littlefield.

Baker, Raymond (2005) *Capitalism's Achilles Heel*, Princeton, NJ: John Wiley & Sons.

Banerjee, D. (1990) 'An appraisal of the profitability of the Indo-British commodity trade during 1871–1887', *Journal of Development Studies*, 26(2): 243–259.

Boughton, James (2002) *Why White, not Keynes?*, www.imf.org/external/pubs/ft/wp/2002/wp0252.pdf (downloaded 15 December 2013).

Bourdieu, Pierre (1987) *Choses Dites*, Paris: Les Editions de Minuit.

Bourdieu, Pierre and Haacke, Hans (1994) *Libre-Échange*, Paris: Seuil.

Burke, Edmund (1789, 1870) 'Speech on the fourth day', 7 May 1789, *Works of the Right Honourable Edmund Burke, Volume VII, The Impeachment of Warren Hastings*, London: Bell & Daldy.

Craig, R. Bruce (2004) *Treasonable Doubt*, Kansas, MI: Kansas University Press.

Epstein, Gerald A. (2005) *Capital Flight and Capital Controls in Developing Countries*, Cheltenham: Edward Elgar.

Habib, Irfan (2006) *Indian Economy, 1858–1914*, New Delhi: Tulika Books.

Helleiner, Eric (1994) *States and the Re-emergence of Global Finance: From Bretton Woods to the 1990s*, Ithaca, NY: Cornell University Press.

—— (2005) 'Regulating capital flight', in Gerald A. Epstein (ed.) *Capital Flight and Capital Controls in Developing Countries*, Cheltenham: Edward Elgar: 289–300.

Horsefield, J. Keith (1969) 'Preliminary Draft Plan for a United Nations Stabilization Fund and a Bank for Reconstruction and Development of the United and Associated Nations (April 1942) H.D. White, Assistant to the Secretary, US Treasury Department', in *The International Monetary Fund 1945–1965, Volume Three, Documents*, Washington, DC: International Monetary Fund.

Hume, David (1758) 'Of money, Essay III', in *Essays and Treatises on Several Subjects, Volume II*, London: A. Millar in the Strand.

Hunter, Lawrence A. (2002) 'Guidance on Reporting of Deposit Interest Paid to Nonresident Aliens: Testimony before the Internal Revenue Service Proposed Rule Making: REG-133254–02 and REG-126100–00', US Congress, 5 December, http://archive.freedomandprosperity.org/ea-hunter.pdf (downloaded 12 February 2014).

India, Government of (2012) *White Paper on Black Money*, submitted to Parliament by Finance Minister Pranab Mukherjee 16 May, http://finmin.nic.in/reports/WhitePaper_BlackMoney2012.pdf (downloaded 3 December 2013).

India, Reserve Bank of (2009) *India's Financial Sector, An Assessment*, Report of the Committee on Financial Sector Assessment, March, chaired by Rakesh Mohan, Deputy Governor, Reserve Bank of India, www.rbi.org.in/scripts/PublicationReportDetails.aspx?FromDate=3/30/2009&SECID=21&SUBSECID=0 (downloaded 13 May 2013).

—— (2012) *Annual Report*, http://rbidocs.rbi.org.in/rdocs/AnnualReport/PDFs/19T_AN23082012.pdf (downloaded 27 May 2013).

206 K. Srinivasan

—— (2013) *Balance of Payments Manual*, www.rbi.org.in/scripts/OccasionalPublications. aspx?head=Balance%20of%20Payments%20Manual%20for%20India (downloaded 13 May 2013).

Jevons, William Stanley (1866) 'Brief account of a general mathematical theory of political economy', *Journal of the Royal Statistical Society*, 29(June): 282–287.

Jones, Geoffrey and Wale, Judith (1998) 'Merchants as business groups: British trading companies in Asia before 1945', *The Business History Review*, 72(3): 367–408.

Kalecki, Michal (1968, 1976) 'The difference between crucial economic problems of developed and underdeveloped non-socialist economies', in *Essays on Developing Economies*, Brighton: Harvester Press, 1976.

Kar, Dev (2010) *The Drivers and Dynamics of Illicit Financial Flows from India: 1948–2008*, www.gfintegrity.org/storage/gfip/documents/reports/india/gfi_india.pdf (downloaded 14 December 2013).

McCulloch, Jude and Pickering, Sharon (2005) *British Journal of Criminology*, 45(4): 470–486.

Misra, A.M. (2000) 'Business culture and entrepreneurship in British India 1860–1950', *Modern Asian Studies*, 34(2): 333–348.

Naoroji, Dadabhai (1901) *Poverty and Un-British Rule in India*, London: S. Sonnenschein.

Norway, Government of (2009) *Report from the Government Commission on Capital Flight from Poor Countries, appointed by Royal Decree on 27 June 2008, submitted 18 June 2009, No. 19 of 2009*, www.regjeringen.no/pages/2223780/PDFS/NOU20092009 0019000EN_PDFS.pdf (downloaded 6 May 2013).

Palme Dutt, R. (1940) *India To-Day*, London: Victor Gollancz.

Patnaik, Utsa (2002) *New Estimates of 18th Century British Trade in the Making of History*, London: Anthem.

Rojas-Suarez, Liliana (1991) 'Determinants and systemic consequences of international capital flows', *IMF Occasional Paper 77*, 15 April, Washington, DC: International Monetary Fund, www.imf.org/external/pubs/cat/longres.cfm?sk=272.0.

Srinivasan, Kannan (1995) '"Private banking" and depreciation of the rupee', *Economic and Political Weekly*, 30(45): 2849–2850.

—— (2007) 'Money laundering and security', in M. Vicziany (ed.) *Controlling Arms and Terror in the Asia Pacific: After Bali and Baghdad*, Cheltenham: Edward Elgar.

Srinivasan, Kannan and Gangoli, Geetanjali (2005) 'India and Middle Eastern oil: 1900–1950', *Contemporary India*, Journal of the Nehru Memorial Museum and Library, 4(1/2): 58–103.

Steuart, Sir James (1770) *Principles of Political Oeconomy*, Dublin: printed for James Williams in Skinner Row, and Richard Moncrieffe in Cape Street.

UK Government (1998) *Review of Financial Regulations in the Crown Dependencies, Andrew Edwards in Cooperation with the Island Authorities*, presented to Parliament by the Secretary of State for the Home Department, November.

—— (2009) *Final report of the Independent Review of British Offshore Financial Centres, October 2009* (Michael Foot), http://webarchive.nationalarchives.gov.uk/+/ www.hm-treasury.gov.uk/d/foot_review_main.pdf (downloaded 29 May 2013).

—— (2010) *House of Commons Justice Committee Crown Dependencies Chaired by the Rt Hon Sir Alan Beith MP, Report, together with formal minutes*, published on 30 March by authority of the House of Commons HC 56–I, London: The Stationery Office, publications.parliament.uk/pa/cm200910/cmselect/cmjust/56/56i.pdf (downloaded 11 February 2014).

—— (2012) *White Paper, The Overseas Territories*, June 2012 Cm 8374, gov.uk/government/uploads/system/uploads/attachment_data/file/32952/ot-wp-0612.pdf (downloaded 11 February 2014).

US Bureau of Economic Analysis (BEA) (2013) *The International Investment Position of the United States at the End of the First Quarter of 2013 and Year 2012*, bea.gov/scb/pdf/2013/07%20July/0713_international_investment_position.pdf (downloaded 11 February 2014).

US Federal Reserve Bank (2013) *Foreign Portfolio Holdings of US Securities as of June 30 2012*, Board of Governors of the Federal Reserve System, Department of the Treasury, April, www.treasury.gov/resource-center/data-chart-center/tic/Documents/shla2012r.pdf (downloaded 11 February 2014).

Von Neumann, John and Morgenstern, Oskar (1944) *Theory of Games and Economic Behavior*, Princeton, NJ: Princeton University Press.

Zdanowicz, John S., Welch, William W. and Pak, Simon J. (1996) 'Capital flight from India to the United States through abnormal pricing in international trade', *Finance India*, 10(3): 881–903.

12 Power-hungry

The state and the troubled transition in Indian electricity

Elizabeth Chatterjee[1]

1 Introduction

India's pre-liberalization power policy was characterized by vast subsidies for irrigated agriculture, widespread theft, scarcity and underinvestment. With regional variations, this description also fits the contemporary power sector. Electricity is critical for capital accumulation – making its comparative neglect in the study of development all the more egregious – and we would intuitively expect India's contemporary pro-business state to alter policy to benefit 'India Inc'. The power sector was indeed one of the first selected for reform in 1991, yet the pro-business transition has substantially failed. What can this failure tell us about the contemporary Indian state and its relationship with capitalist development?

The following review of public policy making in the power sector analyses this question along two dimensions: the state's relations with social classes, and its internal organization. These arise out of the interrelated Marxist and Weberian literatures on the state. To bowdlerize a set of complex debates, Marxists broadly analyse the state in capitalist society as shaped by class relations, whether through external constraints or internal institutionalization, while Weberians draw greater attention to the state's own interests and distinctive logic. Nonetheless, moderate Weberian institutionalists are not unsympathetic to class-analytic theories. The modern state – which is not simply despotic and extractive, but aims to coordinate social life – draws upon sources of social power: it is *embedded*. Even as embeddedness opens the state to capture and proliferating demands, it increases the state's stability, popular legitimacy, information on interest group preferences, and its ability to penetrate society and buy off opponents (Mann 1993: 59–61). The state is socially embedded insofar as bureaucrats are drawn from and partly socialized within (typically elite) social classes. It is politically embedded insofar as societal interest groups can mobilize to influence it. The first line of analysis therefore surveys the state's relationship to dominant social classes.

The second line analyses state *capacity*. The aspirational myth is the Weberian ideal type: bureaucracy as impersonal, meritocratic, competent, neatly hierarchical, and shielded from everyday political interference (Weber 1978:

The state and transition in Indian electricity 209

956–1005). Moderate Weberians accept that in reality 'state autonomy' is not fixed but varies according to (*inter alia*) the state's internal organization and coherence, technical expertise, level of bureaucratic commitment, insulation, and control over investment resources, alongside shifting relations with societal groups (Skocpol 1985). The state's institutional arrangements also structure interactions within society and the political expression of class interests, altering incentives and mechanisms of influence (democratic or otherwise). Its ability to promote long-term capital accumulation, including the ability to channel and discipline capital, therefore depends on both the type and degree of its embeddedness in society *and* its internal institutional characteristics (Evans 1995).[2] Together these inform the *class content* of policy and the state's *capacity* to implement it in practice.

Section 2 examines the state's problematic embeddedness. From the 1970s power policy was substantially captured by non-corporate capitalist groups, especially numerous and well-organized farmers, thus undermining the sector's long-term development. In this context, liberalization may be seen as the central government's attempt to dis-embed itself, 'depoliticizing' the compromised state system through strategies of technocracy and insulation. Yet this marked less the removal of politics than the sector's *repoliticization* in a more technocratic and elitist form. Closer business links have been forged, but there is still no neat capital–state nexus: the state remains the sector's prime mover, thanks to energy security, redistribution and employment concerns, and the (perceived) unreliability of the capitalist class itself. Insulation from popular politics has also proved to be only a partial and uneven success. The persistence of pervasive state ownership means that political contests continue to take place within the state and the context of hybrid state capitalism. Section 3 explores the sector's problematic bureaucratization, which in part reflects its embeddedness. Institutional complexity, bureaucratic pathologies, and especially the federal system militate against a 'Weberian' bureaucracy and policy coherence. The emergent hybrid system continues to struggle.

Section 4 concludes with a call for a disaggregated analysis of the contemporary Indian state. The tense and confused relationship between technocracy and 'politics' is likely to prove unstable. Certain technocratic elements at the apex of the Indian state have unsystematically increased their functional autonomy from non-corporate sections of society, but simultaneously the Indian state remains fundamentally plural, disunited and unevenly embedded, undermining the attainment of its own stated goals.

2 Liberalization as *re*politicization

The power sector provides a useful lens through which to view the contemporary Indian state because electricity is a key issue both for capital and for 'mass politics'. It is not innate to capitalism, but has become 'effectively … a structural feature' of capital accumulation and intensification, especially for big business (McDonald 2009: 3–7). It is a pre-eminent South Asian business concern – *the*

210   *E. Chatterjee*

biggest problem businessmen report facing (Ahmed and Ghani 2007: 11) – and a major target of industrial lobbying.[3] At the same time electricity's unique physical characteristics and social resonance, its 'quiddity', goes well beyond this: it is also a crucial agricultural input, an enabler of human development and modern consumerist life, and, more or less overtly, a vote-winning political asset. It is therefore a pre-eminent issue of 'mass politics' too, lying at the heart of contemporary distributive conflicts.

Pre-liberalization power policy is widely seen as an archetypal victim of short-termist populism: widespread public ownership (along with bureaucratic corruption) and well-organized groups' demands for low tariffs together crippled the sector's long-term development. Liberalization in turn marks an attempt to extract the sector from 'politics', and to wrest control back for technocratic and pro-business fractions at the state's apex on more favourable terms for corporate and energy capital.

The diagnosis: a surfeit of 'politics'

Capitalism as a mode of accumulation and a social relation cannot be reproduced and expanded purely through market relations: the state is necessary to create the conditions for stable long-term accumulation. Historically this has included provision of the material infrastructure that individual capitalists would not be able to provide, as most in the post-war world – and in India – agreed was the case for electricity.[4] After much debate, the 1948 Electricity (Supply) Act enshrined a leading role for the state, while continuing to tolerate private participation.

The 1948 Act also enshrined an uneasy compromise between the central and state governments (Kale 2014). Electricity consequently appears on the Constitution's 'Concurrent List'. The central government formulates long-term plans, provides technical analysis and approves projects. Policy implementation rests with the individual states. The crucial institutions were the state electricity boards (SEBs), vertically integrated monopolies under the control of state governments, with responsibility for tariff setting (today theoretically in accordance with their electricity regulators' recommendations), in practice for almost all distribution, and for a substantial share of generation.[5]

Under this system, industrialists enjoyed lower power tariffs than other consumers until the early 1970s. However, with corporate capital comparatively weak at Independence, state elites increasingly sought allies from other powerful groups, notably agricultural capitalists. Simultaneously these groups mobilized to access public resources, especially within the states. The state's internal fragmentation, incoherence and embeddedness grew as it attempted, often ineffectually, to accommodate growing demands, and as both favoured social groups and bureaucrats sought to expand their jurisdictions (Herring 1999; see also Section 3).

Electricity, a valuable agricultural input, was a key focus of the newly competitive distributive politics. Bolstered by sociocultural change, incomplete land reform and the state-sponsored Green Revolution, well-organized rural lobbies

The state and transition in Indian electricity   211

used their disproportionate influence on electoral politics to demand protection and extension of state support (Bardhan 1998; Rudolph and Rudolph 1987; Varshney 1995; Kale 2014).[6] State politicians gave into the temptation of using agricultural power as a tool of patronage and electioneering. Tolerating power theft, too, became 'part of deliberate political strategy' (Min and Golden 2014: 624).[7] It is effectively a subsidy to the informal economy, and benefits not only larger farmers but also wealthy residential users and some industrialists (Harriss-White 2003: 64). *Paying* industrial and commercial consumers gradually came to cross-subsidize cheap agrarian and residential power through some of the world's highest tariffs.

The magnitude of subsidies and theft threatened to cripple both the power system and state governments. SEB officials had no incentive to secure cost efficiency, but acceded to their superiors' politicized demands knowing they would be bailed out (eventually by the centre). Electricity became the largest single burden on many state budgets. Draining resources, discouraging much-needed investment and providing only erratic power, the sector's development benefited few in the longer term.

The solution: 'depoliticization'

In 1991, the power sector was the first major sector selected for liberalization. The financial crisis permitted a moment of state autonomy, bolstered by an ideologically committed central elite and external champions (or scapegoats) (Shastri 1997). The reforms went through several phases. First, in 1991, came support for independent power producers (IPPs) to invest in generation. By 1993 the World Bank had solidified its template for reform. This provided a neat and purportedly universal prescription: unbundling vertical monopolies, privatization, creating independent regulatory agencies and building competitive markets. The second phase (approximately 1995–1998) comprised a period of regionally led experimentation with regulators and SEB restructuring, with heavy involvement from the World Bank and other international consultants. Several states, most famously Odisha, brought in their own reforms (see Dubash and Rajan 2001). It was not until early 2000 that the centre really re-entered the debate with a draft Electricity Act, which was finally passed in May 2003.[8] This aimed to consolidate and give momentum to earlier developments, and theoretically introduced competition throughout the sector.[9]

The IPP policy aside, the reformers' diagnosis was a surfeit of politics: they argued that India's electricity subsidies developed, persisted and grew due to the short-termist logic of electoral democracy. The World Bank lamented 'the pervasive politicization of most decisions' in the sector by patronage-dispensing state governments (1997: 4), later blaming 'political interference' and its mirror image 'lack of political will' for the continuing gap between rhetorical pro-reform consensus and half-hearted practice. Its Delhi-based officials admitted that 'now we are not sure democracy is a good thing when [politicians'] concern over increasing power tariffs is related to their electoral victory' (quoted in Xu 2004: 59).

212   *E. Chatterjee*

This was not new. For years official studies had analysed the power sector's woes and called for reforms to bolster the centre versus the states.[10] Such reforms have a pedigree stretching back to the establishment of the Rural Electrification Corporation in 1969. In 1975, with extensive World Bank support, the central government established two state-owned enterprises (SOEs), the National Thermal Power Corporation (NTPC) and the National Hydroelectric Power Corporation (NHPC), to give a fillip to generation capacity and act as an instrument of central fiscal discipline upon the profligate SEBs. In 1989 it moved into inter-state transmission with the Power Grid (now another corporatized vehicle to assist in creating markets in the sector).

In this context, liberalization offered a framework for 'removing the economy from politics'. The 'apolitical' nature of the solution was not only a means but also an end in itself: 'The principal objective of reform', as its evangelists in Russia made clear, was 'to *depoliticize* economic life' (Boycko *et al.* 1995: 11, emphasis in original). This meant insulating the technocratic executive apex from the pressures of mass politics and the state's embedded lower reaches; circumventing other bodies seen as compromised; and, at least in the early years, tacitly condoning some furtiveness: citing Jenkins (1999), a World Bank energy consultant concluded: 'since much of [power] reform is politically unmarket-able,... the implementation game is all about stealth, ambiguity, and following the path of least resistance' (Lal 2006: 21; see also Mahalingam 2005). Crucially, some central technocrats agreed that monopolistic state control of such a critical asset was a liability: Gajendra Haldea, drafter of the Electricity Act 2003, warned that 'the government needs to distance itself from the ownership of infra-structure sectors that clouds its judgement' (Haldea 2011: xxxi). The reforms' endorsement by key fractions at the apex of governments at the centre and in some states indicated that they similarly recognized and sought to counter the state's own disunity and porosity, even while they had reason to reject massive (and disastrous) Russia-style privatization. I briefly survey two particularly high-profile 'depoliticization' measures here.

First, the introduction of independent regulators, a sign less of deregulation than 're-regulation', marks one explicit (and internationally fashionable) attempt to create depoliticized expert spaces (Sen and Jamasb 2012: 89). As the World Bank explained for Odisha, the unlikely pioneer, the regulator's purpose was 'to insulate Orissa's [Odisha's] power sector from the government' (quoted in Dubash and Rao 2008: 322). Electricity particularly lends itself to techniques that recast problems in technical, apolitical terms requiring specialist hands. In turn, regulators offered state politicians the chance to shift the locus of unpopular tariff decisions, although not always with much public credibility (Chatterjee 2012). In practice, regulators have been reabsorbed into the political process in several states (appointees are often retired bureaucrats), and have so far proved unable to escape the multiple demands of different kinds of consumers, politicians, investors and international lenders.

Second, with many states remaining recalcitrant (see Section 3), the open-access[11] provisions of the Electricity Act suggest a pragmatic attempt to create a two-track economy that punishes overly politicized laggards, in theory at least. 'Captive' private on-site generation has risen to compensate for the unreliable and expensive state-run system. Open access institutionalizes this exit option for high-value customers. It attempts to bring in competition, increase investment and reform distribution by the back door while avoiding directly antagonizing agriculturalists or state governments (Joseph 2010). This suggests that the centre is prepared to take substantial steps to force fiscal discipline and tariff reform upon the states: such a solution risks ceding 'all the family silver (big cities, industrial areas, and SEZs [special economic zones])' to private players (Kumar and Chatterjee 2012: xiii).[12] Without decent regulation and enforcement, largely lacking so far, this threatens to create a two-tier system that benefits industrialists and the urban middle classes, but leaves rural areas to fall behind with increasingly decrepit public utilities (Joseph 2010; Tongia 2007). This system may come to resemble the notorious SEZs, permitting elites to partially secede from messy democratic realities. To avoid losing lucrative customers, however, state governments are subverting the policy by pressurizing regulators to set prohibitively high surcharges. Once again, the federal division of responsibilities stymies implementation, as the exigencies of popular politics collide with liberalizing orthodoxy.[13]

Although much literature treats the power sector as a technical arena, then, all policy making is emphatically political. Liberalization shifts some of the arenas for these struggles, somewhat diminishing the legislature's power in favour of the executive and (quasi-)judicial organs, to structurally favour certain groups. The result is a 'two-track polity': on the one hand, the messy, deadlocked electoral arena and underfunded social programmes; on the other, the concentration of secretive and technocratic decision-making power (Kohli 2012; Mooij 2007). . Liberalization marks less a qualitative shift in this strategy, which Marxists and Weberian institutionalists alike would argue is a perpetual urge in government (Weber 1978: 990–994), than a strengthened hand for some high-level technocrats and their business allies. These fractions of the state have sought to insulate it from penetration by rural groups and even from its own cost-blind lower bureaucracy, even while seeking to facilitate closer relations – developmental embeddedness – with business.

Embedded autonomy versus state ambivalence

If capture by subsidy-hungry agriculturalists and other theft-prone groups alters the class content of policy to make the long-term development of the power sector difficult, the 'right type' of embeddedness reinforces the state's reform inclination and its access to information, finance and technology. The central state's pro-business turn is visible in the power sector, with corporate lobby groups, personnel and energy capitalists increasingly brought into the policy process in New Delhi. Some things have not changed, however. Bureaucrats retain suspicions about business, due in part to past experience with private energy players. In addition, electricity's social importance and India's growing

214 *E. Chatterjee*

energy worries make the state indispensable, creating a dualistic and ambivalent system, market-oriented but state-led, even as rural groups retain influence in some states.

The contemporary state's 'instrumentalist' links with big business are increasingly strong. Where rural groups relied on electoral weight for influence, energy capitalists are welcomed more directly into the policy-making process. They are better equipped than rural lobbies to cope with the rapid pace and technicalities of complex legislation, repeated policy revisions and legal challenges. Some business lobbies have become more 'developmental' in their mechanisms of influence, favouring PowerPoint policy advice as much as 'briefcase politics'. There are two major power industry lobbies – the Independent Power Producers Association of India (IPPAI) and the Association of Power Producers (APP) – which provide loud, articulate private voices in policy formulation. The centre of lobbying action, too, has shifted from Udyog Bhavan, the industries ministry, to the infrastructure ministries (Kochanek 1996; Sinha 2010).

Many central power bureaucrats are genuine believers in the ability of the market to correct distortions and provide much-needed fiscal discipline.[14] The 'revolving door' between the upper echelons of the bureaucracy, regulators, SOEs and private companies also spins rapidly, so that the state effectively subsidizes expertise for the private sector. Former power secretary R.V. Shahi previously worked for NTPC and for the private Bombay Suburban Electric Supply Ltd (BSES, later taken over by Reliance Energy), for example; he is currently chairman of an energy consultancy and sits on the boards of several other companies, including Jindal Power. Ashok Khurana, director-general of APP, was an IAS officer in the power ministry and later a World Bank consultant. Interview evidence suggests that this embeddedness is two-way, with former bureaucrats bringing at least the rhetoric of public interest to the private sector.[15] The payoff was a surge of private investment into the sector during the Eleventh Plan period (2007–2012).[16]

Energy capitalists are not always 'developmental', however (Herring 1999). Some have proved timid, preferring to follow in the state's wake; or less than competent, as some generation companies' unfeasibly low tariff bids in solar auctions may indicate. Others have sometimes proved willing to use quasi-legal mechanisms of influence and to pursue short-term or predatory strategies, exploiting the credulity or venality of some policy makers. In this way the interests of energy capitalists, and the bureaucrats' attitudes towards them, may not align with those of big business more generally.

The classic case is the initial IPP phase of reform. The policy was flawed anyway, based on the convenient misconception that additional generation was the first priority rather than politically risky distribution reform. More problematically, 'attracting capital became an end in itself, rather than a considered means' (Dubash 2011: 70). Often secretively, IPPs were offered startlingly generous terms, most notoriously in the case of Enron's Dabhol power plant, Maharashtra. Such IPPs' business practices were often deeply sleazy, their finances opaque, and the power generated extremely expensive. A decade after the

The state and transition in Indian electricity   215

government 'fast-tracked' eight projects, only three had produced power; in the latter half of the 1990s public sector capacity grew twice as fast as private generation (Tongia 2007: 140–142). Perhaps the most charitable assessment is that IPPs won new state-level reform converts through the sheer scale of corruption they permitted (Mahalingam 2005). Bureaucrats and academics alike now regard the entire episode as a debacle, and the 1990s as a lost decade for power policy.

Predatory behaviour by energy capitalists and feeble government responses have proved a recurrent theme. As one former state technocrat (now, like many others, safely installed in a private energy corporation) said glumly: 'We regulated them as though they were good guys – but they weren't.'[17] This lack of trust, and the state's visible inability to effectively discipline and regulate energy capital, suggest that power policy does not consistently benefit from Evans' (1995) developmental state–business nexus. Even within the sector, Indian capitalism seems to have both developmental and rent-seeking faces (cf. Gandhi and Walton 2012). The degree of capitalist cohesion, and of business penetration of the state, may have been somewhat overstated. Unsurprisingly the state continues to intervene heavily.

The dual system

Contra Bretton Woods orthodoxy, India has liberalized pragmatically without dramatic expenditure reduction or privatization. In the energy sector it has favoured corporatization of public sector undertakings, the parallel introduction of competition, and public–private partnerships (most strikingly the ultra-megapower projects, supported with unusual proactivity by the Prime Minister's Office) while preserving SOEs. This has created a 'pragmatic hybrid with the state playing a stronger role in steering and guiding developments', even though market rhetoric remains potent (Dubash 2011: 71).

Today some SOEs have 'emerged to occupy a space between the old state-owned system and a hypothetical "textbook" power sector that is dominated by purely private firms'. They have become profit-driven and comparatively efficiently run hybrids (Tongia 2007: 113–116). Long a World Bank favourite, NTPC was explicitly designed 'to become a model of modern operational practices that the SEBs could emulate' (Dubash and Rajan 2001: 3370, quoting the Bank). Like some of its siblings, such as Oil and Natural Gas Corporation Ltd (ONGC) and Gas Authority of India Ltd (GAIL), it has been corporatized, commercialized and declared a *Navratna* company[18] with greater everyday financial and managerial autonomy from ministerial oversight. Dominating the Indian stock market, the *Navratna* companies combine corporate management systems and political connections to a degree matched only in the private sector by Reliance Industries. They have gradually gained prominence for what they reveal about contemporary Indian capitalism: wealth is highly concentrated; SOEs remain powerful and sometimes profitable (41 per cent of the profits of the biggest 100 firms sits in state-controlled firms); and 'old-fashioned', rent-thick sectors predominate (*The Economist* 2011; Gandhi and Walton 2012).

216   *E. Chatterjee*

The SOEs enjoy a complex relationship with the state. They are exposed to competition, and have independent directors and 'an increasingly arm's length relationship' with the government (Rai 2010). Yet their prospectuses make clear that their broad direction is under government control, and the controlling line ministries have had little formal redefinition of role or responsibilities. Beyond corporate profitability they advance state goals, and provide the central government with vast amounts through dividends and disinvestment; this includes periodic 'cosmetic disinvestment', whereby the lucrative energy SOEs buy shares in their less profitable siblings. They continue to generate substantial employment, with state power utilities employing around 900,000 workers and NTPC 25,000 (compared to Coal India's 360,000), though with liberalization these numbers are decreasing somewhat. They sometimes suffer from being unable to pass through full costs (for example, of expensive imports) to end-users, although they have also obtained favourable terms for extracting debts.

The SOEs clearly owe their dominance to their former near-monopolies and close relationship with the state, but the best are proving resilient in the face of the new market turn, and may indicate a new entrepreneurial mode of state intervention. NTPC and its siblings simultaneously act as an instrument for the liberalizing and managerialist impulse, for accessing finance, and for central guidance of a key sector in a technocratic mode less accessible to populist demands. In this, India is not unusual: such huge, reasonably well-managed and politically networked 'dual firms' characterize other major emerging economies like China (Huaneng Power), Brazil (Petrobras) and South Africa (Eskom) (Victor and Heller 2007). They have every interest in avoiding full-blown reform, even while resisting excessive drains on their resources through subsidies and underpricing. In all of these cases Victor and Heller find a distinct and stable outcome:

> a 'dual market', combining attributes of the state- and market-based systems.... While not the most economically efficient outcome, the dual market arises and is held in place by strong political forces that favour a system in which parts of power generation and delivery are profitable even as other parts are plagued by nonpayment, inadequate investment, and economically inefficient operation.
>
> (Victor and Heller 2007: 30)

Continued state control and partnerships rather than privatization may not be such a surprising solution, then, particularly given the development and equity concerns that also characterize power. Electricity also, of course, relies on natural resources. In the West the shift from a nation-state to a market-oriented paradigm depended, *inter alia*, on unproblematic access to resources and assets with long life spans ahead. This looks anachronistic. Today resource-scarce countries like India must contend with volatile prices, unstable producer states, climate change and international scrutiny. In New Delhi the realization that the country has not 200 years but perhaps 40 years of domestic coal reserves is '[t]he single most important fact driving India's strategic rethinking on energy' (Dubash 2011: 67). Consequently a new narrative of energy insecurity and scarcity has increasingly come to dominate in policy circles, in which the state's continued role looks assured, not least in facilitating access to resources through dispossession.[19]

Victor and Heller suggest that the state-market hybrid is durable, but India's power sector is far from flourishing. The attempts at depoliticization have been unevenly and partially successful, and many of the sector's problems remain. At least in India, the balance between technocracy and 'politics' appears less stable than their interpretation credits. This is true not only because of the state's problematic embeddedness, but also its internal incoherence.

3 Another spoiler: state dysfunction

That planners and policies aim to facilitate pro-business development is no guarantee of success. If the developmental state requires the right type and degree of embeddedness, it also requires the right modus operandi (Evans 1995). In contrast to the Weberian ideal type, the state is not a unified, cohesive entity. Internal incoherence, conflict and policy dysfunction are no aberration, but a fundamental part of state operations (Schaffer 1984). The twin trends of embedded populism and 'depoliticizing' liberalization have helped reshape the state's own institutions. Under permanent political and popular pressure, India's power bureaucracy is increasingly riven by institutional proliferation and rivalry, pathological behaviour, and the fundamental fracture line of federalism.

Federalism and disunity

The state not only provides the arena for increasingly competitive distributive conflicts, but also structures these conflicts (and is itself remoulded in the process). Similarly, it is not sufficient for individual bureaucrats to 'think Weberian': 'bureaucratic rationality must also be structured in an appropriate apportionment of *power* among state policy agencies' (Chibber 2002: 952). That is to say, 'planners need to also have the capacity to discipline other *state agencies*' (ibid.: 954). Instead the federal system provides a frame that weakens the technocratic apex, both in terms of interest group management and in directing the allocation of state resources.

With the decline of the Congress system, the rise of regional political parties and the competitive neoliberal environment, India has increasingly become a de facto as well as de jure federal system.[20] As was feared from the outset, electricity's constitutionally 'concurrent' status encourages states to politicize the power sector while the centre looks on. Power reform implementation has therefore been highly uneven (Table 12.1). Not all state administrations are or have been equally pro-liberalization; distinctly different logics may govern the state and central levels, the former sometimes 'predatory' while the latter is 'developmental' (Mooij 1999: 236; cf. Varshney 1995: 181–185).

218   *E. Chatterjee*

Table 12.1 Status of reform across Indian states

Description	States
No change	Arunachal Pradesh, Nagaland
Regulator but no structural change	Jammu and Kashmir, Manipur, Meghalaya, Mizoram, Sikkim
Regulator and one reform	Bihar, Goa (regulator + IPPs) Tripura (regulator + tariff reform)
Regulator, tariff reform, open access, but no IPPs or unbundling	Punjab, West Bengal
Regulator, tariff reform, open access in transmission and distribution, IPPs but no unbundling	Tamil Nadu, Chhattisgarh, Jharkhand, Himachal Pradesh, Kerala; Uttar Pradesh (unbundling but no IPPs)
Regulator, IPPs, unbundled SEB under state ownership, tariff revision, open access	Andhra Pradesh, Madhya Pradesh, Gujarat, Haryana, Karnataka, Maharashtra, Rajasthan, Uttarakhand, Assam
Regulator, IPPs, unbundling, tariff revision, open access, with privatized distribution	Odisha, Delhi

Source: Based on Sen and Jamasb (2012: 130), drawing on Ministry of Power data dated December 2007.

Note
This masks other important variations. Gujarat (successful in attracting investment), Himachal Pradesh (resource-rich), Delhi (reformed tariffs and privatized distribution), and until recently West Bengal (with a combination of plentiful resources and suppressed demand through lack of agricultural mechanization, industrialization and rural electrification) have been in reasonable financial condition despite their differing structures. Tamil Nadu, conversely, does abysmally, in part because it resisted tariff rises for seven years before public outcry over the power situation made a huge 37 per cent hike, and U-turning to back the controversial Kudankulam nuclear power plant, politically feasible. Other previously dubious performers to hike tariffs substantially in 2012 include Uttar Pradesh, Rajasthan, and former early mover Haryana.

Enthusiasm for reform, with its threat of rising tariffs for agricultural and residential users, has varied broadly according to the comparative strength and influence of rising business groups versus rural constituencies (Kale 2014). Where rural political interests are well organized, for example, in Punjab, Tamil Nadu and (after Chandrababu Naidu) Andhra Pradesh, they have slowed or undermined power reforms that would more obviously benefit industrial and urban groups and foreign capital, often despite very poor SEB performance. Where rural interests are numerically insignificant (Delhi) or have remained politically marginalized (Odisha), or the state administration is particularly strong (Gujarat), reforms have proceeded with somewhat greater ease.[21]

Although federalism is perhaps the largest single obstacle to sweeping reform, the centre is not entirely powerless. It uses its not inconsiderable financial sway as both carrot and stick to incentivize reform compliance (Ruet 2003). For

The state and transition in Indian electricity   219

instance, before regulators became mandatory, the centre agreed to grant interest subsidies on Power Finance Corporation loans only to states that had set up regulatory commissions (Kumar and Chatterjee 2012: 5). Centrally sponsored schemes are increasingly used as levers. The well-funded Accelerated Power Development and Reforms Programme (APDRP) incentivizes states to cut urban commercial losses and improve distribution by linking success to disbursements. A level of fiscal decentralization and the encouragement of state-level agreements with international donors and private investors are also designed to harden budget constraints (Kirk 2010). Similarly, the centre uses its substantial control of energy supplies through enterprises like NTPC to discipline SEBs, for example, by threatening to cut supply, even taking over the Talcher thermal power plant in 1995 after non-payment in Odisha (Rudolph and Rudolph 2001: 1547). The centre's ability to intervene directly in the states may have been reduced, but it still retains some instruments to regulate and impose fiscal discipline. However, harder budget constraints are often compromised through debt write-offs, restructuring and payouts to coalition partners. The latest central bailout was announced in September 2012.

As with the overall economy, the sector's 'real centre of gravity' has shifted towards the states, while the centre struggles to employ credible institutional or financial controls (Ruet 2003: 6). In practice, then, 'control of the economy is being wrenched with the greatest difficulty' from state-level populism and non-corporate influence, with 'considerable inertia and indecision in tackling the very largest state transfers' like the vast agricultural power subsidies (Harriss-White 2003: 65; Bardhan 1998: 127–132). As Harriss-White (2003) argues, the fitfulness and pain of reforms over the past quarter-century may be seen as marking the bitter, incomplete transition from an 'intermediate regime' of statist intervention, subsidies and scarcity to a more traditionally capitalist, big-business-dominated, liberalization-minded regime. In this incomplete transition, federalism may dissipate resistance (Jenkins 1999), but electricity's concurrent status also limits the ability of the technocratic apex to enact reforms and further widens regional inequalities, even as it leaves the states open to public blame. In this light, privatization and other central efforts to weaken state control mark an attempt to secure 'the relative recuperation of an advantage by the Centre [*sic*] over the States' (Ruet 2003: 14).

Bureaucratic pathology

The power sector is inseparable from the energy sector more generally, yet India has no overarching energy strategy. Like other elements of the Indian bureaucracy, and again exacerbated by the federal system and 'politics', power policy suffers from institutional proliferation. The Ministry of Energy was split into three in 1992. Today, five ministries directly handle energy policy, and multiple energy teams feed into the Five-Year Plans. This institutionalizes chronic disunity, yet the exigencies of coalition and federal politics, in which allies are rewarded with posts, suggest that multiple ministries are likely to continue.

220   E. Chatterjee

The technical calibre of central technocrats appears generally high, but their vision is not necessarily transmitted through the state system. The comparatively weak Planning Commission struggles to influence large ministries with their own interests and priorities (Dubash 2011: 68). In this way 'a robust bureaucracy can become a weapon *against* state cohesion' (Chibber 2002: 984). To circumvent such bodies, technocrats have resorted to creating new organizations, like the Bureau of Energy Efficiency or the Missions of the National Action Plan on Climate Change. The energy bureaucracy has consequently become 'increasingly byzantine and fragmented', characterized by both vertical complexity (multiple competing jurisdictional levels) and horizontal complexity (multiple ministries and other organizations) (Dubash 2011: 68).[22]

Policy is prone to all the problems that this complexity would suggest: interagency competition over resources and priorities, territoriality, vast transaction costs, multiple conflicting goals, cost-blindness, malcoordination, duplication, secretiveness, prodigious paper pushing, illogical rule following and blame shifting (Schaffer 1984; Ruet 2005; Chatterjee 2012). In addition, politicized transfers and brief appointments are rife at all levels, along with 'incompetence, arrogance, indifference, [and] suppression of dissent', as one distinguished commentator raged after July 2012's severe blackouts (Sethi 2012). This undermines specialized expertise and the coherence of decision making.

As this suggests, the sector's administrative problems are not confined to the lower echelons of the state.[23] There is no single-minded state apex (cf. Kohli 2012), but rather a series of apex-level fractions, some of which are more pro-liberalization and technocratic in their orientation. A collection of essays by the Electricity Act's architect, for example, proudly describes him as 'the most hated man in Delhi's infrastructure ministries' (Haldea 2011). Such liberalizing technocrats, along with finance ministry officials, do not necessarily speak with the same voice as career bureaucrats and politicians in the line ministries. Indian power policy is undermined both by the state's awkwardly embedded character *and* such internal incoherence.

4 Conclusion

Examining both the class content of Indian power policy and the state's institutional arrangements, this review suggests that, contrary to popular anthropomorphism, the state has no simple material reality. Its morphology is uncertain: its boundaries with society are porous and complicated by federalism, institutional complexity, and the incorporation of lobbies and hybrid organizations. Its functions, too, are consequently ambivalent: the Indian state is not monolithic but struggles to act in a unitary fashion.

Consistently technocratic, long-term-minded, pro-business 'developmental' impulses *can* be found, particularly within some central organs and among the leadership of some states, although this is complicated by intra-state competition and frequent dysfunction in planning and practice. The central state's strategies of technocratization, institutional (re)invention, re-regulation and state-market

The state and transition in Indian electricity 221

hybridity attempt to strengthen the hand of the executive against the vagaries of populism, especially at the state level. This survey suggests that this 'depoliticization' of power policy has permitted cautious *re*politicization at elite levels, through a closer relationship with domestic and international capital. Nonetheless, at its local reaches and in various states the state may compromise with or favour different class configurations. Given its fragmentation and malfunctioning, it is unhelpful to talk about a monolithic Indian state. This accords with other scholars' findings that the actually existing Indian state is 'polymorphous', 'pluricentred' and 'multilevelled', or 'protean' and 'complex' (Rudolph and Rudolph 1987; Gupta 2012: 17–18; Harriss-White 2003: 102).

The emergent state-market hybrid system is constrained by the combination of societal resistance, its own organizational structures and physical resources. It is hardly enjoying unreserved success, and is consequently far from stable. The state is still critically important, however. India is not following a 'conventional' trajectory of liberalization. The state's reach and scale remain unique, unmatched by even the greatest capitalists. It structures competition over resources, and continues to dominate popular conceptions of legitimacy. To argue that it is weakening would be to simplify and exaggerate. India's contemporary state remains simultaneously more ambivalently 'capitalist', more indispensable and more chaotic than much theory might suggest.

Notes

1 I am grateful to Barbara Harriss-White, Judith Heyer, and especially the late Jos Mooij for comments on this chapter.
2 In his review, Wright (1996) highlights Evans' fusion of the two sets of state theories – Marxian class-analytic and Weberian institutionalist – in his concept of 'embedded autonomy', something Evans himself does not stress. Evans notes that the state's responsibility for economic transformation has become a source of legitimacy in its own right.
3 The state endorses the business–power linkage by incorporating electrification alongside size into its definition of ('unorganized') enterprise. There is no firm divide between formal and informal enterprises. The ranking of electricity as the top constraint is true for both (World Bank 2011: 28–29).
4 See e.g. industrialists' famous Bombay Plan (Thakurdas *et al.* 1944).
5 The states' share of installed generation capacity is declining but even now remains large: 38.8 per cent in December 2013, compared with 28.6 per cent central ownership and 32.5 per cent private (Central Electricity Authority 2013: 4).
6 Electric tubewells are cheap to use but expensive to install. Medium and large farmers, *not* small farmers or landless labourers, therefore benefit disproportionately from power subsidies, especially where irrigation was most successfully extended through Green Revolution policies (Kale 2014).
7 'Aggregate technical & commercial' (AT&C) losses, including technical losses as well as revenue losses through theft, under-billing, non-payment and subsidy misclassification, still hover around 30 per cent, down from 39 per cent in 2001/2002 (versus 17 per cent in Brazil, 10 per cent in Indonesia and 5 per cent in China in 2009; OECD/ IEA 2012: 40). The share of agricultural subsidies in this figure was frequently calculated as a residual, thus systematically underestimating both theft and urban usage.
8 The Act was amended in January 2004 and June 2007.

222　E. Chatterjee

9　Competition was nominally brought in through delicensed (including captive) generation; mandatory non-discriminatory open access to transmission; consumer open access and multiple licensees in distribution; recognizing power trading; and empowering regulators to frame regulations for market development (see the detailed analysis in Kumar and Chatterjee 2012).

10　For example, the report of the Rajadhyaksha Committee in 1980.

11　Open access allows large consumers to seek sources other than the utility on payment of charges to use the incumbent's infrastructure and cross-subsidize other users; they can also now sell any excess from captive production. Big consumers include commercial customers and the wealthy residential colonies; an amendment to the Act decreed that customers with loads above 1 megawatt would be given the option.

12　From the Foreword by Pramod Deo, Chairman, Central Electricity Regulatory Commission.

13　In any case, the current demand–supply gap (alongside equity and environmental concerns) makes competition problematic. Developed-country liberalization in the 1980s was facilitated by excess supply. This may be seen as evidence that Indian liberalization suffers from pathologies of 'isomorphic mimicry': attempts to gain legitimacy 'through the imitation of the forms of modern institutions without functionality' (Pritchett *et al.* 2010: 20). Imported policy models and agendas have proved problematic in application, accountability and credibility terms (Dubash and Rajan 2001; Xu 2004). The disjuncture between sophisticated best-practice plans and Indian realities leads to persistent dysfunction.

14　Author interviews, New Delhi, February to June 2012.

15　A senior private sector representative in Delhi, where distribution is privatized, said that 'the private sector is called upon to fulfil the functions of the state' (author interview, Delhi, May 2012). IAS members sit on the boards of both BSES distribution entities in Delhi.

16　Many projects have been damaged by India's recent fuel supply crisis.

17　Author interview, New Delhi, May 2012. The same interviewee described schemes to abuse the cheap infrastructural financing that comes with power project approval, and suggested that energy lobbies should assist the state in disciplining their own badly behaved members. Other examples of predatory capitalism include the abuse of solar procurement procedures as exposed by the Centre for Science and the Environment (Bhushan and Hamberg 2012); and private coal blocks being left unmined and instead speculated upon, part of 2012's enormous 'Coalgate' allocation scandal. The suspicion created by these examples tars others: several bureaucrats interviewed also evinced scepticism about Reliance's underproduction from its Krishna-Godavari basin gas reserves, and about Tata and Reliance's attempts to renegotiate power purchase agreements after fuel imports drastically increased in price.

18　NTPC became one of India's 'nine jewels' in 1997; in 2010 it was made a *Maharatna*, the new top class, able to make investments of about US$1 billion (Rs.5000 crore) without explicit government approval.

19　While renewable and energy-efficiency concerns are integrated into the energy security narrative due to India's limited domestic resources (Dubash 2011), environmental concerns are often low priority: at the time of writing (February 2014) the Ministry of Environment and Forests is headed by the petroleum minister. Power generation causes vast environmental damage, including a groundwater crisis from subsidized electric tubewells and 85 to 115,000 deaths a year through pollution from coal-fired plants (Greenpeace 2013).

20　Energy lobbies also realize this, and lobby heavily at the state level.

21　Odisha and Delhi have privatized distribution (Table 12.1), while Gujarat has attracted private capital, innovatively separated out rural household and agricultural supplies, and leads in solar power.

22 This is partly a function of the issue's own complexity: the Empowered Group of Ministers – itself a bureaucratic short cut, sidestepping the huge Cabinet – that examined ultra-mega-power projects included not only the power, coal and environment ministers, but also the defence, law and finance ministers (OECD/IEA 2012: 19). The Ministries of Rural Development, Fertilizers, and even External Affairs also often involve themselves with energy issues.

23 In any case, critiques of 'implementation' by the lower bureaucracy often have unsettling class overtones (Gupta 2012: 25), and the strict analytical separation of planning and implementation is usually meaningless or misleading in practice (Schaffer 1984).

References

Ahmed, Sadiq and Ghani, Ejaz (2007) *South Asia: Growth and Regional Integration*, Washington, DC: World Bank.

Bardhan, Pranab (1998) *The Political Economy of Development in India*, expanded edn, Oxford: Oxford University Press.

Bhushan, Chandra and Hamberg, Jonas (2012) 'The truth about solar mission', *Down to Earth*, 15 February, www.downtoearth.org.in/content/truth-about-solar-mission.

Boycko, Maxim, Shleifer, Andrei and Vishny, Robert W. (1995) *Privatizing Russia*, Cambridge, MA: MIT Press.

Central Electricity Authority (2013) *Executive Summary: Power Sector*, New Delhi: Ministry of Power, Government of India, www.cea.nic.in/reports/monthly/executive_rep/dec13.pdf (accessed 3 January 2014).

Chatterjee, Elizabeth (2012) 'Dissipated energy: Indian electric power and the politics of blame', *Contemporary South Asia*, 20(1): 91–103.

Chibber, Vivek (2002) 'Bureaucratic rationality and the developmental state', *American Journal of Sociology*, 107(4): 951–989.

Dubash, Navroz K. (2011) 'From norm taker to norm maker? Indian energy governance in global context', *Global Policy*, 2(2): 66–79.

Dubash, Navroz K. and Rajan, Sudhir Chella (2001) 'Power politics: process of power sector reform in India', *Economic and Political Weekly*, 36(35): 3367–3390.

Dubash, Navroz K. and Rao, Narasimha D. (2008) 'Regulatory practice and politics: lessons from independent regulation in Indian electricity', *Utilities Policy*, 16: 321–331.

Economist, The (2011) 'Adventures in capitalism', 22 October.

Evans, Peter (1995) *Embedded Autonomy: States and Industrial Transformation*, Princeton, NJ: Princeton University Press.

Gandhi, Aditi and Walton, Michael (2012) 'Where do India's billionaires get their wealth?', *Economic and Political Weekly*, 47(40): 10–14.

Greenpeace (2013) *Coal Kills: An Assessment of Death and Disease Caused by India's Dirtiest Energy Source*, www.greenpeace.org//india/en/publications/Coal-Kills/.

Gupta, Akhil (2012) *Red Tape: Bureaucracy, Structural Violence, and Poverty in India*, Durham, NC: Duke University Press.

Haldea, Gajendra (2011) *Infrastructure at Crossroads: The Challenges of Governance*, Oxford: Oxford University Press.

Harriss-White, Barbara (2003) *India Working: Essays on Society and Economy*, Cambridge: Cambridge University Press.

Herring, Ronald J. (1999) 'Embedded particularism: India's failed developmental state', in Meredith Woo-Cumings (ed.) *The Developmental State*, Ithaca, NY, and London: Cornell University Press.

224 *E. Chatterjee*

Jenkins, Rob (1999) *Democratic Politics and Economic Reform in India*, Cambridge: Cambridge University Press.

Joseph, Kelli L. (2010) 'The politics of power: electricity reform in India', *Energy Policy*, 38: 503–511.

Kale, Sunila S. (2014) *Electrifying India: Regional Political Economies of Development*, Stanford, CA: Stanford University Press.

Kirk, Jason A. (2010) *India and the World Bank: The Politics of Aid and Influence*. London: Anthem.

Kochanek, Stanley A. (1996) 'Liberalisation and business lobbying in India', *Commonwealth & Comparative Politics*, 34(3): 155–173.

Kohli, Atul (2012) *Poverty Amid Plenty in the New India*, Cambridge: Cambridge University Press.

Kumar, Alok and Chatterjee, Sushanta K. (2012) *Electricity Sector in India: Policy and Regulation*, New Delhi and Oxford: Oxford University Press.

Lal, Sumir (2006) *Can Good Economics Ever Be Good Politics? Case of India's Power Sector*, Washington, DC: World Bank.

Mahalingam, Sudha (2005) 'Economic reforms, the power sector and corruption', in Jos Mooij (ed.) *The Politics of Economic Reforms in India*, New Delhi and London: Sage.

Mann, Michael (1993) *The Sources of Social Power, Vol. II: The Rise of Classes and Nation-states, 1760–1914*, Cambridge: Cambridge University Press.

McDonald, David A. (2009) 'Electric capitalism: conceptualizing electricity and capital accumulation in (South) Africa', in David A. McDonald (ed.) *Electric Capitalism: Recolonizing Africa on the Power Grid*, London: Earthscan.

Min, Brian and Golden, Miriam (2014) 'Electoral cycles in electricity losses in India', *Energy Policy*, 65: 619–625.

Mooij, Jos (1999) *Food Policy and the Indian State: The Public Distribution System in South India*, New Delhi and Oxford: Oxford University Press.

—— (2007) 'Is there an Indian policy process? An investigation into two social policy processes', *Social Policy & Administration*, 41(4): 323–338.

OECD/IEA (2012) *Understanding Energy Challenges in India: Policies, Players and Issues*, Paris: International Energy Agency.

Pritchett, Lant, Woolcock, Michael and Andrews, Matt (2010) 'Capability traps? The mechanisms of persistent implementation failure', *Working Paper 234*, Washington, DC: Center for Global Development.

Rai, Varun (2010) 'Adapting to shifting government priorities: an assessment of the performance and strategy of India's ONGC', *Program on Energy and Sustainable Development Working Paper 91*, Stanford, CA: Stanford University.

Rudolph, Lloyd I. and Rudolph, Susanne Hoeber (1987) *In Pursuit of Lakshmi: The Political Economy of the Indian State*, Chicago, IL, and London: University of Chicago Press.

—— (2001) 'Iconisation of Chandrababu: sharing sovereignty in India's federal market economy', *Economic and Political Weekly*, 36(18): 1541–1552.

Ruet, Joël (2003) 'The limited globalisation of the electrical sector: from the pre-eminence of the States to the relative come back of the Centre', *CERNA Occasional Paper*, Ecole Nationale Supérieure des Mines de Paris, Paris.

—— (2005) *Privatising Power Cuts? Ownership and Reform of State Electricity Boards in India*, New Delhi: Academic Foundation, Centre de Sciences Humaines.

Schaffer, Bernard (1984) 'Towards responsibility: public policy in concept and practice', in Edward J. Clay and Bernard Schaffer (eds) *Room for Manoeuvre: An Exploration of Public Policy in Agricultural and Rural Development*, London: Heinemann.

Sen, Anupama and Jamasb, Tooraj (2012) 'Diversity in unity: an empirical analysis of electricity deregulation in Indian states', *The Energy Journal*, 33(1): 83–130.

Sethi, Surya P. (2012) 'Power and no accountability', *Indian Express*, 16 August.

Shastri, Vanita (1997) 'The politics of economic liberalization in India', *Contemporary South Asia*, 6(1): 27–56.

Sinha, Aseema (2010) 'Business and politics', in Niraja Gopal Jayal and Pratap Bhanu Mehta (eds) *The Oxford Companion to Politics in India*, New Delhi: Oxford University Press.

Skocpol, Theda (1985) 'Bringing the state back in: strategies of analysis in current research', in Peter B. Evans, Dietrich Rueschemeyer and Theda Skocpol (eds) *Bringing the State Back In*, Cambridge: Cambridge University Press.

Thakurdas, Purushotamdas, Tata, J.R.D., Birla, G.D., Dalal, A., Ram, S., Lalbhai, K., Shroff, A.D. and Matthai, J. (1944) *A Brief Memorandum Outlining a Plan of Economic Development for India*, Harmondsworth; New York: Penguin.

Tongia, Rahul (2007) 'The political economy of Indian power sector reforms', in David G. Victor and Thomas C. Heller (eds) *The Political Economy of Power Sector Reform: The Experiences of Five Major Developing Countries*, Cambridge: Cambridge University Press.

Varshney, Ashutosh (1995) *Democracy, Development, and the Countryside: Urban–Rural Struggles in India*, Cambridge: Cambridge University Press.

Victor, David G. and Heller, Thomas C. (eds) (2007) *The Political Economy of Power Sector Reform: The Experiences of Five Major Developing Countries*, Cambridge: Cambridge University Press.

Weber, Max (1978) *Economy and Society: An Outline of Interpretive Sociology*, ed. Guenther Roth and Claus Wittich, Berkeley and London: University of California Press.

World Bank (1997) Project appraisal document, Haryana Power Sector Restructuring Project, Report No. 17234-IN.

World Bank (2011) *More and Better Jobs in South Asia*, Washington, DC: World Bank.

Wright, Erik Olin (1996) 'Review of Peter Evans, *Embedded Autonomy*', *Contemporary Sociology*, 25(2): 176–179.

Xu, Yi-chong (2004) *Electricity Reform in China, India and Russia: The World Bank Template and the Politics of Power*, Cheltenham: Edward Elgar.

13 Technology and materiality

South Asia in the twenty-first century

Sanjeev Ghotge[1]

This chapter visits the different concepts of materiality in natural and social sciences, and their impact on the way in which materiality and the destruction of nature has been marginal to capitalist industrialisation (including the industrialisation of agriculture) and the expansion of commodity production under capitalism. The political history of relations between technology, production and energy is examined – particularly between energy and electricity in South Asia, notably India, and their roles in the trio of environmental, climate and energy crises facing the region. The three main elements of India's GDP and alternative approaches to technology for them are indicated. The chapter concludes by asking whether capitalism, in particular India's capitalism, is equal to the task ahead.

1 Production and its consequences

With the acquisition of new productive faculties, men change their mode of production and all the economic relations which are merely the necessary relations 'of this particular mode of production' (Marx, 'Letter to Annenkov', in McLellan 2000: 210).[2] As production changes, so do its environmental consequences, irrespective of whether production takes place in pre-capitalist, capitalist or socialist societies. The material/environmental cause – consequence relationships and networks across space and time involve disciplines in the natural sciences: physics, chemistry, the engineering disciplines, biology and the medical sciences. The tracing of cause–consequence relationships across disciplines has not been easy. Nevertheless, the different sciences have a common focus on materiality. Inverting the relationships between the eco system, the production system and the economic system, Commoner holds that:

> given these dependencies – the economic system on the wealth yielded by the production system and the production system, on the resources provided by the ecosystem, logically the economic system ought to conform to the requirements of the production system, and the production system to the requirements of the ecosystem. The governing influence should flow from the ecosystem through the production system to the economic system. This

Technology and materiality 227

is the rational ideal. In actual fact, the relations among the three systems are the other way around.

(Commoner 1976: 2)

In the social sciences the notion of materiality traverses other disciplines: from historical materialism in philosophy, to the material basis of production in political economy, and the complex relationship between the material base and the ideological superstructure in politics. Materialism in Marx's understanding of private property relates to profit and the structural violence unleashed by capitalists against the subaltern classes. As defender of private property, the state acts as the 'corporation of corporations'. The material interests of the ruling classes and their political and juridical interests are enshrined in, and protected by, the state (see Kovel 2002: Preface and xx; Bellamy Foster 2000: 116; O'Connor 1996: 163). These are the political economic arrangements prevailing in the postcolonial countries of South Asia, despite the largest democracy, India, being constitutionally socialist.

The same equations of mass-energy balances used for the design of factories in the engineering disciplines may be extended beyond the ownership boundaries of factories to reveal the environmental wastes which social science has reluctantly theorized as negative externalities of production. Regulative laws, established for the control of externalities in a democratic society, fall into three categories that correspond to the three states of matter. These laws cover the disposal of solid wastes, liquid effluents and air pollution. Their intent is to prevent damage (prevention being better than cure) and to compensate through tort law. The latter is very poorly developed, possibly by design, in South Asian societies whose judicial and institutional processes follow the Anglo-Saxon model. The biases of state institutions in favour of production-consumption and away from externalities are very evident. The state itself is irrational in following upon its intent and obligations under its own laws, nowhere more so than in relation to climate change. In reflecting upon technology and materiality, three troubling factors in addition to externalities must be introduced at the outset.

First, the laws of nature do not change according to the type of society in which they are tested: similar technological production processes display similar patterns of externalities, whether in capitalist or in socialist societies.

Second, the chasm between the natural sciences on the one hand and the social sciences/humanities on the other can be traced back to their respective roots in natural and moral philosophy.[3] Due to these differing genealogies, notions of 'materiality' differ, that of the social sciences relating to the economy, production and society, that of the natural sciences relating to the properties of matter and energy. Energy transforms matter through heat, work and chemical interactions – dissipating towards entropy. These physical laws also apply to production. However, consider the thought of Adam Smith, the founding father of economics. Worster (1993) has looked closely into Adam Smith's life and sources of thought and asks: 'So how did Adam Smith look on the world around him? Where did nature fit into his thinking? What were the long term

228 *S. Ghotge*

implications that his ideas had for the natural order of Planet Earth?' (p. 214). After examining his life and times, Worster concludes: 'Smith seems to have lived his entire life utterly oblivious of nature around him. He set out to revolutionize the study of economics in total disregard of the economy of nature.' The conceptual sins of the founding father continue to cast a shadow over the profession of economics to this day.

The third factor concerns the types of evidence shaped by these disciplinary concepts, their interpretations and their modes of presentation. For there seem to be insurmountable barriers, in both capitalist and socialist societies, to the acceptance of evidence-based reasoning, in this case particularly about matter and energy.[4] We now turn to the recent history of materialism, in the form of technology and energy.

2 Energy and industrial society

Energy and materials are not free gifts but become valuable through the action of labour, mediated by technology. India's trajectory follows in the wake of developments globally. Commercial electricity operations started in 1881 and 1882 in the US, by harnessing hydro- and thermal power. In 1886, there were 45 hydroelectric dams in the US and Canada, and by 1889 there were 200 in the US alone. Commercial coal-based thermo-electric plants also began life in 1882 in New York and London. Karl Marx died in 1883. In his lifetime there were no automobiles with internal combustion engines – the first workable petrol (Otto) engine was available commercially in 1876, the first commercially workable diesel engine in 1897. Marx's life was spent in the age of coal, with steam-engines virtually the sole source of motive power in the cotton textile industry, railways, steamships, etc. The other large coal-based industry would have been steel. Privately owned railways assured the bulk supply of coal to distant industries and consumers.

The working class that Marx observed was composed of coal-miners, textile workers, steel and railway workers; and the unbearable working and living conditions of those times informed his conclusion that the proletariat was the revolutionary class, interested in the overthrow of capitalism. However, even between Marx's passing and Lenin's October Revolution, new sources of energy – oil and gas – had appeared on the industrial landscape, accelerating and revolutionizing production. From the outset, industrialization has been driven by fossil fuels. Until recently the social sciences have consigned their study to their margins.

The twentieth century saw the expansion of electricity, coal and oil in both the capitalist and socialist countries, with energy technologies growing larger in scale and improving in efficiency. Military-industrial capabilities were developed to secure supplies of fossil fuel (though see Wrigley (2010) for a bloodless history). The First World War was fought over rich coal (and iron ore) deposits. While steel has been identified as a key raw material for industry, insufficient attention has been paid to fossil fuels. Two of Hitler's biggest military offensives

Technology and materiality   229

were launched in order to capture petroleum resources, the Stalingrad campaign to capture the oilfields of the Caspian Sea and the North African campaign under Rommel to capture the oilfields of Egypt (Shirer 1983: 1188–1191).

There is therefore considerable continuity of motives between pre-war and post-war eras, the difference being that waning British influence was replaced by assertive US power, since the US industrial economy, intact following the Second World War, probably represented about half of the world's then industrial output. The Fischer-Tropsch process, invented in Germany for converting coal to oil, is still in use in South Africa and is being introduced in China and India in the twenty-first century as an insurance against the depletion of oil. Motives for the control of oil in West Asia remain the same as they were for Nazi Germany: 'energy security'. The flow of oil connecting the establishment of 'friendly' rulers in Saudi Arabia and the Gulf States, the toppling of the Mossadegh regime in Iran in 1954, the Cold War hostility towards Egypt, Syria and Libya, and finally, the oil war between Kuwait and Iraq and the need to dominate Iran and Afghanistan may reflect similar motives.

The only new energy resource introduced on any significant scale in the twentieth century was nuclear. Yet at its peak it probably never contributed more than 4 per cent of energy in the overall energy scenario of the world. France, where nuclear power makes a major contribution to the grid, is an exception. With overt and covert subsidies and accounts hidden behind veils of national secrecy, nuclear electricity has never competed in open markets. Its prestige in public opinion is related to nuclear weapons. The quantitative contribution of nuclear energy has always been dwarfed by the contributions of coal, oil, gas and hydro in running the world's gigantic industrial economies.

Pared to the bone, the story of twentieth-century energy resources involves coal and oil. The societies made possible by these energy sources and technologies have been dominated by large centres of commodity production, in cities and industries, fed by centralized sources of energy and materials, connected by centralized electricity grids, highways and railways. The large corporations that have dominated these societies seem to fall into natural alliances: coal and gas with electricity utilities; oil with automobiles, highways and construction, petrochemicals, etc. The mass production of automobiles in particular has spanned alliances with steel, machinery, plastics, rubber and so on in conglomerates of capital (Commoner 1976: 189–210).

In market-driven economies, the greater the social consumption of energy, the larger the markets and the higher the profits of the energy corporations and their allies. Corporations have actively promoted increased energy consumption and succeeded in linking energy consumption to prosperity, economic well-being and growth. For the energy corporations, energy conservation threatens a reduction in the sizes and shares of energy markets, an increase in competition and a reduction in profits; hence they have opposed energy conservation (Stobaugh and Yergin 1979: 171–172). Moreover, the tremendous strategic, political and military investments in 'energy security' could be used to mask the profit motive and justify the pursuit of wars in distant countries, 'collateral damage', negative

230 S. Ghotge

environmental externalities and the assault on biodiversity, and to brush aside the extinction of 'distant' victims. 'Trickle-down' theory conveniently promised that their time would eventually come.

It is instructive to ask what kind of emerging global class structure resulted from these material relations of energy towards the closing years of the twentieth century. At one end were the fabulously wealthy, referred to variously through the course of the century ranging from Veblen's 'leisure class' to robber barons, the jet set, the new royalty, the '1 per cent', owners of finance or industrial-commercial capital, buttressed by politicians, bureaucrats and technocrats, military elites and academics, and treated as the holders of permanent power. To this class, the corridors of state power were and are always open, and access is guaranteed, simply by invitation to Davos. Next is a fairly large and growing middle class, defined in terms of status and consumption, upwardly mobile, well content provided that their upward mobility and consumption is sustained, men and increasingly women who are known by the company which keeps them. At the lower end are layers of workers, also referred to by a variety of names: the working class(es), labouring classes, the labour aristocracy, the proletariat, the cybertariat, the precariat, with various strata of skilled blue-collar wage earners shading into unorganized labour, peasants, displaced artisans, all manner of petty producers and agricultural labourers, collectively, an under-class of workers and petty producing more or less dependent micro-capitalists. With their numbers falling in the core capitalist societies, there was a significant change from the proletariat witnessed by Marx during his lifetime. The lowest of the under-classes proliferated throughout postcolonial societies and are well represented in South Asia. Below the under-class are strata of 'waste people', ranging from the unemployed (also known as the reserve army to discipline the labour force) through the destitute (unprotected by society, most vulnerable to environmental destruction and exposure to physical and social hazards) to the culturally defined internal enemies that lurk inside the territories of all societies. In a given social and historical formation, the quality and quantity of energy used provides an unerring indicator of the class to which the individual belongs.

3 Ideas about energy and economic development

We need to introduce here the findings of scientists researching energy and economics which, by overturning the work of Robert Solow, may bring a revolution in the field. In the mid-1950s, most economists believed that the growth of economies could be explained by rising inputs from just two sources – capital and labour. Solow demonstrated that growth could not be explained by these inputs, by applying the Cobb-Douglas production function (used to analyse the relationship between capital, labour and output in companies or sectors) to the US economy as a whole. Solow showed that the growth of the US economy was much higher than predicted by the Cobb-Douglas model. The gap between the real growth and the predicted growth came to be known as the Solow residual and he and neoclassical economists attributed this large residual to technology.

Technology and materiality 231

In the late 1970s, however, German physicists and economists devised a model incorporating energy. Applied to 30-year data of the US, Germany and Japan, this produced startling results, almost completely eliminating the 'Solow residual' previously assumed to technology. The implication of the findings was that energy was about ten times more important in explaining economic growth than implied by Solow (Hall *et al.* 2001).

Further refinement by Ayres and Benjamin (2005) showed that energy was about 14 times more important as an explanatory factor than implied by Solow. This theoretical work led to their conclusion that energy is the third factor of production, a result accepted by Solow if not given prominence in standard economics texts. As a third factor, however, non-human energy is not in contradiction to capital and labour but is subsumed under capital. The importance of this finding cannot be overestimated for South Asian societies pursuing economic growth in the context of constraints posed by 'environmental externalities' and climate change.

Energy technologies have been argued to be capable of driving desirable social change, an optimism shared through the twentieth century by Soddy and Hogben, among many others (Martinez-Alier 1987: 127, 137, 149, 156). Hogbeneven espoused the view that advanced technology did not require an urbanized society, whether capitalist or socialist, but could energize a decentralized, ruralized economy (Martinez-Alier 1987: 150). This vision was also shared by Mahatma Gandhi who was not 'opposed to industrialization but industrialization in the manner of the West' (see also K. Marx and F. Engels, *The Communist Manifesto* (2000), Pt. 9). Gandhi was accepted as a revolutionary by Hobsbawm (1994)[5] but neither by the orthodox Left nor by the revolutionary Left in India. During his lifetime, Gandhi did not have access to energy technologies that could help realize his vision. Even in 1976 when Barry Commoner wrote his classic *The Poverty of Power*, such energy technologies were not available, but in the twenty-first century technology for decentralized energy generation and industrial production is now increasingly available. The next question is whether such technologies/ factors of production can be wrenched from the control of capital. To contribute to an answer we examine the materiality of electricity, the crises that have resulted from its expansion, the use of energy in the major components of India's GDP – agriculture, industry and services – and possible alternatives.

4 Energy and technology in the twenty-first century

The past two decades have witnessed the emergence of energy technologies based on renewable sources of energy, wind, sun, geothermal, biomass, wave, tidal and hydrogen energy, and so on. The rise of the aerospace industry created the ability to manufacture large aerofoil sections employed in the conversion of wind power to electricity. Although Einstein discovered the photoelectric effect in 1905, it has taken nearly a century for solar photovoltaics to mature for power generation. The initial impulse (and public investment) for the development of this expensive technology came from the space sector. Spacecraft needed a

232   *S. Ghotge*

source of electricity in outer space that, in the absence of oxygen, was not based on combustion. Unfurled sails with PV cells provided the answer. Private/ corporate capital now holds intellectual property rights over many technologies whose R&D was supported from government grants and state subsidies (Commoner 1976: 119–120, 141–145). In South Asia, the pursuit of new sources of renewable electricity powering a decentralized, rural–urban (rurban) society is consistent with a socially rational response to harsh constraints being imposed by climate change. Renewable sources of electricity and energy conservation are essential preconditions for other efforts to reduce greenhouse gases (GHGs), and material inputs, and to expand resilience.

5 The quiddity of electricity

All activity has peculiarities, both physical and symbolic. Electricity is no exception. Its quiddity lies in having many sources but being hard to store. Another peculiarity is that over 100 years after its invention, US state courts are unable to decide whether it should be considered a 'good or product' or a 'service' and have judged both ways. As a good or product, electricity becomes strictly liable for damage or injury under tort law, with varying local interpretations under common law. As a service, it is judged under contract law (Ferrey 2000: 211, 223, n. 19). As the matter stands at the start of the twenty-first century, electricity is a service before it enters the meter and becomes a good or product after it crosses the meter. A third peculiarity arises in determining its price. Conventional electricity may be produced in a number of different ways: in hydro, coal, gas or nuclear power plants. Renewable electricity may be produced by wind turbines, by 11 different solar configurations falling into two broad categories (solar PV and solar thermal), by burning biomass, bio-methane or waste. Yet, at its point of consumption, it is exactly the same: a flow of electrons at specified voltage and frequency. It is not like other economic commodities such as bars of soap or toothpaste, where product differentiation is achieved through changes in perfume, flavour, colour or packaging, all backed by strenuous advertising internalized into the cost to the consumer. Each electricity production technology has a different cost of production, yet the electricity is bundled and sold at a uniform price through the grid to consumers.

Even in economics, however, the notion that some forms of electricity are 'cheaper' than other forms is increasingly under challenge, because of the external costs of fuel excavation, fuel transport, environmental and social externalities, overt and covert subsidies, and climate change-related damages ('global externalities'). As indicated earlier, through interdisciplinary efforts natural scientists have studied and evaluated many of the external costs, though the economics profession is yet to formulate a considered view, except to re-invent nature as 'ecosystem services' to human societies, which economists then proceed to value in terms of 'willingness to pay' or 'natural capital', to which economists then assign value. In other words, the problem is starting to be identified in a restrictive way – but is not yet solved.

The peculiarities of electricity and its technologies arise partly because there is no commonly accepted methodology for technology assessment; the various technologies are left to compete on unequal terms in 'the marketplace'. Entrenched conventional technologies including nuclear energy continue to have an overwhelming advantage over renewable energy (RE) technologies which can create a more sustainable and climate-secure economy. Competition between the two sets of technologies fits the paradigm outlined by Piore and Sabel (1984: 49–104) in which the set of firms employing large-scale, rigid, mass production technologies with high investments, dominant market shares, organized labour and supportive policy frameworks battle against new firms employing new technologies. The latter are small–medium scale, flexible, batch-produced, and involve smaller investments; they are firms which have less dominant market shares, smaller but more numerous unions, fighting for state support to ensure their survival. RE technologies fit the latter pattern, being varied, modular, fast in deployment, flexibly sized to suit a range of applications and far superior in terms of their environmental and social externalities.

It is a peculiarity of energy technologies that they tend to transform the structure of everyday activities. This transformative role of electricity, coupled with the decentralization of electricity production and its manufacturing base and the positive externalities of RE may eventually lead to a change in the class structure of society very different from the structure that emerged in the twentieth century in the capitalist countries.

As South Asia enters the twenty-first century, it faces a multiplicity of crises caused by these material and technological arrangements.

6 Three interlinked crises – climate, the peaking of oil and the environment

Three crises which will transform the face of production confront South Asia in the twenty-first century. The three crises are interrelated, with energy being a major constituent of them all. The decisive crisis is that of climate change which will have a major impact on the region for at least a few centuries, and hence deserves more space here than the other two, namely those of hydrocarbon availability/energy security and the immediate physical environment and biological systems.

At its core, the climate crisis arises from the finite carbon-absorption capacity of the Earth, estimated at 3.1 to 3.2 billion tonnes of carbon per annum (tcpa). This is split between the oceanic uptake of 1.7 to 2.2 billion tcpa and the land uptake 1.4 to 0.9billion tcpa (IPCC 2001; 2007). According to IEA (2012: 44), annual global emissions from fossil fuels in 2010 were of the order of 8.3 billion tcpa (43 per cent coal/peat; 36 per cent oil; 20 per cent natural gas). The excess carbon piles up in the atmosphere as CO_2 and is the principal cause of global warming.

The excess heat trapped in the atmosphere is thermodynamically transmitted to the other four major Earth systems. Melting of the cryosphere (the frozen parts of the Earth including the polar regions and glaciers) is accelerated and will eventually lead to sea-level rise. Heating of the hydrosphere (all the water bodies on Earth including the oceans, seas and freshwater bodies) reduces their ability to retain dissolved CO_2 and increases evaporation. The increased water vapour in the atmosphere acts as a greenhouse gas, accelerating warming in a positive feedback effect. Heating of the land system, the lithosphere, will result in its long-term drying (increased desertification) as well as unpredictable changes in precipitation leading to alternating or simultaneous cycles of droughts and floods. It is also a causative factor in the increasing frequency, intensity and destructiveness of cyclones and storms in different parts of the world. Finally, the cumulative impact on the biosphere, the layer of life forms extending across land and oceans, is likely to be disastrous, as life chains unable to cope with rapid changes in temperatures, precipitation and habitats will become extinct.

These are the brute facts and the scientific derivations based on those brute facts.[6] Worse, the climate system is full of positive feedbacks which will accelerate global warming: the reduction of reflection from the ice cover over land and sea, melting permafrost, increasing forest fires, CO_2 emissions from land and seas, and so on. Much scientific evidence indicates that global warming will be faster than predicted by the IPCC (Spratt and Sutton 2008). The Earth being a very large system, there is an estimated time lag of about 40 years between the rise in atmospheric CO_2 concentration and the heat impacts of this change. The impacts measured in 2013 correspond to CO_2 equivalent concentration levels of the 1970s, when the fossil fuel economy was quantitatively much smaller. The worst is yet to come.

The emissions of combined fossil fuels are now so much larger (and rising) than the absorption capacity of the Earth that if heating is to be checked, the total emissions have to be brought well below 3.1 to 3.2 billion tcpa to allow reabsorption from the atmosphere over many decades. The best estimate of the IPCC experts is that global temperature rise has to be contained below 2°C to prevent runaway global warming. However, it may be shown from IPCC (2007: 15, 39)[7] that this limit has already been breached, since the current concentration of CO_2, measured at 400 ppm,[8] corresponds to a CO_2 equivalent of approx 490 ppm. This means a 2.2 to 2.4°C temperature rise. Global negotiations aimed at a 2°C containment are seriously inadequate both in terms of science and politics. Moreover, since the absorption capacity of global biophysical sinks on ocean and land are not within social control, the only available control variable is the reduction of global emissions below 3.1 billion tcpa, and the containment of emissions below that level over centuries, to permit the global sinks to reabsorb atmospheric carbon. Consequently, all sectors of production, in particular the energy sectors which are the largest emitters, need radical technological change.

Further, IPCC (2007) indicates that, under the present emissions trajectory, by the 2060s to 2080s the annual absorption capacities of the land sink may reverse, as the temperature rises beyond 2°C, with land becoming a net emitter of CO_2. This will make the reabsorption of CO_2 even harder and will mean that it will take even longer to re-stabilize the global climate. As of now, in the early

Technology and materiality 235

twenty-first century, it is no exaggeration to state that the spectre of global warming haunts humanity. Even the Stern Review has unequivocally named climate change as the greatest market failure in history (Stern 2006: 3). To rectify this failure essentially means the death of the fossil fuel industry worldwide. Yet the virtues of the market continue to be sung with undiminished vigour, never mind that the invisible hand of the market operates mostly under the table.

The second crisis relates to energy security. The international debate over peak oil has resulted in many experts (e.g. Energy Watch Group 2007: figs 40, 68; Schindler *et al.* 2006: 6) believing that peak oil has arrived (Campbell 2005; Commoner 1976: 36–37; Deffeyes 2001; 2005) and that the peaking of all fossil energy, including coal and gas, will follow shortly.

Irrespective of future fossil fuel reserves, however, the climate constraint means that development trajectories based on the ever-increasing use of fossil fuels are suicidal. The carbon sequestered by nature over millions of years has to be kept underground, rather than inventing and deploying new technologies at great public cost for carbon capture and sequestration. Energy conservation has long been shown to be significantly cheaper than increasing energy supply, but selling more energy by stoking demand and appetite for it leads to greater profits for corporate fossil fuel producers and utilities. Existing climate politics is governed by lobbies representing over 10% of world GDP. Low energy development models have low credibility both with planning experts and the public.

For India, energy price trends indicate that in the long term, (about 24 years @ 3 per cent p.a. increase of the real energy price index), electricity may be priced at double today's levels (even though electricity prices do not reflect externalities, subsidies and climate damage costs).[9] Full ecological pricing is needed. A doubling of electricity prices would not double the consumer's bill if a range of efficiency improvements were applied across devices and systems to reduce energy consumption. In any case, the impact of a doubling of electricity prices is nothing compared to the foreseeable impacts of climate change. Nevertheless, fear of energy insecurity can be fomented to justify partisan political agendas and inadequate progress away from the status quo.

The third crisis involves the global destruction of ecological systems. Current development models ignore their own biological and physical consequences – the destruction of forests and biodiversity, marine habitats, land and water resources, and the depletion of finite mineral resources. Global capital links mass production to mass consumption through mass transport (of people, commodities and raw materials) and the processes are legitimized by mass media. The mass production–mass consumption paradigm creates enormous amounts of environmental waste. The material throughput of the entire global system needs drastic reduction. Technologies exist for this. Yet growth is equated to quantitative expansion – more cars, expressways, petroleum refineries, steel, more Macdonald's producing industrial feed for the masses and so on, despite the fact that unlimited growth in a set of finite eco systems is logically and physically impossible. Incapable of intelligently responding to extrapolations of science or

236 *S. Ghotge*

to foresight, this system of production is more likely to collapse than to change its driving principles.

In dealing with the future of South Asia, we have to keep in mind this complex of global crises from which the subcontinent cannot be extricated.

7 The future of South Asia in the twenty-first century

Most of South Asia's populations are in a drawn-out transition from agrarian to industrialized society. Currently, since India dwarfs its neighbours, the subcontinent's future path will affect all the surrounding countries, for better or for worse. It is not necessary to look beyond the middle of the century, because whatever actions may be taken in the first half, by 2050 climate change effects will become so predominant that all South Asian societies are certain to spend significant resources in their responses to these impacts constantly rebuilding what is being continuously destroyed, in terms of physical/economic assets and human lives.

Beyond the middle of the twenty-first century, Bangladesh and the Maldives are likely to be the most affected due to sea-level rise (Houghton 2004). The destinations of physically displaced people of Bangladesh, other than India, are unknown. Both Sri Lanka and India will also be directly affected. Major coastal cities/centres of economic production in India will be threatened by sea-level rise, Mumbai, Chennai, Kolkata, Mangalore and Vizag among others. Moreover, the coastal areas are densely populated compared to other parts of India (barring the Gangetic plains), worsening the population displacement scenario.

The Report of the Irrigation Commission (Government of India 1972: 163–165) estimates that about half of India consists of semi-arid and arid lands, which will become more desertified with global warming. These lands are in the west, northwest and south of India. Desertification effects will also prevail throughout most of Pakistan and significant tracts of Nepal. Coupled with disturbances to the hydrological system, desertification will threaten food production. The cultivation of temperate crops, corn and wheat among others, may have to be discontinued as these cannot survive high temperatures over long periods of the growing season. It is impossible to predict whether even the traditional dry crops, namely bajra, jowar and other millets, will be able to provide adequate food for a population projected at around 1.6 billion by the mid-twenty-first century. Natural forests would have largely disappeared from peninsular India. Fuel and energy shortages will intensify due to a combination of factors, a shrinking biomass base, a large population, stringent constraints on fossil fuels and so on. The limited supply of energy will constrain industrial production, coupled with shortages of materials and limited availability of transport along with constraints on water and land. The expectation of mass prosperity through industrialization would long since have collapsed. The third leg of the economy, services, is low on energy and material inputs, though it requires an efficient information and knowledge infrastructure, along with an educated and skilled population.

Technology and materiality 237

This dismal scenario will come to pass under 'business-as-usual' and 'politics-as-usual'. Yet a different path is still possible, based on intelligent technology choices. The most important constraints will be water for agriculture, energy for industrial production, and transport and information/knowledge infrastructure for services. Since agriculture, industry and services contribute the largest part of GDP, the transformation of the crucial material relationships deserves attention (the most crucial material relationship which is being examined is with water; the other relationships with fertilizer, ploughing, soil chemistry, etc. would take up too much space to deal with here, but they have been examined elsewhere by the author, and by others (see e.g. Gathorne-Hardy (2013) for rice).

Agriculture conducted on an organically sustainable basis does not require any external inputs other than water under the control of the agrarian household. All other inputs may be produced in situ by the peasant household (Ghotge 2004).The fundamental role of water from solar pumpsets in enhancing and sustaining the productivity of agriculture has been demonstrated in field trials in regions with water-tables varying seasonally between 10 and 20 metres which show that with cropping pattern changes (partially substituting vegetables for food grains) and with assured water throughout the year provided by solar pumping, a five- to ten-fold enhancement of value addition in agriculture is possible (NABARD 2009 in Surendra 2011). The study was conducted in 1999 on small (two-acre) farms in three different locations in Andhra Pradesh and Tamil Nadu. Recent experiments show that an unsubsidized investment of Rs.100,000 per peasant household could transform agriculture using solar pumpsets already available in India and appropriate for the major Gangetic basin states, namely UP, Bihar and West Bengal, as well as southern Punjab and parts of Tamil Nadu. Solar pumps also have great potential for Bangladesh and other Indian river valleys.

Increased farm incomes improve purchasing power and food availability, and increase labour demand; production and consumption linkages may incentivize rural industrialization; and water pumped with solar energy will be more efficiently used and conserved than with industrial agriculture. Yet, state support for low external input/low carbon agriculture is lacking not only in India but around the world.

It may be shown that this approach solves food and water security concerns for a significant part of the rural poor, creates rural employment at a fraction of the cost of industrial employment and so absorbs surplus labour, creates a material base for decentralized rural industrialization, improves both rural and urban nutrition and health through improved food quantity and quality, conserves water quantity and quality, and is likely to be more environmentally sustainable and more climate friendly than the current chemical-industrial agricultural paradigm being propagated. Many agricultural processing industries can recycle organic slurry back to agriculture, thereby closing the carbon cycle at a local level. This indicates that 'economic growth' does not have to be based on centralized, energy-intensive approaches. Yet governments lack the foresight

238 *S. Ghotge*

to promote such alternatives despite a wealth of evidence, both in India and around the world.

Industry, the second major element in GDP, requires a reconsideration of economic sectors, physical quantities and technologies. Recent work (Weizsacker *et al.* 2005; 2009) shows that constant output can be maintained with a quarter or one-fifth of the physical inputs. This has massive implications not only in terms of material and energy throughputs but also reduced systemic production of waste and external damage, including contributions to climate change. India's development plans, requiring greater quantities of energy and material for industrial mass production, are unsustainable. Globally, this materials- and energy-intensive approach to the economy produces societies that are unsustainably urbanized, overconsumptive, financially over-securitized, wasteful of resources, which rely on vast unsustainable supply chains spanning the globe, prone to recurrent crises of material, financial and social security, and shot through with endemic under- and unemployment. It is today possible that technology and practical experience could be used to build economic systems based on RE quite rapidly. As currently assessed, the technical potential for wind energy in India ranges between 100,000 MW to 700,000 MW, while that for solar energy could be in excess of 1.5 million MW. Compared with the current conventional installed capacity of 200,000 MW, we may conclude that it is not technical limits that constrain India from moving in these directions. Transport infrastructure could be based on renewable electricity; industrial systems could develop minimal material throughputs; material systems would have far smaller carbon and ecological footprints; and more resilient social systems would result.

Yet until the value destruction caused to environment, climate and society, conceptualized as negative externalities, is subtracted from the value addition from industrialization, which current mainstream economic procedures for calculating GDP do not consider important, the transition away from the vastly unsustainable global economy in which India is embedded cannot be initiated.

The third contributor to GDP, the services sector, is widely acknowledged as being far less materials and energy intensive per unit of GDP compared with industrial production. The processing and transmission of information underlies many service sector activities. Insofar as information transmission replaces the movement of materials or persons, information is capable of reducing both energy and material consumption, as well as reducing time. This can be appreciated in a wide variety of everyday contexts: replacement of visits to the bank teller by ATMs, electronic billing and payment systems, travel booking, business videoconferencing, office automation through computers and printers, computerized editing and printing of books and journals, improved information systems in health care, social services, welfare monitoring, accounting, insurance, etc. There is little reason to doubt that the application of information systems can create value with low materials and energy consumption. Unfortunately, the massive increases in human productivity achieved so far have not resulted in increases in overall human welfare: computers have replaced human labour and added to business costs rather than adding to overall welfare. While the energy sources are different, the dilemma is exactly the same as at the start of the Industrial Revolution in the cotton textile sector, with the move from hand looms to power looms, when a young man with a 12-year-old assistant could produce 20 times the output of a hand weaver (Landes 1969: 86).

The possibilities for economic growth along technological pathways other than 'business-as-usual' and 'politics-as-usual' confirm that 'another world is possible' in which technology eliminates the drudgery of labour and minimizes the impact of human societies on nature.

But there is no sign from the most powerful single indicator of stress, namely GHG emissions, that India's elite, along with those of almost every other country, are capable of initiating a low carbon transition. While different paths are possible, based on intelligent technology choices, are they possible under capitalism?

Will capitalism survive and prevail at whatever social cost? Underpinning the argument that it will, the logic of capitalism depends on preserving the production relations of commodified labour, and not on fossil fuels. Even as it dematerializes, capitalism will attempt to reinvent itself by replacing black and grey commodities by fraudulent green commodities. The commodity aspect of labour relations will not be allowed to change. The resulting planet may be unattractive and may not even support human life on today's scale, but capitalism aspires to be the final mode of production on Earth (Harriss-White 2012).

Certainly a 'green capitalism' is being created and promoted in India, as elsewhere, under the euphemism of a Green New Deal (Barbier 2010). Yet the proponents of such a 'green capitalism' choose to ignore the logic of growth and accumulation and the historical relations between materials, energy and labour under capital described in this chapter. The range of untried, risky and even as yet impracticable measures envisaged by the 'green capital' school ignores the precautionary principle, which should govern any rational social response to the known risks and unknown uncertainties involved.

Altvater (1993), by contrast, does not believe capitalism can survive. For instance, India is developing an energy-intensive infrastructure whose working life stretches some 40 to 50 years into the future. Much of this infrastructure is unnecessary if RE (wind farms, solar-photovoltaic energy) is developed. Then, the domination of finance capital over manufacturing capital has locked manufacturing into a dependency on fossil fuels. To date, the logic of accumulation and the necessity of growth have overwhelmed gains in materials and energy efficiency per unit of output. A 'green capitalism' that has broken free of this dependency is not evident in the capitalist economy worldwide.

For a low carbon transition to be successful, the changes in the structure of production would have to be massive and would comprehensively affect the relations between social classes. How that mobilization would take place is the biggest political question, not only for India but also for the world.

Almost 40 years ago, Barry Commoner attempted a detailed review of alternatives related to agriculture, transportation, industrial production and the energy sector. He concluded that:

240   *S. Ghotge*

In moving into this more general realm, it is not my intention to transform economics into a branch of thermodynamics, or the relationship between entrepreneur and worker into a branch of ecology. Rather, I intend to pursue the economic leads arising out of the earlier consideration of energy problems wherever they may take us. In particular, I wish to explore the contradictory effects on the productivity of capital and labour that are revealed by the economic behaviour of the new, energy-intensive sectors of the production system. The object of this quest is to discover what fault in the economic system can account for the complex of problems that has been the concern of this book.

This pursuit will trespass into a field that lies outside my own professional training, but ... if those of us who have some knowledge of the scientific and technological features of this knot of problems fail to make contact with its economic facets, then the burden of establishing this essential link will fall on economists, who may be no better prepared to cope with the technical matters. Both sides need to make the effort, accepting the risk of error as a duty that we owe to a deeply troubled society.

(Commoner 1976: 236–237)

These words were written well before the enormity of the climate change crisis confronted humanity. Yet the situation has not changed significantly. Other senior scientists are arriving at similar conclusions with regard to the observance of the limits set by nature (Steffen *et al.* 2011).

Green socialism will not emerge automatically. It is going to have to be built step-by-step, for which collaborative international effort remains to be undertaken. The stakes have never been higher both for humanity and for all life forms on Earth.

Time will tell whether this will happen or not.

Notes

1 I am grateful to Barbara Harriss-White for her detailed and constructive editorial work on this chapter. I am also grateful to Judith Heyer and the participants at the conference, 'Capitalism and Development in the 21st Century', held at Oxford University in July 2012, where a version of this paper was first presented.
2 See also K. Marx, 'The Poverty of Philosophy' second observation in David McLellan (2000: 219–220).
3 Callicott and Ames (1989: ix). The full quotation is as follows:

During the eighteenth century European Enlightenment, what had once been an integral part of philosophy – natural philosophy – evolved into the natural sciences: physics, chemistry, geology, biology and so on. And the remaining part of the western philosophic tradition – moral philosophy – had, by the end of the nineteenth century, begun its metamorphosis into the social sciences: economics, sociology, anthropology and psychology.

4 Martinez-Alier (1987: 143–144) questions the 'silence ... and lack of reception in academic circles'.
5 Photograph no. 56 with caption.

Technology and materiality 241

6 Houghton (2004): p. 90 for coupling of various systems; pp. 91, 94 and 95 for feed-backs; p. 147 for sea-level rise; p. 163 for desertification; p. 173 for deforestation; p. 189 for extreme events.
7 See table SPM 5 and table TS 2 (abridged respectively from) IPCC (2007, Vol III: 39;

Category of CO_2 concentration	CO_2 Conc. (ppm)	CO_2 Eq conc. (ppm)	Global mean temperature increase above pre-industrial at equilibrium (°C)	Peaking year for CO_2 emission
I	350–400	445–490	2.0–2.4	2000–2015
II	400–440	490–535	2.4–2.8	2010–2030
III	440–485	535–590	2.8–3.2	2010–2030

IPCC (2007, Vol I). The Physical Basis states that:

> There is unanimous agreement among ... climate models ... that future climate change would reduce the efficiency of the earth system (land and ocean) to absorb anthropogenic CO_2. As a result, an increasingly large fraction ... would stay airborne in the atmosphere under a warmer climate. Atmospheric concentrations simulated by these models range between 730 and 1020 ppm by 2100.
> (Vol I: 750 under the heading 'Carbon Cycle')

8 Parts per million.
9 A distinction needs to be preserved between local environmental damage or the local 'externality' of production on the one hand and climate damage involving the global externalities of all emissions from the production-distribution-consumption system on the other.

References

Altvater, M. (1993) *The Future of the Market: An Essay on the Regulation of Money and Nature after the Collapse of Actually Existing Socialism*, London: Verso.

Ayres, Robert and Warr, Benjamin (2005) 'Accounting for growth – the role of physical work', *Structural Change and Economic Dynamics*, 16(2): 181–209.

Barbier, Edward B. (2010) *A Global Green New Deal – Rethinking the Economic Recovery*, Cambridge: UNEP/Cambridge University Press.

Bellamy Foster, John (2000) *Marx's Ecology*, New York: Monthly Review Foundation.

Callicott, J. Baird and Ames, Roger T. (1989) Foreword in J. Baird Callicott and Roger T. Ames *Nature in Asian Traditions of Thought: Essays in Environmental Philosophy*, Albany: State University of New York Press.

Campbell, C.J. (2005) *Oil Crisis*, London: Multi-science Publishing.

Commoner, Barry (1976) *The Poverty of Power – Energy and the Economic Crisis*, New York: Borzoi Books.

Deffeyes, Kenneth (2001) *Hubbert's Peak*, Princeton, NJ: Princeton University Press.

—— (2005) *Beyond Oil – The View from Hubbert's Peak*, New York: Hill and Wang.

Energy Watch Group (2007) *Crude Oil – The Supply Outlook*, EWG Series No. 3/2007, http://energywatchgroup.com/oil-report.

Ferrey, Steven (2000) *The New Rules – A Guide to Electric Market Regulation*, Tulsa, OK: Pennwell Corporation.

Gathorne-Hardy, A. (2013) *Greenhouse Emissions from Rice*, www.southasia.ox.ac.uk/sites/sias/files/documents/GHG%20emissions%20from%20rice%20-%20%20working%20paper.pdf.

242 *S. Ghotge*

Ghotge, S. (2004) 'Agriculture: its relation to ecology and society', in 'Financing Agriculture', *Journal of the Agricultural Finance Corporation*, 36(1): 35–48.

Government of India (1972) *Report of the Irrigation Commission, Vol. I*, New Delhi: Ministry of Irrigation and Power.

Hall, C., Lindenberger, D., Kummel, R., Kroeger, T. and Eichhorn, W. (2001) 'The need to reintegrate natural sciences with economics', *Biosciences*, 51(8): 663–673.

Harriss-White, Barbara (2012) 'Ecological economics – in and after Marx', in Ben Fine and Alfredo Saad Filho (eds) *An Encyclopaedia of Marxist Economics*, London: Edward Elgar.

Hobsbawn, Eric (1969) *The Age of Extremes*, London: Michael Joseph.

Houghton, J. (2004) *Global Warming: The Complete Briefing*, 3rd edn, Cambridge: Cambridge University Press.

International Energy Agency (IEA) (2012) *Key World Energy Statistics*, Paris: IEA.

IPCC (2001) *Third Assessment Report*, Cambridge: Cambridge University Press.

—— (2007) *Vol III: Summary for Policy Makers: 15, and Technical Summary: 39*, Geneva: IPCC.

Kovel, Joel (2002) *The Enemy of Nature – The End of Capitalism or The End of the World?*, London: Zed Books.

Landes, David (1969) *The Unbound Prometheus – Technological Change and Industrial Development in Western Europe from 1750 to the Present*, Cambridge: Cambridge University Press.

Martinez-Alier, J. (1987) *Ecological Economics – Energy, Environment and Society*, Oxford: Blackwell.

Marx, K. 'Letter to Annenkov' in David McLellan (2000) *Karl Marx Selected Writings* (2nd edn), Oxford: Oxford University Press.

—— 'The Poverty of Philosophy', in David McLellan (2000) *Karl Marx Selected Writings* (2nd edn), Oxford: Oxford University Press.

Marx, K. and Engels, F. 'The Communist Manifesto' in David McLellan (2000) *Karl Marx Selected Writings* (2nd edn), Oxford: Oxford University Press.

O'Connor, James (1996) 'Socialism and ecology' in Carolyn Merchant (ed.) *Key Concepts in Critical Theory – Ecology*, New Delhi: Rawat Publications.

Piore, M.J. and Sabel, C.F. (1984) *The Second Industrial Divide*, New York: Basic Books.

Schindler, J., Wurster, R. *et al.* (2006) *Where Will the Energy for Hydrogen Energy Come From: Status and Alternatives*, Brussels: European Hydrogen Association.

Shirer, William (1983) *The Rise and Fall of the Third Reich*, New York: Fawcett Press.

Spratt, David and Sutton, Phillip (2008) *Climate Code Red – The Case for Emergency Action*, Brunswick, Victoria: Scribe Publications.

Steffen, Will, Grinevald, Jacques, Crutzen, Paul and McNeill, John (2011) 'The anthropocene: conceptual and historical perspectives', *Philosophical Transactions*, 369: 842–867.

Stern, Nicholas (2006) *The Economics of Climate Change – Summary of Conclusions*, www.hm-treasury.gov.uk/d/CLOSED_SHORT_executive_summary.pdf.

Stobaugh, Robert and Yergin, Daniel (1979) *Energy Future*, New York: Ballantine Books.

Strahan, David (2007) *The Last Oil Shock*, London: John Murray.

Surendra, T.S. (2011) 'Solar photovoltaic power for irrigation and water management', in G.M. Pillai (ed.) *Solar Future for India*, Pune: WISE Press: table 2, p. 201.

Weizsacker, E. von, Lovins A. *et al.* (2005) *Factor Four – Doubling Wealth, Halving Resource Use*, London: Earthscan.

Weizsacker, E. von, Hargroves K. *et al.* (2009) *Factor Five*, London: Earthscan.

Worster, Donald (1993) *The Wealth of Nature – Environmental History and the Ecological Imagination*, Oxford: Oxford University Press.

Wrigley E.A. (2010) *Energy and the English Industrial Revolution*, Cambridge: Cambridge University Press.

Glossary

Adda 'den' of commission agents and traders
Adivasi(s) Scheduled Tribe(s), member(s) of a Scheduled Tribe
Arhatiya(s), Kacha arhatiya(s) commission agents
Arunthathiyar(s) member(s) of one of the three major Scheduled Castes in Tamil Nadu
Asarai(s) member(s) of a caste ranking similarly to Vanniyars (see below)
Bajra millet
Bania trader, trading community
Bazaar market, market area, market street
Bishnoe(s) member(s) of a major landholding caste in Madhya Pradesh
Coolie casual manual labourer
Dal pulse
Dalit(s) here members of the Scheduled Castes. Also used more broadly to include members of Scheduled Tribes and sometimes others as well.
Dharam kata electronic weighing scale, literally 'honest weighing scale'
Gherao blockade
Grahak(s) customer(s)
Gramanis member(s) of a caste ranking similarly to Vanniyars (see below)
Grameen after Grameen Bank in Bangladesh
Gujjars members of a major landholding caste in Madhya Pradesh
Haavi dominant
Hammal(s) porter(s), head load worker(s)
Hawala informal transfer of money system
Jat(s) member(s) of a major landholding caste in Madhya Pradesh
Jhum shifting cultivation
Jowar sorghum
Kachi arhat pratha, Kachi arhat trade, trade licence
Kharif summer or monsoon crop season – crops sown in summer and harvested in autumn
Kisan farmer
Kisan neta farmers' leader
Krantikari revolution
Kulalar(s) member(s) of a caste ranking similarly to Vanniyars (see below)

Glossary 245

Maha yudh   greatest battle
Maligai(s)   silk merchant(s)
Mandal   block, the next-level administrative unit above the revenue village
Mandal Samakhya   block-level organisation of village organisations in Andhra Pradesh
Mandi   a market, a regulated primary agricultural market
Mudaliyar(s)   member(s) of an upper caste in north eastern Tamil Nadu
Munim   accountant
Nagad   cash
Naidu(s)   member(s) of an upper caste in north eastern Tamil Nadu
Nattar(s)   member(s) of a caste ranking similarly to Vanniyars (see below)
Navithar(s)   member(s) of a caste ranking similarly to Vanniyars (see below)
Paraiyar(s)   member(s) of one of the major Scheduled Caste groups in Tamil Nadu – one of the three major Dalit groups in Tamil Nadu
Patta(s)   title deed(s)
Pavala vaddi   3 per cent interest
Rabi   winter crop season – crops sown in winter and harvested in spring
Rajput(s)   member(s) of a major landholding caste in Madhya Pradesh
Rajya   regional state
Reddiyars   member(s) of an upper caste in northeastern Tamil Nadu
Sa-Dhan   agency representing microfinance institutions
Sabzi   vegetable
Settu(s)   member(s) of an upper caste in northeastern Tamil Nadu
Soopda wali(s)   sweeper(s) of spilled grain
Sumangali, Sumangali Thitham   bride scheme
Taulati   trader's weighman
Tehsil   a unit of administration below the district and above the block
Vanniyar(s)   member(s) of a low-ranking farming caste in northeastern Tamil Nadu
Zilla Samakhya   district-level organisation of village organisations in Andhra Pradesh

Index

Page numbers in *italics* denote tables, those in **bold** denote figures.

Accelerated Power Development and Reforms Programme (APDRP) 219
accumulation: capitalist 24, 25, 26, 32, 40; by dispossession 3, 23, 25, 36, 39, 40; *see also* primitive accumulation; regional patterns of agrarian accumulation; spatio-technical regimes of accumulation
adivasis 31, 38
Adnan, Shapan 3, 23–41
agency theory 171, 173–5
agrarian accumulation 4–5; *see also* primitive accumulation; regional patterns of agrarian accumulation
agriculture 2–5, 13, 14, 118, 121–3, 126, 131, 179, 237; agrarian institutions 66–83; agricultural labour 47, *47*, *48*, 118, 125; and credit 105; future of 237–8
agricultural markets 5–6; 84–101; *see also* regulated markets, Madhya Pradesh
Agricultural Produce Marketing Committee (APMC), Harda 85, 87, 93
agricultural productivity, Arunachal Pradesh 71–2; agrarian regions 46–65; structure; *see also* agrarian regions; landlessness; landlords
Andhra Pradesh: microfinance institutions (MFIs) 105–12, *107*, *108*, 113–14; nefarious practices of MFIs 110–12; regulation of microfinance 113–14; self-help group–bank linkage (SHG–BL) microfinance 103–5, 111, 112, 114–15
Andhra Pradesh Economic Restructuring Project (APERP) 114
Annan, Kofi 106
APDRP *see* Accelerated Power Development and Reforms Programme (APDRP)

APERP *see* Andhra Pradesh Economic Restructuring Project (APERP)
APMC *see* Agricultural Produce Marketing Committee (APMC), Harda
armed resistance to land grabbing 31
arms dealing 194
Arni, Tamil Nadu 59, 176–84, *177*, *178*, 185–6, 187n14
Arunachal Pradesh 5–6, 66–79; access to land 69–71; changing agrarian structure 67–8, *68*, *69*; cropping pattern and input use 71–2; ethnicised governance 76–7; institutional diversity 72–8, *73*, *74*; labour use and livelihood diversification 71, 72, 74, *74*; timber trade 74–5
Asmitha Microfinance Ltd 108, *108*
Association of Power Producers (APP) 214
Ayres, Robert 231

Bangalore 30
Bangladesh 236–7
Banias 55, 57
banks (banking) 6–7, 90, 111–15, 155, 192–8, bank credit 104–5; banking crisis 154, 160; bank transfer payments 91; money laundering and capital flight 192–4, 195, 196
Basile, Elisabetta 11, 170–86
Basu, Deepankar 37
Becker, Gary 156
Belgium 198–9
Bermuda 196
Bernstein, Henry 4, 78, 81n21, 119
Bhaduri, Amit 27–9, 33, 41n6, 42n13, 61n5, 86, 149
Bharatiya Janata Party (BJP) 88, *99*

Bharatiya Kisan Sangh (BKS) 95, 96–7
Bhattacharyya, R. 34–5, 38
bio-piracy 163
biodiversity 235–6
BJP *see* Bharatiya Janata Party (BJP)
BKS *see* Bharatiya Kisan Sangh (BKS)
bonded labour/neo-bondage 7; Arunachal
  Pradesh 72, 74, 78, 80n8, 80n14; Tamil
  Nadu 119–21, 123, 127, 131, 182;
  textile industry 143, 144–5, 146
Bourdieu, Pierre 202
Brass, Tom 4, 15n6
Brazil 192
Brenner, Robert 25
bride scheme (sumangali thittam) 143,
  145–6
British Empire 191–2, 201–2
British Virgin Islands 196

canal irrigation 89–90, 121
capital flight 10–12, 190–202; colonial
  origins 191–2; Keynes and White
  201–2; policies to prevent 27–8, 38;
  trade mispricing 193, 200–1; United
  Kingdom 191–2, 193, 194, 195–8, 199,
  201–2; United States 193, 194,
  198–200, 201–2
capitalism/capitalist development: capitalist
  accumulation 4–7, 10–11, 14, 24, 25, 26,
  32, 40, 46–65, 131, 137–40, 153, 161–2;
  172, 239 (clandestine accumulation 3,
  190–207; non-agrarian 4, 53–5, 58, 70–1,
  74–6; politics of 76–8); and circuits 34–6;
  and class 1–2, 4, 6, 10–14, 23, 26–30,
  35–8, 46–50, 58–60, 70–2, 75, 77, 84,
  118–20, 123–4, 130, 154, 157, 161–2,
  171–6, 180–6, 208–9, 213, 220–1, 227–8,
  230, 233; and commodification, 8, 9–10,
  153–66 (*see also* commodification);
  competition 5, 8–9, 28, 32–3, 157, 211,
  213, 215–16, 220–1; consumption 6, 8,
  71, 90, 120, 129–30, 157, 165, 180, 185,
  190, 227, 229–30, 232, 235, 237–8;
  corporate: 10, 14, 25, 29–34, 38–9, 56,
  92, 163, 190, 196,198–9, 209–10, 213,
  215–16, 227, 229, 232, 235 (societal
  corporatism under 183–4); crises 11, 25,
  50, 56, 109, 111–12, 151–4, 157–8, 160,
  165, 175, 185, 200, 211, 226, 233–6,
  238–40 (environmental crises 3, 233–40;
  and energy 2, 13–14, 159, 177, 208–20;
  226–40); exploitation (labour 1–2, 9, 11,
  161, 163 (*see also* labour); through
  markets 35, 88, 98, 102, 162, 165;

resources, 1, 3, 9, 13, 24–5, 29–40, 55,
  71–8, 108, 110, 114, 118, 122, 127–8,
  162, 168, 170, 172, 180–1, 209–11,
  216–17, 220–1, 226, 229, 235–3, 238);
  flight (of capital) 11–12, 27, 38,
  190–202; investment 2–3, 6, 12, 27–9,
  32, 50, 52, 54, 56, 58–60, 72, 74–6, 90,
  104, 108–9, 115, 140, 149, 150, 159–60,
  163, 184, 194, 197–201, 208–11,
  213–16, 231, 233, 237; petty capital:
  4–5, 14, 32–43, 38, 58, 71, 76, 92, 105,
  153, 161, 183–4, 230; primitive
  accumulation 2–4, 23–45; 161; social
  regulation of xx–xxi, 1, 6, 8, 9–11, 12,
  14, 25, 37–8, 46, 71, 75–6, 77, 85–6, 92,
  105, 118, 120, 126, 129–31, 137–41,
  149, 153–66, 172–5, 176, 180–6, 192–4,
  208, 210; spatial arrangements: 71,
  125–6, 136–52 (*see also* spatio-technical
  regimes); technological change 9, 30,
  52, 136–52, 165, 193, 197, 213, 226–43
carbon dioxide emissions 14, 154, 233–5,
  239, 241n7
care, commodification of 154
Carswell, G. 143
caste 6–14, 35, 55–6, 59–60, 91, 96,
  118–30, 137–9, 143, 161, 174, 181–6;
  and consumption 129–30; and
  employment 119–20, 121–2, 123–4; and
  Marxist/Institutionalist framework 181,
  182–4, 186
caste associations 183
casual labour 122–3
Cayman Islands 196, 198
ceremonies, costs of 129–30
CGAP *see* Consultative Group to Assist
  the Poorest (CGAP)
Champdany Jute 191–2
Channel Islands 193, 194–6
Chatterjee, Elizabeth 12, 13, 208–21
Chatterjee, Partha 28, 36, 37
Chhattisgarh 30–1, 47, 53, 55, 59, 68, 218
Chidambaram, P. 111
China 198
CIF *see* Community Investment Fund
  (CIF), Andhra Pradesh
circular migration 119, 125–6, 129
City of London 193, 194–8
civil society 182–4, 186
class structure: and consumption 129–30;
  and employment 119–20, 121–2, 123–4;
  and Marxist/Institutionalist framework
  171–3, 175, 180–2, 184, 185–6; and
  primitive accumulation 23, 24

248 *Index*

climate change 14, 233–5, 241n7; and future of South Asia 236–40
CMSA *see* Community Managed Sustainable Agriculture (CMSA) programme
coercive practices, in loan recovery 110–11
Coimbatore, Tamil Nadu 58–9, 141–5
collective bargaining 141
collective property rights 67
colonial drain 191–2
commission agents (*kacha arhatiyas*) 87–9, 90–1, 92, 93
commission, agricultural markets 86–93
commodification 8, 9–10, 153–66; commodified and uncommodified 160–2, 164; dialectics of 157–8, 162–3; of knowledge 9–10, 160, 162–5; of labour 171–2, 182, 186–7; politics of markets 158–60, 163–4
Commoner, Barry 226–7, 229, 231, 239–40
Communist Party of India 31
Community Investment Fund (CIF), Andhra Pradesh 104
community landownership 67, 71; forests 75
Community Managed Sustainable Agriculture (CMSA) programme 105
compensation for dispossession 3, 14, 30, 35
competition 8–9; *see also* capitalism and competition
Comptroller and Auditor General of India (CAG) 193
Congress Party 88, 114–15
Consultative Group to Assist the Poorest (CGAP) 106
consumer expenditure, rural populations 51, *51*
consumerism 129–30
consumption and employment 120, 129–30
coolie work 122, 123
cooperatives, not-for-profit 112; *see also* self-help group–bank linkage (SHG–BL) microfinance
copyright 163
cost escalations 193
cotton cultivation 89–90
cotton knitwear production 145–8
cotton-spinning industry 141–3
counter-insurgency operations 31, 39
credit 127; agricultural markets 86–93; *see also* microfinance

crisis and commodification 153–4
cropping patterns, Arunachal Pradesh 71–2, *73*
Crown Dependencies, UK 195, 196; *see also* Channel Islands
cutting, machining and trimming (CMT) 145–6

Dalits 8, 15, 99, 119–32, 144
Damodaran, Harish 55–6, 57
Das, Budhaditya 38
Das, Debarshi 37
De Neve, G. 143
debt bondage *see* bonded labour/neo-bondage
debt, commodification of 154, 160
debt traps 111
deindustrialisation 32
Delhi, squatter settlements 30
Deloitte Touche 196
depoliticization, electricity industry 211–13, 217, 221
desertification 236
dialectics of commodification 157–8, 162–3
discrimination, in employment 7–8, 119
dispossession: accumulation by 3, 23, 25, 36, 39, 40; Arunachal Pradesh 74, 76; creation of wage labour 3, 23, 33–4; mechanisms of 26; resistance to 27, 30–2, 38–9; and Special Economic Zones (SEZs) 28–9, 30, 31, 35–6, 37, 39; state acquisition of lands 29–30; without proletarianization 33–7
domestic labour, commodification of 154, 161
dormitories, tied labour 143, 146
Double Movement 157–8
dowries 129
drugs trafficking 190, 193
Dubash, Navroz K. 220

ecological systems 235–6
education costs 129
education, marketisation of 162, 163–4, 165
Edwards Report 195
electricity industry 208–21; liberalisation 209, 211–13, 215–17; reform implementation 217–19, *218*; and state dysfunction 217–20; state embeddedness 208, 209, 213–15; state-owned enterprises (SOEs) 212, 215–17, 219; state ownership 209, 210–11; technology 228, 232–3

Index 249

electronic bank transfers 91
electronic weighbridge 93–5, 96
embeddedness 174; politics of 159, 164;
  state and electricity industry 208, 209,
  213–15
eminent domain 29
employment *see* labour
energy: commodification of 159; prices
  235; and technology 228–33; *see also*
  electricity industry
energy security 229–30, 235
environment: climate change 14, 233–5,
  236–40, 241n7; and commodification
  154; ecological systems 235–6; impacts
  of materiality 226–8; peak oil 235
Epstein, Gerald A. 201
ethnicity 6, 7, 10, 12, 55, 57, 66, 69–70,
  172, 174; ethnicised governance,
  Arunachal Pradesh 76–9
exchange labour, Arunachal Pradesh 71,
  72, *74*
exchange-value 155, 157, 166n4, 200
export manufacturing, textiles 140–1,
  145–8

FDI *see* foreign direct investment (FDI)
federalism 217–19
feminisation of labour 125, 142–3
Ferguson, Niall 166
fictitious commodities 157–8, 162, 163
fictive commodities 163
field-to-factory route of industrial
  transition 55
financial inclusion 111–12
Finlay Muir 191–2
First World War 228–9
Fischer-Tropsch process 229
food markets 5–6
food security 237
Foot, Michael 196
foreign direct investment (FDI) 12, 197;
  policies to attract 27–8, 38
forests 28–9, 38, 66, 71, 75–7, 81n17,
  235–6
fossil fuels 228–9, 234, 235
Foucault, Michel 156
France 229
fruit and vegetables 52, 124

Gandhi, Mahatma 231
garment industry *see* textile industry
gatekeeping 127, 128
GBCs *see* global business companies
  (GBCs)

GDSP *see* Gross Domestic State Product
  (GDSP)
gender 6–8, 12, 14, 118, 139, 154, 172,
  174; and commodification 161; and
  labour 119, 120, 124–5, 137, 145,
  181–2; and livelihood diversification 71;
  and privatisation of land rights 69–70
GHGs *see* greenhouse gas emissions
  (GHGs)
Ghotge, Sanjeev 14, 15, 226–40
global business companies (GBCs) 198
Global Financial Integrity 201
global warming *see* climate change
gold and weddings 129, 130
Gounders 58–9
government contracts, money laundering
  and capital flight 193
government office-related accumulation
  53–4
green capitalism 239
Green Revolution 56, 57, 176
greenhouse gas emissions (GHGs) 14, 154,
  233–5, 239, 241n7
Gross Domestic State Product (GDSP),
  agriculture 48–9, *49*
groundwater 30
group-based lending *see* microfinance
Guérin, Isabelle 8, 118–31

Haldea, Gajendra 212
hand loom industry 140
Harda Mandi, Madhya Pradesh 85; cash,
  credit and commissions 87, 88–92;
  vegetable and fruit market 93; weights
  and measures 93–7
Harrison & Crossfield 192
Harriss, John 13
Harriss-White, Barbara 1–15, 219;
  agrarian accumulation 54, 57, 59; Arni,
  Tamil Nadu 59, 179, 187n13;
  commodification 153, 154–5, 158, 159,
  160–1, 166; institutional diversity in
  Arunachal Pradesh 72, *73*, 74, *74*, 75,
  77; politics of technology 136, 137–8;
  regulated markets 85–6, 89, 98; rural
  urbanism 131; self-employment 34;
  social regulation of labour 118, 119,
  125; spatiality of accumulation 136, 139
Harvey, David 3, 23, 25, 36, 39
Haryana 47, 49, 51, 52, 53, 218
health costs 129
Heller, Thomas C. 215, 216
heterodox framework *see* Marxist/
  Institutionalist framework

250 *Index*

Heyer, Judith 1–15, 54, 125
higher education, marketisation of 162, 163–4, 165
Hobsbawm, Eric 159, 231
Hong Kong 198
Horsefield, J. Keith 201, 202
human capital 162
Hume, David 199, 204n24
Hunter, Lawrence 199, 200
Huws, U. 9, 156, 161
Hyderabad Urban Development Authority 29, 30

IBCs *see* International Business Corporations (IBCs)
IMF *see* International Monetary Fund (IMF)
income: agricultural 50–1; deflation 37
Independent Power Producers Association of India (IPPAI) 214
independent power producers (IPPs) 211, 214–15
Indian Navy procurement 193
indigenous knowledge, appropriation of 162–3
industry: 4, 9, 14, 32, 48, 58–60, 123, 139–44, 148, 154, 214, 228, 231, 235, 237–8; bazaar-to-factory route of industrial transition 55; future of 238; industrialisation and agriculture 47–50, *47*, *48*, *49*; Tamil Nadu 57–9
inequality 42n19, 51, **52**, 53, 58, 69, 75, 131, 170, 172, 175, 181
informal economy 160–1, 211
informal labour 33–6, 118, 122–3
information systems 238–9
institutional change 10–11, 182; *see also* capitalism, social regulation of
institutional diversity, Arunachal Pradesh 72–8, *73*, *74*
Institutionalism 170–1, 208–9; *see also* Marxist/Institutionalist framework
insurance, micro 105
intellectual labour 163
intellectual property rights 160, 162, 163, 164
interest rates: deregulation 102; microfinance institutions (MFIs) 110, 111, 112, 115; subsidised 105
Intergovernmental Panel on Climate Change (IPCC) 233, 234, 241n7
interlinked markets 92, 127
interlocked transactions 86–7, 127
intermediate classes 161–2

International Business Corporations (IBCs) 196
international finance 11–12; *see also* money laundering
International Monetary Fund (IMF) 25, 28, 38, 201, 202
International Year of Microcredit 106
IPCC *see* Intergovernmental Panel on Climate Change (IPCC)
IPPAI *see* Independent Power Producers Association of India (IPPAI)
IPPs *see* independent power producers (IPPs)
Ireland 196, 199
irrigation 52, *53*, 57; Arunachal Pradesh 71, *73*; Harda, Madhya Pradesh 89–90
Irrigation Commission 236
IT corridors 30

Japan 198
Jats 95–7
Jessop, Bob 156–7, 162
Jevons, William Stanley 199–200
Jha, P.S. 10
Jharkand 47, 52, 68
jhum cultivation 67
job brokers 127, 128
jobless growth 33–4

kacha arhatiyas (commission agents) 87–9, 90–1, 92, 93
Kannan, Emumalai 50–1
Kapadia, Karin 129
Kar, Dev 201
Keynes, John Maynard 201–2
Khan, Mushtaq 12, 161, 164
Khurana, Ashok 214
Kisan Credit Cards (KCCs) 90
Kisan Panchayat (KP) 95, 96–7
knitwear production 145–8
knowledge economy 9–10, 160, 162–5
KP *see* Kisan Panchayat (KP)
Krishnamurthy, Mekhala 6, 84–98

labour 7–8; agricultural 47, *47*, *48*, 118, 125; Arunachal Pradesh 67, 70, 71, 72, 74, *74*, 75, 80n8; and caste 119–20, 121–2, 123–4; casual 122–3; children 119; and class structure 119–20, 121–2, 123–4; commodification of 172, 182; and consumption 120, 129–30; cotton-spinning industry 141–3; creation of wage labour 3, 23, 33–4; discrimination in 7–8, 119; elderly people 119;

feminisation of 125, 142–3; and gender 119, 120, 124–5; informal 33–6, 118, 122–3; intellectual 163; knitwear production 146–8; lack of employment 27, 33–4; manufacturing 47, *47*, *48*, 49, 57–8; and neoliberal policies 32; by sector 47, *47*, *48*; self-employment 33–6, 122, 124; and technological change 141–50; weaving industry 143–5; *see also* bonded labour/neo-bondage; migrant labour; social regulation of labour, Tamil Nadu
labour theory of value 199–200
Land Acquisition Act (1894) 29
land: alienation 68, 72
land grabbing 28–32, 37; in Arunachal Pradesh 71, 75–6; land leasing, Arunachal Pradesh 70–1, 72–4, *73*, 80n8; resistance to land grabbing 27, 30–2, 38–9
land sale and land speculation 54–5; land and Special Economic Zones (SEZs) 28–9, 30, 31, 35–6, 37, 39; state acquisition of lands 29–30
landlessness, Arunachal Pradesh 69, 70, *73*, 74
landlordism 127, 128
landownership: Arunachal Pradesh 67, 69–71, 72, *73*, 75; community-based 67, 71, 75
language 14, 15, 111–12, 156, 202
Lawson, Tony 1
lending *see* credit; microfinance
Lerche, Jens 4, 46–60, 119
Levien, Michael 31, 35–6, 40
Leys, Colin 153, 158–9, 160
liberalisation: electricity industry 209, 211–13, 215–17; financial 102; textile industry 140; trade 32; *see also* neoliberal policies
Life Insurance Corporation (LIC) 105
livelihood diversification 118; Arunachal Pradesh 71; Tamil Nadu 122–3
Lloyds of London 196
local politics 128–9
Locke, John 200
Luxembourg 196, 198–9

MACS *see* Mutually Aided Cooperative Societies (MACS)
Madhya Pradesh *see* regulated markets, Madhya Pradesh
Mahatma Gandhi National Rural Employment Guarantee Act *see* NREGA

Mahindra World City SEZ, Rajasthan 35–6
Maldives 236
malpractice, microfinance institutions 110–12
mandi see regulated markets, Madhya Pradesh
manufacturing employment 47, *47*, *48*, 49, 57–8
Maoist resistance to land grabbing 31
market-driven politics 158–9
markets 1–14, 26, 30, 32–4, 35, 40, 48, 54–9, 66–78, 84–98, 103–9, 114–15, 118–30, 136–49, 153–66, 170–85, 197–200, 210–17, 220–1; agricultural 5–6 (*see also* Madhya Pradesh; regulated markets); politics of 158–60, 163–4
Marwaris 55, 57
Marx, Karl 7, 12, 13, 228; commodification 153, 155, 157, 158, 162, 166n1; materialism 227; primitive accumulation 2–3, 23, 24, 25–6, 39; use-value and exchange-value 155, 157, 200
Marxist/Institutionalist framework 10–11, 170–86; analysis of Arni, Tamil Nadu 176–84, *177*, *178*, 185–6; analysis of capitalism 175; caste 181, 182–4, 186; class structure 171–3, 175, 180–2, 184, 185–6; propositions 172–5
materiality 226–8; *see also* technology
Mauritius 197–8
MBTs *see* Mutual Benefit Trusts (MBTs)
Michiels, Sébastien 8, 118–31
micro-insurance 105
Microcredit Summit 106
microfinance 5, 6–7, 102–16; interest rates 110, 111, 112, 115; microfinance institutions (MFIs) 105–12, *107*, *108*, 113–14, 115–16, 127; nefarious practices of MFIs 110–12; regulation 112–14; self-help group–bank linkage (SHG–BL) 103–5, 111, 112, 114–15, 128; Tamil Nadu 127, 128, 130
middle classes 173, 230
migrant labour 7, 119, 129; Arunachal Pradesh 67, 70, 74, 75, 80n8; Tamil Nadu 120–1, 123; *see also* circular migration
migrant settlements, Tamil Nadu 125–6, 127, 128
minimum support prices 91
Mishra, Deepak K. 5–6, 66–79
Misra, A.M. 192

252 *Index*

mobile phones 125, 128, 129, 130
money laundering 190–202; colonial
origins 191–2; Keynes and White
201–2; trade mispricing 193, 200–1;
United Kingdom 191–2, 193, 194,
195–8, 199, 201–2; United States 193,
194, 198–200, 201–2
Money Lenders' Regulation Act 112
moneylending 54, 127
moneylending regulation 113–14
Mooij, Jos 12–13
Moscow, John 195
Most Backward Classes 121; *see also*
Vanniyars
motorbikes 129, 130
Multi-Fibre Agreement (MFA) 145
Mutual Benefit Trusts (MBTs) 107
Mutually Aided Cooperative Societies
(MACS) 108

NABARD *see* National Bank for
Agriculture and Rural Development
(NABARD)
Naidu, Chandrababu 114, 115
National Alliance of People's Movements
(NAPM) 30
National Bank for Agriculture and Rural
Development (NABARD) 103, 104,
111–12
National Hydroelectric Power Corporation
(NHPC) 212
National Knowledge Commission 165
National Social Assistance Scheme
(NSAS) 105
National Thermal Power Corporation
(NTPC) 212, 215, 216, 219
natural resources 13–14; expropriation
28–32, 37; *see also* land grabbing
Navratna companies 215
NBFCs *see* non-bank financial companies
(NBFCs)
Nehru–Elwin policy 76, 81n17
neo-bondage *see* bonded labour/neo-
bondage
neoliberal policies 25, 27–8, 32–3, 37–8,
39
Nepal 236
New Marxism 171; *see also* Marxist/
Institutionalist framework
NGOs 128; microfinance 103, 104, 112,
127
NHPC *see* National Hydroelectric Power
Corporation (NHPC)
non-agrarian accumulation 4, 53–5, 58,

70–1, 74–6; *see also* spatio-technical
regimes of accumulation
non-bank financial companies (NBFCs)
107–12, *107*, *108*
non-farm employment/labour/activities 3,
57, 69, 71, 80n11, 80n15, 119, 120–3,
125–6, 128–30, 139, 179
non-violent protests, land grabbing 31
Norwegian Commission on Capital Flight
197
not-for-profit microfinance 102–5, 106–7,
111, 112, 114–15, 128
NREGA 124, 125, 128, 130
NSAS *see* National Social Assistance
Scheme (NSAS)
NTPC *see* National Thermal Power
Corporation (NTPC)
nuclear energy 229, 233

Odisha: electricity industry 212, 219; land
grabbing 30
oil, peak 235
Old Institutionalism 171; *see also* Marxist/
Institutionalist framework
open access, electricity industry 212–13,
222n11
Operation Green Hunt 31
Overseas Territories, UK 193, 195–6

Paattali Makkal Katchi (PMK) 128
Pakistan 236
Paraiyars 121–2, 123; *see also* Dalits
patenting 160
Patnaik, P. 11, 27–8, 32, 39, 41, 41n9,
41n10
Patnaik, U. 27–8, 32–3, 50, 191
Pattenden, Jonathan 53
pavala vaddi scheme 104, 115
PCP *see* petty commodity production
(PCP)
peak oil 235
peasant production *see* petty commodity
production (PCP)
pensions 105, 122
peri-urban settlements, Tamil Nadu 126,
127, 128
PESA Act (1996) 29
petty commodity production (PCP) 32–3,
34–6, 76, 161
photovoltaics 231–2
Piore, M.J. 233
PMK *see* Paattali Makkal Katchi (PMK)
Polanyi, Karl, 166, 167n9; commodification
155, 157–8, 162, 167n6

policy 12–13; social policies 127–8; *see also* electricity industry
political stability, commodification of 161–2
politics: of embeddedness 159, 164; of ethnic difference 76–7; market-driven 158–9; of markets 158–60, 163–4; revolutionary 3; of state involvement 159, 164; Tamil Nadu 128–9; of technology 136, 137–8
portfolio-interest exemption 199
Power Finance Corporation 219
power industry *see* electricity industry
power looms 140, 141, 143–5
power theft 211
price–specie flow mechanism 199–200, 204n24
primitive accumulation 2–3, 23–41; accumulation by dispossession 3, 23, 25, 36, 39, 40; development resources as reversal of 36–7; dispossession without proletarianization 33–7; of knowledge 162–3; mechanisms of 25–6; and neoliberal policies 25, 27–8, 32–3, 37–8, 39; overview 37–41; and politics of intermediate classes 161; resistance to 27, 30–2, 38–9; and Special Economic Zones (SEZs) 28–9, 30, 31, 35–6, 37, 39; state acquisition of lands 29–30; theoretical aspects 24–7
private banks, money laundering and capital flight 192–4
private corporate investment: and land grabbing 28–9; lifting of restrictions on 28
privatisation/privatization 14, 27, 69, 72, 160, 162, 164, 211, 212, 215, 216, 219
property rights: Arunachal Pradesh 67, 69–71, 72, *73*, 77; and primitive accumulation 23, 24
protests, land grabbing 30–2, 38–9
public expenditure reductions 32, 33
public purpose credit societies 112; *see also* self-help group–bank linkage (SHG–BL) microfinance
public services: commodification of 156, 159, 163; privatisation of 160; *see also* electricity industry
Punjab 49–54, 56–7, 92, 161, 218, 237

Rajasthan 35–6, 54, 61n9
Rajshekhar, M. 3
Ramesh, Jairam 114
Rangarajan Committee 111–12

RBI *see* Reserve Bank of India (RBI)
Reddy, D. Narasimha 7, 102–16
regional patterns of agrarian accumulation 5, 46–60; accumulation within agriculture 50–3, *50*, *51*, **52**, *53*; and economic development 47–50, *47*, *48*, *49*; non-agrarian accumulation by farmers 53–5, 58; Punjab case study 56–7; Tamil Nadu case study 57–9; and wider economy 55–6
regulated markets, Madhya Pradesh 84–98; cash, credit and commissions 86–93; weights and measures 93–7
Regulation School theory 175
religion 6, 7, 10, 12, 118, 120, 122, 127, 129, 130, 172–3
renewable energy 159, 231–2, 233, 238
rent-seeking 35, 75, 77, 161, 163, 164
reproduction, commodification of 154, 166n3
Reserve Bank of India (RBI) 104, 109, 111, 112, 114, 197
resistance to dispossession 27, 30–2, 38–9
retirement benefits 105, 122
rice cultivation: Arunachal Pradesh 67, 70, 74, 80n8; commodification of 161; Tamil Nadu 121
Rojas-Suarez, Liliana 200
Roman, C. 181, 182
rural lobbies and electricity industry 210–11, 218
rural urbanism 131
Russia 193
Rutten, Mario 54, 56

SAARC *see* South Asia Association for Regional Cooperation (SAARC)
Sabel, C.F. 233
sabzi (vegetable) mandi, Harda 92
Salam, Umar 9–10, 153–66
Sanyal, Kalyan 33, 34–5, 36–7, 38
SAPAP *see* South Asia Poverty Alleviation Programme (SAPAP)
SAPs *see* structural adjustment programmes (SAPs)
Scheduled Castes 119; *see also* Dalits
Scheduled Tribes (STs) 67–8, *69*, 70, 76–7, 119; *see also* adivasis
sea-level rise 233–4, 236
seasonal migration 119, 120–1, 125–6; *see also* migration, circular migration
SEBs *see* state electricity boards (SEBs)
Second World War 228–9

254 *Index*

self-employment 14, 33–4, 122, 124, 182
self-help group–bank linkage (SHG–BL) microfinance 103–5, 111, 112, 114–15, 128
semi-agrarian settlements, Tamil Nadu 126
SERP *see* Society for the Elimination of Rural Poverty (SERP), Andhra Pradesh
services 7, 14, 32–5, 47, 58, 70, 87, 95, 96, 103, 106, 109, 113, 122, 127, 138, 154, 156, 159–60, 163–5, 172, 177, 192, 194, 198–9; services sector, future of 238–9
SEZs *see* Special Economic Zones (SEZs)
Shah, Mihir 37
Shahi, R.V. 214
SHARE Microfinance Ltd (SML) 107–8, *108*, 110
SHG *see* self-help group–bank linkage (SHG–BL) microfinance
SIDBI *see* Small Industries Development Bank of India (SIDBI)
silk weaving industry 180–2
Singh, Digvijay 88
Singh, P. 57
SKS Microfinance Ltd *108*, 109, 113
Small Industries Development Bank of India (SIDBI) 109
small producers *see* petty commodity production (PCP)
Smith, Adam 227–8
SML *see* SHARE Microfinance Ltd (SML)
social differentiation 119–20
social policies 120, 127–8
social regulation of labour, Tamil Nadu 118–31; caste and class 119–20, 121–2, 123–4; consumption 120, 129–30; and credit 127; gender 119, 120, 124–5; non-farming employment 119, 120, 122–3, 125; social policies and local politics 127–9; spatial fragmentation of labour 125–7
social service reductions 33
Social Structures of Accumulation theory 175
Society for Helping and Awakening the Rural Poor through Education (SHARE) 107
Society for the Elimination of Rural Poverty (SERP), Andhra Pradesh 103, 104
SOEs *see* state-owned enterprises (SOEs)
solar energy 238; photovoltaics 231–2
solar pumpsets 237
Solow, Robert 230–1

South Asia Association for Regional Cooperation (SAARC) 103
South Asia Poverty Alleviation Programme (SAPAP) 103
South India Spinners Association 142
Soviet Union 193, 201, 202
soybean cultivation 89–90, 94
Spandana Spoorthy Innovative Financials (SSIF) 108–9, *108*
spatio-technical regimes of accumulation 136–50; cotton-spinning industry 141–3; knitwear production 145–8; labour and technological change 141–50; policy shifts in textile industry 139–41, 148–50; politics of technology 136, 137–8; segmented global markets for clothing 145–8; weaving industry 143–5
Special Economic Zones (SEZs) 3, 28–9, 30, 31, 35–6, 37, 39, 58
squatter settlements 30
Sraffa, P. 153
Sri Lanka 236
Srinivasan, Kannan 11–12, 190–202
Srinivasan, M.V. 179
SSIF *see* Spandana Spoorthy Innovative Financials (SSIF)
state 1–14, 24–39, 46–60, 66–78, 84–97, 102–15, 118–21, 128, 131, 136–44, 155–61, 164–5, 182–4, 190–202, 208–21, 227–40; state and policy 12–13; *see also* electricity industry
state electricity boards (SEBs) 210, 211, 212, 215, 218, *218*, 219
state expenditure reductions 32, 33
state involvement, politics of 159, 164
state-owned enterprises (SOEs) 212, 215–17, 219
state procurement 57, 91–2; and tax evasion 88, 190, 191–5,
Stern Review 154, 235
Stewart, Frances 137–8
Straw, Jack 196
structural adjustment programmes (SAPs) 25, 27, 114
STs *see* Scheduled Tribes (STs)
subsidies, electricity 210, 211
subsidies, withdrawal of 32
suicides 110, 112
sumangali thittam (bride scheme) 143, 145, 146; *see also* bride scheme
sustainable agriculture 237–8
Swayam Krushi Sangham (SKS) 109
Switzerland 192–3, 194, 196, 198–9

Tamil Nadu: agrarian accumulation 57–9; Arni 59, 176–84, *177*, *178*, 185–6, 187n14; textile industry 58–9, 141–8; *see also* social regulation of labour, Tamil Nadu
Tawa Dam, Madhya Pradesh 89
tax evasion 190, 191, 192, 199
tax havens 193, 194, 195–9
technological rents 163, 164
technology 8–9, 136–50, 226–40; and climate change 233–5, 241n7; cotton-spinning industry 141–3; and ecological systems 235–6; and energy 228–33; environmental impacts 226–8; and future of South Asia 236–40; knitwear production 145–8; and labour 141–50; and peak oil 235; policy shifts in textile industry 139–41, 148–50; politics of 136, 137–8; segmented global markets for clothing 145–8; weaving industry 143–5
Technology Upgradation Fund (TUF) 140–1, 149
televisions 130
tenancy *see* landlords
textile industry 58–9; cotton-spinning 141–3; cotton weaving 143–5; knitwear production 145–8; labour and technological change 141–50; neo-bondage 143, 144–5, 146; policy shifts 139–41, 148–50; segmented global markets 145–8; silk weaving 180–2
tied labour *see* bonded labour/neo-bondage
Tikait, Mahendra Singh 97
timber trade 74–5
Tiruppur, Tamil Nadu 58–9, 142, 143–8
tractors 52, *53*
trade (commerce) 5–6, 27, 30, 32, 46, 50, 54–7, 60, 84–97, 105, 122, 139, 144, 162, 176, 179–85, 190, 191, 193, 199–201; timber trade 74–5; trade liberalisation 32; trade mispricing 193, 200–1
trading castes 55–6, 57
trafficking 190, 193
Treasury securities 198, 199
tribal knowledge, appropriation of 162–3
tribal lands 29; *see also* community landownership
tribes *see* Scheduled Tribes (STs)
TUF *see* Technology Upgradation Fund (TUF)

un-freedom, labour *see* bonded labour/neo-bondage
under-classes 230
UNDP *see* United Nations Development Programme (UNDP)
unethical practices, microfinance institutions 110–12
United Kingdom 191–2, 193, 194, 195–8, 199, 201–2
United Nations, International Year of Microcredit 106
United Nations Development Programme (UNDP) 103
United States 193, 194, 198–200, 201–2
unity of opposites 160–2, 164
universities: marketisation of 162, 163–4, 165; numbers of new 165
Urban Land Ceiling Act 29
use-value 155, 157, 166n4, 200

value, labour theory of 199–200
Vanniyars 121–2, 123, 128
Veblen, Thorstein 171
vegetable and fruit market, Harda 92; *see also* fruit and vegetables
Venkatasubramanian, G. 8, 118–31
Victor, David G. 215, 216
Vijayabaskar, M. 9, 136–50
violence: land grabbing 30, 31, 37; loan recovery 110–11

wage labour: Arunachal Pradesh 71, 72, 74, *74*; creation of 3, 23, 33–4; lack of employment 27, 33–4; and neoliberal policies 32; self-employment 33–6
Walker, Kathy Le Mons 31
Wall Street 193, 198–200
Warr, Benjamin 231
water security 237
weapons deals 194
weaving industry: cotton 143–5; silk 180–2
Weberian institutionalism 208–9
wedding, costs 129, 130
weights and measures, agricultural markets 84, 93–7
welfare payment reductions 32, 33, 37
West Bengal 29, 30, 31, 92
wet rice cultivation 67, 70, 74, 80n8
wheat cultivation 90, 91–2, 94
White, Gordon 159
White, Harry Dexter 201–2
wind energy 238
Wolf, F.O. 7

Index

women: consumption 130; employment in Tamil Nadu 119, 120, 123, 124–5, 142–3; employment in textile industry 142–3; and microfinance 6–7, 103–4; sumangali thittam (bride scheme) 143, 145, 146; unwaged labour 161

Wood, Ellen Meiksins 25

World Bank 28, 38, 164–5, 201, 202; liberalisation of power industry 211, 212; microfinance 103; structural adjustment programmes (SAPs) 25, 114

Worster, Donald 227–8

Zdanowicz, John S. 200